Routledge Revivals

State Policies and Migration

First published in 1982, *State Policies and Migration* is a study on migration-related government action. This book consists of analyses of various rural reforms and industrial strategies in eight Latin American and Caribbean countries. The emphasis of the studies has been determined by the particular context of the country or region concerned, but in general the studies fall into three categories. The first four chapters are primarily concerned with land reforms, however partial. The next two chapters focus on general industrialisation strategies, considering their impact on urbanisation and the attempts made to achieve population redistribution within the context of the longstanding process of industrialisation. Finally, the third section consists of two very different cases of attempts to alter population distribution in the context of transforming the socio-economic structure. This book will be of interest to students of economics, agriculture, history, public policy and migration studies.

State Policies and Migration

Studies in Latin America and the Caribbean

Edited by Peter Peek and Guy Standing

Routledge
Taylor & Francis Group

First published in 1982
By Croom Helm

This edition first published in 2023 by Routledge
4 Park Square, Milton Park, Abingdon, Oxon, OX14 4RN
and by Routledge
605 Third Avenue, New York, NY 10017

Routledge is an imprint of the Taylor & Francis Group, an informa business

A Library of Congress record exists under ISBN: 0709920288

ISBN: 978-1-032-60486-2 (hbk)
ISBN: 978-1-003-45940-8 (ebk)
ISBN: 978-1-032-60487-9 (pbk)

Book DOI 10.4324/9781003459408

State Policies and Migration

STUDIES IN LATIN AMERICA AND THE CARIBBEAN

Edited by Peter Peek
and Guy Standing

A study prepared for the International Labour Office within the framework of the World Employment Programme with the financial support of the United Nations Fund for Population Activities

CROOM HELM
London & Canberra

Croom Helm Ltd, 2-10 St John's Road, London SW11

British Library Cataloguing in Publication Data

State policies and migration.
Migrant labor—Latin America
I. Peek, Peter II. Standing, Guy
III. World Employment Programme
330.98 HD8110.5

ISBN 0-7099-2078-8

The responsibility for opinions expressed in studies and other contributions rests solely with their authors, and publication does not constitute an endorsement by the International Labour Office of the opinions expressed in them.

The designations employed and the presentation of material do not imply the expression of any opinion whatsoever on the part of the International Labour Office concerning the legal status of any country or territory or of its authorities, or concerning the delimitation of its frontiers.

Printed and bound in Great Britain by
Biddles Ltd, Guildford and King's Lynn

Table of Contents

Page

Page

List of tables

Page

Page

Page

Chapter 8

Chapter 9

Page

Page

List of Charts, Figures and Maps

Page

Chapter 7

Chapter 8

Preface

Movements of people within as well as between country boundaries have always been substantial but have almost certainly increased in recent years. Many governments have introduced policies to affect the flow of migrants in one way or another and for various identifiable reasons. Yet only in recent years has attention been focussed on the rationale and efficacy of such policies and the consequences for those most immediately affected.

Within the ILO's Migration and Employment research programme a series of country studies have been prepared on migration-related government actions. This book is one outcome, consisting of analyses of various rural reforms and industrial strategies in eight Latin American and Caribbean countries. The individual chapters represent the views of the particular authors, though all were discussed by the group of authors and been revised to take account of comments made during the course of a four day discussion. The emphasis of each study has been determined by the particular context of the country or region directly concerned, but in general the studies fall into three categories.

After the introduction, the first four chapters are primarily concerned with land reforms, however partial; these are concerned with Chile, the Chancay Valley of Peru, the Sierra of Ecuador and, in the extent that colonisation schemes can be considered as part of land reform, the Rondonia region of northern Brazil. The next two chapters are more focused on general industrialisation strategies as pursued in Mexico and Colombia, considering their impact on urbanisation and the attempts made to achieve population redistribution within the context of the longstanding process of industrialisation. Finally, the third section consists of two very different cases of attempts to alter population distribution in the context of transforming the socio-economic structure. Recent attempts to affect population distribution and rural-urban movements in Guyana are presented in the context of a long history of successive attempts to concentrate the population in the coastal region of the country, and in the case of Cuba urban decentralisation policies are shown to be closely integrated into the radical social and economic transformation that has taken place since 1959.

It is recognised by all contributors that the analyses are exploratory and should be extended. In most cases the type of data required to adequately portray the process that has been occurring are simply not available. Without more relevant data analyses and policy proposals will both be hampered, and there will be little chance to devise appropriate recommendations.

The studies should also be seen in the context of other studies being conducted in Africa and Asia, and as part of a continuing programme on causes and implications of different types of population mobility in low-income countries.[1] All these studies have been generously supported by the United Nations Fund for Population Activities (UNFPA). In addition to this research programme, the ILO is assisting four Latin American countries - Bolivia, Colombia, Ecuador and Peru - in the collection of migration data and in the design of migration-related policies. Elsewhere in the ILO work is being done on the international dimensions of migration, and objectively it must be recognised that many of the issues associated with internal migration are similar to those associated with international migration; often of course the distinction is at best arbitrary.

This book has taken a long time to prepare and we would most of all like to thank our fellow contributors for their assistance and, in some cases, for making extensive revisions. We are also most grateful to Mary Dominguez for preparing the manuscript so patiently, and for the assistance of other colleagues in the ILO. We have benefited from comments made by Antoinette Béguin, Henry Bernstein, Roger Böhning, Elizabeth Hopkins, Jean Lasserre-Bigorry, Jean Mayer, Carmen Solorío and Vivianne Ventura-Dias. None of course should be held responsible for any part of the text, but their comments were appreciated.

P.P.
G.S.

---

[1] For a general description, see World Employment Programme: Population and Development, a progress report on ILO research on population, labour, employment and income distribution (Geneva, ILO, 1981; 3rd edn.).

Chapter 1

STATE POLICIES AND LABOUR MIGRATION

by Peter Peek and Guy Standing

I. Introduction

The ebb and flow of peasants and the labouring poor moving in distress or in hope is a collective phenomenon of enormous proportions; globally its magnitude has exploded, and in many parts of the world it became a visible and growing reflection of social and economic crises in the 1970s and early 1980s.

In 1978 a UN population inquiry addressed to governments found that the great majority of the low-income countries considered their population distribution to be "substantially" or "extremely unacceptable". In the ECLA region, out of 27 countries no less than 21 reported the distribution to be "extremely unacceptable", and a further four described it as "substantially unacceptable" by which "substantial intervention" was deemed "appropriate" (table 1). In large part the distribution of the population reflected rapid migration in the recent past. That had been associated with population growth, but more fundamentally migration has reflected the changing structure of agrarian relations of production in many parts of the world, nowhere more so than in Latin American countries.

As in previous eras of transition, such as the European Industrial Revolution, rural-urban migration has grown with the emergence of industrialisation (Hobsbawm, 1974). And in that context the most significant form of population movement has been the labour migration of the agricultural population. It is this form with which the present book is primarily concerned, an implicit theme being that the causes of rural migration lie primarily in the changing social relations of production between the producers and the consumers of economic surplus, in other words the changing nexus of relations between peasants or wage labourers and landlords or commercial, agricultural and industrial capital. In rural areas the extent and incidence of population mobility have been strongly influenced by changes in land tenure, and have reflected and influenced the social division of labour, the degree of commoditisation and the development or stagnation of the material forces of production; they have

Table 1: Report of government on acceptability of population distribution (UN Population Inquiry, 1978)

Countries of ECLA region

Distribution*	Country	
Entirely acceptable:	Barbados	
Slightly unacceptable:	Cuba**	
Substantially unacceptable:	Bahamas Brazil** Dominican Republic Nicaragua	
Extremely unacceptable:	Argentina Bolivia Chile Colombia Costa Rica** Ecuador El Salvador Grenada Guatemala Guyana** Haiti	Honduras Jamaica Mexico Panama** Paraguay Peru Surinam Trinidad Uruguay Venezuela

Notes:

* Government perceptions: Entirely acceptable: no intervention appropriate. Slightly unacceptable: limited intervention appropriate. Substantially unacceptable: substantial intervention appropriate. Extremely unacceptable: radical intervention appropriate.

** Country whose government did not perceive that an adjustment in the spatial distribution of population would contribute to the resolution of problems associated with population growth.

Source: UN Fourth Population Inquiry addressed to governments, 1978. UN: World population trends and policies: 1979 Monitoring report, Vol. II: Population (New York, 1980), p. 119.

also been influenced by the legal, ideological and political superstructure coexisting with the prevailing mode of production. Such a combination of influences defies easy generalisations. But unless the process of migration is couched in such terms even the simple realities will be concealed.

II. Analyses of Migration

Formally, migration is a demographic phenomenon but is a reflection of socio-economic change, which can and often does facilitate or impede other types of change. However, the socio-economic functions of population mobility have rarely been illuminated in the burgeoning literature on the subject. This is partly because the over-all process has been obscured by the two analytical perspectives - the dualistic and neo-classical models - that have dominated that literature.

The first is associated with Lewis' general equilibrium analysis by which underemployed labour moves from the "traditional", subsistence, peasant sector, to the "modern", capitalist sector at a constant real wage (Lewis, 1954, pp. 139-91). As the industrial capitalist sector expands, the demand for labour grows and the perfectly elastic supply of (migrant) labour exists because the marginal and average product of labour in the subsistence sector are less than the market wage rate in the capitalist sector. But as development occurs the average and marginal productivity of labour in the "traditional" sector rise, so that eventually market wages rise, which slows the growth of industrial employment and thereby the rate of migration out of the traditional sector.

The second model is the neo-classical approach that places primary emphasis on individualistic, rational behaviour. This could be regarded as being concerned with the "final form" in the explanation of migration, to use Theil's econometric term; perhaps it should be called the lowest level of abstraction. Those working with some variant of this model have explained migration in terms of expected incomes, "human capital" formation, or expected costs and benefits.[1]

Most analyses in this latter tradition have concentrated on individual motivations and choices, and have been dedicated to a remarkable proposition based on a remarkable premise, the premise being that people are rational and the proposition that they will move from areas of low economic opportunity to areas of greater

---

[1] For a very sympathetic review of studies in this tradition, see Todaro (1976).

opportunity. This is true, but trivial. It is made even more trivial, even tautological, if use is made of the concept of "full income", where that term encompasses all sorts of psychic and non-monetary factors. Where these approaches are not simple tautologies - people move because they think it better for them to move, and we know that they thought it was so because they moved - they tend to indicate that one personal or household characteristic is more or less important than another. Such revelations are unquestionably useful, but showing that the rural-urban income differential tends to be positively related to the migration rate should only be a rather minor part of migration analysis. Indeed, even if there is a common tendency, the fact is that average incomes (and even expected incomes) have often differed substantially between areas without inducing a mass movement from the lower-income area, whereas in other cases small income differences have coexisted with high rates of migration, or migration has increased in the wake of a fall in income differentials. In sum, with neo-classical models the level of migration is scarcely explained, the tendency to rationalise any particular statistical result is extremely strong, and most fundamentally of all, such approaches are ill-suited to explaining the role of migration on the transformation of the structure of production and distribution.

However, whereas the neo-classical approach obscures by abstracting from the structure and superstructure of social formations, thus leaving the process of migration essentially unexplained, the dualistic approach obfuscates by postulating the existence of a specific dualistic economy in which the two sectors are basically unrelated other than by the supply of labour and in which it is assumed that the traditional or "subsistence" sector is stagnant and uncommercialised. It is assumed there is a surplus population ready and able to move to urban areas at a constant real wage and that mass "underemployment" exists prior to the existence and growth of the modern capitalist sector. As such, dualistic models have tended to dichotomise "sectors" in an artificial and obscuranist way, employing terms such as "modern" and "traditional", or "formal" and "informal", which are hard to define in any analytically satisfactory manner.

Dualistic models have been attacked because they have been used to justify a policy of promoting "modern" (i.e. capitalist) industrial enterprises, to accelerate a certain type of industrialisation, to the neglect of agriculture and "non-modern" enterprises. In response to criticism they have spawned a host of dualisms supposedly observed in both urban and rural areas. But they have also been criticised for neglecting the awkward fact that to create a labour surplus for a dynamic capitalist sector, diverse State policies and related economic tactics have had to be deployed, either to make participation in the "traditional" sector effectively impossible or more often merely to raise the "effort price" of labour force participation in traditional economic activities.[1] There is considerable evidence - further supported by some of the studies in this volume - that efforts have been made to force down living standards in the rural traditional areas in order to create the underemployment necessary to ensure the supply of labour to industrial wage employment. At the very least they have contributed to the immiserisation of the peasantry.

III. A Framework for Analysing Migration Policies

The last point highlights the major objection to both the neo-classical and dualistic approaches, which is that they divorce the analysis from consideration of the social relations of production and the mechanisms of exploitation used by the powerful to control and manipulate the labouring poor. The first question that so often comes to mind in rural areas of Latin America, or in Africa or most of Asia for that matter, is why there has been so little flight from the countryside given declining or stagnant rural living standards and large rural-urban income differentials. Some neo-classical economists have emphasised the deterrent effect of high rates of urban unemployment, the psychic costs of moving, and the apparent lack of information. But what they have signally failed to do is incorporate in their models of migration the prevailing social relations of production.

For example, in many rural areas relations between powerful landlords and peasants, or even relations between kin, have been such as to effectively preclude rural emigration by the peasantry; moreover, in such circumstances governments have either explicitly represented the interests of the landowners or have acted so as to preserve the existing class structure, in either case

---

[1] See, for instance, Arrighi (1970, pp. 197-234). As an incidental and historiographical aside, it is interesting that dualistic models have tended to present migration as a "good thing" - providing labour for industrialisation - whereas neo-classical models have tended to present it as a "bad thing" - contributing to urban unemployment. It is perhaps no coincidence that the dualistic models emerged in the 1950s, the neo-classical formalisms in the 1970s.

tolerating practices restricting population mobility or on occasion introducing legislation to restrict it. Yet where landlords' power has declined, or where they have evolved into commercial agricultural enterprises, or where industrial capital has become more prominent, the State has been more likely to reflect the interests and needs of the emergent classes, and in such cases population or rather labour mobility has been facilitated or encouraged. Accordingly as governments have come to play a more active role in stimulating industrial expansion they have introduced measures that have directly or indirectly stimulated population mobility. Indeed in so far as industrialisation relies on the existence of a mobile labour force there are numerous historical examples of governments having had to introduce legislation to secure that basic requirement. But where State power has been transferred to such "progressive" elements the more common pattern has been for population mobility to be increased by reforms introduced for other reasons, typically designed to increase the extent of rural surplus and squeeze more of that surplus out of the rural population.

At an abstract level, by reference to the nature of the social formation and the contradictions inherent in it, State policies can be classified by three strategic criteria, even though some will combine elements of several of those criteria. First, there are policies which can be classified as basically defensive, being negative in the sense that they are designed to retrieve a situation in which relations of production are under stress, most likely because they are restricting the development of the material forces of production and thereby inducing stagnation and a series of crises in the composition of the social formation. Thus, to give a simple example, if hacienda owners saw the introduction of railways into the regions they dominated as a threat to their labour supply, in that it would facilitate a mass exodus by the peasantry, they might press to have judicial or legislative barriers erected. Or if peasants were fleeing increasingly heavy rents and labour obligations landlords would be inclined to press for tighter controls on mobility. Analogously, if there was a State in which the contradictions of policies squeezing the peasantry of surplus and releasing previously inhibited mobility had resulted in mass urban unemployment, defensive policies would encompass actions designed to control the threatening social unrest. Such defensive policies might include colonisation or resettlement schemes, or the imposition of licences or quota schemes for restricting urban in-migration.

Second, there are policies which can be classified as progressive, expansive or aggressive, being progressive in the sense that they are introduced to accelerate the transition from one mode of production to another. The most discussed policy supposedly exemplifying this category is land reform in its various guises. But it also includes legal reforms, particularly with respect to private property law and protective labour legislation, both of which have implications for the extent and incidence of population mobility.

Third, there are policies which fit uneasily into either the defensive or progressive categories; these are best described as neutral or reinforcing policies. These encompass political actions introduced by a hegemonic class or at least by a government under no particular threat to its immediate survival. Such policies could be seen, for example, as deepening the penetration of a specific mode of production in regions that had been little more than geographical appendages to the national "developmental" process or as transforming tributory modes that were no particular threat to the stability of the dominant mode, e.g. the industrial capitalist sector. The most apparent example of such policies are colonisation schemes, where introduced to extend the accumulation process, increase agricultural production, and increase the potential for exploitation of rural producers.

This threefold classification of State policies is highly schematic, of course. However some such schema should make it easier to conceptualise the nature of State policies and distinguish between the daily or plan-specific practicalities and longer-term strategies and tendencies of the State. In that context, this volume consists of analyses of the impact on population mobility, intended or otherwise, of policies designed to alter the social relations of production and the pattern of "development". In focussing on a selection of Latin American and Caribbean countries the emphasis of the studies has been on various types of transition, primarily from social formations dominated by quasi-feudal relations of production to systems based on "free" wage labour, in its classic double sense. As Latin American countries have experienced a succession of political and social upheavals, relations of production and the nature of the State have undergone enormous changes in recent decades. There is no need to resort to what is sometimes described as "economism" or "reductionism" by which the State is somehow seen as merely reflecting the class interests of a dominant mode of production. However, changes in the economic structure have occurred in a period when there have been significant changes in the nature of the State, some of which have conveniently "corresponded", some much less so. Here is not the place to try to make a judgement on such theoretical issues, however important. But it is clear that in the late 1970s some States remained dominated by landlord interests, though they were rarely hegemonic any longer; some had vacillated uneasily but had become increasingly dominated by industrial or agrarian monopoly capital; others had long since passed into the control of the latter; others were in the throes of populist coalitions, seemingly unable to move into a more dynamic, capitalist era; and of course several had moved into an uneasy phase of transition to some form of socialism. The nature of State policies, with respect to migration, the labour process generally, or other aspects of its concern for that matter, could hardly be expected to be similar in each of those countries.

Most of the studies in this volume concentrate on agrarian reforms and their impact on mobility. In an attempt to put the various historically specific studies in a general context the remainder of this introduction briefly presents an overview of the elements constraining and influencing population mobility in rural areas. No attempt is made to present an ideal type, but the focus must be on the changing labour relations and modes of exploitation, and most particularly on the changing mechanisms by which surplus is squeezed out of the peasantry and rural proletariat. To analyse the impact of reforms on migration, through their impact on class differentiation, proletarianisation, and the pattern of accumulation, it is useful to start by briefly considering elements of previously established social relations of production which in themselves have impeded or controlled population mobility.

IV. Quasi-feudal Relations of Rural Production

In many countries of Latin America, Asia, Africa and the Middle East, elements of what could be described as feudal or quasi-feudal relations of production have lingered for generations.[1] There has of course been an extended debate on the exact character of the mode of production in Latin American agriculture, a debate which suffered from an unnecessary tendency to regard Latin America as essentially homogeneous.[2] For the present

---

[1] Their extent in rural areas of Latin America was vividly documented by the Inter-American Committee for Agricultural Development (CIDA) in the 1960s (see Barraclough and Collarte, 1973).

[2] The debate centred on the work of Frank, who claimed that Latin American agriculture had been capitalist since the sixteenth century (Frank, 1967). This view was most forcefully criticised by Laclau, who emphasised the dual character of a mode of production and Frank's neglect of relations of production (Laclau, 1971, pp. 19-38).

purpose, it is merely necessary to observe that a common feature has been non-reliance on free wage labour. Typically small groups of landlords have owned huge estates on which numerous peasant households worked in return for the usufruct of small rented plots. On the estates themselves much of the arable land has been left uncultivated or undercultivated, for reasons which have been extensively discussed elsewhere.[1] Most of those reasons have reflected the nature of the prevailing mode of production (see, for example, Stavenhagen, 1970). Here we need only note that by restricting the peasants' access to the uncultivated land, landlords have accentuated the dependent status of the peasants, thereby preventing them from raising their incomes through more extensive cultivation while forcing them to work for the estates. For such "internal peasantries" the dependency and the precariousness of their position as tenants have been associated with pervasive forms of patron-client paternalism. They have been forced to rely on the landlords and their intermediaries for a modicum of protection against destitution - for as long as they reciprocated with subservient loyalty.

Though there have been various means by which peasants have been confined to estates or villages or to mining communities, in almost all such societies strict limits have been placed on geographical mobility.[2] This is not to imply there has been no mobility in such circumstances, but what mobility there has been has tended to be either directed mobility, through coercive mechanisms, or a reflection of a social formation under stress. Often the landlord class has attempted to restrict mobility by economic methods complemented by a web of legal and extra-legal devices, doing so because of a low population density and their need to extract economic surplus through rent, labour services, taxes and related forms of exploitation. At times the methods used to restrict mobility, and thus preserve their source of surplus, have consisted of little more than coercion based on their localised power; in other circumstances elaborate systems of indentured labour have tied workers to the estates through long-term contracts, as was the case with

---

1 For instance, it was estimated that in the 1960s there was more than twice as much idle land as crop land on latifundios in the combined area of Argentina, Brazil, Chile, Colombia, Ecuador, Guatemala and Peru (see Feder, 1971, p. 68).

2 The issues mentioned in this section are discussed more extensively in Standing (1981).

the colonos in Brazil and indentured immigrant labour in many plantation colonies in the West Indies and elsewhere (ibid.; see also Balán, 1978). The role and legacy of such a system in Guyana are considered in Chapter 9 of the present volume. But besides contracted arrangements it has been common for landlords, aided by the political and legal apparatus in the areas they have dominated, to oblige peasants wishing to leave an estate to obtain permission before doing so. The implied power of landlords has reflected the fact that most large estates have existed as virtually isolated, semi-autonomous communities, creating their own legal codes and accepted patterns of conduct. The very isolation of such communities restricted mobility by making travel and communications with other areas both difficult and costly.

There have also been induced behavioural factors impeding mobility, for both "internal" and "external" peasantries, the latter being defined by their lack of formal ties to estates or plantations. Typically, in their productive activities, peasant households have had to rely on the combined efforts of family members, often supported by informal exchange labour arrangements with relatives and neighbours. In such circumstances any individual's ability to migrate or to change conventionally fixed patterns of behaviour has been limited by the likelihood that his departure would disrupt the fragile basis on which the family survived. Involvement in wider social relations of production could be expected to further control mobility. Sharecropping is an example. In many cases the landlord, as a monopsonist, has been able to demand levels of output that the peasant has been unable to attain without the labour input of family members, given the primitive technology and undeveloped division of labour at his disposal. Similar adaptive responses have characterised internal peasantries, where the various members of the peasant household have been obliged to provide a range of labour services for the landlord and other dominant groups in the community, notably church dignitaries (Pearse, 1975; Hobsbawm, 1969).

Yet of all factors restricting peasant migration one should single out the various forms of debt bondage or debt peonage, partly because of their extensive role and partly because of the lack of theoretical and empirical attention paid to the issues involved. With limited access to cash or productive assets and highly vulnerable to the vagaries of climate and the consequences of ill-health, accidents or ill-luck, peasants have been easily lured into debt. In many cases landlords or their agents have instituted the practice of making cash advances to entice peasants into debt, sometimes thereby obliging them to remain on the estate until the debt has been paid, as in the classic enganche system in rural Peru, and sometimes obliging them to make short-term seasonal moves to accept short periods of low-paid wage labour. Often usury has induced debtors into a status of almost permanent debt bondage, where the debtors have had little or no prospect of securing sufficient income to pay back the original loan and the interest (see, for example, Rutledge, 1977, pp. 205-28). In many cases landlords have been only too willing to lend at high rates of interest when peasants were faced with unforeseen adverse circumstances, such as an illness or crop failure. In many areas of Latin America campesinos have been forced to sell their food crop to the landlords, often as a means of paying off part of a debt, and then have had to buy the food back later at higher prices, often through the means of a loan. Such vicious circles have severely limited potential mobility.

In many peasant communities usury has been rife, and mobility has been restricted by peasants being enmeshed in debts to local moneylenders.[1] Those may also have been the landlords or local traders, shopkeepers or millowners. Often peasants have been forced deeper into debt through being compelled to pay rents in advance for land, housing or the use of a landlord's mill. Even where money wages have been paid, debt has arisen through payment in arrears or as a result of arbitrary deductions. In short, in Latin America as in many other parts of the world, debt bondage has been a pervasive means of tying the rural poor to rural areas and to pre-capitalist relations of production.

Though of course there has always been some migration, other mechanisms have existed by which landlords and others could restrict population movements, if they wished to do so. In social formations dominated by quasi-feudal elements the role of the state has been essentially passive. But national governments have contributed to a pattern of immobility, notably by abstaining from intervention in labour relations in agriculture or in local judicial and administrative processes. Where the State has directly intervened, it has typically done so to

---

1 To give just one example, in Ecuador fewer than 1 per cent of the peasants had access to institutional credit, the rest being obliged to borrow from moneylenders at much higher interest rates. See Stitzlein (1967).

reinforce the existing social relations of production.[1] Thus where landlords or a plantocracy have been economically and politically powerful, labour laws protecting agricultural workers have either not existed or been ineffectual. Governments in effect either have been unable to control the abuses and forms of exploitation governing relations of production or have tolerated or condoned them. Moreover, the decentralised State apparatus characteristic of landlord-dominated social formations have allowed estate owners to impose their own rules and disciplinary procedures, in whatever form needed to preserve the peasantry or some part of it in a state of subordination.[2]

In such circumstances powerful landowners, individually or as a co-ordinated body, have often actively discouraged modernisation; it has even been argued that in some Latin American countries, such as Chile and Ecuador, hacienda owners long opposed railway construction in the regions they dominated for fear that it would allow outsiders into the province concerned and provide peasants with a means of leaving (Mellafe, 1971, p. 11; see also Costales and Costales, 1964). Indeed in landlord-dominated societies estate owners and their representatives have typically dominated the organs of urban local government as well as those in rural communities, and have used municipal legislation to consolidate their control of the land (Glade, 1969, pp. 61-62).

Such are the principal elements of the pre-capitalist relations of production which have restricted population mobility in rural areas. In some cases there has of course been fairly substantial migration despite the apparent hegemony of a landlord class, but there has usually been some special factor involved or the social relations have been in the throes of a crisis, or most particularly, the migration has been a clear reflection of a transition in the relations and forces of rural production. It is the analyst's primary task to determine which has been or is the case.

---

1 The classic example was the attempt by the crisis-ridden state in Tsarist Russia before 1917 to strengthen the landlords' control of the rural economy, notably by means of the land reforms introduced by Stolypin. See, for example, Baran (1967).

2 For instance, at least until recently, peasants on haciendas in some parts of Latin America have had to work without pay to gain the right to use paths and bridges on the estate, and corporal punishment is not unknown (Barraclough and Collarte, 1973, pp. 20-21).

V. Agrarian Transitions: The Shift to Wage Labour

The diversity of agrarian relations of production has been matched by the variety of forms of transition. While traditional, quasi-feudal relations have persisted in certain regions and remained prominent in a few countries, in the great majority they have been steadily eroded. In most places, it is possible to distinguish between the contradictions that eroded the viability of traditional labour relations and the factors that facilitated specific types of transition and particular alternative relations of production. But any general review would be well beyond the purpose of this introduction, which is only designed to put the changing patterns of migration and the role of major state policies into an appropriate context.

Changes in pre-capitalist productive relations could be induced primarily by increasing opposition of the direct producers to landlords or their agents or social equivalents. Or it could be introduced by the landlords themselves because external pressures and opportunities make such relations increasingly inefficient. But that somewhat oversimplifies the situation, for whatever the impact of external factors, it is the inefficiencies and inherent tendencies in the rural economy which are crucial. In some cases, landlords have found it impossible to "squeeze" any more surplus out of the labouring population and have found themselves frustrated in their efforts to increase revenue to allow the potential improvement in their lifestyle and consumption. In other cases, the ability of the peasantry to provide conventional levels of surplus, or rent, has been undermined by restrictions making it impossible to develop the forces of production on the land. In the latter situation, a notable factor has been population growth which, coupled with shrinking access to fertile land and sometimes dysfunctional inheritance customs, has accelerated land fragmentation, thereby aggravating impoverishment and increasing the opposition of subordinated producers to the social relations afflicting them. Often the landlords' efforts to increase the revenue and product obtained from the peasants has coincided with the decreasing ability of the peasants to meet their obligations. And in those circumstances conflicts have erupted as landlords have tried to increase their control of land while peasants have tried to acquire more or reobtain some of what they had lost. Land invasions, of course, have marked the desperate reality in numerous areas of Latin America and elsewhere; and much has been written about the background to such desperate actions, as well as the futility so often associated with them (for useful analyses, see Migdal, 1974;

Paige, 1975).

In response to such conflicts, or in response to the prospect of them, some groups of landlords have replaced peasant cultivators by commercial farming themselves, relying increasingly on wage labourers, often hired from outside the region, thus doubly reducing their contact and "dependency" on the peasantry. In some cases, production levels have stagnated or declined on the land utilised by peasant cultivators, perhaps reflecting soil erosion, increasing indebtedness and general impoverishment. In those cases, the landlords' rentable income has declined while cultivators have tended to abandon the land, or have been easily dispossessed of it.

In some areas affected by transition to wage labour production, there has been a process of "peasant involution" whereby whole areas have become little more than labour reserves for profit-oriented farming elsewhere. Initial patterns of seasonal or short-term migration to work as harvest labour have tended to give way to longer-term out-migration as the dislocation and stagnation of the local economy progressed, partly because of the seasonal unavailability of part of its workforce.

These factors that have contributed to change could reasonably be described as internal to the rural economy. But a factor accelerating the transformation of agrarian relations of production has been the growth of urban-based industry, which has been in inherent conflict with an uncommercialised agricultural sector, since the latter impedes the potential growth of industry by not providing sufficient surplus for investment, by not providing adequate quantities of low-cost food for urban workers, by restricting the expansion of the domestic market for commodities, and by restricting labour supply and labour mobility. In one way or another, a quasi-feudal agrarian structure becomes a serious obstacle to industrial expansion. For that expansion to occur, agriculture is required to provide a source of foreign exchange or at least a means of preventing the outflow of scarce foreign exchange on imported food. At the same time, industry requires a mobile, low-cost labour supply to facilitate rapid accumulation.

For those reasons, urban-industrial groups have tended to be at the forefront of efforts to change government policies so as to transform the agrarian structure. In some cases landowners have modified productive relations because new access to cheap credit encouraged commercial farming, credit facilities in the hands of urban-based institutions being used to foster an agrarian transformation. But commonly market pressures and opportunities have had to be complemented by the types of government policies discussed in later sections.

In addition to urban pressures, foreign influences cannot be ignored. Some landlord-dominated élites have been under pressure to introduce land reforms and related agrarian policies without there being a powerful internal pressure forcing them do so. This was particularly so in some parts of Latin America in the 1960s, when the Alliance for Progress was used to get changes. Created in 1961 in the wake of the Cuban revolution, the Alliance's programme promoted certain types of social and economic reforms designed to forestall the revolutionary threat in the region. But apart from such official strategies, foreign capital has generally fostered productive relations in its own image.

The nature of agrarian change has had implications for the pattern and extent of migration, hinging on the labour relations that have become established. In those societies in which capitalist agriculture has become the main form of production, by no means have all rural workers become a landless proletariat working full-time in regular wage employment. Such may be the long-term tendency, but in many areas quasi-feudal relations have been modified only gradually as the peasantry have been progressively squeezed, supplying more of their time as seasonal wage workers, subsidised with increasing difficulty by subsistence production carried on by themselves and in their absence by their families. Particularly where there have been plantations, semi-proletarianisation has meant attached wage workers having rented plots of land on which to produce their means of subsistence; in some cases agricultural estates have acquired part of their labour locally and part from groups of permanent migrants, landless workers such as the Torrantes in Chile or the bóias frias in Brazil.

Corresponding to the changing patterns of labour use and supply, land tenure patterns and distributions have changed, sometimes through land reforms as discussed in the next section, and in part through the effects of population growth that has taken place without such changes as would have been required to allow pre-existing landholding patterns to be reproduced. For example, as discussed in Chapters 4 and 7, in Ecuador and Colombia, the average size of small-scale farmholdings declined, while state policies turning the terms of trade against agriculture were making it necessary to increase the size of farms to maintain subsistence living standards. Such trends have fuelled seasonal and longer-term migration, which in turn has helped nascent capitalist farmers acquire cheap labour and transform productive relations in areas hitherto relying on other forms of production.

With the growth of urban-industrial areas and with the agrarian transformation, a vast number of the rural landless and underemployed have moved to urban areas. But the rural exodus has been greatly facilitated by changes in government policies accompanying the shift in economic and political centres of gravity. And it is here that we can usually identify the clear conflict of interests between landowners and the industrial middle class. The latter have favoured reforms that would release labour and accelerate capitalist industrialisation, the former have tended to see reforms as merely a series of palliatives to reduce tensions without fundamentally altering relations of production in rural areas. In either case - and the history of reforms indicates a wide variety of compromises which have often allowed a retrenchment by landowners - the rural poor have scarcely benefited at all and have often experienced further deterioration in their standard of living.

Government policies in times of emerging industrialisation have helped to create a "free" and mobile labour force. Some of the most blatant quasi-feudal abuses have been controlled by legislation, and in some cases legislation has been passed which landlords accept as pre-empting stronger and more effective policies. A classic case has been the regulation of tenancy contracts, ostensibly introduced to give peasants greater security of tenure and being an integral part of the formalisation of property law. Often such laws have made the legal processes so complicated as to be extremely hard to enforce. But non-enforceable laws have often pre-empted more effective action (Barraclough and Domike, 1970, p. 77).

Initial changes in government policy have commonly been presented as modifying quasi-feudal controls over rural workers. Whether they have benefited the peasants or not, they have manifestly tended to stimulate rural-urban migration. Such legal changes have included regulation of both tenancy and labour contracts and the establishment of minimum wage levels. Perhaps the most fundamental and certainly the most discussed government policy has been land reform, a loose concept covering a vast array of legalistic devices for modifying land tenure systems.

VI. Land Reform and Rural Emigration

Most countries have resorted to some type of land reform programme in the early stages of industrialisation; it has been rare for fundamental agrarian change to take place without it. Usually land reform has been presented as having two purposes, to increase production and to improve the welfare of the peasants. Implicitly in some cases, and explicitly in others, two further objectives have been the transformation of quasi-feudal relations of production in agriculture and the reduction of growing rural-urban migration due to land fragmentation and population growth in the face of limited availability of land (see, inter alia, World Bank, 1975; Thiesenhusen, 1971, pp. 57-76).

A major impetus to agrarian reform in Latin America was provided by the realisation that traditional social relations of production, and the land tenure system in particular, had impeded agricultural growth and, in the wake of population growth, had meant increasing poverty and unemployment. Moreover, for the expansion of industrial capital, it became essential to transfer a larger agricultural surplus to the growing urban-industrial areas, which in many countries already accounted for the majority of the population. The type of land reform introduced was primarily concerned with replacing traditional landlordism with capitalist, mechanised, "modern" farming. In some cases, as in the Colombian Land Reform Act of 1961, landowners were forced to modernise and to increase the area under cultivation by the threat of expropriation if they failed to cultivate more than a certain proportion of the arable land, or if land productivity was not above a certain level (Ridler, 1978, pp. 37-45). In other cases, as with the Ecuadorian land reform of 1964 discussed in Chapter 4, the traditional use of servant labourers (principally huasipungueros) was prohibited (CIESE, 1977). In many countries the introduction of tenancy contracts was the first step in modifying the agrarian system, the ostensible objective being to increase the security of peasant cultivators and thereby encourage investment, soil conservation and related practices, while reducing rural-urban migration (see, for example, Barraclough and Domike, 1970, pp. 74-78; Rudra, 1978, pp. 28-34). In some circumstances land reform has been supposedly designed specifically to redistribute land, often by fixing a maximum size of holding. Such programmes have been introduced in many countries, including Mexico (1910-17), the Republic of Korea (1950), Bolivia (1952), Egypt (1952), India (from the early 1950s), Venezuela (1960), Cuba (1959 and 1962), Chile (1967-73), Peru (1969) and Algeria (1971). However, these policies have varied greatly in their practical application, and in some cases have had little redistributive impact. Almost invariably they have been presented as a means of improving equity and production while encouraging small-scale cultivators to remain in rural areas.

Yet arguably most of these policies have stimulated rural-urban migration. Thus the introduction of tenancy contracts in countries such as Argentina, Colombia and Peru led to a mass eviction of peasant tenants (Barraclough and Domike, 1970, p. 76). To have allowed security of tenure would have meant the landlords ceding control of the land they owned. The abolition of servant labour in Ecuador had a similar effect. It was accompanied by a rule stipulating that peasants were to be granted ownership of the land they cultivated as well as credit and extension services. Landowners interpreted this as a threat to their local control and began to consolidate their landholdings and mechanise production. As a result the peasants became worse off than before, especially as non-farm employment declined substantially (Peek, 1979). Correspondingly, there was a rapid increase in rural emigration (Saenz Andrade, 1978, pp. 102, 141).

Indeed, land reform has rarely resulted in extensive land redistribution; often legislative loopholes have allowed landlords to retain much of the land, notably the most fertile, as well as vital assets such as equipment, mills and irrigation points. A few examples should suffice to illustrate the small redistributive impact. In Ecuador the effect of the 1964 land reform was mainly confined to state-owned lands and such lands as the Church and private landlords were willing to sell (USAID/Ecuador, 1970, p. 75). In Venezuela the terms on which landlords were obliged to sell land were so generous that the reform agency had to limit severely the number of farms purchased (Wing, 1970, p. 27). In Colombia only land inadequately utilised was subject to expropriation, which meant there was no land reform in the fertile valley areas (Feder, 1971, pp. 197-202). This is not to suggest that such reforms had no redistributive effect. Some did have, but mainly by providing temporary gains that were soon eroded.[1] Some reforms, notably in Bolivia after 1952, redistributed what had been semi-feudal holdings but in doing so created minifundias, which resulted in a drop in food output and further emigration from the areas affected (see, for example, Hiraoka, 1980, p. 332). However, most have had little effect because of diverse exemption clauses or because they were never really implemented.

In many cases of reform, exemption clauses have allowed large landlords to avoid expropriation. In

---

1 This point is argued in a recent ILO study by Ghai, et al (1979); in particular, see the studies of Egypt and the Republic of Korea. See also Clark (1970).

Colombia "well managed" holdings were exempt, in Peru estates registered as stock companies, in Brazil all those classified as "rural enterprises", in Ecuador "efficiently run" farms, and so on. These loopholes have had one overriding consequence, that of motivating landowners to cultivate commercially with wage labour. At the same time governments have generally provided low-cost agricultural credit to large farmers for labour-saving innovations, which has further marginalised the peasantry and driven many to migrate (Pearse, 1970, pp. 201-209; Shaw, 1974, pp. 123-132).

What these various reforms did manage to do was accelerate agricultural commercialisation, mechanisation, extensive cultivation, and the associated shift to wage labour. But as they sought to become the efficient profit-oriented farmers the legislators had in mind, large landowners increasingly dispensed with tenants and only required large numbers of wage workers at certain times of the agricultural cycle. The result was that the peasants' precarious livelihood was worsened rather than improved, since they lost their previously insecure source of subsistence altogether. For many of them rural emigration became practically the only option.

Another effect of land reform was an acceleration of urban growth. Paradoxical though this may seem, it is better appreciated when it is noted that a major objective of land reform was the transfer of economic surplus to urban areas. This was done by generating agricultural profits that could be invested in manufacturing and other urban industries and by supplying urban populations with more food at lower cost, which would allow lower money wage rates and thus accelerate capital accumulation in urban areas. But urban growth has also often benefited more directly and immediately from land reform. Thus in some cases even the threat of land reform was enough to make landowners shift investments to urban areas (King, 1977, p. 67). After the initiation of land reform in Mexico, for instance, landlords transferred investments in this way, first into construction, then into other industries (Flores, 1956, pp. 243-246). This boosted the urban economy at the expense of agriculture, and by raising urban incomes and job opportunities encouraged rural-urban migration. Such migration was a direct consequence of the land reform policy as actually implemented, even though it was scarcely the stated objective.

There have been other effects of land reform tending to increase migration. To the extent that the reforms and the associated provision of credit have led to technological innovations, greater land utilisation and productivity, and hence higher agricultural output, there has been a tendency for unit prices of agricultural products to fall. Where small farmers have been unable to raise production to offset falling prices, their propensity to migrate has increased.

VII. Colonisation or Resettlement Schemes and Migration

As an alternative to land reform, many governments have turned to elaborate and costly colonisation or "human resettlement" schemes. These have been introduced in many countries of South and Central America, including Bolivia, Brazil, Chile, Colombia, Guatemala, Guyana, Peru and Venezuela, as well as in many other parts of the world.[1] As with land reform, the main objectives have included increasing agricultural production and the surplus available for urban-based industrialisation; the schemes have also been presented as a means of absorbing part of the surplus population in depressed areas. Yet many observers have seen them as a convenient substitute for land reform[2] - indeed as a means of easing the pressure for land reform in the face of rising unemployment, poverty and rural emigration.

One purpose of colonisation schemes has been to shift workers from densely to sparsely populated regions, thereby not only stimulating production in the newly settled areas but raising the average living standards of those remaining in the more settled areas (Nelson, 1973, pp. 29-31). In practice, however, colonisation and resettlement schemes have in most cases not arrested rural-urban migration, either from the newly settled areas or from the settlers' home areas. And where they have had some success it has generally been at enormous financial cost (Barraclough and Schatan, 1973, pp. 175-194). A few successes can be cited, but usually some special factor has been involved (Katzman, 1978, pp. 709-724; idem, 1975, pp. 75-107). One can catalogue various reasons for the persistent failure of colonisation schemes, such as lack of infrastructure, inappropriate choice of settlers, and the difficulty of adapting

---

[1] Perhaps the most controversial have been the transmigration schemes in Indonesia, where even limited land reform was abandoned in the 1960s (Tjondronegoro, 1972). Among the many analyses of the transmigration policy, see Hardjono (1977) and Perez-Sáinz (1979).

[2] See, for example, Lipton (1974), p. 272. Albert Hirschman concluded that "colonisation may be expected to be amply tried out in a country where the landowners are powerful and where virgin, state-owned lands are plentiful" (Hirschman, 1963, p. 138).

traditional techniques of cultivation in unfamiliar terrain; studies of such schemes in Bolivia, Brazil, Guyana and Peru, for example, have pointed to these and related obstacles (see, inter alia, Dozier, 1969; Nelson, 1973; Standing and Sukdeo, 1977, pp. 303-313).

But there are other reasons that are more fundamental. Thus the effect on living standards in the rural areas from which the settlers are drawn depends crucially on the social relations of production prevailing there. If the community consists mainly of independent smallholders, then living standards, productivity and output may indeed rise. However, there is no guarantee that a reduction in population pressure will lead to improved output. Indeed some economists have argued that an increase in population pressure is a necessary stimulus to technological change and agricultural production (Boserup, 1965). If that is so, colonisation schemes designed to reduce population pressure may actually postpone technological change and slow down the growth of agricultural production, at least in those areas.

If, however, the relations of production in the settlers' home areas are characterised by landlord domination, then any improvement in living standards following their out-migration is likely to be small or negligible. This is because any surplus over traditional subsistence requirements is likely to be absorbed by the landlords and middlemen. Indeed that fact alone would be a powerful disincentive to an expansion of peasant production. And in such circumstances the tendency of the poor to leave the rural areas will persist.

The same argument applies where traditional hierarchical relations of production become established in the settlement areas. This emerges in the case of the Rondônia settlement schemes discussed in Chapter 5 below and in a way in the settlement schemes introduced in Guyana in recent years, as discussed in Chapter 9. In many colonisation schemes the settlers have not been given ownership of the land on which they have been settled, and the result has been that once cleared, the land has been reclaimed by the owners (Barraclough and Domike, 1977, p. 86). Schemes of this sort have quickly bred disillusion among smallholders who had settled in the hope of becoming prosperous independent farmers. In many cases, from Indonesia to the Amazon areas of Brazil, such disillusion has speedily led to migration and economic stagnation.

One of the major reasons for the limited success of these schemes is that, like many types of land reform, they have been introduced to stimulate manufacturing industries in urban areas as much as to benefit the rural population directly involved (Gutelman, 1974). In Chile and Guatemala, to take just two of many examples, colonisation agencies are said to have created such small farm units that the settlers had to supplement their meagre incomes by seasonal migration to work for wages on estates or in urban areas (King, 1977, p. 86). In such cases colonisation schemes have had little chance of redistributing the population or discouraging rural outmigration.

VIII. Government Wage Policies and Rural Emigration

Agrarian reforms typically have encouraged urban population growth through the rural-urban migration of peasants and workers displaced by mechanisation and land consolidation. In turn, that migration has been associated with rising urban unemployment and poverty (Bairoch, 1973). Two factors have been identified as contributing to these trends. The first is the inability of urban employment growth to keep up with the growth of the urban population. The rate of employment growth has often been rapid; the problem has been that the initial base has usually been too small.[1]

The second factor is the rural-urban wage differential. Indeed, many economists have argued or implied that the most effective way of reducing rural-urban migration and urban unemployment is to reduce that differential (Todaro, 1976, pp. 211-225). Although some attempts have been made to reduce urban wage levels, it has been widely recognised that the main reason for the substantial differentials has been the low level of rural wages.[2] Many governments have implicitly recognised this by introducing minimum wage legislation, often with the active support of industrialists as well as workers. Such legislation has often been directed at estate-owners who have traditionally paid their peons little or nothing in the form of a money wage.

However, minimum wage legislation has almost certainly failed to reduce rural-urban wage differentials substantially, if only because it is the urban-based

---

1 For instance, between 1968 and 1975 urban employment in Ecuador expanded at the same rate as urban population (6 per cent annually), but labour absorption declined because of the much smaller initial level of employment. As a result, urban poverty greatly worsened (Peek, 1979, and Chapter 4 below).

2 Among those wanting to hold down urban wage levels, see Tidrick (1975) especially pp. 322-324; and Todaro (1971), pp. 402-403.

industrialists who have benefited most from low rural wage levels. That is because the rural wage is a major determinant of the cost of wage labour and food prices in the urban areas.[1] Moreover, whereas minimum wages have typically represented a "floor" in urban industries, in rural areas they have tended to form a "ceiling". Employers in the remoter rural areas, taking advantage of their monopsonistic position in the labour market, have also been able to circumvent the legislation to a greater extent than has been possible in the more regulated urban economy. One common practice of rural employers has been to pay a large part of the wage "in kind", and to overvalue the non-monetary elements. As a consequence it has been shown on several occasions that many groups of rural workers have received substantially less than the prescribed minimum wage.[2] Often agricultural employers have successfully circumvented minimum wage laws by replacing permanent labourers with casual workers (a practice by no means restricted to rural employers). Especially when paying workers on a piece-rate basis, rural employers have been able to hire temporary workers at wage rates that reflect the workers' weak bargaining power rather than the legal minimum. Casual workers have been least protected by social security benefits, and rural employers have commonly used seasonal migrants to avoid paying either the minimum wage or, where provision is made for them, social security contributions. Such migrant workers, like the so-called <u>bóias frias</u> of Brazil, have virtually no bargaining power or security of employment and have to accept what wages they are offered. Yet because they have been used to displace more permanent workers, rural unemployment has risen and rural wage rates have declined, despite minimum wage legislation. It is therefore scarcely surprising that such legislation has done little to lessen rural-urban wage differentials and has even contributed to rural-urban migration.

---

[1] This is consistent with the fact that urban industrialists have favoured the establishment of wage laws, for they have been a means of "freeing" rural workers from the restraints on mobility represented by the sort of non-wage relations of production discussed earlier.

[2] For instance, one estimate found this applied to cane cutters in rural Brazil (Barraclough and Collarte, 1970, p. 45). In Mexico agricultural workers "receive ...incomes, which are generally below minimum official wages" (Stavenhagen, 1970, p. 245). Similar findings have been reported in Peru (PREALC, 1978).

Conversely, where such legislation has been effective in rural areas, as in large-scale capitalist enterprises, it has tended to accelerate labour-saving mechanisation. In Brazil, for example, this process contributed to a rapid increase in rural emigration (Brandao Lopes, 1977, pp. 59-71). Thus even the successful application of minimum wage laws in rural areas has encouraged rather than discouraged rural-urban migration.

IX. Other Agrarian Policies

Although academics and planning specialists have proposed numerous other policies to reduce rural emigration, a common difficulty has been the likelihood that they may conflict with other state objectives. To recommend measures that do not take account of such realities is not particularly useful.

One popular suggestion is tax reform. In many countries agricultural produce has been taxed to finance urban-based industrialisation, a policy which has widened rural-urban income differentials and thus stimulated rural-urban migration. The advantages have been that the large size of the agricultural sector makes the tax income potential also large, and that sales taxes have been convenient to collect. So, those recommending some alternative tax strategy have to show that the benefits more than offset such perceived advantages.

Some analysts have suggested taxing urban wages as a means of reducing rural-urban migration (Todaro, 1976a, p. 403). The practical objection to this (and there are others) is that it will lead to countervailing actions by urban workers, and unions in particular, and is merely likely to increase wage inflation. If the tax is passed on to the employer in increased labour costs it will discourage the growth of urban employment, which governments would presumably be loath to do when faced with mass unemployment.

Another suggested tax measure is the reform of property taxation, making it more progressive and high enough to induce land redistribution through the sale of parts of large rural landholdings. The two drawbacks to this are that such taxes are easy to evade in the absence of an effective land title system, a common enough situation, and that they have often been largely or wholly passed on to consumers, thus tending to raise labour costs (workers needing higher wages to compensate for higher food prices).

A related approach has involved altering the rural-urban terms of trade through agricultural price support systems or subsidies to agricultural production. These also have serious drawbacks, being costly to administer and typically contrary to the development strategy of rapid industrialisation. To the extent that price support systems raise food prices they not only encourage the persistence of inefficient forms of production but, more importantly, raise the cost of living. In doing so they put upward pressure on urban wage rates, and thereby hinder employment growth outside agriculture. In sum, given a commitment to rapid industrialisation, price support systems have inherent limitations.

Agricultural subsidies have been introduced in many countries, but there is no evidence that they have reduced rural-urban migration, whether they have taken the form of tax credits or waivers, subsidised interest rates, or direct investment subsidies. Almost certainly they have raised rural unemployment - and thus migration - by inducing labour-displacing technological innovations.

Other suggestions have included programmes of "integrated rural development" involving the wholesale provision of social services and infrastructure as well as fiscal and other incentives to rural development. In practice such approaches share some of the drawbacks of colonisation schemes, requiring a massive commitment of government resources and being fraught with administrative, political and economic difficulties. Moreover, there is no assurance that they will check rural-urban migration; after all, the opening of roads and railways to remote areas has often provided a convenient means of migrating out of those areas.

Finally, it is worth mentioning three strategies which appear to have a relatively high probability of reducing rural emigration. The first is the creation of integrated rural communities based on a fundamental change in the social relations of production. That would encompass rural co-operatives, including schemes of the Ujamaa village type advocated if not effectively implemented in Tanzania. A fundamental difficulty is that the establishment of "self-reliant", profitable and equitable rural co-operatives has been extremely hard to achieve in communities conditioned by quasi-feudal or competitive traditions where a sense of close community co-operation is novel or long-forgotten.[1] A second approach pursued in some countries such as Brazil and the Republic of Korea is the creation of new "urban growth poles" designed to draw migration away from the primate cities.

---

[1] Guyana is an example of a country in which rural co-operatives have been established largely on a voluntary basis, with limited impact on rural development or rural emigration. For a brief account see Standing (1979, pp. 70-76).

As with integrated rural development strategies, this has the cardinal drawback of being extremely costly. It has the added disadvantage of being likely to stimulate rural-urban migration rather than reduce it, since it merely presents potential migrants with new locations from which to choose. That of course is less important if the primary objective is to reduce population concentration in specific urban centres.

A third approach combines elements of the previous two, and involves a more integrated form of development based on changing the social relations of production in urban as well as rural areas. In particular it implies a commitment to break down the rural-urban dichotomy and to stimulate what is sometimes known as the "urbanisation of the countryside". The country in Latin America which has favoured something like that is Cuba, whose policy has been characterised as "a minimum of urbanism and a maximum of ruralism" (Fidel Castro, quoted in Landstreet and Mundigo, 1978, p. 20). There, the capital Havana has received relatively little in the way of resources while over 300 new small towns have been set up since 1964 in an attempt to make the country a web of small urban communities comprising a predominantly agricultural population. The relative success of this strategy in checking the type of migration and urban unemployment found in other Latin American countries can be assessed in the light of a few telling statistics. In the past two decades or more, it seems that no country in Latin America has experienced such balanced growth in its rural and urban populations or such low rates of urban population growth. Perhaps most striking of all, and contrary to the recent experience of most other countries, the growth of the capital city has lagged behind over-all population growth (ibid.; see also Landstreet, 1975, pp. 127-158). Significantly too, in the UN Population Inquiry in 1978 Cuba was one of only two countries in the ECLA region with a population distribution that could be described as completely or largely acceptable (table 1).

It seems these results have been achieved by the establishment of "rural-urban" communities equipped with the necessary infrastructure and productive organisation to make then economically and socially viable. The experience, critically analysed in Chapter 10 below, suggests that it is possible to check rapid urbanisation and rural-urban migration, but to do so probably requires a commitment to change the direction of economic development as pursued in most countries.

X. Concluding Remarks

It is clear that while many governments have expressed their concern over high rates of rural-urban migration and their determination to curb it, their policies have substantially contributed to that migration.

This has posed a dilemma few governments have been able to resolve. Article 13(1) of the Universal Declaration of Human Rights states that everyone has the right to freedom of movement and residence within the borders of his own State. Yet many governments have introduced legal restrictions on movement or have attempted to discourage rural-urban migration by discriminating against migrants in the provision of social services or jobs.

Perhaps the best known example of direct controls on urbanisation is the "rustication" of urban secondary school graduates in China, which coincided with restrictions on travel to urban areas.[1] Elsewhere attempts have been made to limit entry to large cities: the notorious pass laws in Southern African townships are a case in point. In many countries vagrancy laws have allowed the deportation of jobless migrants. And in Jakarta, Indonesia, a decree issued in 1970 required migrants to register on arrival and if without a job after six months to leave the city. Although many thousands of migrants have been sent back to their village of origin for lack of the necessary identification card, the various administrative restrictions have had only a modest impact and have given rise to petty corruption (Simmons, 1979, pp. 92-93). Such schemes have been no more successful elsewhere, but have created resentment and bitterness wherever implemented. Other methods of restricting entry to cities have been tried, including controversial urban slum clearance programmes, designed in part to discourage migrant squatters. These have figured prominently in Brazil and in other Latin American countries, but many observers have argued that they have not only caused extensive human suffering but have failed to arrest migration.

Some analysts have concluded that controlling migration would worsen rural-urban inequality, primarily because it would reduce the downward pressure on urban

---

[1] For a detailed account of Chinese schemes to reverse rural-urban migration, see Bernstein (1977).

wages while allowing rural poverty to increase.[1] Whether or not that is a realistic or generalisable conclusion, it is likely that many governments introducing migration controls have been primarily concerned with defusing political unrest that is harder to control when the unemployed and poor are concentrated in urban centres than when they are dispersed in the countryside.

The fact remains that the early stages of industrialisation in all market economies have been associated with rapid rural-urban migration, which in turn has been linked to the transformation of traditional rural production relations impeding the growth of agricultural output and of urban-industrial employment. This migration, typically accompanied by urban unemployment and poverty, has undoubtedly been stimulated by government policies introduced to accelerate economic growth. In order to bring about a change in that pattern of migration, it will be necessary to make corresponding changes in the broader strategy of economic growth.

---

[1] An empirical study of the Philippines suggested that migration controls would have that effect, as did a similarly detailed study in the Republic of Korea. See Rodgers, Hopkins and Wéry, 1978, pp. 323-324; and Adelman and Robinson (1978, pp. 1-26, especially table 3, p. 20).

References

Adelman, I. and Robinson, S. (1978): "Migration, demographic change and income distribution in a model of a developing country", in J.L. Simon (ed.): Research in population economics, Vol. I (Greenwich (Conn.), Jai Press).

Arrighi, G. (1970): "Labour supplies in historical perspective: A study of the proletarianisation of the African peasantry in Rhodesia", in Journal of Development Studies, Apr., Vol. 6, No. 3.

Bairoch, P. (1973): Urban unemployment in developing countries (Geneva, ILO).

Balán, J. (1978): Agrarian structure, capitalist development and labour markets in Latin America: Cityward migration in a historical perspective (Buenos Aires, CEDES).

Baran, P.A. (1957): The political economy of growth (New York, Monthly Review Press).

Barraclough, S. and Domike, A.L. (1970): "Agrarian structure in seven Latin American countries", in R. Stavenhagen (ed.): Agrarian problems and peasant movements in Latin America (New York, Anchor Books).

Barraclough, S. and Collarte, J. (1973): Agrarian structure in Latin America (Lexington, Massachusetts, Heath and Co.).

Barraclough, S. and Schatan, J. (1973): "Technological policy and agricultural development", in Land Economics, May, Vol. XLIX, No. 2.

Bernstein, T.P. (1977): Up to the mountains and down to the villages (New Haven, Conn., and London, Yale University Press).

Boserup, E. (1965): The conditions of agricultural growth: The economics of agrarian change under population pressure (Chicago, Aldine).

Brandao Lopes, J. (1977): "Développement capitaliste et structure agraire au Brésil", in Sociologie du travail, Jan.-Mar., Vol. 19, No. 1, pp. 59-71.

CIESE (1977): Impacto de la reforma agraria en la distribución de la población en Ecuador (Quito).

Clark, R.J. (1970): "Land reform in Bolivia", in AID Spring Review of Land Reform, Vol. VI (Washington, DC, US Agency for International Development).

--- (1970): "Land reform in Ecuador", in AID Spring Review of Land Reform (Washington, Agency for International Development), Vol. VI.

Costales, P. and Costales, A. (1964): Aspectos socio-económicos de la estructura agraria ecuatoriana, Vol. II of Historia social del Ecuador (Quito, IEAG).

Dozier, C.L. (1969): Land development and colonization in Latin America: Case studies of Peru, Bolivia and Mexico (New York, Praeger).

Feder, E. (1971): The rape of the peasantry: Latin America's landholding system (New York, Anchor Books).

Flores, E. (1956): "Agrarian reform and economic development", in K.H. Parsons, R.J. Penn and P.M. Raup (eds.): Land tenure (Madison, University of Wisconsin Press).

Frank, A.G. (1967): Capitalism and underdevelopment in Latin America (New York, Monthly Review Press).

Ghai, D., Khan, A., Lee, E. and Radwan, S. (eds.) (1979): Agrarian systems and rural development (London, Macmillan, for the ILO).

Glade, W. (1969): The Latin American economies: A study of their institutional evolution (New York, American Books).

Gutelman, M. (1974): Structures et réforme agraire (Paris, Maspèro).

Hardjono, J.M. (1977): Transmigration in Indonesia (Kuala Lumpur, Oxford University Press).

Hiraoka, M. (1980): "Settlement and development of the Upper Amazon: The East Bolivian example", in The Journal of Developing Areas, Apr., Vol. 14, No. 3.

Hirschman, A.O. (1963): Journey toward progress: Studies of economic policy-making in Latin America (New York, Twentieth Century Fund).

Hobsbawm, E.J. (1974): The age of revolution, 1789-1848 (London, Abicus).

--- (1969): "A case of neo-feudalism: La Convención, Peru", in Journal of Latin American Studies, Vol. 1, No. 1.

Katzman, M.T. (1978): "Colonization as an approach to regional development: Northern Paraná, Brazil", in Economic Development and Cultural Change, July, Vol. 26, No. 4.

--- (1975): "Regional development policy in Brazil: The role of growth poles and development highways in Goias", in Economic Development and Cultural Change, Oct., Vol. 24, No. 1.

King, R. (1977): Land reform: A world survey (London, Bell and Sons).

Laclau, E. (1971): "Feudalism and capitalism in Latin America", in New Left Review, No. 67.

Landstreet, B. (1975): "Cuba", in A.L. Segal (ed.): Population policies in the Caribbean (Lexington, Mass., Heath and Co.).

Landstreet, B. and A.I. Mundigo (1978): Development policies and demographic change in socialist Cuba, paper presented at the annual meeting of the Population Association of America, Atlanta, April 13-15 1978.

Lewis, W.A. (1954): "Economic development with unlimited supplies of labour", in The Manchester School of Economic and Social Studies, Vol. 22, No. 2.

Lipton, M. (1974): "Towards a theory of land reform", in D. Lehmann (ed.): Agrarian reform and agrarian reformism: Studies of Peru, Chile, China and India (London, Faber and Faber, 1974).

Mellafe, R. (1971): The latifundio and the city in Latin American history (Toronto, Toronto University Press).

Migdal, J.S. (1974): Peasants, politics and revolution: Pressures towards political and social change in the Third World (Princeton, Princeton University Press).

Nelson, M. (1973): The development of tropical lands: Policy issues in Latin America (Baltimore, Johns Hopkins University Press).

Paige, J. (1975): Agrarian revolution: social movements and export agriculture in the underdeveloped world (New York and London, Macmillan).

Pearse, A. (1975): The Latin American peasant (London, Frank Cass and Co.).

--- (1970): "Urbanization and the incorporation of the peasant", in A.J. Field (ed.): City and country in the Third World (Cambridge, Mass., Schenkman).

Peek, P. (1979): Urban poverty, migration and land reform in Ecuador (Geneva, ILO; mimeographed World Employment Programme research working paper; restricted).

Perez-Sáinz, J.P. (1979): Transmigration and accumulation in Indonesia (Geneva, ILO; mimeographed World Employment Programme research working paper; restricted).

PREALC (1978): Perú: Estrategia de desarrollo y grado de satisfacción de las necesidades básicas (Santiago de Chile).

Ridler, N.B. (1978): "Government policy options for agrarian reform in Colombia", in Desarrollo rural en las Américas (Bogotá), Vol. X, No. 1.

Rodgers, G.B., Hopkins, M. and Wéry, R. (1978): Population, employment and inequality: BACHUE-Philippines (Farnborough, Saxon House, for the ILO).

Rudra, A. (1978): The basic needs concept and its implementation in Indian development planning (Bangkok, ILO-ARTEP).

Rutledge, I. (1977): "The integration of the highland peasantry into the sugar cane economy of northern Argentina, 1930-1943", in K. Duncan and I. Rutledge (eds.): Land and labour in Latin America: Essays on the development of agrarian capitalism in the nineteenth and twentieth centuries (Cambridge, Cambridge University Press).

Saenz Andrade, A. (1978): El proceso de transformación de la estructura agraria, estructura ocupacional y migraciones en la parroquia Cutuglahua, en el periodo 1959-1974 (Quito).

Shaw, R.P. (1974): "Land tenure and the rural exodus in Latin America", in Economic Development and Cultural Change, Oct., Vol. 23, No. 1.

Simmons, A.B. (1979): "Slowing metropolitan city growth in Asia: Policies, programs, and results", in Population and Development Review (New York), March, Vol. 5, No. 1.

Standing, G. (1979): "Socialism and basic needs in Guyana", in G. Standing and R. Szal: Poverty and basic needs (Geneva, ILO).

--- (1981): "Migration and modes of exploitation: The social origins of immobility and mobility", in Journal of Peasant Studies, Jan., Vol. 8, No. 2.

Standing, G. and Sukdeo, F. (1977): "Labour migration and development in Guyana", in International Labour Review (Geneva, ILO), Nov.-Dec., Vol. 116, No. 3, pp. 303-313.

Stavenhagen. R. (ed.) (1970): Agrarian problems and peasant movements in Latin America (New York, Anchor Books).

--- (1970): "Social aspects of agrarian structure in Mexico", in Stavenhagen, 1970, ibid.

Stitzlein, J.N. (1967): The characteristics and significance of the non-institutional credit market in rural Ecuador, AFC Research Publication No. 117 (Columbus, Ohio State University, Department of Agricultural Economics and Rural Sociology).

Thiesenhusen, W.C. (1971): "Employment and Latin American development", in P. Dorner (ed.): Land reform in Latin America: Issues and cases, Land Economics Monograph No. 3 (Madison, University of Wisconsin Press).

Tidrick, G.M. (1975): "Wage spillover and unemployment in a wage-gap economy: The Jamaican case", in Economic Development and Cultural Change, Jan., Vol. 73, No. 2, pp. 306-324.

Tjondronegoro, S.M.P. (1972): Land reform or land settlement: Shifts in Indonesia's land policy 1960-1970, Land Tenure Center Paper No. 81 (Madison, University of Wisconsin Press).

Todaro, M.P. (1971): "Income expectations, rural-urban migration and employment in Africa", in International Labour Review (Geneva, ILO), Nov., Vol. 104, No. 5, pp. 387-413.

--- (1976): Internal migration in developing countries (Geneva, ILO, 1976).

--- (1976a): "Urban job expansion, induced migration and rising unemployment", in Journal of Development Economics, Sep., Vol. 3, No. 3.

Wing, H.E. (1970): "Land reform in Venezuela", in AID Spring Review of Land Reform, Vol. V (Washington, DC, AID).

World Bank (1975): Land reform (Washington, DC).

Chapter 2

AGRARIAN CHANGE AND MIGRATION IN CHILE

by Cristobal Kay*

I. Introduction

Migration in Chile, as elsewhere, should be analysed in terms of the changing structure of production.[1] The extent and pattern of migration in Chile have been largely determined by changes in Chile's insertion in the world capitalist system, the over-all development of the productive forces, the land tenure system, social and technical relations of production, state policy and, of course, the rate of population growth. A comprehensive analysis of migration processes taking into account the above factors is beyond the scope of this paper. The analysis is limited mainly to the various forms of capitalist penetration in agriculture and the implications of this for migration from a long-term perspective. A historical view is essential to single out the key factors relating to migratory processes. Attention will concentrate on the recent agrarian reform and current counter-reform periods.

Vergopolous, in his stimulating book on the agrarian question and capitalism, criticises the classical Marxist position which contends that the development of capitalism in agriculture leads to land concentration, the multiplication of large-scale enterprises, and the proletarianisation of small landowners (Vergopolous, 1975). On the contrary, he contends that the development of the capitalist mode of production has led to the persistence of small peasant ownership. Similarly Nun, Murmis and Marín sustain the thesis that the penetration of capitalist relations into subsistence agriculture in dependent countries does not dissolve the old links of the worker with the land thereby maintaining and even recreating the subsistence economies (Nun, Murmis and Marín, 1967). Evidence from the Chilean case (and I suspect from a few

---

* University of Glasgow.

1 For some efforts in developing a political economy approach to migration see Portes (1978); Standing (1979); and Peek and Standing (1979).

others as well) suggests, however, that the original propositions are still partly valid. Of course the patterns of development of capitalism in agriculture have not always taken the forms envisaged by Marx nor have they always evolved for the reasons he states but the essentials are still correct or, at least, provide extremely useful insights. I hope, in what follows, to demonstrate this proposition for the Chilean case. The implications of my proposition are that labour mobility and rural out-migration developed earlier and were more accentuated in Chile than in other contexts where the landlord road to capitalist agriculture was not so predominant or did not succeed.

Amin also sustains that the development of the capitalist mode of production in peripheral social formations has reproduced and not proletarianised small peasant producers (Amin, 1975, p. 44). However, the effect of capitalism in Chile was to turn tenants (inquilinos) into wage labourers, and small peasant-proprietors (minifundistas) into seasonal labourers for the landlord or into migrant urban workers. Thus the landlord road to capitalist agriculture predominated in Chile (see below). Small peasant proprietorship (minifundistas) survived but were articulated with and subordinated to the needs of the capitalist transition of the landlord economy.

It is crucial to study the hacienda system, its transformation and relationship to the internal and external peasant enterprises, to understand the dynamics of agrarian change and rural migration. As the hacienda system concentrates most of the land and capital and is the largest employer of rural labour, it exercises a determining influence over the rates of labour absorption and expulsion in the countryside. By internal peasant enterprises I refer to the various types of tenant enterprises within the hacienda and by external peasant enterprise to the traditional small peasant proprietorships. Both rely on unpaid family labour; little or no wage labour is contracted. Both mainly produce use values (production for subsistence consumption) rather than exchange values (production for the market) and in both simple commodity production predominates, as the commercialised surplus is only sufficient to purchase some essential commodities. Thus little or no capital accumulation takes place. The internal and external peasant enterprises are distinguished by ownership, for whereas the peasant proprietor owns a plot of land, the tenant does not.

The central feature of the landlord road to capitalism is the slow transformation of the hacienda system based on tenant labour into one relying solely on wage labour.

In the tenant-labour hacienda system two processes of production take place simultaneously: one undertaken by the tenant enterprise and the other by the landlord enterprise (demesne). The labour time spent by the tenant family on the tenancy plot can be considered as necessary labour as it satisfies subsistence needs. The labour time worked by the tenant family on the demesne is surplus labour whose product is appropriated directly by the landlord. The tenant provides a certain amount of unpaid labour to the landlord enterprise as labour-rent payment for the lease of a subsistence plot of land. This is the original and most simple organisation of the hacienda system which in Chile was partly transformed by the mid-nineteenth century.

The penetration of capitalism resulted in the destruction of the tenant enterprise and the centralisation of the hacienda's process of production into a single one on the landlord enterprise. I refer to this as the internal proletarianisation process, as the tenant is changed into a full proletarian employed for a wage by the landlord enterprise, or is even expelled from the estate, having to search for alternative employment as a wage labourer (Kay, 1971). The penetration of capitalism into the small peasant-proprietor areas leads them to seek seasonal wage employment on the landlord enterprise or to emigrate to the urban sector as proletarians. I refer to this process as external proletarianisation. The internal and external proletarianisation of subsistence peasant agriculture takes slightly different forms, being influenced by different factors and proceeding at completely different speeds. The internal proletarianisation is much faster and more ruthless, being under the landlord's direct control, unlike the external. Minifundistas on the external peasant enterprise are more able to resist full proletarianisation, as seasonal wage employment - a partial proletarianisation - enables them to retain small plots of land. It also serves as a cheap labour reserve for capitalism. These different forms of proletarianisation have led to different types and degrees of migration.

II. Rural Migration: An Overview, 1865-1970

Before embarking on a more detailed analysis, it may be helpful to present an over-all picture of rural migration by region between 1865 and 1970 (see table 1). For simplicity the country has been divided up into three regions - Northern, Central and Southern. The Central region is the most important from the population and agricultural points of view as it is here that the hacienda system has been traditionally dominant. In 1865 this region accounted for two-thirds of the rural population and probably over three-quarters of cultivated land, falling to just under a half of rural population and over a third of cultivated land by 1965. What is remarkable is that for the whole country there was a continuous net rate of rural out-migration for the whole period. The southern region was partly colonised in the second half of the nineteenth century[1] and was an area of significant net rural immigration until the mid-1880s. It started to lose population from 1930 and in an accelerated fashion from the 1950s, surpassing the traditionally high rate of net out-migration of the Central region. The northern mining region exhibited a pendular pattern of migration during the second half of the nineteenth century and the beginning of this century. Periodic crises brought a fluctuating demand for labour, particularly in the nitrate mines. In times of expansion the net rate of migration tended to be negative and during crises to be positive, i.e. some unemployed miners returned to peasant subsistence agriculture. As for the total rate of net rural migration, it is significant that its sudden acceleration in 1940 and thereafter is linked to the end of the period of continuous expansion of cultivated land and to the beginnings of a process of rapid mechanisation in agriculture.

Table 1 also indicates the rate of growth of the rural and total populations. During the economic crisis of the 1930s, the rate of growth of the rural population temporarily increased (or, in other words, the rate of rural out-migration fell) only to stagnate as from 1940 and to become negative from 1960 for the first time in Chilean history. Stagnation in the growth of the rural population coincided with the introduction of the import-substitution industrialisation policy by the Popular Front government in the late 1930s. At the same time the urban population exceeded the rural. The drastic increase in the rate of rural out-migration from 1950 also coincided with the start of the population explosion, i.e. the rate of population growth doubled from 1940-52 to 1952-60 and remained high, declining only slightly. As a result of both effects (the stagnant and negative rate of rural population growth and the population explosion), the rate of urban growth accelerated, especially in the capital city which accounted for over 40 per cent of total urban population by 1960, leading to the emergence of vast urban slums and shanty-towns. This continuous

---

[1] Partly because most of the relatively small indigenous population were already settled there before the Spanish Conquest. Complete military control over the area was only established after Independence.

Table 1: Rate of net rural migration per year by region and rate of rural population and total population growth, 1865-1970
(Rate per 100 population)

Period	Rate of net rural migration per year[a]				Annual rate of total population growth	Annual rate of total population growth
	Northern region(b)	Central region(c)	Southern region(d)	Total		
1865-75	-1.84	-1.16	1.18	-0.73	0.8	1.33
1875-85	0.68	-1.74	1.43	-0.60	1.5	1.90
1985-95	-1.06	-1.30	-0.16	-0.93	0.0	0.73
1895-1907	1.03	-1.57	0.05	-0.66	1.1	1.52
1907-20	-1.49	-1.36	0.32	-0.79	0.5	1.11
1920-30	-4.23	-1.26	-0.27	-1.23	0.4	1.41
1930-40	-0.38	-1.09	-0.47	-0.72	1.1	1.60
1940-52	-2.32	-1.50	-1.47	-1.57	0.0	1.40
1952-60	-3.01	-2.03	-3.23	-2.64	0.8	2.78
1960-70				-4.51	-1.3	2.42

[a] The rate of net rural migration per year has been calculated by the author on the assumption that the annual natural rate of rural population growth is the same as the annual rate of total population. The probably higher mortality rates in the rural areas may result in a slight over-estimation of the rate of net rural out-migration mainly until the 1940s.

[b] Northern region includes the provinces of Tarapacá, Antofagasta, Atacama and Coquimbo.

[c] Central region includes the provinces of Aconcagua, Valparaíso, Santiago, O'Higgins, Colchagua, Curicó, Talca, Maule, Linares and Nuble.

[d] Southern region includes the provinces of Concepción, Arauco, Bío-Bío, Malleco, Cautín, Valdivia, Osorno, Llanquihue, Chiloé, Aisén and Magallanes.

Source: Data for 1865 to 1960 calculated by author from Hurtado (1966, p. 144); Data for 1970 are calculated from CELADE (1979, p. 29).

and, in recent decades, increasing rate of rural out-migration has meant that by 1970 only a quarter of the total active population was engaged in agriculture.

From colonial times to the agrarian reform in 1965 Chile had one of the highest indexes of land concentration in the world, and the hacienda system dominated the countryside. However, no major social crisis or political upheaval occurred in the rural areas. Contrary to the commonly upheld view among social scientists, the hacienda system had displayed a high degree of flexibility in adapting to the changing needs of capital so that by the middle of the nineteenth century it could no longer be characterised as a static, quasi-feudal institution. Landlords changed the social and technical relations of production of the hacienda system when over-all economic circumstances indicated it was profitable to do so. Paradoxically, it was in the late 1930s when the hacienda system started to undergo its most significant transformation that the economic crisis of agriculture began. From this time on the rate of growth of agricultural production per capita became negative.

The hacienda system's flexibility was made possible by the existence of large reservoirs of land and labour. The labour surplus existed both within the large landed estates and more significantly in the surrounding minifundia areas which provided abundant and cheap labour for the hacienda system. The changing and varied relationships which the landlord enterprise was able to forge with the internal and external peasant enterprises allowed it to adapt to circumstances. The continuity in the rate of rural out-migration in the Central region disguised the varied causes of migration and the different origins of the migrants (from internal or external peasant economies) which changed according to the various phases of the penetration of capital into the rural sector. This development of capitalism in agriculture was accomplished with relatively little resistance from the peasantry, largely because rural out-migration provided a safety valve which together with the expansion of the arable land helped to avoid the ecological and demographic crisis which constantly threatened peasant agriculture (de Janvry and Garramón, 1977).

III. The Commercialisation of Agriculture, Colonisation and Labour Mobility

In the late 1840s new export markets opened up for Chilean wheat. This gave a tremendous boost to agricultural production as wheat was the principal crop. Prior to this there had been little incentive to increase production as the urban market was small, and most of the rural population obtained its own means of subsistence. The new export markets provided the stimulus for expanding production and the annual average rate of growth of wheat production between 1860 and 1880 was as high as 5.3 per cent. Exports accounted for about a third of total production during this period. After 1880 export opportunities diminished and wheat output increased by only 0.9 per cent yearly between 1880 and 1908 (Kay, 1977, p. 109). Most of the wheat production came from the hacienda system which owned an estimated 85 per cent of the country's arable land.

What effect did the growing commercialisation of the hacienda have on the relations of production, forms of labour exploitation, and migration? The increase in agricultural production was mainly achieved by expanding the cultivated area and by employing more labour. No major change occurred in the technical relations of production. Given the existence of a large reservoir of surplus labour in the hacienda and, especially, in the minifundia areas, the easiest way for landlords to increase their profits was by exploiting labour. The tenant labourers (inquilinos) now had to provide more labour services on the landlord's central enterprise, more inquilinos were settled but with smaller plots of land and, above all, large amounts of seasonal wage labour were employed chiefly from the surrounding minifundia areas but also by employing itinerant workers (Bauer, 1975).

With the growing commercialisation of agriculture, land concentration further increased and, as land values rose, landlords preferred to employ extra labour without granting too many new tenancies to inquilinos (Hagerman Johnson, 1978). Where possible, they employed seasonal labour, particularly as wheat production entails seasonal employment. Growing land concentration intensified population pressure on the minifundia areas and obliged minifundistas to undertake seasonal wage employment for landlords. With the expansion of agricultural production a large part of the floating mass of rural labour, derisively referred to as vagabundos (vagabonds), were settled on the hacienda and on minifundia areas, as by seasonally working on the estates they could survive on small plots of land (Góngora, 1966). On the hacienda they were mainly settled as allegados (residents) in existing inquilino households, so landlords avoided providing them with a tenancy.

From 1850 to 1880 the increase in production in the Central region was achieved by expanding the so-called internal frontier of the hacienda system, by enlarging the cultivated area within the estate's boundaries, as much land was still available. After 1880 wheat production was partially transferred to the Southern (or colonised) region which later became the country's main wheat region. In this case the increase in production was obtained by expanding the external frontier through the colonisation of new areas. According to Bauer, the expansion of wheat production between 1859 and 1875 in the Central region required between 35,000 and 50,000 additional workers (Bauer, 1971). I estimate that the natural growth of the active agricultural population in the region during this period accounted for more than double the amount of additional labour required. This explains how agricultural production could expand substantially in the Central region and yet be associated with a negative rate of net rural migration. This out-migration was largely destined for the Southern colonisation region (table 1).

This steady, relatively early and high rate of rural out-migration has important implications for the discussion on the characterisation of the mode of production in rural Chile. Frank, in his historical study of Chile, maintains that Chile and indeed Latin America have been capitalist since their integration into the world capitalist system during the Colonial period (Frank, 1967). He reached such a conclusion because, in his definition of the capitalist mode of production, exchange relations take primacy over production relations, and he did not examine carefully the prevailing social relations of production. Laclau gives primacy to the relations of production in his conceptualisation of mode of production and maintains that a feudal mode of production existed in many regions of Latin America which was articulated to a dominant capitalist system (Laclau, 1971). While Frank views the Chilean growth of agricultural exports as further consolidating capitalist underdevelopment, Laclau argues that these exports strengthened servile relations of production and the use of extra-economic coercion (Laclau, 1969). Frank considers that the inquilino is further proletarianised while Laclau clearly states that it is erroneous to interpret the increasing extraction of a surplus from the inquilino as evidence of proletarianisation. In his turn, Ratcliff disputes Laclau's characterisation of the nineteenth century inquilinos as serfs and the large estates as feudal institutions (Ratcliff, 1973). Ratcliff's argument is that a quasi-capitalist mode of production based on large agrarian estates predominated in Chile. In certain aspects landowners performed as a capitalist class by responding aggressively to expanding market conditions but they instituted a labour repressive mode of production (a term borrowed from Barrington Moore) that is distinct from a capitalist, free labour system (ibid., pp. 82-83).

In my view, Laclau is incorrect in stating that extra-economic coercion was prevalent. Nor do I agree with Ratcliff's interpretation of a labour repressive mode of production. Landlords did not need to resort to extra-economic coercion to secure a supply of labour; the evidence indicates that a large number of surplus labourers existed who willingly settled as tenants or worked as subcontracted day labourers or directly as seasonal wage labourers on the hacienda when the opportunity arose. Of course, the monopolisation of the land by landlords helped to bring about this relative overpopulation in the minifundia areas. Labour mobility was in fact quite intense, particularly in the Central region where the hacienda system predominated. The annual rural population growth rate of the Central region between 1865 and 1907 was 0.2 per cent while the total population growth rate was 1.4 per cent, indicating the large emigration of labour from rural central Chile (Hurtado, 1966, p. 144). However, both seasonal and permanent migrant labour mainly came from the minifundia areas and from the vagabonds who lived on the fringes of villages, minifundia areas and the hacienda system (Tscherebilo, 1976). But this in no way indicates that the inquilino was attached to the hacienda by extra-economic coercion. On the contrary, they were attracted to settling on the estate by economic factors. The prospect of acquiring a tenancy of good irrigated land acted as a powerful incentive not only for landless rural workers but for minifundistas who were often confined to dry hill farming on the coastal range (Bauer, 1975, op. cit.). Despite the hard working conditions, inquilinos were seen as privileged as they had higher living standards than other rural labourers and a more secure subsistence income, not being compelled to migrate in search of seasonal work or extra income; some even did subcontract labour. Thus, far from being compelled to stay on the estates, inquilinos feared expulsion which sometimes occurred when the landlord enterprise expanded direct cultivation during the wheat export boom and expelled the original inquilinos in favour of new settlers who were willing to work under less favourable conditions (Hagerman Johnson, 1978, p. 638). Thus there were no restrictions on hacienda tenants, and labourers could leave the estate and look for alternative opportunities. In short, the labour employed by the hacienda was free labour and not forced.

Frank's characterisation is also deficient because wage relations did not then predominate in the countryside and most peasants were not divorced from their means of subsistence. A more detailed examination of the social relations of production is surely necessary.

As for the external peasant enterprise it was clearly not a capitalist form of production and can best be analysed in terms of a system of petty commodity production. However, minifundistas became increasingly dependent on a partial wage income for their subsistence reproduction which they obtained by working as seasonal wage labourers on the hacienda. It is very difficult to form a precise picture of the relative importance of the external peasant enterprise in relation to the internal peasant enterprise for the second half of the nineteenth century. The scanty evidence available seems to suggest that the inquilino economy was at least as important as the minifundia economy, at least in terms of land cultivated and number of animals owned. The small external peasant producers constituted roughly 50 per cent of rural proprietors, generated an estimated 15 per cent of total agricultural production, probably cultivated not more than 10 per cent of the arable land and employed about 33 per cent of the active agricultural labour force (Bauer and Hagerman Johnson, 1977).

As for the social relations of production within the hacienda system, a proper understanding of the _inquilinaje_ is of key importance. The inquilinaje was a complex institution indeed, as the inquilino was neither a pure subsistence producer nor a pure wage labourer. The inquilino's payment took the form of usufruct of a patch of land, some consumption goods and a small cash payment. He received two plots of land as production fringe benefits (_regalía de tierra_). One was the _cerco_ or garden plot, which was a small piece of land around the house in which the inquilino family lived. Generally potatoes, beans, maize, vegetables, a few fruit trees and small animals, such as pigs and hens, were kept on the _cerco_. The other plot of land was larger, where wheat was sometimes cultivated. The inquilino also had rights to pasture a certain number of animals on the estate (_derecho a talaje_). As consumption fringe benefits, he received housing rights and sometimes he would collect wood from the forest for fuel. During the days worked on the landlord enterprise, he would receive lunch and for breakfast bread and tea. The inquilino was under an obligation to work nearly all the year around on the landlord's enterprise when required, and often had to provide an additional member of his household during the period of sowing and harvesting. This additional worker was referred to as _peón obligado_ or _ganán_. He could be a relative of the inquilino or just an _allegado_ (resident) of the family household. Both the inquilino and the peón obligado received a small monetary wage as well as a food ration for the days worked on the landlord's enterprise. A very gross estimate would seem to indicate that this monetary payment was about a quarter of the monetary wage of a nitrate worker and probably constituted at most a third of the total inquilino's income.

The inquilino was able to acquire some simple instruments of production such as a wooden plough and a few working (draft) animals. But it is unlikely that his production was sufficient to cover the subsistence needs of the household; accordingly the monetary wage and the food ration were a necessary income. This raises the point of whether the inquilino should be considered as a producer who paid labour rent for his tenancy or as a labourer who received a tenancy as part of his payment. If he paid labour rent then the inquilino must be characterised as a servile labourer unless it is possible to speak of a capitalist labour rent. However, from the second half of the nineteenth century with the transformation in the inquilinaje system arising from the rapid expansion of wheat production, the inquilino has to be analysed in terms of a proletarian partly paid with productive resources as a type of payment-by-results acting as an incentive. He thus can be considered as a semi-proletarian.

Laclau is very emphatic in denying that the transformations in the inquilinaje system can be seen as the emergence of an agricultural proletariat in that the monetary wage did not constitute the principal part of the inquilino's means of subsistence (Laclau, 1969, p. 305). However, this is too narrow a view. The inquilino labour was used by the landlord as a form of valorising capital and as a mechanism for increasing capitalist profits. For landlords the inquilinaje was not so much a source of labour rent income as a way of obtaining cheap and permanent labour. The centralised market production of the landlord enterprise was more important than the inquilino's subsistence production. For the employer the price of inquilino labour was less than its value not only because he paid him a wage which did not cover his reproduction needs but also because the opportunity cost of the tenancy was very low for the landlord.[1] The employer took advantage of certain

[1] For the inquilino the value of his labour equalled payment in cash plus payment in kind plus value of production generated on land plot in usufruct. For the landlord the price of inquilino labour equalled payments in cash plus payments in kind plus opportunity cost of land plot for landlord. As long as the value of production generated on the land plot in usufruct was higher than the opportunity cost of that land plot for the landlord, the landlord was paying a price for the inquilino's labour below its value.

characteristics of the peasant enterprise to overexploit inquilino labour. The family labour in the inquilino enterprise partially supplied the necessary use values for the reproduction of the unit and when faced with a reduction in the regalías and the wage, as occurred in the second half of the nineteenth century, they were forced to increase the intensity of the work on their reduced tenancy and seek additional wage employment. Owing to the overexploitation of family labour on the tenancy, the values generated on the plots were higher than those which would have been created if the landlord had cultivated this land directly with wage labour. So long as the technical relations of production of the landlord enterprise were not greatly superior to those of the inquilino enterprise, it remained profitable for landlords to employ inquilino labour. This situation did not arise until the 1930s.

Landlords increased wheat production not only by settling more inquilinos on the hacienda system and demanding a greater amount of labour days to be worked on their central enterprise but also by employing more seasonal workers (afuerinos). The afuerinos were paid a monetary wage, a food ration and sometimes received primitive accommodation. The wage was higher than the one paid to inquilinos and peones obligados in order to attract labour during periods of high labour demand. It was also higher because they did not receive production perquisites. To encourage greater speed and longer daily hours of work part of the payment was made on a piece rate system (Kaerger, 1901). Most of the afuerinos came from minifundia areas and many were migrants.

Again, afuerino labour was a cheap form of wage labour for landlords as it was only contracted when required, particularly in view of the great seasonality of wheat production. They worked for a few days, weeks or months on the hacienda enterprise and could be dismissed at any moment. Furthermore, unlike the inquilinos, they placed no demands on the productive resources of the hacienda. Their wage was of course also insufficient to cover their subsistence needs. Thus landlords paid a price for afuerino labour (the wage payment) which was below its value and which could be depressed to the point where it became equal to the difference between the subsistence needs of the worker and his family and the production of use values that he and his family were able to obtain on the minifundia.

In conclusion, the growing commercialisation of agriculture and the resulting transformations in the social relations of production are major factors in explaining the early and substantial rate of rural out-migration between the 1850s to 1930s.[1]

IV. Proletarianisation and Rising Rural Out-migration

In the late 1930s agricultural imports exceeded agricultural exports for the first time and from then on the deficit in the agricultural balance of trade has continually increased. By the late 1930s the urban population exceeded the rural, and rural-urban migration continued to increase thereafter. Agricultural production was evidently unable to keep up with the increasing internal demand. To expand production became more difficult as the incorporation of new land into cultivation became progressively more expensive. Both the so-called internal and external colonisation frontiers had reached their limits by the late 1930s. The irrigated area has remained the same since the 1930s and the cultivated area has even declined slightly. Thus the main way open for augmenting agricultural production was through increasing productivity. This happened in a variety of ways. The most important was through mechanisation, and indeed mechanisation grew at about 8 per cent yearly in value between 1945 and 1965 (Ballesteros, 1965). Another way was to change the crop pattern from lower to higher value crops - the area cultivated with high value industrial crops expanded significantly, and the area of fruit plantations almost doubled between 1930 and 1965. Furthermore, the greater use of fertilisers, pesticides and insecticides also contributed in raising productivity.

As most of the technical innovations mentioned above were capital intensive they resulted in a growing rate of rural out-migration and a relatively high increase in labour productivity. In agriculture labour productivity grew at about 2.2 per cent annually between 1940 and 1965 which compares quite favourably to industry's 2.6 per cent (Mamalakis, 1976). Not surprisingly, the active labour force engaged in agriculture increased by only 0.5 per cent yearly between 1935 and 1965 and its relative importance within the total active labour force fell from 37 per cent to 28 per cent during the same period (Hurtado, 1966). According to estimates by McBride, in 1935 approximately 60 per cent to 70 per cent of rural population of central Chile lived on large properties (McBride,

---

[1] This does not mean to say that the rapid development of the mining sector played no role, either directly or indirectly, in stimulating rural out-migration. However this paper is essentially concerned with examining the relation between agrarian change and migration.

1936). By 1965 they only supported about 35 per cent of the rural population in this area (Bloom, 1973, p. 70). Most of the increases in productivity occurred on the medium and large agricultural enterprises.

Thus the employment of workers on haciendas actually fell by about 20 per cent in the 10 years between 1955 and 1965. The composition of the labour force also changed as the proportion of wage labour, particularly temporary labour, to tenant labour increased (Chile, Dirección de Estadísticas y Censos, 1969).

The particularly sharp increase in labour productivity on the haciendas led to the complete proletarianisation of most inquilinos from the mid-1930s and in an accelerated fashion from 1950. The significant change in the technical relations of production made it more profitable for landlords to employ wage labour instead of inquilino labour. The increase in productivity of the landlord enterprise meant that the payment of fringe benefits to inquilinos became more costly for landlords and, as a consequence, a substitution process replaced the regalías productivas with money payments.

It would be useful to present some data at this stage in order to assess the relative importance of the tenant-labour enterprises and the external peasant enterprises. The best data exist for the year 1955 reflecting the situation in the middle of the process of proletarianisation of the inquilinos. Table 2 indicates that in 1955 the labour force of the inquilino enterprise was as important as that of the minifundia, but in terms of value of production the former produced more than twice the value of the latter. Thus the complete proletarianisation of the inquilino had a significant influence on the destruction process of the subsistence sector in rural areas and on the rate of rural out-migration. Table 2 also shows the concentration of land among the medium and large enterprises.

The proportion of labourers engaged in the inquilino enterprise within the total economically active agricultural population diminished from its maximum of 40 per cent in 1935 to 25 per cent in 1955 and to 12 per cent in 1965 (Oficina Central de Estadísticas, 1938; Chile, 1960; and Chile, 1969). Furthermore the proportion of wage labourers within the active agricultural population increased remarkably from 17 per cent in 1955 to 41 per cent in 1965 (Chile, 1960; Chile, 1969). Thus the absolute number and relative proportion of inquilinos in the labour force employed by the landlord enterprise diminished. Nevertheless in the central region where the hacienda system predominated, inquilinos still accounted for 28 per cent of the workers employed by the landlord enterprise in 1965 while voluntarios - semi-

Table 2: Chile: Relative importance of the various types of agricultural enterprises, 1955

Type of agricultural enterprise	Percentage of enterprises	Percentage of active agricultural population	Percentage of arable land	Percentage of annual cropland	Average size (in arable hectares)	Percentage of value of production
Tenants:						
Inquilinos	39	25	2.5	7.5	1.2	9.9
Sharecroppers	9	6	7.0	30.0	13.0	13.8
Proprietors:						
Minifundias	19	26	1.0	1.7	1.0	3.8
Family	21	16	10.6	9.8	9.8	12.2
Medium & large	12	27*	78.9	51.0	128.8	60.3
Total	100	100	100	100	100	100

* Most of the active agricultural population of the inquilino enterprise has to be added to this figure as the majority worked in medium and large enterprises as well.

Source: CIDA (1966, pp. 162, 206).

permanent employed wage labourers often resident in the inquilino household - accounted for 20 per cent.

The proletarianisation of the inquilino is also revealed by the increase in the proportion of his income derived from wage labour. It is estimated that in the early 1940s approximately a third of his total income came from his money wage and food ration (Chile, Dirección de Estadística, 1945) while in 1965 this had risen to about a half (ICIRA, n.d.). The remainder of his income was derived from his role as a producer on his enterprise. Legislation also required employers to pay an increasing proportion of the inquilino's minimum wage in cash. This proportion rose from 25 per cent in 1953, when minimum wage legislation was introduced in the country-side, to 75 per cent in 1965. Furthermore the number of implements and working animals owned by the inquilinos steadily declined. Data for the central region show that in 1965, 45 per cent of inquilinos had no iron ploughs and 66 per cent had no working animals (Schejtman, 1970). As many as 82 per cent of inquilinos were dependent on landlords or other peasants to provide them with some sort of instruments of production. The landlord enterprise, through its ownership of vastly superior instruments of production, particularly machinery, expanded its productive participation in the inquilino's enterprise by undertaking their ploughing and harvesting. The same data reveal that in 60 per cent of the inquilino enterprises the landlord enterprise was in charge of the soil preparation prior to sowing. Already, in 9 per cent of the haciendas landlords gave a <u>ración cosechada</u> to inquilinos - i.e. they took away the <u>regalía de tierra</u> (except the goce) and replaced it with the equivalent production, which inquilinos had previously obtained by cultivating it directly themselves.

The inquilino and sharecropping systems were only profitable for landlords as long as the surplus value appropriated from inquilino labour remained above that extracted from workers paid purely with a cash wage and as long as the sharecrop rent remained higher than the profit landlords could obtain by exploiting the land themselves. When the productivity of the landlord enterprise increased, pushing up profits per hectare and therefore the opportunity cost of the land, a substitution process in favour of the employment of pure wage labourers took place. As a consequence rural wage labourers were increasingly important in the total labour supply of the hacienda system. Landlords employed two types of wage labour. One was the voluntario who lived in the inquilino household. But these were only employed when necessary, receiving a wage and food ration for days worked. On average voluntarios worked for 188 days per annum on the landlord enterprise, as opposed to 254 days of inquilinos.[1] The other type of labour contracted by the estates was the afuerino. He was termed "outsider" because he did not live permanently on the hacienda, nor was he attached to it as he only worked seasonally. On average afuerinos worked 67 days on a particular landlord enterprise (Kay, 1971). Afuerinos were either minifundistas, village labourers or permanent migrant workers (torrantes). Perhaps as many as 30 per cent to 50 per cent of afuerinos were linked in one way or another to some sort of subsistence production, but many were also unemployed for various months (Marín, 1969). Nevertheless 85 per cent were employed as afuerinos for more than six months of the year by working on various haciendas (Zemelman, 1967). Thus by 1965 the labour force of the landlord enterprise in the central region, where the inquilinaje had been predominant, was composed of only 28 per cent inquilinos, 20 per cent voluntarios and as many as 40 per cent afuerinos. However, in terms of annual working days afuerinos represented only a fifth of the total (Kay, 1971).

Marx considered the proprietorship of small land parcels to be only a transitional stage in the development of capitalist agriculture. He argued that the following factors would destroy small landed property: destruction of rural domestic industry by large-scale industry, gradual impoverishment and exhaustion of the cultivated soil, usurpation of common lands by big landowners and competition from large-scale capitalist agriculture (Marx, 1966, p. 807). Whilst agreeing in general with these propositions, it has to be acknowledged that in the process of capitalist development in agriculture, peasant proprietorship has displayed a remarkable capacity of survival. While it has disappeared in some countries, it has remained in others, particularly in the dependent countries. Despite the apparent inability of capitalism to destroy peasant proprietorship, capital has managed to progressively subsume peasant producers, leaving them with only formal ownership of their land.

It is certain that most rural domestic industry has vanished in Chile, thereby reducing the peasant's ability to earn extra income through non-agricultural activities. Common rights to pasture land, which allowed peasants to rear livestock and maintain their working animals, were already eliminated during the colonial period. The minifundia areas also experienced an ecological crisis which has been particularly acute in some Coastal areas due to

[1] Data refer to Central region in 1965. See Kay (1971).

soil erosion. Between 1919 and 1936 the proportion of minifundia within the total number of farms rose slightly from 41 per cent to 44 per cent. After 1936 this proportion fell slightly to 37 per cent in 1955, after which it dropped more rapidly to 28 per cent in 1965 (Chile, Dirección General de Estadística, 1933; Chile, 1960; Chile, 1969). In absolute terms the number of minifundia enterprises increased between 1919 and 1936 but fell continually from then on. The average size of these farms remained similar between 1930 and 1955, 1.6 hectares and 1.4 hectares respectively, increasing to 2.0 hectares in 1965 (Chile, 1933; Chile, 1960; Chile, 1969). This could indicate that the smallest minifundia tended to disappear as their labour force became completely proletarianised; but additional information would be required to permit a definite conclusion.

A further factor making petty commodity production less viable was the growing population pressure on the limited land resources. In Chile between 1955 and 1965 the minifundia absorbed an increasing amount of the rural labour force not only in absolute terms (38 per cent) but in relative terms as well, from 13 per cent to 17 per cent respectively.

Given the factors mentioned above which, among others, operated against the minifundia, how could its persistence be explained? First, there is the dependency relationship. The persistence of the subsistence sector was a result of the process of dependent capitalist development which, in turn, required the continual reproduction of the former. It may be helpful to clarify this with an example. Chile, like many other Latin American countries, embarked on a process of import-substitution industrialisation as a result of the 1930's crisis. Through the internationalisation of capital, the industrialisation process in dependent countries resulted in distorted production and consumption patterns and in the adoption of inappropriate technologies. Such an industrialisation process created insufficient employment opportunities, making it impossible for many small-scale producers to abandon subsistence production. Thus a large reservoir of surplus population was continually reproduced in the subsistence sector, keeping wages in the industrial sector well below increases in productivity. This might have increased profits in the industrial sector or allowed certain inefficient industries to continue to exist. In effect, the industrial strategy of the dependent system is not concerned with enlarging the internal market by reducing unemployment or redistributing income in favour of subsistence sectors.

Secondly, small proprietors can work for simple reproduction and subsistence and not for profit. As part of an abstract answer it has been noted that:

> "For the peasant owning a parcel, the limit of exploitation is not set by the average profit of capital, in so far as he is a small capitalist; nor, on the other hand, by the necessity of rent, in so far as he is a landowner. The absolute limit for him as a small capitalist is no more than the wages he pays to himself, after deducting his actual costs. So long as the price of the product covers these wages, he will cultivate his land, and often at wages down to a physical minimum." (Marx, 1966, pp. 805-806).

With parcellised farming, capital in general can appropriate part of the "rent" and "profit", while the peasant views his enterprise as a means of subsistence. This formal subsumption by capital of peasant proprietors had already reached such a high degree in Chile that according to my estimates, based on data from CIDA and ICIRA, income per capita of the minifundistas was slightly lower than that of the various kinds of workers and tenants in the hacienda system (Kay, 1971; CIDA, 1966; ICIRA, n.d.). This indicates that despite all the efforts small peasant proprietors had made to increase their surplus production, either via the absolute or relative surplus mechanism, their technology had fallen so far behind that of landlords and other capitalists that the latter groups, as well as appropriating rents and profits, could pay higher wages to workers than the small proprietor paid to himself. Of course, the growing population pressure on the minifundia also explains why his income had fallen behind that of estate labourers. One advantage which minifundistas had over wage labourers, however, was permanent employment and thus greater security of income throughout their lifetime. But even this became less certain.

Finally, small subsistence proprietors became more able to find seasonal wage employment. With increasing demographic pressure on the minifundia sector it became vital for them to secure additional forms of income. This became possible through increasing temporary employment as compared to permanent employment offered by landlord enterprises and other capitalist enterprises not only in the rural sector but also in the urban sector, which was quick to take advantage of the very cheap labour of subsistence producers. Thus minifundistas became semi-proletarians.

In conclusion, the sharp rise in the rate of rural out-migration after 1940 was essentially due to the rapid mechanisation of the haciendas. Between 1955 and 1965 alone the estates expelled about a fifth of their labour force, reducing their employment of the total agricultural active population from 50 per cent to 45 per cent (Chile, 1960; Chile, 1969). This high rate of labour expulsion from the haciendas accelerated demographic pressures on the minifundia as never before. It forced a net immigration of labour into the minifundia, increasing their active population by 3.8 per cent during the same period (ibid.). Most of the rural out-migration came from the haciendas. But as a counterpart to the capitalist modernisation of estates, the minifundia were increasingly forced to perform the function of a rural labour reserve, particularly for the capitalist agricultural enterprises.

Recent detailed and sophisticated statistical analyses generally support these conclusions. Studies using regression and path analyses both identify the significant and positive effect which the level of mechanisation had on the rate of rural emigration in Chile (Weiss-Altaner, 1975; Long, 1974). Weiss-Altaner's research, which covers the period from 1910 until 1960, also stresses the importance of land availability in shaping income opportunities in agriculture and thereby affecting demographic change. In his view, the end of land expansion after 1940 also explains the inability of agriculture to absorb labour and the consequent rising rate of rural out-migration. Meanwhile Long, whose analysis dates from 1952, also points to the increasing rate of rural unemployment and underemployment as well as technological rural push as significantly affecting net rural out-migration.

The study by Lira, limited to a few provinces in the Central Valley, established the following statistically significant correlations. Factors which increased the rate of net migration were a greater degree of mechanisation and land concentration, and those which decreased it were a growing number of minifundia enterprises, and an increase in cultivated land and in the vegetable crop area (chacras) (Lira, 1976). Applying Lira's correlations to the national level it has to be concluded that the rate of rural out-migration increased between 1955 and 1965, because mechanisation and land concentration increased (although the latter very slightly) while the number of minifundia, cultivated area, and the vegetable crop area decreased (Chile, 1960; Chile, 1969).

A more general comparative study of Chile, Colombia, Costa Rica and Peru provides further support for my analysis (Shaw, 1976). Shaw's statistical model for the Chilean case indicates that the variables reflecting provincial differences in the land-tenure system and population growth were very highly associated with the rate of net rural migration. He found that Chile had both one of the highest indexes of land concentration in Latin America and one of the highest rates of rural out-migration. Furthermore it was one of the few Latin American countries where the absolute rural population declined. By way of contrast, Costa Rica had a considerably less uneven land tenure structure and one of the lowest rates of rural out-migration in Latin America.

A factor often neglected in migration analysis is the role of the State. In Chile the State played a key role in the economy from the 1930s onwards. The economic policies of the State certainly had an important influence on the rising rate of rural out-migration in Chile after 1940. The import-substitution industrialisation strategy discriminated against, or neglected, the agricultural sector. The cheap food policy which operated through price controls on agricultural products and subsidies to agricultural imports had a negative effect on the rate of return of investments in agriculture. The situation whereby agricultural output grew at a higher rate than population radically changed after 1930. Agricultural production grew at a yearly rate of 1.8 per cent between 1930 and 1964 while population increased at 2.2 per cent per annum and agricultural demand rose at over 3.0 per cent yearly. During the 1930s agricultural exports still exceeded agricultural imports, but because of the increasing gap between internal production and demand, the trade balance became more and more negative up to the point where agricultural imports consumed a fifth of the country's foreign exchange earnings in 1964. Owing to the low rate of return on investment in agriculture, the cultivated area even declined between 1955 and 1965, exerting a negative effect on rural employment. The rural-urban income differential continued to move in favour of the urban sector, further encouraging rural out-migration.

Furthermore, government policy aggravated the high rate of rural out-migration by subsidising the imports of agricultural machinery. Instead of encouraging technological changes which displaced labour, the government should have attached more importance to land-augmenting technologies. By this is meant improved seeds, fertilisers, pesticides, etc., which generate a greater demand for labour, especially if they lead to more labour-intensive crop patterns. Of course the principal obstacle to overcoming the low rate of agricultural growth and to adopting labour-intensive technologies is the land tenure system. Thus the monopolisation of the land and capital by landlords was one of the major factors behind the high rate of rural out-migration as it resulted in a process of capitalist modernisation with a very low rate of production increase and with a very high rate of labour expulsion. It was only during the Christian Democrat government that an attempt was made to change the land tenure structure through an agrarian reform programme.

V. The Agrarian Reform: 1964-1973

During this period a major agrarian reform was implemented, beginning with the Christian Democrat government of 1964-70 and finishing with the Popular Unity government of 1970-73. The agrarian reform and the unionisation of rural workers gave peasants a major political influence for the first time. Under both governments the role of the state changed considerably and a new relationship was sought with foreign capital. The two regimes also relied, though to a different extent, on the mass political mobilisation of the middle class, urban workers and the peasantry. Politics became mass politics. Both governments also attempted to solve the crisis of dependent capitalism. However, while the Christian Democrats tried to reform the dependent capitalist system, Popular Unity intended to challenge it and initiate a socialist system.

The model of capital accumulation based on the "easy phase" of import-substitution industrialisation (i.e. production of consumer goods) entered into crisis during the late 1950s. The crisis was mainly due to market constraints for industrial products and to foreign exchange limitations - both hindered the transition from consumer-goods to capital-goods production. The reformist Christian Democrat government of Eduardo Frei sought to solve the political and economic crisis. Politically it tried to establish a new system of class alliances centred on the modernising fraction of the bourgeoisie and the middle class while incorporating unorganised popular sectors, chiefly shanty town dwellers and peasants, as subordinate elements. The middle class acted as a political class, administering the political system and the state. Through such a popular alliance and by using the state apparatus the Christian Democrats hoped to modernise traditional sectors of the bourgeoisie and, at the same time, ward off the challenge to the capitalist system from the Marxist parties, the organised industrial and mining proletariat and some sectors of the peasantry.

The Christian Democrat régime attempted to resolve the economic problem by negotiating a new relationship of dependency with foreign capital and by implementing an agrarian reform. Its policy with respect to foreign capital was based on the "Chileanisation" of the large US owned copper mines and the creation of joint ventures with foreign capital for the development of an intermediate and capital goods industrial sector. The state bought 51 per cent of the shares of the large copper companies and at the same time offered tax incentives to foreign companies to encourage investment and expansion of production. The growth of copper exports was to be one of the main solutions to the foreign exchange constraint.

With the agrarian reform, the Christian Democrats aimed to stimulate agricultural production, to raise the peasants' standard of living and gain their political support. The Frei government then planned to complete the agrarian transition to an efficient capitalism while completing the political incorporation of marginal groups in society. Rising peasant income would enlarge the internal market for industrial products while the increase in agricultural production would reduce the need for agricultural imports. Such policies were designed to lead to economic growth with some redistribution of income and to political stability.

Agricultural production was to be raised by two types of policy - the expropriation of all estates which were inefficient and which did not reach stated efficiency norms by a certain period, and the granting of incentives to medium and large producers willing to modernise. Incentives took the form of special subsidised credit facilities for the purchase of machinery, improved seeds, superior breeds of cattle, fertilisers, and so on. The agrarian reform legislation also contained special provisions in the form of prompt cash compensations for large landowners who were expropriated despite having undertaken investments since the Frei government came to power. The government also raised agricultural prices, subsidised the price paid to producers and guaranteed minimum prices for some products with state purchasing agreements. These policies bore fruit as agricultural investment increased and large landowners raised productivity on their farms (Ringlien, 1971). Agricultural production more than doubled its yearly growth rate compared with the previous period. Paradoxically, most of the production increase came from the private farm sector and not the expropriated farm sector (referred to as the reformed sector) (Smith, 1975). However, this is not so surprising as less than 18 per cent of the land was expropriated (expressed in basic irrigated hectares - BIH - which means that land of different quality was standardised). One of the main intentions of the agrarian reform was to put pressure on landlords' to modernise. Less than a third of the large landed estates were expropriated and most of them were able to retain the best part of their hacienda as a <u>reserva</u> (a smaller farm of up to 80 BIH). It has also to be taken into account that landlords withdrew most of their machinery and livestock when expropriated. Indeed taking into account the low level of capitalisation, the reformed sector performed relatively well in terms of output (ibid.). Nevertheless, it absorbed a considerable amount of the State's financial, technical and bureaucratic resources.

The objective of raising the peasants' standard of living was achieved in a variety of ways. Those peasants who benefited from land redistribution had their incomes greatly enhanced, but this was the case of only about 7 per cent of rural labourers. The increase in the agricultural minimum wage and the government's enforcement of social security legislation had a wider impact. The organisation of rural workers into trade unions also forced many employers to respect minimum wages and social security benefits. Organised workers often managed to negotiate wage rises above the minimum. It is estimated that incomes of permanent workers on estates and expropriated farms rose by 30 per cent between 1965 and 1970, while income per capita of all nationals increased by only 13 per cent during that period (Cortázar and Downey, 1976, p. 3).

With respect to the government's aim of political incorporation, legislation facilitating unionisation and actively promoting peasant organisation was introduced. The number of rural workers affiliated to unions shot up from about 2,000 in 1965 to 140,000 in 1970. Minifundistas were organised into peasant committees and co-operatives, which embraced around 100,000 members by 1970. Thus roughly 40 per cent of rural workers became affiliated to trade unions or peasant committees.

Although the agrarian reform created more employment opportunities, migration continued to rise between 1965 and 1970. As indicated in table 1, during the decade 1960-1970 the rural population actually fell in absolute terms for the first time and the rate of rural out-migration increased. The absence of a population census for 1965 prevents a clearer picture of the effect of the agrarian reform on migration but it is possible to obtain data at five yearly intervals for the total active agricultural population by combining the population censuses of 1960 and 1970 with the agricultural censuses of 1955 and 1965. It is likely that the trends in the active agricultural population reflect fairly closely those of the whole rural population. In a careful study, Corvalán corrected some of the errors, such as double counting, in the agricultural census data (Corvalán, 1976). On the basis of his data (p. 13) I have calculated the yearly rate of change of the active agricultural population as follows: 1955-60, 0.73 per cent; 1960-65,

-0.48 per cent; 1965-70, -1.44 per cent. This shows that during the years of the agrarian reform the rate of out-migration actually rose further, thereby confirming indications in the 10 year interval data. According to Corvalán this increasing rate of rural out-migration largely explains the fall in the rate of agricultural equivalent unemployment from 21.7 per cent in 1955, to 17.2 per cent in 1965, and to 13.2 per cent in 1970.

A study of central Chile by Lira showed that in a province where the agrarian reform was intense the rate of rural emigration diminished between 1960 and 1970 whilst in another province where little land was expropriated the rate of rural emigration experienced one of the highest increases (Lira, 1975, pp. 42-43). However these data are far too general to permit firm conclusions about the effect of agrarian reform on migration. Fortunately data from a survey of large haciendas in central Chile facilitate a more detailed analysis of some possible effects of the agrarian reform on migration. Information was obtained from a representative sample of 105 haciendas for the agricultural year 1965-66 by ICIRA, the main research institute on agrarian reform in Chile at the time. Five years later (1970-71) the Land Tenure Centre of the University of Wisconsin re-interviewed those estates, now formed into 215 farms through private subdivision to escape expropriation and through reservas granted to landlords. Thus a precise view of the impact of agrarian reform on the haciendas during the Frei government can be obtained. Particularly relevant for this study are the data on employment.

It has already been mentioned that between 1955 and 1965 the haciendas reduced the number of labourers employed by about 20 per cent. The agrarian reform reversed this trend as the number of active people increased by 6 per cent between 1965 and 1970, which was 1.2 per cent expressed as a yearly rate of growth (Ortega, 1975, p. 29). This was about half the annual rate of population increase. However, most of the increase in the number of workers employed was accounted for by the expropriated farms (asentamientos) whose permanent labour force rose by 21 per cent.[1]

Another study of 100 asentamientos in central Chile in 1970 showed that the total and permanent labour force increased by 30 per cent and 22 per cent respectively compared with pre-expropriation (Departamento de Desarrollo Rural, Universidad Católica, 1972, p. 71).

---

[1] Calculated from data presented by Cortázar and Downey (1976, p. 26).

It is interesting that the structural composition of the labour force changed quite significantly. The permanent workers (inquilinos and voluntarios), who became asentados and socios respectively on the asentamientos, increased on the expropriated enterprises and to a lesser extent on the reserves but remained stagnant on the haciendas and fell on the privately subdivided haciendas. All types of enterprise, except for the reserves, employed more afuerinos.[1] However, in terms of the total number of days worked by afuerinos two opposing situations are observed. While the number of days worked per year by afuerinos greatly increased on the haciendas, the remaining types of enterprise, particularly the asentamientos, reduced the number. The result was that employment of afuerinos, expressed in total number of days worked, only increased on the haciendas and fell on the other enterprises, with the effect that it very slightly diminished for the sample as a whole (Cortázar and Downey, 1976).

In short, the expropriated farms absorbed labour, but only permanent workers, while the private farm sector absorbed little labour and this was restricted to seasonal employment.

The reformed sector created more permanent employment opportunities because of a shift to a more labour-intensive crop pattern. This made sense given their shortage of capital. Meanwhile the private sector employed very little additional labour and altered its labour demand pattern to seasonal labour for a variety of reasons. Rural wages had risen considerably as had social security payments. These could be avoided by employing non-unionised, seasonal workers who furthermore, did not exert great pressure for the expropriation of the estate.

The reformed sector could have absorbed even more labour but for the scarcity of working capital and its particular organisational structure. When setting up the asentamientos the government largely had in mind their evolution into private family farms which could retain some co-operative features if their members so wished. Therefore, in calculating the number of families to be settled after expropriation, the criterion of family farm predominated (the so-called "cabida potencial"), effectively limiting the number of families able to benefit. These beneficiaries also had a direct interest in limiting the entry of new members to the asentamientos as this would have reduced the amount of land to be eventually

---

[1] Calculated from data presented in Cortázar and Downey (1976).

distributed individually and the amount of profit to be shared from the collective enterprise. The scarcity of working capital hampered the expansion of the cultivated area and reinforced the shift to labour-intensive crops. A large percentage of land continued to be dedicated to natural pastures and extensive crops like cereals.

Given that the large farm sector as a whole increased the number of people employed by 6 per cent, what factors accounted for the rise in the rate of rural emigration? Firstly, it should be recalled that the 1970-1971 survey refers to central Chile where the agrarian reform was most intense. Much of the rural emigration may have come from other regions. Secondly, the capitalist farm sector of less than 80 BIH took advantage of government subsidies for machinery and equipment and increased the capital intensity of their operation with a resulting displacement of labour (Echeñique, 1970). This was further justified by the large rise in labour costs. In my view it is this highly productive farm sector of 20 to 80 BIH which accounted for most of the rise in the rate of rural emigration. Thirdly, it is possible that the minifundia sector, which had accumulated an excess population, released a greater number of its members to the urban sector. As most seasonal workers were minifundistas their employment opportunities were curtailed by the drop in the demand for seasonal employment - expressed in number of days - particularly on asentamientos. Some minifundistas were also sharecroppers and this arrangement practically disappeared on the asentamientos (Departamento de Desarrollo Rural, 1972, p. 71). It probably became less frequent on private farms owing to new legislation which among other stipulations specifically prohibited sharecropping on reformed land. Thus as another source of income for minifundistas was curtailed, they were pushed towards emigration (Bloom, 1973). A further factor might have been the greater ease with which it was possible to move to the urban shanty towns. The government policy of providing more resources for shanty towns and the great expansion in urban housing, together with a less repressive policy towards urban land invasions by rural-urban migrants, must have encouraged minifundistas to migrate to urban areas.

The agrarian reform and the unionisation of rural workers were major factors dividing the bourgeoisie and strengthening support for a socialist alternative among the rural population. The middle and large agrarian bourgeoisie increasingly opposed the Christian Democrats through fear of future expropriations and the government's increasing inability to control escalating peasant militancy and demands for higher wages and expropriations. On the other hand, peasants became increasingly dissatisfied with the government as they realised that the great majority would not benefit from land redistribution. Their expectations had been greatly raised and their organisational ability enhanced, but only a minority could hope to obtain land from the Christian Democrats' agrarian reform. They demanded an extension, an acceleration, and a radicalisation of the agrarian reform (Affonso et al, 1970) which the left-wing coalition of parties grouped under Popular Unity promised to do if their candidate, Salvador Allende, was elected in the 1970 Presidential elections.

The Popular Unity represented an alliance between the working class and sectors of the middle class, with the former as the main force. Popular Unity's strategy was to use those parts of the state apparatus it controlled to set the conditions for initiating a process of transition to socialism. The Allende government hoped to transform the relative electoral majority into an absolute one by expropriating monopoly and oligopoly capital, by raising the standard of living of the mass of the population and by organising and mobilising popular sectors. Popular Unity was under the impression that such a majority would enable them to win a plebiscite and introduce new key legislation which would further a socialist transition. The strategy and tactics of Popular Unity for initiating a transition to socialism rested on the assumption that the democratic system would permit such a transition to take place through electoral means. The Allende government pledged to respect the institutional system as it believed in the feasibility of achieving its aims by constitutional means.

Allende attempted to break out of the dependency situation by nationalising the large foreign enterprises. The major copper companies were nationalised and placed under total state control. Large local capitalists were also expropriated and most of the major industries, farms, banks and commercial agencies passed into the hands of the state. Workers' councils were formed in the expropriated enterprises to strengthen workers' political support for the government and a socialist transition. It was hoped that these expropriations would allow a greater degree of state control over the economy and that this, together with the capture of part of the economic surplus previously appropriated by foreign and national capital, would enable the implementation of a new development strategy geared to satisfying the needs of the majority of the population.

Great efforts were made to extend unionisation. Between 1970 and 1973, the number of rural workers belonging to unions more than doubled, covering the great majority of peasants who qualified for membership. A novelty was the organisation of peasant councils throughout the country. These councils grouped together representatives of different peasant organisations such as those of the small-owners, the wage labourers, and the peasants from the reformed sector. However, the peasant councils in the end did not have the importance they were supposed to have due to differences within Popular Unity as to their exact function and to opposition from the Christian Democrat party.

Popular Unity utilised the existing agrarian reform legislation but gave it a radical twist by expropriating practically all farms above 80 basic irrigated hectares without considering their efficiency. Furthermore very few reservas were granted to expropriated landlords and those which were granted did not generally exceed 40 BIH. The terms of compensation were also less generous than under the previous regime. The expropriation of almost all farms which could be legally expropriated transformed the reformed sector into the dominant one within the agrarian structure in terms of ownership of land, as it possessed over 40 per cent of the land, expressed in BIH. In terms of production it contributed almost a third of total production and employed just over a fifth of the active agricultural population, according to estimates (Barraclough and Affonso, 1973, p. 81; Barraclough and Fernández, 1974, p. 132). The changes in the land tenure structure brought about by the agrarian reform under Frei and Allende can be assessed in table 3.

According to projections by CELADE the annual rate of population growth fell to 1.7 per cent between 1970 and 1975.[1] And what is truly remarkable, the rate of growth of the rural population became positive again, increasing by 1.0 per cent annually (CELADE, 1978). On the basis of these data I have calculated the rate of rural emigration per year for this period as 0.9. Unfortunately no information is given about how these projections were calculated but if the data are accurate the fall in the rate of rural emigration was dramatic, reaching one of the lowest levels since the last century (see table 1). Such figures are possible, but they should be treated with great caution as they appear to overestimate the fall in the rate of rural emigration.

As the projection refers to the period from 1970 to 1975 it is impossible to distinguish between the effect of

---

[1] The substantial emigration from the country after Allende's overthrow most certainly had a major influence in this fall of the population growth rate.

Table 3: Chile*: Land tenure structure, 1965-1973 (percentage distribution)

Farm sector by size in BIH	1965		1970		1973	
	No. of farms	Amount of land in BIH	No. of farms	Amount of land in BIH	No. of farms	Amount of land in BIH
Less than 5	81.4	9.7	79.7	9.7	79.3	9.7
5 - 20	11.5	12.7	11.3	12.7	11.3	13.1
20 - 80	5.0	22.2	7.5	43.3	7.0	36.6
More than 80	2.1	55.4	0.9	16.7	0.0	0.0
Reformed sector	-	-	0.6	17.6	2.4	40.6
Total	100.0	100.0	100.0	100.0	100.0	100.0

* Includes provinces from Coquimbo to Llanquihue, which is most of the country. The inclusion of the few remaining provinces would not alter the figures significantly.

BIH = Basic irrigated hectare (i.e. the different qualities of land have been standardised).

Source: Barraclough and Fernández (1974); Caballero and Silva (1975).

Popular Unity's agrarian reform on the rate of rural emigration from that of the military government's agrarian counter-reform. Thus the analysis can only be speculative until other data are available. However, it is likely that the policies of both Popular Unity and the military government contributed to the decline in the rate of rural out-migration, though for opposite reasons. It is probable that the counter-revolutionary strategy of the military régime had the more drastic effect, reducing rural emigration to a considerable extent. Despite the tentative nature of this exercise, the data unmistakably reveal the profound effect state policies can have on rural emigration.

The Popular Unity administration made some effort to incorporate minifundistas and afuerinos into the land redistribution process. For this purpose it attempted to replace the asentamiento with the CERA (Centro de Reforma Agraria). The CERA was to group together adjacent expropriated estates, eliminate the internal differentiation between asentados and socios which had existed under the asentamiento organisation, and eventually incorporate afuerinos and some minifundistas as well. However, this advanced form of collective organisation found little favour among the permanent workers on the former estates. In the end few CERAs were established and they bore scant resemblance to the original conception (Kay, 1978). Nevertheless, internal differentiation among members of the reformed sector was reduced and a large number of new members were incorporated with equal rights.

The number of land reform beneficiaries per irrigated hectare of estates expropriated by the Popular Unity government was about 20 per cent higher than on those expropriated by the previous government (Barraclough and Fernández, 1974, p. 44; Maffei, 1979, pp. 35, 36). It is possible that the haciendas expropriated under Popular Unity were more labour intensive, as their average size was smaller. But on the assumption that there was no appreciable difference in the land/labour ratio between those estates expropriated under Frei and those under Allende, this greater incorporation of members under the latter's regime provided an estimated 0.5 per cent additional permanent employment per year among the active agricultural population. It is important to note that this figure is in addition to the number of workers absorbed by the reformed sector during the Christian Democrat government. Thus Popular Unity's agrarian reform seemed to have had a significant impact on the reduction of the rate of rural emigration.[1]

It is possible that the rate of rural emigration from the minifundia sector also diminished, though to a lesser extent. Different forces were operating on this sector. On the one hand, the substantially enlarged credit and technical assistance given to minifundistas (both in terms of number of recipients and amount of money) increased their incomes and tended to reduce their rate of emigration (Barraclough and Fernández, 1974, pp. 56-64, 90-96). On the other hand, the enormous rise in real wages and the tremendous reduction in the rate of urban unemployment worked in the opposite direction. Thus the outcome is uncertain, although the first set of factors were probably more important.

The economic and political crises reached new heights under Popular Unity as it challenged national and international capital. After a vigorous economic expansion during the first half of the Allende government the economy plunged into disarray. As it lacked power the government was unable to replace the capitalist economy by introducing a socialist planning system. The economic offensive of foreign and national capital was co-ordinated by means of a much bolder political offensive against the Popular Unity government. After the first half of Allende's rule the various fractions of the bourgeoisie, who had been divided by the reformism of the Christian Democrat administration, re-united. When they failed to defeat Popular Unity in the Congressional elections of March 1973, it was left to the military to overthrow Allende. For Popular Unity the solution to the agrarian question lay with socialism, but it was overthrown by a military coup d'état in September 1973.

VI. The Agrarian Counter-reform, 1973 Onwards

To restore the economic and political dominance of international and national capital the military dismantled the formal democratic system and suppressed the revolutionary sectors of the working class and its political representatives. The Constitution of 1925, which had allowed the increasing political participation of the whole population, was replaced by the rule of a military régime. This made it possible to return to private capital all the

---

[1] Evidence from other sources bears witness to the large increase in the number of labourers on the expropriated farms, although underemployment also increased. A study of ICIRA of 15 reformed units indicated a rise of 51 per cent in the number of permanent workers (ICIRA, 1973).

means of production which had been expropriated under Popular Unity. The military even transferred many state enterprises which had been created before the Allende government to private capital. The aim was to greatly strengthen the latter's economic base and reduce that of the state, so that any future civilian government would be under its control, and that of the military. The new authoritarian state being developed reduces the economic power of the state while increasing its repressive power.

The economic model which inspires the military government is that of the monetarists, as expounded by Milton Friedman and the "Chicago school". Monetarist policies are expected to resolve the crisis of the import-substitution industrialisation strategy of capital accumulation. In following this model, the economy is being restructured to link it more closely to the world capitalist system. To achieve this, every possible facility is being provided to foreign capital, and protective tariff barriers are being progressively reduced. Price controls have been abolished to make internal prices mirror international prices, and most state subsidies have been removed. Conversely small groups were able to obtain huge amounts of capital in the sale of public enterprises at undervalued prices. The government argues that in order to increase efficiency it is necessary to reallocate productive resources to those economic activities enjoying comparative advantages in relation to the international market. As a result, some industries have gone bankrupt, while a few agro-industrial industries and agricultural exports have expanded. As a result of the restructuring of capital under this new scheme of the international division of labour, oligopolistic conglomerates have reappeared largely under the control of financial capital. The severe limitation of the rights of workers and peasants is crucial for this policy, as it serves to lower wages, increase profits and increase the firms' international competitiveness.

Within that model the agricultural sector plays a key role as it is seen to possess great comparative advantages enabling it to become one of the most dynamic sectors - particularly in exports. The economic and political strategy has defined the following policies towards the reformed sector. Part of the expropriated land is being returned to former owners; part is being auctioned to large capitalists and the remainder is gradually being subdivided into family farms and mainly sold to some of the peasants in the reformed sector. Coupled with the expulsion of politically active peasants, these actions have drastically curtailed the economic base and political power of the peasantry and enormously enhanced that of the landlords. Privatisation of the reformed sector means economic doom for some peasants and reconcentration of the land for some landlords. The parcelisation into family farms also signifies the fragmentation of the peasantry which belonged to the reformed sector, thereby weakening their political power.

By late 1978, 28 per cent of the expropriated farms had been totally returned and 37 per cent partially returned (Garrido, 1979, p. 162). Considering that some landlords had managed to retain a reserve at the time of expropriation and that two-thirds of the expropriated farms were reconstituted, most of the former landlords were left with part or all of their old estates. It is important to notice, however, that in terms of land only 30 per cent has been returned, although this slightly underestimates the amount given to former landowners, for it is expressed in physical hectares and they received better land. A further 12 per cent of the land which belonged to the reformed sector has been sold to financial conglomerates (grupos financieros). Some 27 per cent of the land remained as state property in the reformed sector (ibid, pp. 161-163).

By the end of 1978 only 31 per cent of the expropriated land had been splintered into _parcelas_ or _unidades agrícolas familiares_ (agricultural family units), as they are technically called. Over 40,000 parcelas had been sold mainly to peasants belonging to the former reformed unit, but it is estimated that 15 per cent of these were sold to outsiders who were not peasants (Franco, 1979, p. 640). Because _parceleros_ have to pay for the land and as they no longer receive technical assistance and state credit, many have insufficient capital to make their farms viable and it is estimated that already 40 to 50 per cent have had to sell their land to capitalists (ibid., p. 640; Maffei, 1979, p. 53).

It is likely that only another 5,000 parcelas will be established, for most of the land which remains in state ownership will eventually be sold directly to capitalists. Thus in the end only about 45,000 parcelas will be created. If, as estimated, the reformed sector had around 75,000 members, then 30,000 will have been excluded. Furthermore if it is considered that 40 to 50 per cent of already established parceleros have had to resell and that this proportion will hold for the remaining 5,000 parcelas to be assigned and that 15 per cent have been sold to non-peasants, then the number of former land reform beneficiaries who will be transformed into landless peasants will be between 41,000 and 49,000. This means that between 55 per cent and 65 per cent of the former peasants from the reformed sector will join the ranks of the rural proletariat.

The government's economic policy is shaping a new process of socio-economic differentiation by orienting agriculture to exports. The rural bourgeoisie is being divided by the split of agriculture into two productive sectors. First, there are those fortunate enough to find sufficient capital and whose farms have the appropriate soil and climatic conditions and are thus able to switch to the export market. Second, there are those not able to undertake productive changes who remain primarily attached to the internal market. The dynamic of capital accumulation will vary according to the sector. Those producers who become linked to the export market are favoured by government economic policies, are finding exports profitable, and are faced with an enormous export potential. Those producers who remain tied to the internal market suffer from the depressed and increasingly competitive internal market conditions; depressed because of high unemployment and low wages, competitive because of the reduction of import restrictions on farm products. Thus it is mainly the export farmers who are capitalising, intensifying production, and using wage labour. Those attached to the internal market have even suffered a technological regression and reverted to the use of tenant labour (inquilinos) and sharecropping (mediería).

The parceleros will remain tied to the stagnant internal market. They do not possess the necessary financial resources, nor can they risk specialising in one or two export products. Also, as the main export products (i.e. fruit and forest products) require major investments they are ill-suited for peasant agriculture. In some cases they might be able to produce for export under a contract system with an agro-industry, export agency, etc. But they would become wholly dependent on these capitalists, have little entrepreneurial control over their farm, and would indirectly become wage labourers even though they remain the formal owners of the land. As a consequence of the withdrawal of the state's financial and technical support, a technological involution has occurred and yields have dropped considerably. With the continuation of the stagnation of the internal market, the parceleros have seen their incomes fall sharply and have increasingly shifted to a regressive production pattern geared to self-consumption. An additional number will become proletarianised (Olavarría, 1978, p. 54).

The proletarianisation and exclusion from the reformed sector arising from the agrarian counter-reform would seem to point towards an increase in rural emigration. But the projections of CELADE already mentioned seem to indicate that the reverse has in fact occurred. One major explanation for this is the lack of alternative employment opportunities in the urban sector and the steep fall in wages without precedent in modern Chilean history. Urban unemployment after the military coup shot up spectacularly from around 4 per cent to over 16 per cent and has remained just below 15 per cent in recent years (Riveros, 1979, pp. 185-192). Furthermore urban squatting was no longer possible because of repressive action by the government. Thus potential rural emigrants have had no urban physical space into which to migrate. Despite the odds, however, some have migrated to urban areas and others have left for Argentina. But the majority have been forced to find a living in the rural sector.

It should also be noted that although many former beneficiaries of the agrarian reform have been excluded from the parcelisation process or have had to re-sell their parcel, not all were expelled from the former reformed unit. Many have been able to earn a living of a sort by entering into a complex of informal leasing and labour relationships. In some cases those not favoured by the sale of a parcela have been granted temporary usufruct rights for three or more years over a plot of land in the former co-operative, as way of compensation. In other cases they have managed to retain their house and the small adjacent garden plot. Furthermore, a large number of informal sharecropping sub-tenancies, or other forms of rental agreements have been arranged between parceleros and former members of the reformed sector, ex-parceleros and other landless peasants. In cases where parceleros have lacked the financial means to exploit their land, they have sometimes reached a sharecropping arrangement with a local merchant, truck owner, or even the former landlord who provided the capital (Gómez, Arteaga and Cruz, 1977). Thus a complex system of subsistence units is developing which Maffei refers to as the "informal minifundia" (Maffei, 1979, pp. 158-159). In this case the social relations of production could be characterised as semi-proletarian.

The less fortunate among those excluded or forced to re-sell their parcela have become subproletarians. By this I mean that they are only able to find occasional work. Where they have been casually employed by parceleros, they are not paid in money but with food and agricultural produce because of the financial problems of the parcelero himself (ibid., p. 136). Thus the agrarian counter-reform has unleased a process of differentiation among the former peasants of the reformed sector.

Of course, many rural labourers have found no employment at all, as indicated by indirect evidence. According to CELADE projections for 1975, the active rural population remained constant (CELADE, 1976b, p. 24). When it is recalled that the annual rate of rural population growth for the same period was 1.0 per cent, one must conclude that unemployment has risen. However these factors - exclusion from distribution of land parcels, proletarianisation, fall in the peasants' standard of living and rising rural unemployment - have not increased the rate of rural emigration as one would expect in normal circumstances. Indeed the reverse has happened. For the first time since Chile gained political independence - except perhaps to a minor extent during the world crisis of the 1930s - urban conditions have not permitted rural out-migration as required by changes in the rural sector. Thus it is possible to speak of a forced retention of rural labour through unemployment and underemployment.

VII. Summary and Conclusions

The long-term analysis of agrarian change and migration in Chile has shown that the following factors have exerted a crucial influence on patterns of migration: the type of dependent insertion of the Chilean socio-economic formation within the world capitalist system, the pattern of internal capital accumulation, State policies, the land tenure structure, and the way in which capitalism has developed within the rural sector.

Within peripheral socio-economic formations, Chile represents a case of early development of capitalist relations of production in agriculture on the basis of the landlord road. In that context, a continuous, fairly steady stream of rural emigration developed from the middle of the last century when capitalism began to penetrate significantly into agriculture. In broad terms it is possible to distinguish four phases in the development of rural capitalism to which different types and intensities of migration are related.

During the first phase from the middle of the last century to the 1930s, the formal subsumption of peasant labour by capital predominated. The hacienda system increasingly produced for the market by extending the cultivated and irrigated land and employing more labour. Thus landlords increased capital accumulation by enlarging the absolute surplus value extracted from rural labour. As the external minifundia areas already contained an excess population and as the rate of rural population growth was higher than the demand for additional labour by the hacienda, the rural sector was able to release labour to the expanding urban sector. Most rural emigrants stemmed from the external minifundia sector. Population shifts also occurred within the rural sector between regions. For instance, the rural zone of the central region transferred labour to the southern region in a process of colonisation. The southern region was an area of net rural immigration until 1920. The State actively promoted the colonisation of this area by waging a war against the native population ("la pacificación de la Araucanía"), and encouraged European immigrants to settle in the frontier region. In the North the State also expanded Chilean territory by winning the rich northern nitrate region in the war against Peru and Bolivia of 1879 ("la Guerra del Pacifico"). The rural areas of the central region again supplied part of the required labour for the mines.

The second phase ran from the exhaustion of the expansion of the cultivated area in the late 1930s to the beginning of the agrarian reform in 1965. The haciendas expanded production by raising productivity, a move which was encouraged by a series of State policies. The State facilitated the mechanisation of the haciendas, greatly increasing labour productivity. But as the productivity of the land did not grow sufficiently to meet the rising urban demand the gap had to be met by burdensome food imports. Capital accumulation now proceeded on the basis of extracting relative surplus value from the internal permanent labour force but also by overexploiting seasonal labour (in Meillassoux's sense of that term). With the rapid change in the hacienda's technical relations of production, tenant labour became proletarianised, the permanent resident labour force fell and temporary labour became relatively more important. The external minifundia sector partly retained labour at decreasing levels of productivity, but an increasing proportion of its labour force were hired for wages by landlords. Thus the transition from formal to real subsumption of internal minifundia labour by capital was almost completed and the formal and partially real subsumption of capital over external minifundia labour was greatly extended. This led to a turning point in that the rate of rural population growth stagnated for the first time and even declined in the 1960s as a result of an increased rate of rural emigration. Such high rates of expulsion of rural labour more than satisfied the State's promotion of an import-substitution process that started in the late 1930s, and that required an abundant supply of cheap labour.

The third phase of agrarian change was the land reform period of 1965 to 1973. The Christian Democrat administration (1964-70) pursued a dual policy in the rural sector. On the one hand, it further intensified changes in the technical and social relations of production in the private commercial farm sector. On the other, it expropriated inefficient haciendas and transformed them into peasant co-operatives. In spite of the agrarian reform, the rate of rural emigration probably continued to increase or at most slowed down very slightly. As mentioned before, the absolute size of the rural population fell between 1960 and 1970 - probably one of the first cases in a peripheral country - but though no census data are available for 1965 it is possible that the decrease was largely confined to the years 1960-65. The reformed sector did employ more labour, though this was limited by the reduced number of expropriations and by its internal organisation, which conspired against a larger incorporation of peasants. The government policy of raising rural wages, subsidising machinery and unionising rural labour produced a further expulsion of workers from the private commercial farm sector. The increased employment opportunities in the reformed sector certainly did not match the reduction in employment in the capitalist farm sector. The drastic and rapid expropriation of all remaining haciendas by the Popular Unity administration (1970-73) did considerably slow down the rate of rural emigration. The organisation of the reformed sector also changed to allow a larger incorporation of additional members. The reduction in peasant differentiation and the greater economic assistance by the State to the small farm sector also helped to diminish rural out-migration.

Finally, the fourth phase is marked by a counter-agrarian reform started by the military government in 1973 and still underway. The new model of capital accumulation centring on the export market benefits only a few capitalists and condemns many workers and peasants to poverty and unemployment. Much of the expropriated land has been handed back to former landlords or sold to capitalists. The remainder has been subdivided into land parcels and sold to some former members of the reformed sector. Many of these, however, have had to sell or rent out their land through lack of capital, as the state has withdrawn the economic support it used to give to the peasant farm sector during the agrarian reform period. Despite this exclusion and proletarianisation of many peasants, rural emigration seems to have diminished further. Unlike the Popular Unity period, however, rural labour is now trapped in the rural sector, being forced to remain there because urban unemployment has soared, urban wages have plummeted through the state's economic policy and urban squatting is repressed. A series of informal non-monetary land rental arrangements have spread and many non-wage relationships appeared in the rural sector. This is explained by peasant farmers' and even some landlords', lack of capital and the sub-proletariat's and semi-proletariat's desperate need to find ways and means to subsist. In the end it is likely that a sharply differentiated and yet closely connected dualist agrarian structure will emerge, constituting a modern version of the latifundia-minifundia complex. The old latifundia have become smaller, more capital intensive, efficient and largely export-oriented farms, while the minifundia have multiplied considerably through the fragmentation of part of the reformed sector and the emergence of an informal minifundia sector. The capitalist farm sector will largely rely on cheap seasonal wage labour provided by the formal and informal minifundia sector whose members will come to depend on such a wage income for subsistence. The effect this will have on the rate of rural emigration is uncertain. Much will depend on how long the present State policy and pattern of capital accumulation persist.[1]

---

[1] One study estimated that a change in state policy to shift the present crop pattern to a more intensive one would create employment opportunities for an additional third of the present active agricultural population over the next three decades (Corvalán, 1976, pp. 36-39). A more detailed investigation, although confined to fewer provinces, reached a similar figure (Aranda, 1978, pp. 440-441). However, given the present circumstances, it is extremely unlikely that such a policy will be pursued.

References

Affonso, A. et al. (1970): Movimiento campesino Chileno (Santiago, ICIRA).

Amin, S. (1975): "El capitalismo y la renta de la tierra", in S. Amin and K. Vergopoulos: La cuestión campesina y el capitalismo (Mexico, Editorial Nuestro Tiempo, 1975).

Aranda, X. (1978): Interrelaciones entre potencial productivo, estructura, agraria y migración en Chile (Santiago, FLACSO).

Ballesteros, M. (1965): "Desarrollo agrícola chileno, 1910-1955", in Cuadernos de Economía, Vol. II, No. 5.

Barraclough, S. and Affonso, A. (1973): "Diagnóstico de la reforma agraria chilena", in Cuadernos de la Realidad Nacional, April, No. 16.

Barraclough, S. and Fernández, J.A. (1974): Diagnóstico de la reforma agraria Chilena (Mexico, Siglo XXI Editores).

Bauer, A. (1971): "Chilean rural labour in the nineteenth century", in The American Historical Review, Vol. LXXVI, No. 4.

--- (1975): Chilean rural society from the Spanish Conquest to 1930 (Cambridge, Cambridge University Press).

Bauer, A. and Hagerman Johnson, A. (1977): "Land and labour in rural Chile, 1850-1935", in K. Duncan and I. Rutledge: Land and labour in Latin America: Essays on the development of agrarian capitalism in the 19th and 20th centuries (Cambridge, Cambridge University Press, 1977).

Bloom, R.J. (1973): The influence of agrarian reform on smallholder communities in Chile's central valley 1965-70, unpublished Ph.D. dissertation (Los Angeles, University of California).

Caballero, L. and Silva, R. (1975): The reformed units in Chilean agriculture (Uppsala, Swedish University of Agriculture).

CELADE (1976): Boletín Demográfico, No. 24.

CELADE (1979): Boletín Demográfico, No. 23.

Chile, Dirección de Estadística y Censos (1960): III Censo Nacional Agrícola-ganadero 1955 (Santiago).

Chile, Dirección de Estadística y Censos (1969): IV Censo Nacional Agropecuario - Año Agrícola 1964-65 (Santiago).

Chile, Oficina Central de Estadísticas (1938): Censo Agropecuario 1935-36 (Santiago).

Chile, Dirección de Estadísticas (1945): Veinte Años de legislación social (Santiago).

Chile, Dirección General de Estadística (1933): Censo agropecuario, 1929-30 (Santiago).

CIDA (1966): Chile: tenencia de la tierra y desarrollo socio-ecónomico del sector agrícola (Santiago, Imprenta Hispano-Suiza).

Cortázar, R. and Downey, R. (1976): "Efectos redistributivos de la Reforma Agraria", in Estudios de Planificación, No. 53 (Santiago, CEPLAN, Universidad Católica).

Corvalán, A. (1976): "El empleo en el sector agrícola: Realidad y perspectivas", in Estudios de Planificación No. 52 (Santiago, CEPLAN, Universidad Católica).

Departamento de Desarrollo Rural, Universidad Católica (1972): El problema agrario en cien asentamientos del valle central (Santiago, Ediciones Nueva Universidad).

Echeñique, J. (1970): "Las expropiaciones y la organización de asentamientos en el período 1965-70", in D. Alaluf et al.: Reforma agraria chilena: seis ensayos de interpretación (Santiago, ICIRA).

Franco, J. (1979): "El modelo actual y la experiencia agraria", in Mensaje, Vol. XXVIII, No. 283.

Frank, A.G. (1967): Capitalism and underdevelopment in Latin America (New York, Monthly Review Press).

Garrido, J. (1979): "El sector agrícola", in Camentarios sobre la situación económica: Segundo semestre 1978 (Departamento de Economia, Universidad de Chile).

Gómez, S., Arteaga, J.M. and Cruz, M.E. (1977): Cambios estructurales y migraciones en el sector rural, Chile 1965-1978, Documento de Trabajo (Santiago, FLACSO).

Góngora. M. (1966): "Vagabundaje y sociedad fronteriza en Chile (Siglos XVII a XIX)", Cuadernos del Centro de Estudios SocioEconómicos, No. 2.

Hagerman Johnson, A. (1978): "The impact of market agriculture on family and household structure in nineteenth century Chile", in Hispanic American Historical Review, Vol. 58, No. 4.

Hurtado, C. (1966): Concentración de la población y desarrollo económico: El caso de Chile (Santiago, Instituto de Economía de la Universidad de Chile).

ICIRA (n.d.): Proyecto de investigación sobre fundos de gran potencial productivo en el valle central de Chile, 1965-66, unpublished survey data (Santiago).

ICIRA (1973): Estructura organizativa y productiva de los sectores reformados y no reformados (Santiago; mimeographed).

de Janvry, A. and Garramón, C. (1977): "The dynamics of rural poverty in Latin America", in The Journal of Peasant Studies, April, Vol. IV, No. 3.

Kaerger, K. (1901): Landwirtschaft und Kolonisation in Spanischen Amerika (Leipzig, Verlag von Duncker and Humblot).

Kay, C. (1971): Comparative development of the European manorial system and the Latin American hacienda system, unpublished Ph. D. dissertation (University of Sussex).

--- (1977): "The development of the Chilean hacienda system 1850-1973" in K. Duncan and I. Rutledge (eds.): Land and labour in Latin America, (Cambridge, Cambridge University Press, 1977).

--- (1978): "Agrarian reform and the class struggle in Chile", in Latin American Perspectives, Vol. V., No. 3.

Laclau, E. (1969): "Modos de producción, sistemas económicos y población excedente: Aproximación histórica a los casos argentino y chileno", in Revista Latinoamericana de Sociología, No. 2.

--- (1971): "Feudalism and capitalism in Latin America", in New Left Review, No. 67.

Lira, L.F. (1975): "Estructura agraria y población: Análisis del caso chileno", in Documento de Trabajo No. 4 (Santiago, PISPAL, CELADE).

--- (1976): Estructura agraria, crecimiento de la población y migraciones: El caso de la zona central de Chile, 1952-1970, Documento de Trabajo No. 14 (Santiago, PISPAL, CELADE).

Long, J.F. (1974): Rural out-migration in Chile from 1952 to 1960 and from 1960 to 1970, unpublished Ph.D. dissertation (University of North Carolina at Chapel Hill).

Maffei, E. (1979): "Cambios estructurales en el sector reformado de la agricultura, su efecto en la demanda de fuerza de trabajo campesina y las migraciones rurales: 1964-1978", Documento de Trabajo (Santiago, FLACSO).

Mamalakis, M. (1976): The growth and structure of the Chilean economy (New Haven, Yale University Press).

Marín, J.C. (1969): "Asalariados rurales en Chile", in Revista Latino-americana de Sociología, No. 2.

Marx, K.: Capital, Vol. 3 (Moscow, Progress Publishers, 1966).

McBride, G. (1936): Chile: Land and society (Baltimore, Baltimore Press).

Nun, J., Murmis, M. and Marín, J.C. (1967): La marginalidad en América Latina, Documento de Trabajo del CIS No. 53 (Buenos Aires, Instituto Di Tella).

Olavarría, C. (1978): La asignación de tierras en Chile (1973-1976), sus efectos sobre el empleo agrícola, Monografía PREALC, No. 9 (Santiago, OIT).

Ortega, H. (1975): Efectos de la reforma agraria sobre las técnicas de producción 1965-70, Estudios de Planificación, No. 49 (Santiago, CEPLAN, Universidad Católica).

Peek, P. and Standing, G. (1979): "Rural-urban migration and government policies in low-income countries", in International Labour Review (Geneva, ILO), Nov.-Dec., Vol. 118, No. 6.

Portes, A. (1978): "Migration and underdevelopment", in Politics and Society, Vol. 8, No. 1.

Ratcliff, R. (1973): Kinship, wealth and power: capitalists and landowners in the Chilean upper class, unpublished Ph.D. dissertation (Madison, University of Wisconsin).

Ringlien, W. (1971): Economic effects of Chilean national expropriation policy on the private commercial farm sector, 1964-69, unpublished Ph.D. dissertation (Maryland, University of Maryland).

Riveros, L. (1979): "La situación del empleo", in Comentarios sobre la situacion económica segundo semestre 1978 (Santiago, Departamento de Economía, Universidad de Chile).

Schejtman, A. (1970): Peasant economies within large haciendas of central Chile, unpublished B. Litt thesis (Oxford, Oxford University).

Shaw, R.P. (1976): Land tenure and the rural exodus in Chile, Colombia, Costa Rica and Peru (Gainesville, The University Presses of Florida).

Smith, S.M. (1975): Changes in farming systems, intensity of operation and factor use under agrarian reform situations: Chile, 1965/66 - 1970/71, unpublished Ph.D. dissertation (Madison, University of Wisconsin).

Standing, G. (1979): Migration and modes of exploitation: The social origins of immobility and mobility (Geneva, ILO; mimeographed World Employment Programme research working paper; restricted).

Tscherebilo, S. (1976): Estructuración y funciones de las aldeas y espacios urbanos intermedios en un contexto agrícola: Zona central de Chile, 1840-1875, unpublished Licenciatura en Historia (Santiago, Universidad Católica de Chile).

Vergopolous, K. (1975): "El capitalismo disforme", in S. Amin and K. Vergopolous: La cuestión campesina y el capitalismo (Mexico, Editorial Nuestro Tiempo, 1975).

Weiss-Altaner, E.R. (1975): Population pressure and labor absorption in Chilean agriculture, 1910-1960, unpublished Ph.D. dissertation (Pennsylvania, University of Pennsylvania).

Zemelman, H. (1967): El trabajador no permanente en la agricultura (Santiago, ICIRA; mimeographed).

Chapter 3

CASUAL WORK, SEASONAL MIGRATION AND AGRARIAN REFORM IN PERU

by José Matos Mar and José Manuel Mejía*

I. Introduction

Every year Peruvian agriculture experiences a phenomenon of singular importance: when the dry season comes, thousands of poor peasants from the highlands flock down to the coastal valleys where they remain for varying periods of time, usually until work becomes scarce or the rainy season begins again in their home communities. In the valleys they find jobs as casual workers, at rates much below those paid to permanent farm workers and without their job and social security. This constant movement over many years now has become one of the most dramatic expressions of the imbalances and internal contradictions of agriculture in Peru.[1] It was also one of the problems which the radical agrarian reform programme initiated in 1969, sought to solve. This report will attempt to analyse the over-all aspects of the problem in the light of the impact which that programme has had on migration and employment.

In doing so, it will be necessary to describe the background of labour formation in the capitalist

---

* Institute of Peruvian Studies (IEP), Lima.

[1] A more detailed account of these problems is to be found in several previous works of the authors. For a general analysis of migration movements in the structural context of Peru, see Matos Mar (1968). For a more specific analysis of the casual migrant sector in the Chancay valley, see Manuel Mejía, Ramírez, Díaz Suárez and Campos Riveras (1979). Some of the ideas contained in this report were put forward in Matos Mar and Manuel Mejía (1978) submitted to the Symposium on Trends in Internal Migration and Policy Issues in Developing Countries held at Cuernavaca in September 1978 under the joint auspices of the Latin American Council for Social Sciences and UNESCO. Acknowledgements are due to Jorge Balán, Juan Carlos Reboratti, Alicia Unger and Peter Peek for their valuable comments on these texts.

agricultural sector, the various stages in the process and the main consequences for the different segments of the working population. The chief characteristics of the casual migrant population in the period prior to the reform will also be described, and an attempt made to define the specific class conditions resulting from the status of migrant and casual workers. The general features of the reform - its aims, scope and achievements, as well as the obstacles encountered - will then be outlined, with special attention to the way the government attempted to solve the problem of migration. And an assessment will be made of its policies at the national level. Lastly, taking the Chancay Valley as a case study, an analysis will be made of the impact and consequences of the agrarian reform on the sector of casual migrants in the circuit formed by this coastal area and the Callejón de Huaylas highlands.

The central thesis of this study is that, contrary to its explicit objectives, the reform has led to an increase in casual work and seasonal migration and resulted in a situation that tends to aggravate rather than alleviate the problems which they create.

II. Capitalist Organisation of Agricultural and Casual Workers

The existence of a large body of peasants made up primarily of seasonal migrants, who year after year continue to be casual workers, can be properly understood only by analysing the historical development of the capitalist sector of agriculture and the formation of its own labour.

Briefly, an examination of the agrarian structure at the end of the last century shows that it was composed of three major segments. One, situated on the coast, was made up of large, extensive-farming units and organised according to traditional labour relations, while relying heavily on foreign manpower (Chinese and Japanese workers in particular). The second was made up of the indigenous communities in the highlands, where individual holdings existed side by side with communal land and bartering was still a form of trade. The third was made up of the highland estates of large landowners employing indigenous labour in conditions of serfdom or semi-serfdom.

This structure began to change with the growing demand from outside markets, the direct penetration of foreign capital and the rise of a local agricultural middle class that in turn encouraged the development of a capitalist pole of attraction and produced far-reaching changes in the status of labour. At the same time, the processes of change and modernisation unevenly affected the development of the various regions, with marked differences especially between the northern coastal area and the highlands in the south.

In the first two decades of this century the first nuclei of a rural proletariat were formed in the sugar plantations along the northern coast. The technical and administrative modernisation of these plantations and their conversion to intensive farming methods required the permanent presence of a large number of day-labourers. The method used here was the so-called enganche or "enlisting" scheme under which large numbers of peasants moved from the highland provinces of Cajamarca (Chota, Bambamarca, Cutervo and Cajabamba) to the coastal plantations of Lambayeque and La Libertad. Bringing these workers under a wage-earning system was not enough, however, to constitute an agricultural proletariat. It would be several decades before the status, behaviour and attitudes of people who had been self-employed peasants became those of workers selling their labour alone. In trying to define their specific character, the first workforces in those enclaves have thus been called a "mixed proletariat" or a "transitional proletariat" (Sulmont, 1975).

A proletariat took longer to form in the valleys along the central and southern coast. The hacienda or estate system, in the capitalist form, was established there in the 1940s, when most of the landowners took direct control of their estates or leased them to capitalist contractors. Previously these farming units were not worked by members of the proletariat but by a varied group generally made up of a small number of regularly employed wage-earners, a large number of yanaconas[1] and a large number of casual workers most of whom were migrants from the highlands moving back and forth between the valleys and the estates.

Later on, the capitalist operation of the estates was consolidated and the yanaconaje system gradually displaced, leading to a complete conversion of the workers into a proletarian workforce. Two concurrent factors contributed to this process. First, the level of internal capitalisation reached by the estates because of the traditional production relations employed, the new technical possibilities afforded by scientific and technological advances and the threat of land-claiming movements (such as the movement between 1945 and 1948 demanding a

---

[1] Small and medium-sized tenants of cotton plantations who paid a rent in kind. For a description of the yanaconaje system, see Matos Mar (1976).

Yanaconaje Act), worked towards a definite transformation of the labour system and the adoption of wage-paid work as the basis of operation. Secondly, the growing gap between population and resources in peasant communities and the spread of commercialisation (which, by causing internal divisions completely disrupted some communities), automatically steered manpower towards the capitalist sector.

However, while these factors laid the groundwork for the emergence of a diffferentiated and stable agricultural proletariat, this did not occur at once. The peasant from the highlands, used to migrating only periodically so as not to lose control of his small plot of land, showed great reluctance to settle on the estates. Thus, while wage-earning work predominated in the 1950s, it occupied migrant peasants only temporarily as they alternated between the estates and their communities without losing their original class status.

In this initial stage, the status of the casual worker was different from what it is today. A casual worker then still had possibilities of becoming a permanent worker and was not differentiated so sharply as he is today from the latter. His living and working conditions, moreover, were fairly similar.

As new trends developed, the picture began to change. Farming was gradually mechanised or semi-industrialised and jobs became increasingly specialised. This resulted in the need for permanent integration of the labour force and meant that higher salaries had to be paid and additional benefits granted, such as free housing and other facilities on the estate or plantation itself. There were also the limitations of the peasant economy, whether a market or subsistence economy, communal or individual. Not only were its possibilities for expansion as a system of production seriously limited by the capitalist sector but its reproduction process could not keep up with population growth, so that more and more of the domestic workforce became "redundant" in relation to resources. It was only natural in these circumstances that people should turn towards proletarian working conditions.

Casual migrants who were not inclined to turn in this direction at the time, later suffered adverse consequences as manpower requirements on the plantations gradually reached saturation. The trend would subsequently be reversed, with permanent workers being laid off and replaced by casual workers. This happened when the plantations saw that they could take advantage of this new situation to manipulate the redundant population and devise a strategy for exploitating labour through a combined use of different categories of workers in order to achieve maximum profitability.

For this reason the status of casual worker acquired a specific connotation, referring only to people who were unable to obtain steady jobs because the plantations could not absorb more permanent workers in profitable conditions. Casual workers thus came to be regarded as those whose status of insecure seasonal integration was prolonged indefinitely.

Consequently, in addition to the agricultural proletariat made up of permanent wage-earners, there was a large body of workers which the capitalist plantations did not seek, as they did during the initial stage, to make stable. On the contrary, the existence of this fluctuating body would enable them to maintain a given level of wages for the permanent workers and be able to count on additional manpower for peak periods of demand.

The main effects of this situation were three: (a) the "élite" nature of the permanent agricultural proletariat which, as a result of the capitalist development of agriculture, became a relatively favoured sector of rural labour in relation to the whole both because of the job security enjoyed and because these workers had succeeded in organising trade unions;[1] (b) the existence of a growing "sub-proletarianisation", if this word may be used to describe the situation resulting from the continuing non-absorption of labour, whose chief effect was to consolidate an unsettled proletariat subject at one and the same time to many employers and to none; and (c) the consolidation of a permanent migratory movement between the capitalist agricultural units and the peasant communities, making available to the plantations cheap labour at times of greater demand, especially the sowing and harvest seasons.

---

[1] At that time, permanent farm workers had, by being unionised, put through demands of varying kinds including those for wage adjustments, to offset the rising cost of living, reduction of the working day in the fields to six or seven hours, social security, job security, and a number of services provided directly by the plantations (free schooling, health care for the families, housing and the sale of some foodstuffs at subsidised prices). These benefits placed such workers in a middle slice of national income distribution. Casual workers, on the other hand, lacked all such labour benefits and were among the poorest segments of the population. For a description of the status of permanent farm workers on the coast, see Manuel Mejía and Diaz Suárez (1975). In connection with income levels, see Webb and Figueroa (1975).

It may be estimated that in the late 1960s, just before the agrarian reform, the major sugar, rice and cotton plantations alone employed one casual worker seasonally for every permanent worker, or approximately 100,000 in all. This figure is significant considering that in 1961 the total number of wage-earners was only 265,236, or 25.2 per cent of the country's total agricultural labour force of approximately 1 million workers (table 1).

Table 1: Composition of the agricultural labour force by status, 1961

Status	Number	%
Wage-earners	265,236	25.18
- skilled	26,500	2.51
- unskilled	238,736	22.67
Non-wage-earners	137,426	13.04
- sharecroppers	34,728	3.29
- tenant farmers	87,156	8.28
- cotton plantation tenants (yanaconas)	15,542	1.47
Self-employed farmers	650,639	61.78
- joint holders and small landowners	650,639	61.78
Total	1,053,301	100.00

Source: Based on CIDA: Tenençia de la tierra y desarrollo socio-económico del sector agricola, Peru (Santiago, 1966), Appendix I-IV, p. 51.

III. Seasonal Migrants

Now that their background has been described in historical and structural terms, we may go on to ask who these casual migrants were, where they came from, how and in what numbers, and what their specific status was on the plantations. In answering these questions, we shall be able to define their specific characteristics.

Let us begin by identifying the geographical axes along which these migratory flows moved to and from the coast (see chart 1). From available information it is possible to identify at least four major routes. The first linked the highland areas of Piura and Cajamarca with the cotton plantations of the lower and middle Piura, the sugar plantations of the Chancay-La Leche and Zaña valleys and the rice plantations of Jequetepeque. The second ran from the Callejón de Huaylas area (Ancash) and the peasant communities in the departments of La Libertad, Ancash, Lima and Ica on the western spurs of the Andes, to the sugar plantations at San Jacinto, Nepeña and Pativilca, Supe and Barranca, and the cotton and citrus fruit plantations at Huaura, Huaral-Chancay, Chillón-Rímac-Lurín, Mala and Cañete. The third connected the highlands in the departments of Junín, Huancavelica, Ayacucho and Apurímac with the valleys of vineyards and cotton fields in the department of Ica. Lastly, the fourth route followed the coast from north to south, the flow starting in Piura at harvest time and ending in Ica.

Another major flow existed in the south, round Arequipa, Moquega and Tacna, which attracted people from Cuzco and Puno and the highland areas of these departments. Here the major poles of attraction were not the farming centres but the urban and mining centres of the area.

Each of the flows was characterised, on the one side, by the type of farm work available at the pole of attraction and the months of the year in which the movements took place and, on the other, by its components. The flows were determined chiefly by two sets of factors, one ecological and the other socio-economic.

Ecologically, the determining factors were the particular features of the farming region between the coast and the highlands.

The coastal farming region, formed by the rivers flowing down from the western range, was the only region that could be irrigated all year round, and its subtropical climate was suitable for growing sugar cane, rice and cotton. The existing cycles, for their part, produced periods in which manpower requirements rose considerably, as happened when the sugar cane was cut, the cotton picked and the rice transplanted.

In the highland region, on the other hand, only seasonal farming, subject to the rains, was possible. The rough topography, the limitations due to the altitude (from 2,000 to 4,500 metres above sea level), and the scarcity of arable land were such that only highland cattle-raising and the farming of a few food crops peculiar to the Andes (or brought in from outside and adapted to

CHART 1

Coast-Callejon de Huaylas
Regional circuit

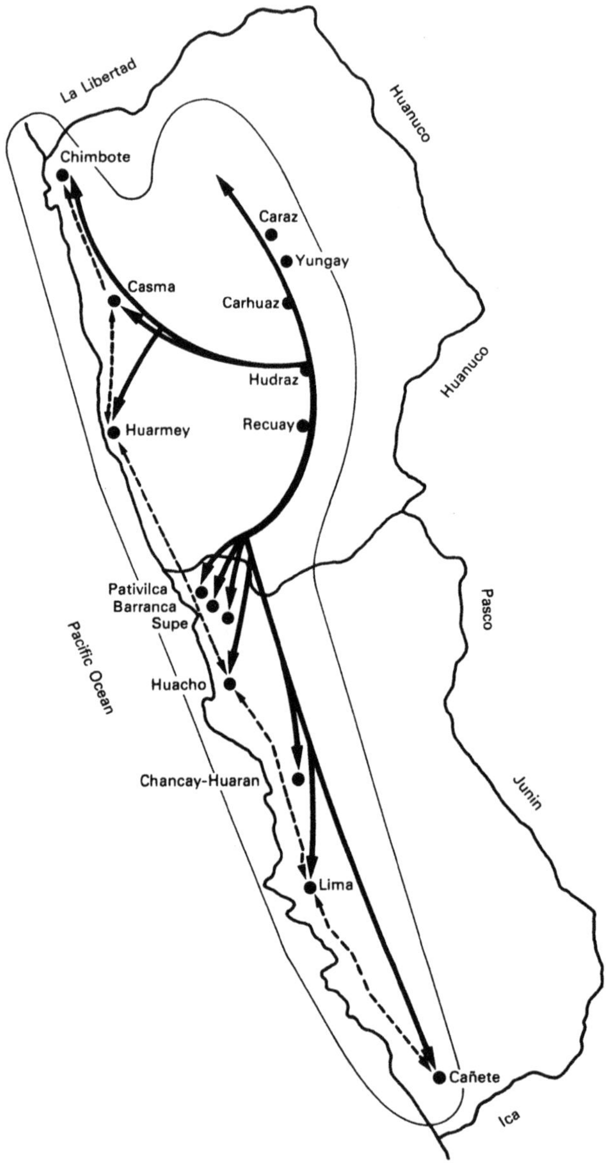

the region) could be developed.

In the distant past, the two regions complemented each other vertically, which allowed harmonious development and made it possible to meet the basic needs of their inhabitants. Such complementarity, however, was disrupted first by the breakdown in the traditional structures of the Andean economy caused by colonialisation, then by the greed of the large landowners and their destructive farming methods, and lastly by the development of capitalist enterprises. The highlands became wholly dependent on the coast.

From the socio-economic standpoint, the migratory flow sprang from the different structures of the two regions. The coastal area was controlled primarily by the large capitalist holdings and its economy based on export crops, while the predominant form of ownership in the highlands was small communal and individual holdings producing food crops. The interest of the capitalist holdings lay in meeting their manpower requirements in conditions that would allow them the highest possible profits, even if that meant overexploiting labour. The peasant economy on the other hand, had to find some use for the part of the domestic workforce that seasonally became redundant.

Furthermore, the geographical distribution of the agricultural working population, as historically consolidated, was marked by great differences in line with the country's unequal regional development. While they do not afford an accurate idea of the imbalance existing at the time, the official reports nonetheless stated that underemployment in agriculture reached an extremely high level: 45.9 per cent. Subsequent studies have brought out gross errors in the theoretical and practical methods of arriving at this figure and at the same time the existence of a shortage and a surplus of seasonal labour. It will therefore be instructive to review the regional data that most accurately reflect the situation, in our case for the circuit Huaral-Chancay-Callejón de Huaylas, in the light of labour supply and demand. These data (see, in this connection, Convenio para Estudios Económicos Básicos, 1970) show, for the provinces of Cañete, a typical coastal area drawing on labour from the highlands, and of Carhuaz, a highland area supplying labour, how migration was required for the operation of the system as a whole (see charts 2 and 3).

In these circumstances, regional migration was the appropriate "outlet", despite the fact that it benefited only one of the parties concerned.

However, this did not necessarily mean that the migrant population was homogenous. While the basic feature which all had in common might be ownership of a

CHART 2

Labour supply and demand and seasonal shortages in the coastal area of a regional circuit (Cañete, 1967)

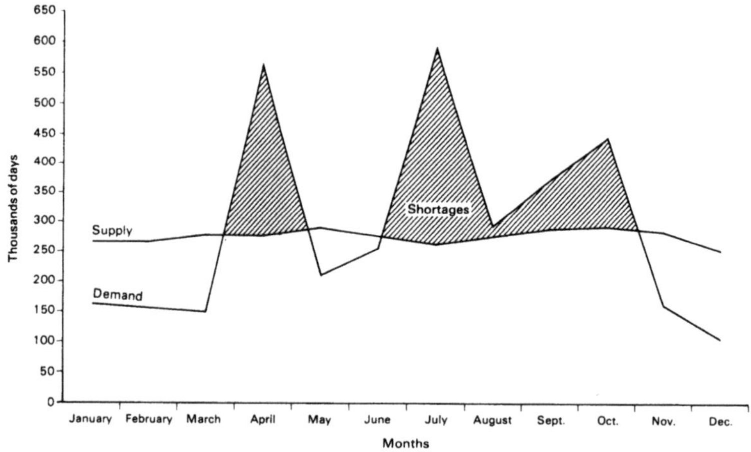

CHART 3

Labour supply and demand and seasonal surpluses in the highland area of a regional circuit (Carhuaz, 1967)

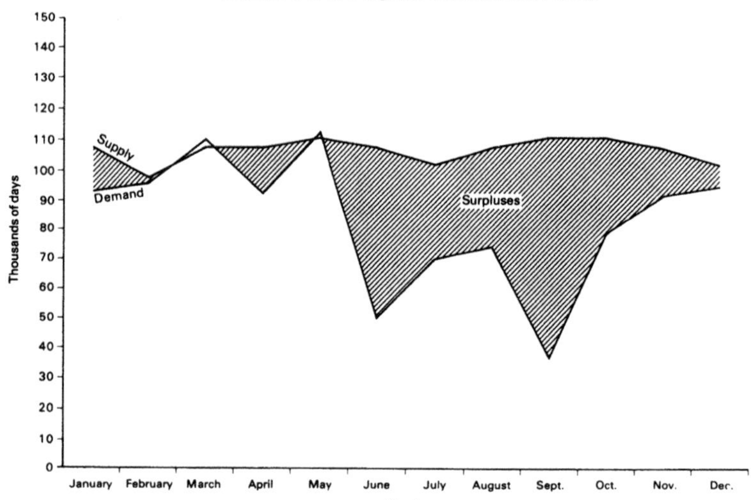

small plot of land, at least three types of migrants could none the less be distinguished:

(i) Migrants who were dependent primarily on earning a wage because of the small quantity or poor quality of the land owned, i.e. whose status was that of semi-proletarian peasant suffering from considerable poverty. Though he spent most or much of his time on his plot, this migrant was really a wage-earner, subject to overexploitation. This meant however that his wage did not cover his basic necessities but had to be supplemented by what he could make from farming or handicraft work in his home community.[1]

(ii) Migrants who depended primarily on farming their own plots of land. Wages had a different meaning for such migrants since they were intended for purchasing goods which their domestic work could not provide.[2] Oddly enough, wage-earning work in this case contributed to the continuance of the non-capitalist form of production and not its dissolution. Thus, casual migration was merely the specific form of articulation tending to reproduce continuously the non-capitalist relationship and to channel economic exploitation to the advantage of capitalism.

(iii) Migrants from large estates where they were employed as serfs or semi-serfs. Paradoxically, it was sometimes the owners of the estates themselves who encouraged these workers to migrate seasonally so as to ease the social pressures created by their status of serfs or semi-serfs. This is the least representative case of the three (as shown in the preliminary analysis of Callejón de Huaylas) but brings out the ultimate consequence of the link which seasonal migration provided between different systems of production.

---

[1] Sulmont (1975) put his finger on this characteristic of the semi-proletarian peasant populations though without pointing out that it is a permanent characteristic which does not disappear at a given time (when the industrial proletariat is formed) but persists as a phenomenon inherent in Peruvian society.

[2] In an excellent theoretical analysis, Guillermo Rochabrún shows how, in this case, wages serve as a mere means of payment and not as an expression of capitalist class relationship since neither the material conditions nor the social environment of the producer depend on wages (see Rochabrún, 1977).

IV. The Agrarian Reform

Of all the policy measures adopted by the military government over 11 years in office, the introduction in 1969 of a new agrarian reform programme was one of the most far-reaching (in this connection, see Matos Mar and Manuel Mejía, 1980).

The programme aimed not only at the effective transfer of land ownership but at the over-all reorganisation of the rural economy and society, as is clear from the objectives laid down in the National Development Plan of which it was a part.

The target set concerning the transfer of land ownership was, in a period of six years (1970-1975), to appropriate 15,000 farms covering an area of 9,687,091 hectares out of an estimated total of 30 million hectares, for the benefit of 342,000 peasants and 1,200,000 rural workers. At the same time, it set as a target for agricultural production an annual growth rate of 4.2 per cent, which was an appreciable increase over the 1.5 per cent annual average recorded during the previous decade. For the same period, though without defining how, underemployment was to be drastically reduced through the creation of 307,800 new jobs. It was hoped that these measures would have a favourable impact on rural income, raising the living standards of the peasant population.

Also, it was planned to foster participation at the grass-roots level through a new type of organisation (defined in 1972 by Legislative Decree 19400) and by developing traditional cultural patterns which up to then lay outside the mainstream of society and were signs of marginality.

The reform was also to play a vital part in altering existing patterns of geographical distribution and migration by influencing the factors that in previous years had led to the growth of definite movements both from the countryside to the towns and, seasonally, between different rural areas.

For those reasons alone, the programme initiated with the enactment of Legislative Decree 17716 was the most resolute project for rural change undertaken under the republic. Its far-reaching scope is all the more clear considering that the structures which were intended to replace the estate system entailed:

(a) implementation of the reform by area and not by unit, i.e. steered towards a geographical reorganisation;
(b) support for the formation of co-operative associations both in the areas covered by the reform and in those that were not;

(c) establishment of a model of micro-regional economic co-ordination based on co-operative federations.

The method of implementation known as Integrated Rural Settlement Projects (PIAR) consisted in carrying out agrarian reform measures by territorial areas defined as micro-regions according to ecological, economic, social and cultural criteria. Thus the land was not appropriated farm by farm but for each micro-region as a whole (one or two valleys) so as to ensure that the reform could be carried out faster and on a broader scale.

This procedure, which was applied after the initial experiments had been assessed, was intended to ensure a future geographical reorganisation inasmuch as the limits of the estates would not have to be taken into account in determining the number, size and type of units to be allocated. Accordingly, the new reformed undertakings could result from the division, merger or even maintenance of the former units. These enterprises automatically took it upon themselves to join a co-operative federation and to undertake co-ordinated planning and execution of production, marketing and provision of services at the micro-regional level.

The intensity and speed with which the agrarian reform measures were implemented was due largely to the adoption of an organisational model of the reformed sector whose main feature was the allocation of land to collective or co-operative undertakings. By the end of the reform those undertakings were to have 70 per cent of the total land allocated, thus becoming the backbone of Peruvian agriculture. The most important types now are the agricultural production co-operative (cooperativa agraria de producción - CAP), and the agricultural collective association (sociedad agrícola de interés social - SAIS).

The agrarian reform also envisaged a co-operative structure of the areas not covered by the reform by reorganising peasant communities in such a way that they could run undertakings of their own, and by organising small self-employed landowners into agricultural services cooperatives (cooperativas agrarias de servicios - CAS), and agricultural integrated land co-operatives (cooperativas agrarias de integración parcelaria - CAIP). This model did not include medium-sized agricultural enterprises, which were maintained under special conditions within the system of private property.

Peasant undertakings in the areas covered by the reform and those that might be formed in the areas not covered by it were to merge ultimately in micro-regional co-operative federations. These would perform a key function since they would serve as a module through which the agricultural sector could operate in a planned and co-ordinated manner, compensating for social and economic differences arising from unequal appropriation of resources and the different characteristics of the production units.

For that purpose, each member undertaking would pay to the federation between 45 and 70 per cent of its profits in order to constitute a co-operative capital fund for productive investments and the provision of services, whose ownership would not be divisible between the members, i.e. the undertakings. Managed by representatives of its member undertakings, the federation would be responsible for planning and carrying out production and marketing and ensuring maximum profits at the micro-regional level. In the most advanced projects, the possibility was even considered of establishing a joint fund between two or more federations for extending the scope of joint investments and services and levelling personal income at the regional level. The possibility of regulating the use of manpower was also considered, with the federation serving as a clearing-house for balancing supply and demand in its member undertakings. Even though such plans did not materialise in legislation, they reflect the directions sought at the time.

Lastly, it was provided that each federation, associated with one or more neighbouring federations, would constitute a minimum geographical unit to serve as a basis for future regional industrial development, as oriented by Integrated Development Projects (PID) when these were established on the broader regional bases. It was hoped that such a rural reorganisation would benefit not only farm workers but workers in the slums around the former estates.

The federations and the PIDs thus rounded out the model of a new agrarian structure, characterised by its co-operative nature. It was assumed in the project that such a structure, resulting from the redistribution of land, would be able to cope with the serious problem of unequal regional development and the imbalance existing between agriculture and industry.

After ten years, three general conclusions may be draw about the results of the agrarian reform. First, it must be recognised that a redistribution of land ownership, unprecedented in Peru, has been accomplished. Secondly, that redistribution has been accompanied by the establishment of a co-operative system involving the most important sector, economically, of Peruvian agriculture. And lastly, despite these two appreciable and probably lasting accomplishments, the targets set of overcoming agricultural underdevelopment and unequal regional development have not been achieved.

Up to June 1979 the agrarian reform had achieved most of the targets concerning the appropriation and allocation of land and the organisation of new operating units or undertakings, though it had failed to do so within the periods originally set because of various political and administrative difficulties. Initially set for 1975, the end of the first stage - that of transferring land ownership - had to be officially extended to 1976; in 1979, however, the administrative steps involved had not yet been completed.

Ten years after the law was enacted, the results stand as follows. The appropriations involve 15,826 agricultural units, comprising 10.5 million hectares of farm and pasture land. Of these, 7,789,811 hectares have been allocated to 337,662 peasant families and 1,569 co-operative undertakings and communities, i.e. 74.6 per cent of the total amount of land it was proposed to transfer and 90.9 per cent of the total beneficiaries envisaged.

Preference in the allocation of land has been given to co-operative associations: 581 agricultural production co-operatives, 12 co-operatives organised as agro-industrial complexes, 60 agricultural worker-owned associations, and 11 worker-owned enterprises, accounting for 62.3 per cent of the beneficiaries in respect of the land allocated and 45.2 per cent in respect of the number of beneficiaries themselves. On the other hand, individual allocations made to self-employed peasants or peasants organised in groups and to peasant communities account for the lowest proportion so far (see table 2).

The target finally set for production differ considerably from those initially planned. It should be noted however that the agrarian reform in Peru has not led to a crisis in production as has happened in other such experiments; even so, the average annual growth rate from 1969 to 1975 did not exceed 2.4 per cent or even keep pace with the rate of growth of the population. What is worse, production continued to be export-oriented to the detriment of local consumption, thus aggravating the deficit of the sector's trade balance.

It was initially estimated that the total amount of redistributed income as a result of the agrarian reform would be between 1 and 2 per cent of the national income. The extent of the redistribution, however, was likely to be quite limited as that amount would have been distributed among the most favoured quartile; and during the reform itself this indeed proved to be the case, with only the members of the most developed units receiving significant benefit.

Table 2: Position of the 1963-1979 agrarian reform: summarised (as on 24 June 1979)

	Units allocated	Areas allocated		Beneficiaries	
		Hectares	%	Number	%
Co-operatives	581	2,196,147	25.5	79,568	21.2
Agro-industrial complexes	12	128,566	1.5	27,783	7.4
Agricultural worker-owned associations	60	2,805,048	32.6	60,954	16.2
Worker-owned enterprises	11	232,653	2.7	1,375	0.4
Peasant groups	834	1,685,382	19.6	45,561	12.1
Peasant communities	448	889,364	10.3	117,710	31.4
Self-employed peasants	-	662,093	7.7	42,295	11.2
	1,907	8,599,253	100.0	375,246	100.0

Source: Dirección General de Reforma Agraria y Asentamiento Rural: Reforma Agraria en Cifras, table 6 (Lima, 1979; mimeographed).

The members of the sugar-growing co-operatives on the northern coast, for example, received a 62 per cent increase in real wages between 1968 and 1972, while the permanent workers of the agricultural worker-owned associations also experienced a rise in wages, though not so much. Those two groups, however, constitute only a small fraction of the intended beneficiaries of the agrarian reform, most of whom received income that did not exceed the level economic experts considered as that of extreme poverty.

A similar discrepancy between targets and achievements has occurred in the case of employment. Though accurate information is not yet available, it can be said that the unemployment gap not only has not been narrowed in the expected proportions, but has widened. Estimates based on information issued by the Ministry of Labour indicate that in 1976 the economically active population in agriculture was made up of 2,150,700 workers, i.e. 43.3 per cent of the country's total economically active population. Of that number, only 815,000 workers, or 37.9 per cent of the economically active in agriculture, had adequate jobs, while 6,500 workers (0.3 per cent) were unemployed and 1,329,200 (61.8 per cent) were underemployed. However provisional these figures may be, they are completely out of proportion to the target set.

These shortcomings may be ascribed both to the mistaken conception of the employment problem mentioned earlier and to the fact that small landowners in the highlands, where the problem of structural and seasonal unemployment is most acute, have hardly been touched by the reform. In the modern sector covered by the reform, on the other hand, the behaviour adopted by the undertakings has resulted in the creation of a limited number of new jobs. Nearly all of them however are jobs related to services or administrative work and not directly related to production. Also, the tendency on the part of the undertaking's members, as the "boss-underling" relationship has disappeared, to take a less active part in the work has given rise to a demand for labour to perform the jobs left vacant. Wage-earners from outside the undertaking are usually hired to fill those vacancies. Thus the net increase in permanent employment associated with the reform is insignificant.

Despite the lack of exact figures, the results were so clearly insufficient that in 1976 the government decided to implement a project for creating jobs in rural areas (GEAR). This is a supplementary programme designed solely to cope with the problem of employment in rural areas, especially in the most depressed and heavily populated areas where the direct effects of the agrarian reform have not been felt and there are few opportunities for permanent employment.

Such rural unemployment is the inevitable result of the sector's limited possibilities of productive reinvestment and of insufficient government backing and investment.

Basically, two factors account for the meagre results obtained by the agrarian reform at this advanced stage: (a) the fact that the changes in land ownership were not accompanied by changes in the orientation and behaviour of agriculture and its role in the national economy as a whole, and (b) the fact that the reform has not equally affected the sectors concerned, having introduced significant changes only in the modern co-operative-run sector while leaving the traditional sector intact.

The transformation achieved by the agrarian reform in the system of land tenure, while maintaining production on the same lines as before and, above all, the under-capitalised state of the sector, may be said to be its Pyrrhic victory.

Price policy plays a basic role here. The reform enabled the government to establish an unfavourable price policy for the sector. This trend, as part of a protective policy of dependent industrialisation, has aggravated the burden already placed on agriculture to generate the necessary surpluses for incipient capitalisation. Accordingly, it has not been possible to reverse the steady decline since 1937 of agricultural prices in relation to industrial prices. The situation has reached especially serious proportions as regards the unequal growth of production costs and consumer prices of agricultural products. For example, between 1972 and 1978 the price of pesticides and fertilisers rose by 1,000 and 600 per cent, respectively, while the price of such crops as rice, Indian corn and potatoes, which are extensively used, rose by only 400 per cent.[1]

A similar part is played by the investment and tax policy. The budget for agricultural investment, whose total amount has been insufficient, was largely devoted to carrying out costly irrigation projects on the coast, disregarding the rest of agriculture which was heavily taxed at the same time by unequal levies. The income tax paid by reformed peasant undertakings during the period under study, for example, may be estimated at 10,000 million soles.

A third obstacle to capitalisation is the payment of the agricultural debt. The beneficiaries were to pay 15,000 million soles over 20 years to cover the land allocation costs which the State, in turn, would pay to the former owners. At the end of 1979, when slightly over 3,000 million soles had been paid, this payment was waived in response to various requests by the beneficiaries, though the pending obligations of the State to the former owners were known. Since the latter have left the countryside, the flow of the money has been from rural areas to the towns.

For these various reasons, then, the agricultural sector continues to play a secondary role in the economy,

---

[1] Estimates of the ECO economic research group, based on official data and data of Bayer and Shell.

though with the difference now that those who suffer most directly from the situation are the reformed undertakings and the peasants, a fact that severely limits their possibilities for economic and social advancement. Within agriculture as a whole, however, the general situation has had different concrete effects on the sector covered by the reform and that which is not, widening the already existing gap between the two.

Before analysing this aspect, it should be noted that the organisational model adopted has proved inconclusive. Although its first target of redistributing land and establishing a co-operative sector has been attained, this has not been the case for the operation of the co-operative federations in the conditions planned. Integration at the micro-regional level, consequently, has not been achieved.

With the failure of regional integration to materialise as projected, the possibility of any real planning has shrunk, and even the minimum co-ordination required is lacking. Without anybody to guide their activities, the units operate with no other reference than the market itself, and are not always successful in their individual efforts to obtain better results. The consequences are inadequate use of resources (e.g. idle machinery in one undertaking and a shortage in the next, duplication of equipment and services etc.), overproduction of certain products, with adverse results in the marketplace, and an unequal and contradictory development of the units in relation to their previous situation, resulting in a wide variety of outputs and inputs. Efficiency in the management of one undertaking thus does not necessarily mean optimum results for all.

Furthermore, the proposal to carry out Integrated Development Projects did not get beyond the experimental stage. Consequently, each undertaking took it upon itself to develop activities to supplement its farming activities with - given the disconnected and isolated nature of each attempt - predictable results. The undertakings with the largest capacity were of course the only ones to make any headway, and only in a direction favouring their own interests. As a result, the conditions of unequal development prevailing before the reform were reproduced. Even with those difficulties, however, the modern pole of agriculture has substantially changed, for it is now centred on co-operative undertakings. This has not happened in the case of the traditional pole. Co-operation there has not worked: despite the attempts at reorganisation, the indigenous community remains intact and small individual holdings have kept their importance. While the reformed sector has shown signs of economic growth, the weight of the negative trends has fallen on the traditional sector as the general agricultural situation has deteriorated.

Generally speaking it may be said that the imbalances between agriculture and industry and between rural and urban areas have grown. Despite the institutional changes introduced, the structural heterogeneity of agriculture has increased.

In these circumstances, the results that the reform has had for migration - for which its implementation aroused great expectations of change - are understandable. The programme was expected to lead to a significant if not rapid change in the pattern of geographical redistribution that had worked to the disadvantage of the countryside, by concentrating the population in a few large towns, especially Lima. Even though it seems sufficient demographic data are not available, it may be inferred that that goal has not been achieved.[1] Some migratory flows may have taken other directions, towards new centres of activity, or may have slackened slightly, but by and large rural-urban migration continues and indeed has tended to increase.

While employment problems are due primarily to the undercapitalised state of rural areas, those concerning migration are directly related to the persistently unequal regional development in the country. The cause of continuing migration must be sought in the continuance of that lack of balance.

V. The Agrarian Reform and Seasonal Migration

It would be a mistake to assume that the process of agrarian reform has merely maintained the pre-existing situation in respect of migration; the specific modes of organisation introduced in rural institutions have affected not only the numbers but the conditions under which casual workers are employed in reformed undertakings.

The most obvious impact here lies in the growing increase in the casual migrant population, employed only seasonally by large co-operative undertakings or medium-sized privately owned undertakings and completely lacking the job security, basic minimum wages and social security benefits granted to permanent workers (health-care, severance pay, paid leave, etc.).

---

[1] The National Population Survey (EDEN) of 1975 has provided valuable information about migratory movements. However, it is based on different criteria from those used for the censuses of 1961 and 1972, and a comparative analysis of the two sources is still pending.

Two main causes account for this increase in seasonal migration: the growing demand for labour on the part of co-operative undertakings, especially those on the coast, and the greater supply in depressed rural areas which have traditionally provided temporary workers.

The growing demand in the co-operatives and the agricultural collective associations is due primarily to the relaxation of the rigid labour relations that formerly prevailed on the estates and the decrease in the amount of work now performed by their members. Soon after the estates had been appropriated, the workers rejected the working conditions that had hitherto been imposed on them. In their new status as owners, it was argued, they would not do so well as members to maintain oppressive systems of exploitation. That attitude, consented to when not actually encouraged by the government authorities then responsible for conducting the reform, led to a reduction of working hours and tasks. Later on, when the undertakings were established and formally under the management of the workers, one of the claims most staunchly defended was a reduction of the work volume to a minimum; in some cases the members even refused to perform jobs considered to be hard or difficult. In most undertakings, consequently, the members shortened the working day from six to five hours or from five to four, converted "daily" tasks into piece work, and slowed down the pace of work while making performance assessment standards more flexible. For those reasons there are undertakings today where the work involved in many of the jobs has been reduced by as much as half.

The decrease in the work performed by the members naturally has to be made up by non-member workers. This has given rise to an increase in the demand for such labour in conditions in which supply seems to be highly elastic. The example only needs to be cited of the high level of casual work in nearly all the co-operatives on the northern and central coast, ranging from 9 to 51 per cent (see table 3).

For their part, the communities supplying workers have increasingly responded to the greater demand for labour on the coast, because they are situated in areas that, socially and geographically, have hardly been touched by the agrarian reform. For peasants living in areas where the population is constantly growing and poverty constantly increasing, who lack opportunities for steady employment on the coast, seasonal migration continues to be virtually the only possible source of earnings to supplement their subsistence farming.

Thus, far from diminishing the major seasonal movements between the active areas and units on the coast and the backward ones in the highlands, have increased

Table 3: Use of casual labour by co-operatives in various coastal valleys

	Number of co-operatives	Year	Proportion of casual workers in the work-force (%)
Piura	6	1975	55
La Leche	2	1972/77	30
Chancay (Lambayeque)	10	1972/77	19
Zaña	3	1972/77	27
Jequetepeque	8	1972/77	51
Sugar-growing co-operatives	8	1972	15
Santa-Lacramarca	8	1974	36
Puarura-Sayán	18	1974	27
Ica			
Large (over 700 hectares)	6	1973/77	40
Medium-sized (500-700)	4	1973/77	20
Small (less than 500)	8	1973/77	10
Agricultural Area IV			
Large (over 1,000 hectares)	23	1976	19
Medium-sized (500-1,000)	40	1976	17
Small (less than 500)	12	1976	9
	156		23

Source: Caballero (1978), pp. 57-80.

considerably. Besides these major migratory circuits, others have been created by the demand of non-cooperative agricultural units or by non-agricultural activities, increasing the volume of seasonal migration. Principal among these is the mountain circuit linking depressed areas in the departments of Huánuco, Pasco, Huancavelica and Ayacucho with dynamic units in the department of Junín or in the coffee- and fruit-growing valley of Chanchamayo. There are also other circuits in the south round the highlands of Collao, Ceja de Selva and the mining centres.

In the course of ten years of agrarian reform, various provisions for the incorporation of casual workers as members of the undertakings have been adopted, but not observed. Failure to comply with those provisions is due to at least two concurrent factors. First, intentions could hardly override in practice the economic laws on which the undertakings are run and whose operation rejects a solution to the problem. Secondly, the casual migrants themselves are not attracted by such a solution, which would mean uprooting them from their home communities.

It is not yet possible to assess accurately the extent to which casual work has expanded. By way of illustration, however, the general features of this trend will be outlined below by analysing a regional case (the Chancay valley and Callejón de Huaylas) where an active coastal area is linked with a depressed area in the highlands.

1. Increase of casual workers

The first aspect that stands out from an analysis of the situation of casual workers in the co-operatives is their numerical growth. This is explained by the behaviour of the wage-earning members: as they began to work shorter hours and at a slower pace, the need arose to make up the gap by taking on casual workers. Consequently, though some casual workers became members of the co-operatives on their formation, in absolute figures their number grew.

Two different patterns have to be distinguished, however, in the growth of casual labour. First, there is the large-scale movement of seasonal migrants which usually occurs only at harvest time. Secondly, there is the body of casual workers remaining at the undertakings or nearby, who are employed on jobs of every sort or at especially busy times of the year, and whose growth is rapid. This is facilitated both by the vegetative increase of the local population and by the growing tendency of some former migrants to settle down. The extent to which this segment of the population has expanded is clear from the mushrooming along the coastal valley of numerous quarters or settlements, such as Pampa Libre, La Huaquilla, Cerro del Estanque and El Trébol, made up exclusively of such migrants. From an examination of the labour registers of the co-operatives surveyed, it may be estimated that the increase in casual work between 1969 and 1978, in number of working days, was about 15 per cent.

An analysis of the information available on these undertakings for the 1974-75 campaign, in turn, shows that of the 970 skilled workers deemed to be members under the agrarian reform, an average of only 711 worked regularly. This was a result of retirements, holidays, sick leave and leave for the co-operative and trade union leaders. The average number of casual workers permanently employed by the agricultural production co-operatives, casual workers living nearby who are taken on at various times of the year, and seasonal migrants, came to 528 (see table 4). In other words, the number of permanent workers in these undertakings accounted for, on average, 57.3 per cent of the workforce and the number of casual workers for 42.7 per cent. This is a clear indication of the importance this form of labour integration has acquired.

Casual work is not evenly distributed over the year but increases appreciably with greater seasonal demand, which occurs primarily at harvest time. The number of casual workers thus varies according to the time of year; while not less than 26.1 per cent of the total labour force at any time, it reaches over 50 per cent at the peak of the cotton-picking. During picking not only does the number of casual workers increase but so does absenteeism on the part of the members, while the number of days worked by them decreases to less than 50 per cent for several weeks after approximately the nineteenth week of picking. Moreover, during most of the year the proportion of days worked by the members is less than their numerical proportion of the workers as a whole (see charts 4 and 5), which means that they perform fewer days of work than the casual workers, not counting the fact that their working day is shorter. Consequently, the actual number of casual workers in peak periods of demand is considerably higher than the average given above. In the twenty-ninth week of the 1974-75 campaign, for example, there were 839 casual workers, i.e. more than 100 per cent of the average number of permanent workers in the agricultural production co-operatives.

The main reason why the undertakings resort to casual workers is that the wages paid under temporary

Table 4: Permanent and casual workforce in seven cotton-growing co-operatives in the Chancay Valley: 1974-75 campaign

Co-operatives	Members	Weekly average number of permanent workers	Weekly average number of casual workers	Average proportion of casual workers in total workforce (%)
Palpa	283	243	249	50.6
Villa Hermosa	131	118	56	33.7
San Martín	117	100	36	26.4
Jesús del Valle	128	82	70	46.0
La Candelaria	108	96	79	45.1
Boza	113	n/a	n/a	n/a
Jecuán	90	80	38	32.2
	970	711	528	42.7

Source: Based on information contained in the undertakings' payrolls.

CHART 4

Manpower employed in seven co-operatives in the Chancay Valley by type of workers (1974–75)

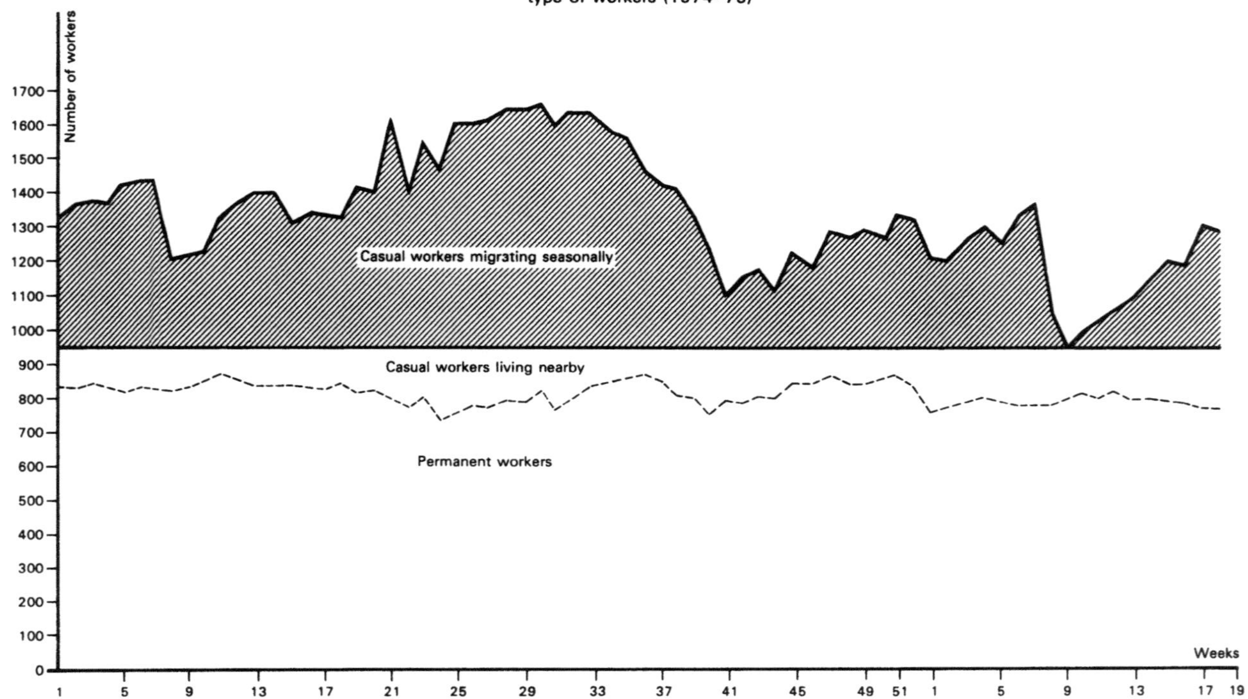

CHART 5

Proportion of member workers and member's wages and working days in semen no-operatives in the Chancay Valley (1974–75)

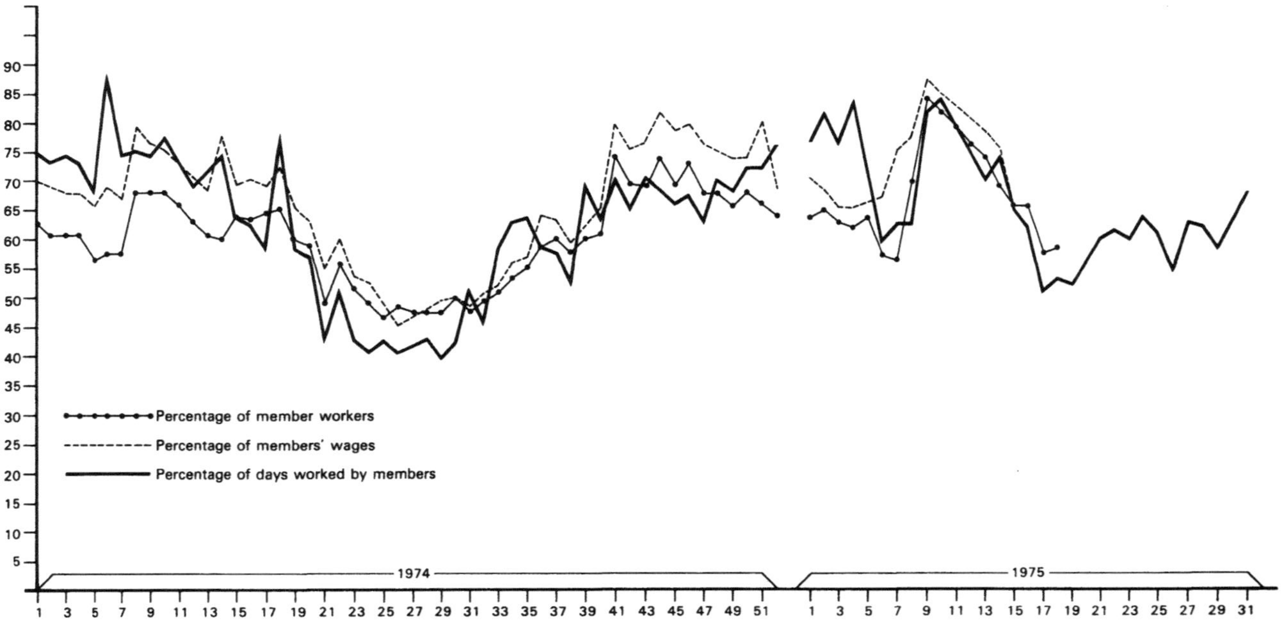

contracts are less than the replacement costs, thus permitting higher earnings. The wages are less for two reasons: first, because labour regulations, as mentioned earlier, are not observed and, secondly, because the day actually worked by casual workers is longer. In cotton-picking, the main activity, they work as many as 10 to 12 hours daily.[1] Most of the casual workers do only this job though many of them are assisted by their wives and children, who perform various tasks: the wife may either pick or clean the cotton, while the younger children look after it and the older ones help in the picking. This extra individual or family work, however, is not remunerated.

In nearly all the co-operatives the wages of the casual workers are much less than those paid to the members. Wages for day-labourers are fixed according to the legal minimum rate for the region and are usually from 25 to 40 per cent less than the average wages of the members. For harvest work, as in the case of cotton, the rate per quintal picked is so fixed that the worker must work ten to twelve hours to earn the wage of a member. Casual workers, besides, do not enjoy social security benefits, paid holidays or other entitlements. Most are excluded from the profit-sharing schemes and the payment of fringe benefits.

Furthermore, no possibility is open to casual workers to reduce the pace of work. They are assigned the hardest jobs by the co-operative, jobs which its members refuse to perform, and are picked by the co-operatives and the contractors according to their output. The best way of ensuring that the pace of work is kept up is to pay piece-work rates. Not satisfied with this, some undertakings require casual workers to bring their own working tools. Despite all this, the seasonal migrants accept the situation. How could we explain that they work so hard for so little pay?

---

[1] The working day of a casual worker is more or less the following: the worker gets up between 4 and 5 a.m. to make his breakfast and prepare the lunch he will take with him to the field. At 6.30 he sets out for work and begins to pick at 7 a.m., if not before. At noon he takes a short break for lunch, 30 minutes at most, then he continues picking until 3 p.m., when he begins to clean the cotton he has picked. This takes roughly two hours, after which he must queue up to have the cotton weighed, the amount being noted by an employee of the co-operative and credited to the worker's account. This takes till 6 or 7 p.m., when the worker returns to his lodging to prepare his supper and from time to time to wash his clothes.

It is simply that in this way they are able to earn an income that is essential for their peasant economy. Seasonal migrants from the rural communities have no choice but to accept the hard conditions in which their contracts have to be carried out. Furthermore, owing to their unstable link with the undertakings, their dependence on the latter both for work and socially, and the difficulties they have in organising themselves - in short, the characteristics inherent in their status as migrants - they have no possibility of demanding better wages through claims or collective bargaining. The only possibility for families to bring in more earnings, therefore, is to step up the pace of work, work more days on the coast or set to work more of their members.

Even in these hard conditions, however, casual work has increased. It must therefore be asked how, despite the agrarian reform in the highlands, such conditions continue to exist.

2. Increase of seasonal migration

Greater casual manpower requirements in the co-operatives have gone hand in hand with greater availability of labour in the traditional centres of supply. This is due to the gradual process of impoverishment that inevitably creates a surplus of domestic manpower and makes temporary wage-earning activities a necessity, even for landowners.

There is little the agrarian reform can do to check this progress, given its limited possibilities for redistribution which fail to afford a solid alternative. In the three communities dealt with below, the reform has reproduced the structure of small holdings that underlies the need for temporary wage-earning work. Only Mishqui appears to differ in the tendency since the beneficiaries of the reform are prevented by a formal measure from continuing to leave. Although this measure is accepted by the peasants since compliance is a requisite for the allocation of land, there is no assurance that, once the immediate objective has been achieved, migration will not acquire again its previous course and magnitude.

The decline in the migration of peasants from Mishqui has been more than offset by the increased flows from Amashca and Hualcán. This expansion occurred even though the agrarian reform stipulated restrictive regulations for organisations established by the reform, which authorises the absence of members

> "... for temporary work of up to three months. In this case, the worker shall, at the end of this period, pay to the community the cash

> equivalent of the work which he would have performed as community tasks during his absence, according to the daily rate for the region." (Comunidad Campesina "Jose Carlos Mariátegui", Reglamento Interno, Chapter III, Article 9(a)).

Though this legal provision attempts to introduce a limit to the length of absence, this is not observed at all, as we shall see later.

In the case of Amashca, 35 per cent of the economically active population migrated to the coast in 1977 to work as temporary farm wage-earners. Considering that most of these migrants were men since women do not leave in large numbers, it may be assumed that at least 60 per cent of the economically active male population left the community. This means, as far as families are concerned, that one of the family members migrated in 66 per cent of the cases. As for Mishqui, the number of peasants who migrated temporarily that year was less than in previous years, primarily because of the impact of the agrarian reform on the community: only 18 per cent of the economically active population migrated or, given the composition of the migrants by sex, 35 per cent of the economically active male population. Similarly, the number of families in which a member migrated would come to 34 per cent. In the case of Hualcán, 38 per cent of the economically active population migrated that year and, considering that 95 per cent of these migrants were men, roughly 70 per cent of the men left their community to work as wage-earners, 20 per cent working as day labourers in the area (Carhuaz and surroundings) in farming and building and the remaining 50 per cent moving to the coastal valleys. Thus, in the case both of Amashca and of Hualcán, one-third of the local economically active population, or two-thirds of the economically active male population, migrated to the coast to seek casual work (see table 5).

The central coastal valleys continue to be a market for the migratory movements from the peasant communities of the region since they generate labour demand that coincides with the period of greatest surplus manpower in Callejón de Huaylas. The migrants go primarily to Chancay and Huaral (47 per cent), secondly to Chimbote (19 per cent) and Casma (17 per cent), and thirdly to other valleys or towns such as Barrança, Huacho, Lima and Callao. It is significant that in 1977 a small number went beyond the traditional frontiers of the circuit, to Trujillo and Cañete which lie just beyond (see table 6). In addition, within the same highland area new poles of

Table 5: Economically active population in the communities of Amashca, Mishqui and Hualcán and number of temporary wage-earning workers, 1977

Peasant communities	1972 Census			
	Total population	No. of families	Economically active population	Number of temporary wage-earning workers
Amashca	655	186	341	121
Mishqui	413	110	214	38
Hualcán	770	202	400	150

Source: IEP interviews, 1977.

attraction have arisen, as for example the community of Huayopampa, a fruit-growing centre in the Chancay valley; previously a labour-supplying community, owing to modernisation it has become a centre offering a demand for casual workers from Ancash.

Particular directions may be noted within the circuit. From Amashca, for example, there is a direct flow to Huaral where the migrants work as cotton-workers or fruit-pickers, and a smaller flow to other valleys or towns, such as Trujillo or Lima, where they find jobs as building workers or day-labourers on various types of farms. The migrants from Mishqui follow more or less the same routes as those from Amashca. The peasants of Hualcán, on the other hand, migrate mainly to Huaral, Chimbote and Casma, where most of them are contracted for three months from the beginning of the cotton harvest. Afterwards, they move south individually, some stopping at Barranca or Huacho, though most go directly on to Huaral. Other casual workers from Hualcán move from place to place between Chimbote and Huaral. Unlike those from Amashca, quite a few of these migrants work as hoers.

As for the jobs performed at present, it should be noted that the older migrants began as hoers, then became pickers and finally, in some cases, building workers. In recent years, however, the casual workers have begun as pickers, hoers and building workers,

Table 6: Migratory movement of peasants from the communities of Amashca, Mishqui and Hualcán to the coastal valleys, 1977

Peasant communities	Coastal valleys or towns								
	Lima Callao	Huaral	Huacho	Barranca	Casma	Chimbote	Trujillo	Canete	Total
Amashca	5	50	12	9	17	11	6	3	121
Mishqui	1	22	-	-	12	1	2	-	38
Hualcán	5	145	-	11	23	46	-	-	150
TOTAL	11	145	12	20	52	58	8	3	309
Per cent	3.6	47.0	4.0	6.2	17.0	18.8	2.3	2.3	100.0

Source: ibid.

which points to a social broadening of the knowledge of the coastal working environment: the young people obtain information about the coast through the experience of their parents. Even so, the tendency to specialise continues since most of the migrants concentrate on the cotton harvest (63 per cent) and only a minority work as hoers, building workers, public utility workers in towns or itinerant peddlars.

Wage-earning work is performed during the months of the year in which demand for farm labour in Callejón de Huaylas is slack and the demand for manpower in the coastal valleys is high. Available data indicate that most of the peasants remain away three to six months of the year, between February and July. At Amashca, 77 per cent of the casual workers were away between three and six months and at Hualcán 88 per cent (see table 7). These temporary migrations recur every year. At Amashca, for example, 56 per cent of the casual workers migrate every year for from 1 to 10 years, 30 per cent every year from from 11 to 20 years, and 14 per cent every year for over 21 years. These figures call in question the "temporariness" of casual work, which tends rather to become seasonally recurrent work. The same situation occurs at Hualcán: 59 per cent migrate for between 1 and 10 years, 29 per cent for between 11 and 20 years, and 12 per cent for over 21 years (see table 8). There are many peasants who have been denied and continue to be denied the social security benefits to which they are entitled as workers. It is thus easy to understand their reluctance to give up their plot of land, which after all is their only source of security, their "social security" so to speak, in which they seek protection from the instability of the employment market and the tendency for wages to remain at low levels and even decline.

What is most significant is that the situation in Callejón de Huaylas does not seem to be an exception but an example of what has occurred in rural areas with similar features, such as Ayacucho, Cajamarca, Alto Piura, etc., whose settlers have also been compelled to turn frequently towards the coast.

Generally speaking, it may be said that this trend is the way out for migrant labour who continue to find work in co-operative undertakings. If the agrarian reform had not been carried out, a crisis would certainly have erupted in the traditional patterns of seasonal migration, shifting them away from the regional circuit and obliging migrants to seek other alternatives, probably in the towns and in branches other than agriculture. Such a prospect, however, has not been definitely ruled out but only postponed, since the possibility of a capitalist

Table 7: Number of temporary wage-earning workers grouped by annual period absent from home communities: Amashca and Hualcán, 1977

Annual period of temporary wage-earning employment (months)	Amashca		Hualcán	
	Number	%	Number	%
1 to 2	8	9	-	-
3 to 4	45	51	20	31
5 to 6	23	26	37	57
7 to 8	6	7	5	7.5
9 to 10	2	2	-	-
11 to 12	4	5	3	4.5
Total	88	100.0	65	100.0

Source: ibid.

Table 8: Number of temporary wage-earning workers grouped by continuous annual absences from home communities: Amashca and Hualcán, 1977

Continuous annual absences for temporary wage-earning employment (years)	Amashca		Hualcán	
	Number	%	Number	%
1 to 5	26	30	20	31
6 to 10	23	26	10	28
11 to 15	13	15	14	22
16 to 20	13	15	5	7
21 to 25	9	10	6	9
26 to 30	3	3	1	1.5
More than 30	1	1	1	1.5
Total	88	100.0	65	100.0

Source: ibid.

reorganisation of co-operative farming and the growing skills of itinerant labour on the coast, are potential threats to the continuing use of the manpower that still exists in the highlands.

VI. Concluding Comments

In the light of what has been said up to now, it may be concluded that after ten years of implementation the agrarian reform carried out by the military government has fallen far short of the targets set and, though generating major changes in other sectors of the nation's life (mobilisation of the peasantry, break with the traditional political system etc.), has proved a failure as far as the problem of migration is concerned. A few comments are made below on the causes of the failure, the significance of this experience, and the prospects it opens up for policies that could come to effective grips with the problem of migration.

1. First it should be stressed that one of the major socio-economic problems connected with seasonal migration is that it permits a specific form of exploitation - and indeed overexploitation - of rural labour. Given the characteristics of the environment and production in the rural areas, seasonal migration will no doubt continue to be one of the basic features of Peruvian agriculture for many years still. Consequently, it is not so much a matter of doing away at all costs with every form of migration, as the theoreticians of the agrarian reform postulate, as of doing away with the exploitation of migrants.

Even so, the negative results of the reform itself still have to be accounted for. It has already been pointed out that not only was the agrarian policy incompatible with the programme for the transfer of land ownership and the reorganisation of rural institutions but in the end proved to be at odds with it. The changes introduced were limited to organisational aspects without affecting the pattern of structural relations that underlie migration, to such an extent indeed that the government's agrarian policy, rather than attenuating the undercapitalisation of rural areas and the regional imbalances, accentuated them. The following conclusions must be drawn in this respect:

(a) These negative results were due not only to the agrarian policy but to the over-all economic policy. The development plans of the military government were concentrated on mining, petroleum and industry. Large-scale investment projects were undertaken in the mining and petroleum sectors but did not contribute much to regional development. The efforts to develop industry, in turn, were made at the expense of agriculture. Even the investments devoted to rural areas were concentrated on large-scale irrigation projects on the coast for increasing farm exports.

(b) Though directed towards regional reorganisation the agrarian reform programme, because of the limitations it ran up against, achieved changes only at the micro-regional level without affecting the relations between micro-regions. Besides, the notion of region implicit in the official programmes was largely an administrative notion and had little to do with the actual geographical areas delimited by employment markets, economic relations, migration and social and cultural identity. Accordingly, without really knowing what they were about, the reform programmes, by modernising certain developed poles and overlooking the traditional ones, merely increased the unequal levels of development already existing in the country.

In this connection, one of the principal reasons for the limited effects of the agrarian reform was undoubtedly its failure to attenuate undercapitalisation and regional imbalance.

Nevertheless, while undercapitalisation and regional imbalance are decisive factors, they do not wholly explain the phenomenon of migration. Literature on the subject brings out a number of other factors exerting an influence, such as the type of economic organisation and individual and family attitudes, which are not discussed in this chapter. We are aware of the need to study the impact of the reform on these factors as well, since only such a study could explain how phenomena that are similar at the macro level could produce different reactions at the micro level, enabling us to understand, for example, differences in migration patterns between or within communities.

2. In attempting to understand problems of development, the situation in Peru obliges us to revise some of the most commonly held notions about the causes of migration.

(a) First, it is clear that problems of rural underdevelopment and, by extension, of migration are not due to the dichotomy between the large estates (latifundias) and small holdings (minifundias) but to the functional relationship between the capitalist units and the peasant small-scale farm economy. Consequently, even when the estates had been converted into co-operative undertakings, the relationship between these and the peasant economy maintained migratory movements. In that sense, not only the backward segment of agriculture needs to be changed in order to bring about a structural reorganisation of the sector, but the underlying social and economic relations nationally.

(b) It has been proposed on a number of occasions that production should be organised on a worker-owned basis as an alternative means of attenuating employment and migration problems. As a matter of fact, as in other experiments in reform and co-operation in the past, the introduction of co-operative formulae in the case of Peru has had some positive effect on employment and has certainly helped to check emigration of the population covered by the reform. Nevertheless, an examination of the Peruvian experience, where seasonal migration has not only continued but grown, points to the need to integrate the process of organisational change into a national policy affecting the underlying economic, social and political structure so as to influence rural migration. Otherwise, co-operative forms of organisation will have little impact.

3. Lastly, there is no doubt that any policy designed to overcome rural underdevelopment in Peru will have to give priority to agriculture and will have to foster regional development. It is obvious that such a change can only take place along with a qualitative change in the current political and economic conditions created by capitalist development. In the short term, however, measures to correct sectoral undercapitalisation and regional imbalances can help to attenuate the problem by making good the limitations of the agrarian reform programme.

It must above all be kept in mind that one of the major challenges facing the country today is the pressing need to overcome, once and for all, the extreme poverty and the political marginality that are associated with the seasonal migration of peasants.

References

Caballero, J.M. (1978): "Los eventuales en las cooperativas costenas peruanas: Un modelo analítico", in Economía, Aug., Vol. I, No. 2 (Lima, Departamento de Economía, Universidad Católica del Perú).

CIDA (1966): Tenencia de la tierra y desarrollo socioeconomico del sector agricola, Perú.

Comunidad Campesina (n.d.): "José Carlos Mariátegui", in Reglamento Interno, Chapter III, Article 9(a).

Convenio para Estudios Económicos Básicos (1970): Primera estimación del sub-empleo de la población económicamente activa en areas rurales por meses, provincias y regiones en el ano 1967 (Lima, Nov.).

Dirección General de Reforma Agraria y Asentiamento Rural (1979): Reforma agraria en cifras (Lima; mimeographed).

Matos Mar, J. (1968): "Dominación, desarrollos desiguales y pluralismo en la sociedad y cultura peruana", in Perú Problem, 5 ensayos (Lima, Instituto de Estudios Peruanos).

--- (1976): "Yanaconaje y reforma en el Peru", in Perú Problema 15 (Lima, Instituto de Estudios Peruanos).

Matos Mar, J. and Manuel Mejía, J. (1978): Desarrollo desigual, reforma agraria y migración en el Peru paper submitted to the Symposium on Trends in Internal Migration and Policy Issues in Developing Countries held at Cuernavaca in September 1978 under the joint auspices of the Latin American Council for Social Sciences and UNESCO.

--- (1980): Reforma agraria: Logros y contradicciones 1969-1979 (Lima, Instituto de Estudios Peruanos).

Manuel Mejía, J. and Diaz Suárez, R. (1975): Sindicalismo y reforma agraria en el valle de Chancay (Lima, Instituto de Estudios Peruanos).

Manuel Mejía, J., Ramírez, J., Díaz Suárez, R. and Campos Riveras, C. (1979): Los eventúales del valle de Chancay: Migración estacional, proletarización rural y reforma agraria en un circuito regional (Lima, Instituto de Estudios Peruanos).

Rochabrún, G. (1977): "Apuntes para la comprensión del capitalismo en el Perú", in Análisis (Lima) Jan.-Feb., No. 1.

Sulmont, D. (1975): El movimiento obrero en el Perú, 1900-1956 (Lima, Fondo editorial de la Pontificia Universidad Católica del Perú).

Webb, R. and Figueroa, A. (1975): Distribución del ingreso en el Perú (Lima, Instituto de Estudios Peruanos).

Chapter 4

AGRARIAN CHANGE AND LABOUR MIGRATION IN THE SIERRA OF ECUADOR

by Peter Peek

I. Introduction

Since the early 1970s, Ecuador has experienced high and unprecedented rates of economic growth. The annual growth rate of real gross domestic product averaged more than 10 per cent, nearly twice as high as in the 1960s. The production and export of oil, started in 1972, is one of the main reasons for this accelerated expansion. It stimulated the growth of manufacturing, other industries and construction, which had started, very modestly, during the previous decade. As a result, the output of these sectors rose by around 15 per cent annually in recent years.

Rapid growth of the urban economy was accompanied by important modifications in the agrarian structure. A growing number of traditional, or semi-feudal, haciendas were transformed into modern, capitalist farms. Simultaneously, the number of very small farms, or minifundia, increased rapidly. These changes were, partly, the result of a series of land reforms started in 1964. In this study it is argued that these were among the major causes of the changing patterns of migration.

Census data from Ecuador appear to indicate that the level of permanent rural emigration from the rural Sierra decreased after the land reform of 1964 (JUNAPLA, 1977). Other evidence seems to point out that temporary migration to urban areas, as well as within rural areas, increased considerably after 1964 (Ministerio de Agricultura y Ganadería and ORSTOM, 1978a). The main objective of this study is to explain these changes in the migration pattern in terms of the process of economic growth in Ecuador.[1]

---

[1] This analytical framework has been described in an earlier working paper (Peek, 1978); see also Peek and Standing (1979).

II. The Agrarian Structure in the Sierra before 1964

Until the early 1960s, production of export crops, mainly bananas, was the principal economic activity in Ecuador. This was largely concentrated in the coastal lowlands, the Costa. During the late 1940s and 1950s output increased substantially, largely as a result of the inflow of foreign capital. US companies owning banana plantations in Central America had experienced increasing difficulties there because of strikes and bad harvests and they decided to withdraw their capital. At that time, the Ecuadorian government strongly favoured the development of the agro-export sector and it adopted a number of measures to attract foreign capital. As a result, several US companies transferred many of their operations to the coastal regions of Ecuador. Besides producing bananas, these companies also controlled their marketing in the USA, together with those grown by local producers. Because these companies exercised a considerable influence over the import quotas set for each country by the US government, banana exports increased substantially. This expansion of the foreign market further stimulated banana production so that the area cultivated increased rapidly during this period.

While the production of export crops rose sharply, production of food crops, largely concentrated in the Sierra, stagnated. Data for the same period show that per capita production remained practically constant (FAO, 1960-65). The low level of production was associated with extensive rural poverty, much more than in the Costa. Evidence shows that the incomes of the great majority of the rural population were extremely low (Barraclough, 1973, pp. 192-228). This co-existence of stagnating production and extensive poverty can largely be explained by the prevailing system of land tenure and distribution.

In 1954 there were around 3,000 large haciendas in the Sierra, with an average size of 650 hectares (table 1). While these large holdings constituted only 1 per cent of the total number of farms, they occupied nearly two-thirds of the available land. Most of these large farms had a quasi-feudal structure; they used different forms of servant labour, such as the huasipungo system, whereby small plots of land were given in usufruct to peasant farmers in return for certain obligations to the landowner. These commonly included working a certain number of days - usually four to six a week - on the lands of the hacienda for which only a nominal wage was paid, much below the wage paid to full-time wage workers. In addition, they were often required to accept specific jobs such as the construction of roads, fence repairs, etc. Furthermore, other members of the huasipunguero households, mostly female, were frequently obliged to work, as servants in the house of the hacienda owner. In return for these obligations the huasipungueros received a plot of land, and the hacienda owner provided financial assistance in situations of special need such as illness, bad harvest, etc. The system of servant labour prevented severe deprivation among the peasantry but it kept peasants largely dependent on the landowners who controlled the land.[1]

Table 1: Number of operational farms and cultivable area by farm size: Sierra, Ecuador (1954)

Farm size	No. of farms	% total	Area (has.)	% total
Less than 1 ha.	83,714	32	40,400	1
1-5 ha.	128,439	50	301,300	10
5-20 has.	33,013	13	296,700	10
20-100 has.	11,316	4	438,700	15
More than 100 has.	3,087	1	1,943,400	64
Total	259,569	100	3,020,400	100

Source: Arias (1972), table A-2.

Besides these servant farmers there were other farmers with small plots of land. Although most of them owned this land, they were dependent on the hacienda owners in many ways. Sometimes they had to borrow from them or they were obliged to sell them their harvests at low prices if they lacked proper means of transport. In addition, they usually occupied infertile land. Data show that land productivity for most subsistence crops was much lower on smaller farms even

[1] The economic rationale of practising servant labour has been discussed in de Janvry and Garramón (1977) and Peek (1978).

holding the level of technology constant (van Binsbergen, 1974). It has been estimated that this group comprised two-thirds of all peasant farmers in the early 1960s, the remaining consisted of servant farmers such as huasipungueros (table 2).

Table 2: Agricultural workers by tenure status: Sierra, Ecuador (1952-58)

Tenure status	Number	% total
Servant labourers		
Huasipungueros	88,029	7
Comuneros	237,069	20
Partidarios	49,967	4
Ayudas	25,907	2
Owner cultivators	826,308	67
Total	1,227,280	100

Source: CIDA (1965, pp. 78 and 80).

Like servant labour, indebtedness also contributed to the impoverishment of the farm population. Insufficient income often forced the peasants to borrow money from landowners or local moneylenders to pay rents in advance for their plot of land, to tide them over until harvest time, to compensate for a poor harvest, or to meet the cost of social customs (Standing, 1981). Often such loans carried exorbitant rates of interest. A survey carried out in the early 1960s showed that, in rural areas, the interest on non-institutional credit was more than twice as high as on institutional credit (table 3). The high levels of interest, often combined with the ready availability of credit on the part of many landowners, reduced many to permanent indebtedness. In other cases, debt peonage was practised forcing debtors to work on the haciendas until their debts were paid. Although this practice was abolished legally in 1918 it still existed in the early 1960s (Pearse, 1962). Its eradication in practice proved extremely difficult because of the political and economic power of the landowners.

Table 3: Mean annual rate of interest on institutional and non-institutional credit rural Ecuador (1965)

Type of credit	Mean annual rate of interest (%)	Median annual rate of interest (%)
Institutional	8.3	8.0
Non-institutional	16.9	22.0

Source: Stitzlein (1967, pp. 29 and 34).

The third factor limiting the incomes of the peasant farmers was the scarcity of rural employment opportunities outside their small farms. Clearly the small farms only provided minimal employment. Table 4 provides data on annual employment per hectare cultivated with different food crops. These crops accounted for nearly 90 per cent of the area cultivated on farms of less than 5 hectares. It is calculated that average employment per hectare is 56 man days per year. Realising that average size of farms with less than 5 hectares is only 1.6 hectares, it can be seen that very little labour is absorbed on these farms. Thus small farmers were dependent on the large farms for providing employment. But the large farms although they controlled most of the land, employed only a relatively minor proportion of the rural work force because they cultivated only a small part of their arable land. Data show that farms of over 50 hectares cultivated on average only 15 per cent of their land in 1954 (table 5). Evidence shows that only 60 per cent of the under- and unemployed on the small farms were able to find employment on large farms (Guerrero, 1975). It appears that land cultivation was deliberately restricted so as to limit the output and to sell it much above the costs of production (calculated from van Binsbergen, 1974, table 8). The bulk of the commercial food crops was cultivated on the haciendas while, until the mid-1960s, food imports were insignificant so that the large landowners controlled the market of commercialised food as monopsonistic producers, and they were motivated to collude to restrict output. This lack of incentive to increase output may also have been reflected in the fact that few landowners mechanised production or used modern inputs. In 1954, only 16 per cent of farms over 200 hectares used mechanised equipment (table 6).

Table 4: Annual labour use per crop: Sierra, Ecuador, 1963

Crop	Annual man-days per hectare
Wheat	35
Corn	38
Barley	30
Potatoes	100
Beans	38
Weighted average	56

Source: JUNAPLA (1964), table 6A, p. 69.

Table 5: Land cultivated by farm size: Sierra, Ecuador (1954)

Farm Size	% of land cultivated on average farm
Less than 5 has.	85
5-50 has.	50
More than 50 has.	15

Source: Arias (1972), tables I-2A to I-2D.

Table 6: Level of mechanisation by farm size, Ecuador, 1954

Farm size (in has.)	No of farms	In percentages					
		None	Animal power	Mechanical power	Animal and mechanical power	Without information	Total
0-4.9	251,250	32	64	-	-	4	100
5-9.9	36,117	51	46	-	-	3	100
10-49.9	40,927	70	26	-	-	4	100
50-199.9	11,957	79	15	1	2	3	100
More than 200	3,697	61	21	6	10	2	100
Total	343,948	41	55	-	-	4	100

Source: Computed from data in ECLA (1961), p. 74, table 10.

Fourthly, the incomes of the peasant farmers constantly eroded because the terms of trade moved systematically against the food producing sector. Between 1954 and 1963 the prices of foodstuffs declined 12 per cent relative to the prices of all other items (table 7). This decline was, to some extent, a result of government policy which largely controlled the price of food. Since the government strongly supported the growth of export agriculture, it sought to keep the cost of wage labour down by controlling food prices.[1]

Table 7: Agricultural terms of trade: Ecuador (1954-1963)

Year	Prices of foodstuffs (A)	Prices of all other items* (B)	(A)/(B) x 100
1954	100	100	100
1955	98	101	97
1956	95	102	93
1957	98	107	91
1958	97	107	91
1959	95	107	88
1960	93	101	88
1961	98	111	88
1962	97	116	83
1963	100	119	84

* Includes some non-food agricultural products.

Source: Zuvekas (1977, p. 372).

The available evidence shows that the incomes of the peasantry were very low during this period. A study carried out in the early 1960s estimated that 90 per cent of all farms were too small to adequately support a household (CIDA, 1965, p. 149).

1 Clearly, food prices would have been lower if the large landowners were not in a monopsonistic position. However, as is shown later, up until the early 1960s government policy was unsuccessful in eliminating this situation because of the political influence of the landowners at that time.

Other data show that farm households with less than 5 hectares earned an average gross farm income of 3,900 sucres a year, which amounted to slightly more than 200 US dollars at that time (table 8). It is also shown that the servant households earned substantially less than the average small-scale farmer. Table 9 indicates that their average total income amounted to only 1,900 sucres a year.

The incomes of the peasant farmers were not only very low, they also constituted a minor proportion of total agricultural income in the Sierra. As table 8 shows, 82 per cent of all farm households earned only 28 per cent of total gross income, while the largest landowners, 1 per cent of the total, earned 25 per cent of total gross income.

III. The Land Reform of 1964

This agrarian structure largely dominated by quasi-feudal haciendas changed substantially in the course of the 1960s. Servant labour was gradually being abolished and an increasing number of hacienda owners began to modernise production and to cultivate the land more intensively. Many farms were being transformed into modern, capital-intensive agricultural enterprises utilising predominantly wage labour. The land reform programme introduced in 1964 played an important role in bringing about this transformation. This can be understood by explaining the reasons why this programme was adopted.

There were three main factors which led to the adoption of the 1964 land reform. They were to a large extent related to the opposed interests of different groups: on the one hand, the "traditional" landowners and, on the other hand, the small but growing urban industrialists, the peasantry and the small group of large landowners who had already modernised their farms.

In the early 1960s the US companies sold most of their plantations in the Costa and reinvested their capital in the banana plantations previously abandoned in Central America. The investment climate there had become more favourable again, and it was felt that a greater return on their investments could be obtained than in Ecuador. As a result, the local producers in the Costa saw their export of bananas to the USA greatly reduced, because the withdrawal of US companies led to a substantial reduction in the import quota for bananas from Ecuador. As efforts to locate other markets were not successful, the local producers began to transfer an increasing proportion of their capital to other sectors of the economy, notably to industry and manufacturing. At that time these sectors were still quite small and it was felt that

Table 8: Average gross farm income by farm size: Sierra, Ecuador (1954)

Farm size (in has.)	No. of farms		Total gross income (millions of 1954 sucres)		Average gross income (1954)
0-5	212,153	82%	829.9	28%	3,900
5-20	33,013	12%	591.3	20%	17,900
20-50	7,722	3%	351.6	12%	45,500
50-200	4,971	2%	452.6	15%	91,000
More than 200	1,710	1%	722.9	25%	422,700
Total	259,569	100%	2,947.1	100%	11,300

Source: Facultad de Ciencias Económicas e Instituto de Investigaciones Económicas de la Universidad Central (1958), table 4, p. 25.

Table 9: Gross average income of huasipungueros and other servant labourers: Sierra Ecuador (1959-60)

Sierra Provinces	Gross average annual income (in 1959-60 sucres)
Azay	1,340
Bolivar	2,688
Cañar	1,745
Carchi	2,019
Cotopaxi	1,650
Chimborazo	1,763
Imbabura	1,679
Loja	2,500
Pichincha	1,723
Tungurahua	1,865
Average Sierra	1,895

Source: Arias (1966, p. 89).

potential profits were high. This transfer of capital was one of the principal factors which led to the development of a national industry in the early 1960s.

However, it was soon realised that the agrarian structure in the Sierra was a serious obstacle to the rise of industrial and manufacturing activities in urban areas. Far from encouraging the expansion of industry and manufacture, it was more likely to limit these. First of all, local industrial development was largely dependent on the size of the internal market. But the majority of the population lived in rural areas and produced most of its own consumption, and any cash income was largely spent on food.[1] The large landowners also bought little industrial and manufacturing output. As mentioned earlier they used little capital. Thus the rural Sierra, the most populous region, constituted a very small market.

Besides an internal market, industrial growth also requires an adequate supply of urban labour at low cost so as to increase profits and stimulate capital accumulation. Generally speaking, wages in the "modern" industrial sectors will be low if, among other things, the opportunity costs of labour are low, i.e. if wages in the "informal" sector are low. But this probably requires migration from the rural areas so that the growth of the urban labour supply exceeds the absorption of labour in the industrial sectors. However, permanent migration of the peasantry conflicted with the interests of the Sierra landowners who wanted to maintain a large pool of rural labour. The cost of labour also depended on the price of food. Although the terms of trade were systematically turned against the agricultural sector, the food price was relatively high because large landowners deliberately restricted output.

Thus the existing traditional agrarian structure limited the development of urban industry and manufacture in various ways. The bulk of the potential labour force was kept in rural areas where it consumed little of urban production, while food crops were produced at relatively high cost. In order to overcome these obstacles, many of those with financial interests in the industrial sectors argued that land reform should be introduced to change the agrarian structure. It was felt that without such reforms urban economic growth was unlikely to proceed.

---

[1] A consumption survey in the rural Sierra indicated that its population spent, on average, more than 70 per cent of its cash income on food (see JUNAPLA, 1976, p. 41).

Similar pleas were made by the few large landowners who had already modernised their farms before land reform was introduced (Barsky, 1978, pp. 74-126). Although most large farms still used servant labour, some had been modernised, employing predominantly wage labour and cultivating the land intensively with modern inputs. Some had done so because they felt that a land reform programme would soon be adopted and so, to avoid government intervention, they voluntarily provided plots of land to the huasipungueros (table 10).[1] Many of them also considered that the profits of capital-intensive farming would soon be much higher than the land rent obtained through servant labour. Urbanisation proceeded rapidly as a result of high population growth and rural-urban migration in the 1950s and 1960s, sharply increasing the demand for food and making it more profitable to expand production by bringing more land into cultivation and using modern inputs so as to increase land productivity. These changes led to a substitution of servant labour for wage labour, because the latter is more profitable in capital-intensive farming (de Janvry and Garramón, 1977).

Table 10: Abolition of huasipungo labour before 1964: Sierra, Ecuador (1959-64)

Year	No. of huasipungeros	Total size of their plots (has.)
1959	88	405
1962	899	3,661
1963	1,310	3,909
1964 (until 15 July)	722	1,929
Total	3,019	9,304

Source: Data from the Departamento de Cuestiones Sociales, Ministerio de Previsión Social y Trabajo, quoted in Barsky (1978, p. 216).

[1] Evidence indicates that these landowners obtained much better terms than those who were forced to do so under the land reform of 1964 (Barsky, 1978).

Another reason why some landowners had decided to abolish servant labour before 1964 was the increased opposition of the peasant farmers. Although their demonstrations and protests were relatively mild compared with the peasant rebellions in some other Latin American countries, their increasing demands for a more equitable distribution of land and higher wages motivated a number of landowners to abolish servant labour (Barsky, 1978). These "modern" landowners, however, also realised that the quasi-feudal agrarian structure was contrary to their interests. Like urban industry and manufacture, they were better served by a large internal market and by ample supplies of cheap labour. Starting in the late 1950s, therefore, the "modern" landowners increasingly pressed for government action to reform the existing structure of production, arguing that large farms which were run "inefficiently" should be expropriated and the land distributed among the peasantry while "efficiently-run" farms should be exempted from such measures (ibid.).

Still another factor contributing to the introduction of land reform was the Alliance for Progress. After the Cuban revolution in 1958 there was an increasing international concern about the agrarian sector in Latin America. Many felt that its backward structure kept the bulk of the rural population in poverty, thus threatening political stability. The Alliance for Progress programme, created in 1961, hoped to remedy this situation by promoting social and economic reforms. This was done, for example, by providing substantial financial aid to countries adopting measures of agrarian reforms. In a report reviewing the socio-economic situation in Ecuador, the Alliance considered that the land tenure structure was highly inequitable posing "the fundamental obstacle to economic progress in the private sector" (Blankstein and Zuvekas, 1973, pp. 79-94). Therefore it strongly urged that measures be taken to modify the system of land tenure. This recommendation was accompanied by different forms of financial aid to improve the rural infrastructure.[1]

When a new government came to power in 1963, it designed a national economic plan in which land reform played a key role. This reflected the diminished political influence of the "traditional" landowners who were unable to mount effective opposition to the demands for land reform.

---

[1] For example, in 1963 the Inter-American Bank, through the Alliance for Progress, contributed around US$ 2,000,000 to improve road conditions and housing facilities in rural areas of Eduador.

The stated objective of this first major land reform was to improve the standards of living of the rural poor and to raise agricultural production. It intended to do this, in the first place, by abolishing the various types of servant labour. According to the 1964 law, huasipungueros and other servant labourers were to receive ownership of the land they cultivated and IERAC, the newly created land reform agency, was to provide credit and technical assistance and, to the extent possible, organise these peasant farmers in co-operatives. Secondly, it was stipulated that land used "deficiently" would be expropriated. This included primarily land that had not been cultivated for three years or more. Furthermore, unused public lands were to be distributed among the peasantry and, in the Sierra, a landholding ceiling was set at 800 hectares, plus 1,000 hectares of pasture land. These measures were complemented by others introduced later. For example, in 1973 another law was accepted which stipulated that land which did not fulfil its "social function" would be expropriated and distributed among the peasant farmers. This largely concerned haciendas that were still using servant labour and on which more than 20 per cent of the total area was uncultivated.

IV. The Agrarian Structure in the Sierra after 1964

As a result of the land reform measures servant labour was practically abolished. In 1974 there were only around 2,600 huasipungueros left in the Sierra, compared with an estimated 90,000 in the early 1960s (Ministerio de Agricultura y Ganadería and ORSTOM, 1978b; Galarza, 1976). On the other hand, the distribution of land did not change substantially. While in 1954 farms of less than 5 hectares, 82 per cent of the total, occupied 11 per cent of the area, in 1974 these percentages were respectively 78 and 12 (table 11).

The fact that land distribution remained practically unchanged largely reflected the political situation at that time. While certain segments of the régime which took power in 1963 were genuinely interested in land redistribution, it met increased opposition from both the "modern" landowners and those representing the interests of the industrial sector. Both groups considered land reform primarily as a means of modernising agriculture rather than an instrument to redistribute wealth and incomes (Velasco, 1979).

To accommodate their interests the programme set up initially was of quite modest proportions. During the period 1964-69, it was planned to redistribute 600,000 hectares, only 20 per cent of the land of large farms.

Table 11: Number of farms and cultivable area by farm size: Sierra, Ecuador (1974)

Farm size	No. of farms	% total	Area (has.)	% total
Less than 1 ha.	113,537	35	49,574	2
1-5 has.	130,370	43	315,924	10
5-20 has.	47,333	14	436,528	14
20-100 has.	19,812	7	789,909	26
More than 100 has.	3,534	1	1,482,339	48
Total	332,506	100	3,074,274	100

Source: JUNAPLA (1978).

In fact, as it turned out later, only 12 per cent of the earmarked land was actually redistributed (AID, 1970). In addition the land reform law had a number of loopholes through which landowners could avoid expropriation, for example, by modernising their production, cultivating more land and abolishing servant labour. Other landowners avoided expropriation simply by dividing up the land among family members (Blankstein and Zuvekas, 1973; Griffin, 1977, Chapter 5). This partly explains the fairly large increase in the number of medium-sized farms (20-100 hectares) and the decrease in the number of larger farms between 1954 and 1974.

Although the highly unequal distribution of land remained practically the same, the structure of production underwent important changes. Many landowners decided to cultivate a much larger proportion of their land. The available data showed that the area of cultivated land and artificial pastures on farms larger than 5 hectares more than doubled between 1954 and 1974 (Arias, 1972; INEC, 1979a). Secondly there was a substantial rise in credit absorbed by the agricultural sector. Between 1960 and 1975, the volume of agricultural credit increased nearly seven times in real terms, its share of total credit rising from 9 to 25 per cent (Lozada, 1975).

It appears that many landowners felt threatened with expropriation and decided to modernise production (Barsky, 1978). Realising that their dominance over the peasantry was being seriously undermined by state policy, many decided to discontinue the recourse to servant labour and to cultivate the land more intensively using modern inputs. Thus it was not actual expropriation but the threat of it which began to transform the agrarian structure.

It is important to note that a large part of the newly acquired agricultural credit was invested in livestock farming and dairy production, particularly on the largest farms. In 1974, the area of land used for pastures was 35 per cent higher than in 1962, while the proportion of "artificial" pastures increased from 21 to 40 per cent during the same period (Barril, 1978, pp. 59-78). Credit to buy livestock was supplied on a large scale by the government and various international agencies, not only because livestock farming was profitable, owing partly to the climatic and soil conditions in the Sierra, but also because it was compatible with the pattern of economic growth. It responded to a rapidly growing urban demand for dairy products, and, in addition, it absorbed a substantial amount of capital.

On the medium-sized farms credit was mainly used to modernise and mechanise the cultivation of crops. A growing number of these farms introduced improved seeds, fertiliser and mechanised equipment in the cultivation not only of traditional crops such as wheat and beans but, increasingly, of fruits and vegetables as well.

V. Migration and Agrarian Change

The transformation of the agrarian structure, noted above, was associated with substantial changes in the patterns of migration. These can largely be explained by analysing how the incomes of small-scale farming were affected. As mentioned earlier, the two principal objectives of the land reform were to modernise agriculture and to raise the standard of living of the peasant farmers. Although it was quite successful in changing the agrarian structure, it seemed to have largely failed in realising the second objective, judging by the data on small-farm incomes. First, although the practice of servant labour virtually disappeared in the Sierra, this did not imply that the labourers themselves were therefore better off. It has even been argued that the land reform measures actually worsened the position of the ex-servant households (Paredes Barros, 1967). With the abolition of servant labour landowners no longer felt the obligation to provide for their subsistence in situations of special need, such as illness. The peasants also lost the right to gather wood and to graze their cattle on the hacienda land. In addition, many servant labourers were not given the plot of land they cultivated but other less fertile land.

Secondly, since land redistribution was rather insignificant the proportion of total land cultivated on small farms did not change substantially. In fact, the small farms became even smaller. Between 1954 and 1974, the average size of farms with less than 5 hectares decreased from 1.61 to 1.45 hectares (see tables 1 and 11). This seems to indicate that, as their families grew, the small farms were increasingly divided up through inheritance. Also, small farm credit did not improve very much. Although the land reform law stipulated that more credit, as well as extension services would be made available to the small farmers, very few of them received these. It has been estimated that only 1 per cent of the ex-servant labourers benefited from the increased credit (AID, 1970).

Thirdly, land productivity on the small farms either stagnated or declined. Without access to additional land and faced with high rates of population growth the peasant farmers intensified land cultivation so as to obtain higher incomes to support their growing families. This, however, seemed to lead to a more inefficient use of the land mainly because of deteriorating soil quality. Evidence shows that the land productivity of subsistence crops such as beans, potatoes and corn either stagnated or declined during the 1960s (FAO, 1970).

The available sources of information point out that, on average, the farm incomes of the peasants declined in real terms between 1954 and 1974. Although gross income on farms of less than 5 hectares increased from 3,900 sucres to 8,100 sucres in current prices, prices rose much faster (Facultad de Ciencias Económicas e Instituto de Investigaciones Económicas de la Universidad Central, 1958, p. 23; Ministerio de Agricultura y Ganadería and ORSTOM, 1978c). Deflating by the general price index and the one for food prices, real gross income on small farms dropped by respectively 16 and 31 per cent (INEC, 1979b). This indicates that, in terms of farm earnings, peasant farmers became worse off after land reform was introduced.

As farm income declined, the peasantry was forced to look for work outside their farms. Available data suggest that an increasing number of them migrated on a short-term basis in order to supplement their declining farm income.

Already before land reform there had been extensive short-term migration, often from the rural Sierra to the Costa. During the harvest seasons labour demand increased sharply in the Costa and its labour force was insufficient to meet it. The rural Sierra had, on the other hand, labour to spare since most households cultivated plots that were too small to provide sufficient employment for all adult members. Moreover, agricultural work in the Sierra was concentrated in a few months of the year which differed from the times of the harvests on the Costa. For example, around two-thirds of the labour time required for cultivating wheat, barley and soft corn, all important crops on small farms, was concentrated in four to six months (Banco Central del Ecuador, 1978, p. 6.). Furthermore, the landowners did not oppose short-term migration of individual family members. This was considered to be in their interest because it raised the incomes of the peasant farmers and enabled them to hold wages at a low level.

Available data suggest that temporary migration increased after the land reform. Unfortunately, direct information does not exist but some conclusions can be drawn from data on earnings of small-scale farmers outside their farms. These show that the percentage of off-farm earnings of small-scale farmers increased substantially between 1962 and 1974. Whereas 20 per cent of their total income in 1962 was earned in wages, this had increased to 62 per cent in 1974 (Ministerio de Agricultura y Ganadería and ORSTOM, 1978c). It is very probable that this rise in off-farm earnings implied an increase in temporary migration. Clearly, small farmers may have been able to obtain employment close to their plots so that they could return home after their work and did not have to migrate. However, it is very probable that the number of wage-earning farmers who found work away from their farm and had to migrate, increased as well. This is also suggested by the very steep increase in the percentage of off-farm earnings. The available data also show that, in 1974, more than half of off-farm income was earned in the non-agricultural sector. It would have been unlikely that the large increase in off-farm employment only consisted of wage work close to the plots, thus not involving migration. Since non-agricultural activities in rural areas are very limited, most of this income must have been earned in urban areas. Although a certain percentage of the small farms may have been close to the cities, the bulk of the peasantry lived at a sufficiently long distance to require temporary migration in order to be employed in an urban job. Thus, in the absence of any firm evidence, these data suggest at least that temporary emigration from the small farms increased.

The increase in off-farm wage income not only resulted from the lower returns to small-scale farming but also from the rise in wage employment in rural areas, particularly in the Sierra. As already mentioned, large farms cultivated more land so that, despite greater mechanisation, the demand for labour rose (ILO/PREALC,

1975). But the use of modern inputs resulted in a more pronounced seasonal pattern of labour demand. Table 12 provides census data on the distribution of the labour force by category. As regards the category of wage workers, these data refer to permanent workers only. It is shown that the proportion of permanent wage workers in agriculture declined. Furthermore, data on farm employment indicate that most wage employment is directed to temporary work. Table 13 shows that nearly 90 per cent of total wage employment was temporary in 1974.

Despite the decline in farm income it appears that the rate of permanent rural emigration did not increase, in fact it seems to have declined after land reform was introduced. Again, there is no direct evidence supporting this. The census data in table 14 show that between 1962 and 1974 the population in the rural Sierra declined only from 34 to 30 per cent of the total population in the country, while it declined from 43 to 34 per cent during the previous 12-year period. This suggests that the rate of permanent rural emigration slowed down after 1962.[1]

Thus, while the incomes from small-scale farming were declining, it appears that the peasantry substituted temporary for permanent migration so as to make up for their income losses.

This substitution may seem paradoxical. Given that small farm incomes declined, one would expect that both permanent and temporary migration increased. The most likely and simplest explanation is that temporary employment grew more rapidly, both in urban and rural areas. Table 12 suggests this for rural areas. As regards urban areas, data show that employment in the so-called "modern" sectors, where most of the stable and permanent jobs are found, grew at a low rate. Whereas the urban work force increased by 6 per cent annually, the growth of employment in the "modern" sectors was less than 3 per cent per year (Gordillo, 1979). On the other hand, employment in sectors like construction and services, largely characterised by temporary and unstable employment, grew rapidly. This trend seems to suggest that it

---

[1] In principle, of course, the hypothesis of a slowing down in the rate of permanent rural emigration is only valid if the natural population increase in the rural Sierra was substantially the same as that in the rest of the country. In fact, however, even if there had been significant differences in the rural and urban natural increase, this would not greatly affect our conclusion because the rest of the country includes the rural Costa.

Table 12: Agricultural labour force by category of occupation rural Sierra, Ecuador (1962 and 1974)

Category of occupation	1962		1974	
	Total	%	Total	%
Own account	250,343	58	222,114	54
Unpaid family worker	49,876	12	69,637	17
Wage employed	130,706	30	114,868	28
Other	189	-	1,517	1
Total	432,114	100	408,136	100

Source: JUNAPLA (1964, pp. 108-124); INEC (1978, various volumes).

Table 13: Employment on farms by size: Rural Sierra, Ecuador (1974) (in thousand days)

Farm size	Family labour	Wage employment		Other	Total
		Seasonal	Permanent		
Less than 5 has.	15,600	3,900	100	1,700	21,300
5-100 has.	11,200	12,000	1,100	800	25,000
More than 100 has.	300	3,800	800	-	4,900
Total	27,100	19,700	2,000	2,500	51,300

Source: Ministerio de Agricultura and ORSTOM (1978b, p. 220).

Table 14: Rural Sierra population as percentage of total population of Ecuador (1950-1974)

Year	Total population rural Sierra (A) (in thousands)	A as % of total population of Ecuador
1950	1,371	43
1962	1,527	34
1974	1,944	30

Source: JUNAPLA (1977, p. 20).

became increasingly difficult for a rural migrant to secure to secure a stable job in urban areas, which may explain why more and more people in the rural Sierra opted for temporary rather than permanent migration. This way they could keep their plot of land, which provided a small but secure income, and do temporary work whenever it was available.

VI. Final Remarks

Finally, it is worthwhile conjecturing what might have been the effects of a successful land reform. If the peasant farmers had been provided with substantially more land and credit so that their farm incomes had increased, it is likely that the flow of temporary migration would have been smaller. However, an expanded system of small-scale farming in the rural Sierra would probably have been less compatible with the pattern of urban economic expansion pursued since the early 1960s. Earlier it was pointed out that, generally speaking, urban growth depends on the transfer of an adequate agricultural surplus to the towns, the existence of a reasonably large internal market and the flow of sufficient labour supplies to urban areas. Modern large-scale farming probably has better prospects of satisfying these conditions than small-scale farming. Firstly, because land cultivation on small farms is more labour-intensive, it leads to a much smaller transfer of labour to urban areas, thus increasing upward pressures on urban wages. Secondly, although small farms can be as efficient as large farms (Berry and Cline, 1979), they tend to market a smaller surplus because part of the output is consumed by the farm household. This is also likely to lead to a slower expansion of the internal market. As small-scale farmers produce for their own consumption, their monetary transactions will be less.

Taking account of these factors, it appears that modern large-scale farming is more conducive to urban economic growth than small-scale farming. It was therefore perhaps inevitable that the results of the land reforms did not include higher farm incomes for the peasants. Such an outcome might well have benefited them, but at the expense of urban economic growth which since the early 1960s has had the highest priority in government policy.

References

AID (1970): "Land reform in Bolivia, Ecuador, Peru", in AID Spring Review of Land Reform, Vol. VI (Washington, DC).

Arias, M. (1966): "Probable efecto de la applicación de la reforma agraria sobre la producción y el consumo", in Economía (Quito), March.

--- (1972): Estructura agraria del Ecuador (Quito, Junta Nacional de Planificación y Coordinación Económica).

Banco Central del Ecuador (1978): "El fondo de desarrollo para el sector rural marginal: FODERUMA" (Quito).

Barraclough, S. (1973): Agrarian structure in Latin America (Lexington, Mass., Lexington Books, Heath and Co.).

Barril, A. (1978): "Modernización agropecuaria y economías campesinas", in A. Barril et al: Ecuador: Tecnología agropecuaria y economías campesinas (Quito, Centro de Planificación y Estudios Sociales (CEPLAES)).

Barsky, O. (1978): "Iniciativa terrateniente en la restructuracion de las relaciones sociales en la Sierra Ecuatoriana, 1954-1964", in Revista de Ciencias Sociales, No.5 (Quito).

Berry, A. and Cline, W. (1979): Agrarian structure and productivity in developing countries (Baltimore (Maryland) and London, Johns Hopkins University Press).

van Binsbergen, A. (1974): El empleo agrícola y las perspectivas para el desarrollo de la agricultura en Ecuador (Rome, FAO).

Blankstein, C.S. and Zuvekas, C. (1973): "Agrarian reform in Ecuador: An evaluation of past efforts and the development of a new approach", in Economic Development and Cultural Change (Chicago), Oct., Vol. 22, No. 1.

Comité Interamericano de Desarrollo Agrícola (CIDA) (1965): Tenencia de la tierra y desarrollo socio-económico del sector agrícola: Ecuador (Washington, Organization of American States).

Facultad de Ciencias Económicas e Instituto de Investigaciones Económicas de la Universidad Central (1958): Boletín Trimestral de Información Económicas (Quito), Jan.-June, Vol. XI, Nos. 36-37.

FAO (1960-65): Production Yearbook (Rome), 1960-65 issues.

FAO (1970): Production Yearbook, 1970 (Rome).

Galarza, J. (1976): Los campesinos de Loja y Zamora (Quito, Ediciones Solitierra).

Gordillo, J. (1979): La fuerza de trabajo en el Ecuador, paper prepared for the Population and Development Committee of the Latin American Council for Social Sciences (CLASCO) (Lima, May).

Griffin, K. (1977): "Systems of labour control and rural poverty in Ecuador", in K. Griffin: Land concentration and rural poverty (New York, Holmes and Meier; London, Macmillan Press).

Guerrero, A. (1975): La hacienda precapitalista en América Latina y su inserción en el modo de producción capitalista: el caso ecuatoriano (Quito, Eds. Escuela de Sociología).

ILO, Programa Regional del Empleo para América Latina y el Caribe (PREALC) (1975): Situación y perspectivas del empleo en Ecuador (Santiago, Chile, Feb.).

Instituto Nacional de Estadística y Censos (INEC) (1978): Tercer censo de población (Quito, various volumes).

--- (1979a): II Censo agropecuario 1974: Resultados (Quito).

--- (1979b): Indice de precios al consumidor, No. 309 (Quito).

de Janvry, A. and Garramón, C. (1977): "The dynamics of rural poverty in Latin America", in Journal of Peasant Studies, Apr., Vol. 4, No. 3.

Junta Nacional de Planificación y Coordinación Económica (JUNAPLA) (1964): Programa de desarrollo agropecuario (Quito).

--- (1964a): Segundo censo de población y primer censo de vivienda (Quito), Vol. III.

--- (1976): Desarrollo y perspectivas de la economía ecuatoriana, Vol. I (Quito).

--- (1977): Características demográficas de la población de Ecuador y su distribución en el territorio nacional (Quito).

--- (1978): Censo agropecuario, 1974 (Quito).

Lozada, P. (1975): El credito agropecuario en el Ecuador, 1970-1974 (Quito, Ministerio de Agricultura y Ganadería and ORSTOM).

Ministerio de Agricultura y Ganadería and ORSTOM (1978a): Diagnóstico socio-económico del medio rural ecuatoriano, Vol. 2: Tierra (Quito).

--- (1978b): Diagnóstico socio-económico del medio rural ecuatoriano, Vol. 3: Población y empleo (Quito).

--- (1978c): Diagnostico socio-economico del medio rural Ecuatoriano, Vol. 7: Ingresos (Quito).

Paredes Barros, C.H. (1967): Incidencia económica y social del proceso de liquidación del huasipungo en la Provincia de Pichincha thesis, (Quito, Department of Economics, Pontificia Universidad Católica del Ecuador).

Pearse, A. (1962): The Latin American peasant (London, Frank Cass and Co.).

Peek, P. (1978): Agrarian change and rural emigration in Latin America (Geneva, ILO; mimeographed World Employment Programme research working paper; restricted).

Peek, P. and Standing, G. (1979): "Rural-urban migration and government policies in low-income countries", in International Labour Review, Nov.-Dec. Vol. 118, No. 9.

Standing, G. (1981): "Migration and modes of exploitation: The social origins of immobility and mobility", in Journal of Peasant Studies, Jan., Vol. 8, No. 2.

Stitzlein, J.N. (1967): The characteristics and significance of the non-institutional credit market in rural Ecuador (Columbus, Agricultural Finance Center, Ohio State University, Dec.).

UN Economic and Social Commission for Latin America (1961): Boletín Económico de America Latina (Santiago de Chile), Vol. 6, No. 1.

Velasco, F. (1979): Reforma agraria y movimiento campesino indígena de la Sierra (Quito, El Conejo).

Zuvekas, C. (1977): Government policy and economic development in Ecuador: 1950-1974 (Washington, DC; mimeographed).

Chapter 5

COLONISATION IN RONDONIA: CONTINUITIES AND PERSPECTIVES

by George Martine*

I. Introduction

An effective migration policy can be defined as one which leads to a significant increase in stable employment opportunities, at adequate levels of income, in strategic spatial units.[1] The pervasive viewpoint that the Brazilian Amazon has a practically unlimited absorptive capacity for rural population has perenially thwarted attempts to search for alternative employment-creating solutions, whether in traditional agricultural areas, in the urban labour market, or in the structuring of the prevailing mode of political and economic organisation. Given the diversionist role played by the promises of the unlimited potential in the Amazon region, it becomes extremely pertinent to evaluate the real significance of recent Amazonian colonisation experiences for the absorption of the relative surplus rural population in Brazil.

A recent paper described the results of the three most prominent colonisation experiences which have been carried out in the Brazilian segment of Amazonia during recent decades and concluded that their impact, in terms of creating stable employment opportunities, and of effectively absorbing the rural population, has been insignificant.[2] The present paper focuses specifically on the territory of Rondônia, which has experienced one of the more massive influxes of rural population ever witnessed in Brazil and whose colonisation projects have received considerable government support during the past few years. The object of the paper is to analyse the short- and medium-range perspectives for permanent

* Social Policy Project, National Human Resources Council, Ministry of Planning, Brasilia.

[1] A broader discussion of migration policies and their application to Brazil are presented elsewhere (Martine, 1979a, pp. 9-38).

[2] See Martine (1979b). The initial section of the present document is partly based on the foregoing paper.

settlement by small farmers in this privileged colonisation area. On-going processes and future developments, in turn, are viewed in the context of the prevailing growth model in Brazil. In essence, it is argued that both the over-all inability of colonisation projects to absorb large numbers of migrants and the internal shortcomings of projects which have been implemented have a common origin in the prevailing pattern of economic organisation; thus, the structure and conditions of the nation's agricultural system in more established rural areas - which tend to reflect the prevailing model of economic growth in Brazil - are currently being reproduced in Rondônia, thereby limiting the possibilities for effective and permanent settlement of large numbers of migrants.

II. Recent Colonisation Experiences in Brazil: The End of the Open Frontier

Current patterns of migration and settlement in Rondônia have to be set against the context of recent events in other parts of the Amazon. Indeed, it is essential for the understanding of the Rondônian situation to bear in mind that, since 1974, when the government reversed its policy with respect to the occupation of the areas along the Trans-Amazon highway, this territory has been looked upon by both would-be settlers and government agencies alike as one of the few remaining outlets for the absorption of rural surplus population. The open frontier, in other words, is undergoing constriction - if not being closed down entirely - thus accentuating problems in areas such as Rondônia, which are still relatively accessible to rural migrants. Prior to current events in Rondônia, the two most prominent recent experiences with respect to Amazonian colonisation were undoubtedly those which were carried out along the Belém-Brasília highway and on the Trans-Amazon highway.[1]

The Belém-Brasília highway was built in the late 1950s in response to expansionist pressures emanating from capitalist interests located in the Centre-South. Construction of this road undoubtedly helped to occupy and integrate an enormous tract of uninhabited land into the nation's economy but little explicit attention was given to the process of agricultural settlement in bordering areas. Thus, for the most part, settlement along the

[1] See Martine (1979b) for a detailed discussion of these processes and for the supporting bibliography. A recent review of colonisation in Brazil is provided in Ianni (1979).

highway was undertaken in a haphazard manner by spontaneous migrants who began practising an itinerant form of agriculture. The results of this type of occupation have not been very promising in terms of the massive absorption and productive establishment of rural labour; only a minority of the migrants who came to the region settled in permanent fashion on a given piece of land. On the whole, spontaneous settlements have given way to latifundia and large cattle ranches via the consolidation of smaller plots which have been abandoned, assimilated or taken over by force. On the other hand, the few government-oriented projects which were initiated are leading to the proliferation of the minifundia; in both cases, a new rural exodus is taking place and a limited number of permanent economic opportunities have been created for rural labour.

The initiative of constructing the Trans-Amazon highway and of settling massive numbers of small farmers along its margins was supposedly launched in response to the great drought which ravaged large segments of the North-Eastern region in 1970. This phase of Amazonian intervention is distinguished from previous experiences both in terms of the accelerated pace at which it was supposed to develop and in terms of the fundamental role which was to be performed by the State in initiating and implementing colonisation activities. It was claimed that 100,000 low-income families would be settled over a four year period on 100 hectare lots, as part of a grandiose colonisation scheme.

In effect, however, the project was shelved before it could be effectively tested. Moved initially by a singular concern with the rural inhabitants of the most depressed areas, the programme was soon divested of its social content in order to make it conform to the canons of "economic rationality". Problems of a more technical nature, such as the inadequacy and inefficiency of the super-structured colonisation model devised by the technocrats, and difficulties inherent to the occupation of jungle areas, exacerbated the existing land rights problem. All of these difficulties were invoked to justify an inversion of the socially-oriented objectives, which had purportedly generated the Trans-Amazon programme, and to rationalise the incursions of large-scale national and multi-national capital into the area. Instead of settling 100,000 families, the programme absorbed, in precarious conditions, some 6,000 families, and the stage was set for subsequent conflicts between squatters, colonists and the large companies attracted to the area by government subsidies.

Reflecting on these and other recent developments, several authors have argued that, despite the quantity and enormity of the tracts of Amazonian land in disuse, the agricultural frontier in Brazil is being closed down from within and from without.[1] Externally, the frontier is being constricted as a result of government policy which entices large companies, whether national or multinational, into the Amazon Region. Such companies have been ceded enormous tracts of public land and have received generous government subsidies with which to implement "rational" development projects in the region. In most instances, only showcase projects have been effectively implemented, thereby demonstrating that the main interest of these companies consisted, all along, in land speculation; but the central point remains that the amount of open land has shrunk considerably as a result of government generosity towards large enterprises. Internally, the frontier is also being reduced both by the expulsion of the numerous *posseiros* who previously practised subsistence agriculture on bits of the huge tracts which were recently ceded to large enterprises, and by the ineffectiveness and virtual abandonment of government-oriented colonisation projects in other regions.

Such is the historical setting for the most important current process of frontier settlement in Brazil, namely that which is occurring in the Territory of Rondônia. Several conditions lend particular relevance to the Territory's colonisation experience. Firstly, it has been receiving, over the past five years, the single largest flow of frontier migration in Brazil. Secondly, several characteristics of its settlement process would tend to favour successful colonisation and large-scale absorption of rural manpower. Thus, Rondônia was, until recently, largely unpopulated and relatively free of land rights disputes; the majority of migrants who arrive in the region are selective of the more capable and experienced farmers who bring with them some working capital, as well as pioneering knowledge acquired in Paraná and Mato Grosso. Moreover, although its qualities have apparently been exaggerated, the land in Rondônia tends to be somewhat better than in other Amazonian regions.[2] Lastly,

---

[1] The internal and external closing down of the Amazonian frontier are discussed for the first time in Jatobá (1979, pp. 623-624) and Osório (1979, pp. 603-619).

[2] For a recent review of colonisation in Rondônia see Mueller (1979); for an evaluation of the quality of Rondônian soils based on maps prepared by the Projeto RADAM, see Furley (n.d.).

perhaps in compensation for its futile efforts on the Trans-Amazon highway, the government agency in charge of colonisation has expended considerable energies in an attempt to transform the Rondônian project into a going concern for small farmers.

Despite these advantages, the settlement experience of Rondônia has been chaotic and the government is being hard-pressed to simply institutionalise and legitimise situations which it is unable to plan or control. The purpose of the following sections will be to analyse the recent process of colonisation in Rondônia and to discuss its significance and prospects for the absorption of rural population.

III. Migration and Colonisation in Rondônia, 1970-1979

Although covering an area of 243,000 square kilometres (greater than all of the Federal Republic of Germany) and generously covered with patches of fertile soil, Rondônia had only 37,000 inhabitants in 1950. The construction of a dirt road (the BR-364) between Porto Velho, the Territory's capital, and the city of Cuiabá at the end of the 1950s, provided Rondônia with its first link to the Centre-South and, as a result, the Territory increased its population to 111,000 by 1970. This road was improved somewhat in 1970 and, shortly thereafter, the Instituto de Colonizaçâo y Reforma Agraria (INCRA) instituted colonisation projects along it. The opening of access roads and the discovery that a sizeable proportion of Rondônian soils were of good quality combined with push factors in other regions, especially in Paraná and Mato Grosso, to generate a rush of migrants to Rondônia. Since these developments occurred within the context of a growing concern for a shift to domestic capital which had been stimulated by the Programme for National Integration in 1970, the displacement of population to Rondônia brings to mind, in terms of its dimensions and chaotic nature, the gold rush of the western United States. Thus, it can be estimated that Rondônia's population which was set at 111,000 at the time of the 1970 census, multipled some seven times between 1970 and 1980.

The first colonisation project set up by INCRA in Rondônia - the Integrated Settlement Project of Ouro Preto (PIC-Ouro Preto) - was initiated as an attempt to resolve the problems of 300 families who had been attracted to the Territory (and later left stranded) by a private colonisation enterprise. News of the soil's good quality and the information that the government was supposedly giving away land in Rondônia was rapidly disseminated, provoking the interest of other small farmers in the Centre-South and attracting the attention

MAP 1

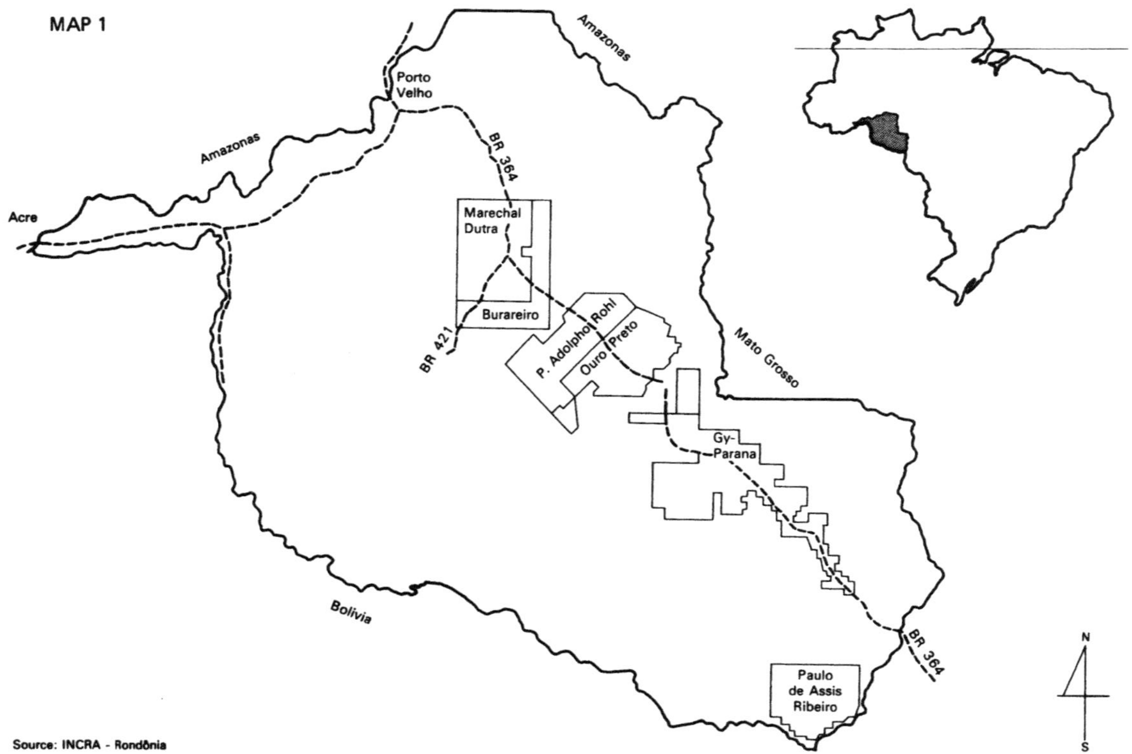

Source: INCRA - Rondônia

of all sorts of adventurers and grileiros (i.e. land grabbers, groups who take illegal and often violent possession of the land for the purpose of selling it to unwary or unscrupulous third parties). Under these conditions, the PIC-Ouro Preto project, which had originally been designed for 500 families was expanded tenfold, yet INCRA's capacity for coping with the mass influx was rapidly depleted.

The invasion led by the grileiros and extemporaneous settlement companies, and the growing influx of spontaneous migrants in search of land, created an untenable land-rights situation, precisely in that part of the country which seemed least susceptible to this type of problem. Indeed, in addition to the good quality of much of its soil, the feature that made Rondônia an outstanding site for large-scale colonisation was its relative absence of disputes over property rights. Thus, when the first national cadaster of rural properties was carried out in 1967 (at a time when the first speculators had already made a few incursions into the Territory), nine people claimed to own tracts of over 100,000 hectares each. Their total claims alone would have added up to some 12 per cent of the Territory's land area; however, INCRA's final analysis established the existence of only 155 legitimate claims, comprising 7 per cent of the total land area. In sum, 93 per cent of Rondônia's surface area was still controlled by the Union in 1967 (MINTER, 1979, p. 41).

Subsequently, private companies - passing themselves off as colonisation enterprises - began to take "possession" of large tracts of land (spilling over onto Indian reservations, forest reserves and national-security areas), dividing them up into lots and selling them to unwary settlers. Thus, when the second INCRA cadaster was taken in 1972 (i.e. two years before the beginning of the largest invasion) a survey revealed that:

> "3,200 properties having the most diverse modalities of ownership have been claimed: these include provisional titles, licences of occupation, definitive titles, long-term lease letters and, in many cases, pure and simple take-over, lacking any sort of documentation" (ibid., pp. 40-41).

It is generally accepted that many grileiros had their land rights legalised through "usocapiao" (a form of squatters' rights). Thus, the total area reserved for redistribution among settlers in INCRA's seven colonisation projects (2,619,000 ha.) would be several times smaller than the total land area which was unduly appropriated and concentrated into large properties in the five-year interim between the two agricultural censuses (Paiva, 1977, p. 9).

In an attempt to cope with the growing influx of hopeful migrants arriving in Rondônia and with the internal problems created by the speculative activities of the grileiros, the government agencies tried to multiply their projects and to accelerate the pace of settlement. However, several circumstances impeded government action from keeping up with demand. Initially, the adverse conditions of the jungle region greatly hindered the delimiting action of the surveyors as well as the construction of access roads - essential preliminary steps in INCRA's scheme of action. Moreover, the colonisation agency never had sufficient financial resources to cope with the magnitude of the task of promoting massive colonisation in accordance with its preconceived schema. Subsequently, the violence generated by the speculators and grileiros, as well as the dissatisfaction of the disillusioned settlers, sabotaged all attempts at rationalising the settlement process. Deficiencies in the administrative and legal structure of the Territory, which would have made efficient operation impossible under normal conditions, made it easy for the grileiros to promote chaos and manipulate existing powers for their own benefit. An illustration of the difficulties encountered is the fact that the municipality of Porto Velho, with an area roughly equivalent to the size of East Germany, had only one judicial district to decide on the numerous lawsuits that sprang up almost daily from the persistent conflicts over land.

Finally, the very size of the continuous flow of settlers to Rondônia stimulated the activities of profiteers and minimised the effectiveness of Government efforts to organise the occupation of the Territory. Available data on in-migration to Rondônia are understandably shaky but a receiving centre for migrants located in Vilhena (a town located on the main access road just inside the Territory) has collected valuable information on such movements since 1975. Although data-collection practices in this centre have been altered over time (and were discontinued altogether for a brief period), it is clear from these data and from other accounts that in-migration to the Territory began to assume substantial proportions during the 1970-74 period, was accentuated as of 1974, when the government reversed its policy with respect to the Trans-Amazon region, peaked sharply in 1976, and then declined in 1977, as a result of the government's intervention - which involved counter-propaganda campaigns in sending areas and police action on the highways. Since then, migration has begun to pick up again such that 1979 witnessed the most intensive movement ever registered (table 1). The rate of migration to the area tends to increase during the dry season (June, July and August) when the dirt roads are passable and when the land is prepared for seeding.[1] Should current plans to asphalt the highway between Cuiabá and Porto Velho be carried through - thus transforming it into an all-weather road - it can be expected that in-migration to the area will reach even greater heights.[2]

IV. Frontier Expansion and the Reproduction of the Traditional Agrarian Structure

As was to have been expected, the ability of government agencies to absorb migrants into the Territory of Rondônia is rather limited. Thus, as shown in table 2, by the end of 1978, the government agency in charge of colonisation (INCRA) had settled a total of 16,482 families and distributed definitive title to 7,007 of these. In addition, the agency expected to distribute an additional 3,485 plots during the course of 1979 and declared that the final number to be settled in existing government projects would eventually reach 23,438. Meanwhile, some 5,000 settlers were to receive title to their land during 1979, and the remaining 11,000 in subsequent years.

These figures, when contrasted to the total inflow of population to the Territory during the past decade, accurately depict the dilemma faced by government authorities with respect to Rondônia and, by extension, with respect to the colonisation process as a whole. Despite hectic efforts dedicated to the processes of demarcation, roadbuilding, settling of disputes, provision of services, etc. - in the face of considerable obstacles - all of INCRA's efforts since 1970 in Rondônia have so far succeeded in establishing less than 20,000 families in

---

[1] It should be noted that the data shown in table 1 refer only to those migrants arriving by truck or bus and registered at the migration-assistance centre in Vilhena. This is indubitably the most common form of travel but it should be noted that other types of traffic or other points of entry (and possibly some unregistered movement through Vilhena) are not covered by these data.

[2] Plans to asphalt the Cuiabá-Porto Velho road are currently being negotiated between the World Bank and the government of Brazil. The probable repercussions of such a move are discussed in the next section of this chapter.

Table 1: Migrants enumerated in Vilhena, Rondônia, by month of arrival and selected states of origin: 1978 and 1979

Month of arrival		No. of migrants	% from Paraná	% from Mato Grosso
Aug.	1978	1,116	39.7	33.0
Sept.	"	1,189	32.5	38.6
Oct.	"	1,801	37.5	25.2
Nov.	"	855	37.8	23.3
Dec.	"	626	36.3	20.3
Jan.	1979	823	39.0	23.5
Feb.	"	836	33.6	23.5
March	"	941	48.6	20.1
April	"	1,393	49.8	16.0
May	"	4,199	38.5	23.1
June	"	6,861	*	*
July	"	7,746	*	*
Aug.	"	7,185	*	*
Sept.	"	4,575	*	*
Oct.	"	4,423	*	*
Nov.	"	3,009	*	*
Dec.	"	2,287	*	*

Source: Various unpublished data from SIMI (Sistema Nacional de Migracões Internas), Ministério do Interior, Brasília.

* Unavailable

Table 2: Federal colonisation projects, Rondônia, 1979

Project	Total area (has.)	No. of families settled			Land titles distributed	
		Until 1978	Expected 1979	Final objective	Until 1978	Expected 1979
Ouro Preto	512,585	4,414	719	5,133	2,932	876
Gy-Paraná	486,137	3,922	834	4,756	1,294	1,000
Paulo de Assis Ribeiro	293,580	2,463	511	2,974	712	1,568
Adolpho Rohl	413,552	2,247	500	4,341	1,131	340
Sidney Girao	60,000	485	15	500	383	90
Marechal Dutra	494,661	2,220	703	4,520	397	673
Burareiro	304,925	731	203	1,214	158	401
Total	2,565,440	16,482	3,485	23,438	7,007	4,948

Source: Ministério da Agricultura, INCRA/CETRO (1979).

colonisation projects; the final count, according to current provisions, will not reach 24,000 families.

Yet, as INCRA itself is quick to point out in evaluating its achievements in Rondônia, the settlement of close to 24,000 families is no mean feat:

> "Evaluation of the process of occupation leads to the conclusion that Official Colonisation, contrary to what was previously observed, is being carried out within a relatively structured planning framework and is furnishing technical and economic support to the settlers established in colonisation projects. The identification, settlement and titling of approximately 24,000 families in 9 years, who are now cultivating and producing what was previously imported, has permitted the Territory to stop importing and to start exporting its products, not only to other states, but also to other countries..." (Ministério de Agricultura, INCRA/CETRO, 1979).

Thus, when viewed in the light of past colonisation experiences in Brazil, the magnitude of the Rondônian enterprise does represent something of an achievement and, to our knowledge, constitutes the largest single outlay of government effort ever expended in Amazonian colonisation. For purposes of comparison, for instance, it can be noted that the state colonisation agency in Pará - one of the most active in the country - settled a total of 20,516 families during the entire 1940-78 period over its huge land area (Sawyer, n.d., p. 9). Other colonisation efforts rarely absorbed more than a few thousand families.[1]

However, the relevant standard by which to judge the efficacy of colonisation efforts should not be in terms of the futility or prior government endeavours at the federal or state level, but in terms of the size of the demand for a piece of land, whether in national or local terms. Thus, it has been estimated elsewhere that the minimum number of lower-class rural families which would have to be resettled in frontier areas of Brazil, in order for colonisation schemes to absorb the surplus rural population, would be in the order of 2.4 million families (Martine, 1979b). At the level of Rondônia, given the size of the influx into Rondônia and the non-existence of any sizeable industrial or other source of employment

---

[1] For a review of government-sponsored colonisation projects in Brazil, see Tavares et al (1972).

opportunities (except in extractive activities where job expansion is very limited), it is clear that the settlement of 24,000 families in official projects constitutes a very partial solution to the problem of the rural poor in Rondônia, and an insignificant one for the rural poor of Brazil.

It is also pertinent to point out that, even for those colonists fortunate enough to be included among the recipients of government lots, severe difficulties are sometimes encountered. An evaluation carried out on the PIC-Ouro Preto Project, the first, largest and most firmly established colonisation project (and one in which the soil, climate and topography are quite favourable), highlighted a great variety of problems faced by both INCRA and the settlers (Turchi, 1971, pp. 109-126). As in most projects, the demand soon overwhelmed INCRA's physical ability to open up roads, delimit plots and provide effective assistance to settlers; consequently, since 1974, INCRA has limited its actions to legitimising de facto situations. This, in turn, has generated considerable conflict among grileiros and would-be settlers. Secondly, the services which INCRA was to have provided in terms of credit, transport, roads, commercialisation, warehousing and social infrastructure were generally defective. Another appraisal of the same project concluded that the administration of the project was marked by excessive bureaucracy and yet by a shortage of technical personnel; moreover, it asserted that the project itself has experienced a high rate of turnover among settlers and that disease and isolation, resulting from poor planning, severely weaken the spirit of settlers and their families (Tcheyan, 1979).

If such is the situation in the privileged Ouro Preto project, it can be deduced that, when viewed in global terms, the Rondônian settlement experience is far from having fulfilled expectations. By mid-1977, the number of agricultural families who had not managed to obtain a lot either by legal or illegal means was already being estimated at 30,000. Since, as shown earlier, the migration flow has become even greater over the past two years, it is evident that the number of families who have arrived in Rondônia and who have been unable to obtain a plot of government land is sure to have increased substantially.

The interesting question at this point thus becomes: how do these "excess" families manage to survive and what implications do their survival strategies have for future developments in Rondônia? Although it is impossible to answer this question in quantitative terms, it is clear that these groups turn to one of the four following alternatives:

(a) re-migration to other frontier areas or return migration,

(b) search for employment in commerce, services or the informal sector of one of the many towns which are booming along the main highway,

(c) employment as a salaried (either stable or part-time) worker or as a sharecropper on one of the lots in existing colonisation projects,

(d) invasion of apparently open lands.

These last two alternatives are particularly crucial for our concern with the continuity, stability and absorptive capacity of colonisation efforts in Rondônia. Indeed, the inability of small farmers to obtain a plot of land in one of the official projects has led them to adopt solutions which are themselves changing the structure of land tenure and of agricultural production in the region, thereby affecting the character as well as the future prospects of colonisaton schemes.

In this sense, it is interesting to observe that a growing number of migrants who have not been recipients of a lot are taking up residence on open lands or on another settler's plot - either with or without the latter's permission. Invasion invariably leads to conflict and the brief history of Rondônia is already notorious for its violent disputes over land. However, the repercussions of the other type of invasion - wherein a settler accedes to or invites the presence of other settlers - are perhaps of even greater impact for the future of Rondônia. Given the difficulties encountered by colonists in clearing their tract of jungle land and carrying out planting and harvesting activities without capital or machinery, many of them have turned to contracting sharecroppers to help them with their tasks. Thus, the relations of production which prevail in areas of origin are being recreated in Rondônia with foreseeable consequences in terms of the proliferation and acceleration of the process of "minifundisation", of disputes over land and of the eventual expulsion of agricultural labour.

The case of the PIC-Ouro Preto project, as analysed by Turchi, is again particularly revealing in this connection (Turchi, 1971, pp. 147-149). She noted that almost one quarter (24.3 per cent) of all the lots in this project were being occupied by more than one family. Most of the extra families had been hired as sharecroppers to help clear the jungle forest and cultivate the land; an additional 12 per cent rented a piece of the colonist's plot and another 9 per cent were salaried workers. The great majority of sharecroppers and renters dedicated themselves to subsistence agriculture. Although government officials in the area claimed that most of the extra families were only provisionally residing on lots while waiting to receive a plot of their own, Turchi points out that a survey carried out by INCRA itself showed that less than one-tenth of such families had actually been the recipient of a lot (and were waiting for conditions to improve before moving on to it), while 75 per cent of them had been rejected in INCRA's selection process.

In short, not only are the colonisation projects incapable of effectively absorbing more than a small proportion of the demand but also, within the colonisation projects - which constitute privileged islands in the over-all picture - the prospects for the re-creation of conditions which prevail in traditional areas appear to be strong.

In this vein, it is of some interest that the other main deficiency of the Brazilian agricultural system - i.e. the accentuated concentration of land in the hands of a small number of individuals - is being reproduced, and possibly surpassed, in Rondônia. As shown earlier, INCRA's first cadaster survey, carried out in 1967, reported that only 7 per cent of Rondônia's land area did not belong to the Union. Previous cadaster surveys, however, already reflected the results of the feverish invasion and struggle for land and demonstrated how effective the expansion of the capitalist frontier has been.

Table 3, which shows the distribution of farms by size in 1972 and 1976, portrays an extraordinary concentration of land in Rondônia. Thus, in 1972, less than 5 per cent of these establishments controlled 83.6 per cent of the occupied land area, while farmers with less than 100 hectares, who owned 50 per cent of all farms, controlled only 2.8 per cent of the land area. Moreover, it appears that this has not changed substantially. In 1976, farms with less than 100 hectares, 45 per cent of the total, controlled only 2.2 per cent of the land. It is observed that the number of farms with 2,000 to 5,000 hectares increased greatly, accounting for 8.3 per cent of all farms and 26.2 per cent of the land in 1976, while farms with more than 5,000 hectares made up 1.2 per cent of the total number but controlled 58.4 per cent of the land.

The figures for Rondônia and for all Brazil in table 4 clearly demonstrate the similarity in the level and trends of land distribution. In both cases, the great majority of farms are of the minifundio type while over three-quarters of the land belongs to large landholders. The proportion of minifundios as well as that of the land they occupied diminished slightly in Rondônia between

Table 3: Rural farms by land size, Rondônia, 1972 and 1976

Size category (in hectares)	1972				1976			
	Farms		Area		Farms		Area	
	No.	%	Hectares	%	No.	%	Hectares	%
0-10	122	3.6	596	-	137	3.2	685	-
10-50	1,043	31.1	27,361	1.3	1,198	27.9	31,411	1.0
50-100	528	15.7	31,363	1.5	603	14.1	36,249	1.2
100-200	1,198	35.7	124,028	5.8	1,515	35.3	157,121	5.1
200-2,000	304	9.1	167,318	7.8	424	9.9	252,318	8.1
2,000-5,000	124	3.7	317,990	14.9	357	8.3	812,651	26.2
5,000-50,000	30	0.9	423,247	19.8	44	1.0	717,105	23.2
50,000+	9	0.3	1,045,106	48.9	9	0.2	1,090,147	35.2
Total	3,358	100.0	2,137,001	100.0	4,287	100.0	3,097,687	100.0

Source: Estatisticas Cadastrais/1 and 4. Ministério da Agricultura/INCRA (1974 and 1978).

Table 4: Agrarian structure, Rondônia and Brazil: 1972 and 1976

Type of establishment	Rondônia				Brazil			
	1972		1976		1972		1976	
	% of estab.	% of land area	% of estab.	% of land area	% of estab.	% of land area	% of estab.	% of land area
Minifundio	76.9	7.1	72.6	6.2	71.9	12.5	71.8	11.4
Modern Agric. Firms	1.3	9.4	1.4	6.9	4.8	9.7	4.8	9.5
Latifundio	21.8	83.5	26.0	86.9	23.2	77.8	23.4	79.1
Total	3,356	2,136,921	4,287	3,097,687	3,387,173	370,275,187	3,842,235	464,428,929

Source: Estatisticas Cadastrais/1 and 4. Ministério da Agricultura/INCRA (1974 and 1978).

1972 and 1976 while a compensatory increase was registered in the proportion of latifundia. These trends were, in general terms, identical to the patterns at the national level. If anything, current land distribution in Rondônia would appear to be even more skewed than that of the rest of the country since a greater proportion of all establishments in Rondônia control a smaller share of the land area.[1]

Exactly how this concentration has come about in the face of government efforts to assist small-scale producers is difficult to decipher. A first hypothesis would be that the data are deficient; the continuity of observed patterns over time, however, and their fit with other data lend them a certain credibility. One factor involved is that government efforts have not been directed solely to small farmers; thus, the Programme for Directed Settlement (PAD's) is addressed explicitly to larger-scale agriculture. Probably of greater importance is the fact that a few powerful groups have succeeded in having their claims to huge tracts of land honoured while some of the scattered long-time residents who roamed over large areas of jungle territory (e.g. the seringalistas or rubber-gatherers) have also managed to retain possession of their original domains. In any case, it is certain that considerable violence and treachery are involved in the take-over and consolidation of many large landholdings.

Be that as it may, for our purposes one particular type of consolidation is particularly relevant for the evaluation of the colonisation experience in Rondônia and

---

[1] The definitions of minifundio, latifundio and modern agricultural firm (empresa rural) are based on the concept of "rural module" which was defined in the Land Statute (Estatuto da Terra) of 1964. The definition of this module is flexible, varying according to region and land use; in essence it involves "an area of family property", understood as "a rural establishment which, directly and personally explored by the farmer and his family, absorbs their entire work force and guarantees their subsistence as well as their social and economic progress". The possibility that hired labour will eventually be used is also contemplated. A minifundio is a rural establishment which has a total area amounting to less than one module. The latifundio has two subcategories; if it is a latifundio by dimension, it has over 600 modules of land area and if it is a latifundio by exploitation, then it has from one to 600 modules which are insufficiently exploited. An empresa rural also has from one to 600 modules, but these are being exploited in a "rational and economic form" (see Graziano da Silva, 1978, pp. 37-38).

for its prospects for the medium term; we refer to the consolidation which results from the sale, barter or take-over of land within the colonisation projects themselves. According to Tcheyan, official statistics show that 14 per cent of all lots have been transferred to new owners with INCRA's approval since the inception of the PIC-Ouro Preto project (Tcheyan, 1979, p. 8). However, the official picture is a very partial one in this respect:

> "... estimates of illegal or extra-legal transfer are double or triple the INCRA figure. In a random sample of 10 lots in the field, four of them were occupied by persons other than the one listed by INCRA. While no systematic study has been done, it appears that illicit transfers of land are often made for the price of a few bags of rice or small amounts of cash which are far below the actual or potential value of the land. Settlers apparently do not realise how potentially valuable land in Rondônia is and sale prices usually meet only their most immediate needs." (Tcheyan, 1979, p. 8).[1]

What is the significance of this type of land transfer for the future of colonisation projects? Again, it seems clear that the prospects for permanent settlement of the rural poor are being reduced by this manifestation of capitalist expansion. To the extent that large tracts are being cleared, roads are built, crops planted and labour becomes accessible, the land in Rondônia will acquire additional monetary value which will inevitably lead to the selling-out and re-migration of a majority of the colonists.

Thus it would appear that the independent but complementary analyses made by Martins and Oliveira of the role played by squatters and advance settlers in the expansion of the capitalist frontier will prove to be accurate even with respect to government-sponsored projects. Martins posited the existence of two basic sequential moments in frontier development: an "expansion front" in which squatters and itinerant farmers establish a subsistence, consumption-oriented agriculture

---

[1] The fact that settlers have no sense of the monetary value of land should not come as a surprise since, for much of the rural lower class - and, especially for squatters or <u>posseiros</u> in frontier regions - land basically has a use value and it is only with the penetration of capitalist forms of production that it acquires monetary value. This point is clearly made in de Souza Martins' (1975) seminal work.

and, a subsequent takeover by the "pioneer front", expressly oriented to profit and accumulation. In this process, the land which had a use value acquires a monetary or exchange value (ibid., pp. 45-46). Oliveira pointed out that the squatters who clear the land and prepare it for eventual takeover by large-scale producers, who then plant permanent crops or turn it over to pasture, serve to reduce the costs of production and to elevate the price of land (de Oliveira, 1976, p. 16).

In this light, it is worth pointing out that the proposed paving of the main thoroughfare which cuts through Rondônia and links its capital to the Centre-South will have an ambivalent function in the Territory. On the one hand, a permanent link with the more developed regions will help resolve one of the principal problems of the colonisation projects, namely access to Centre-South markets for their agricultural produce. Paradoxically, the capacity of colonisation projects to retain population will be simultaneously reduced since the provision of an all-weather road will help quicken the process of capitalist penetration and, ultimately, accelerate the expulsion of small farmers. That is, paving the Cuiabá-Porto Velho highway will cause an immediate upswing in land values, while increasing the economic viability of agricultural production in the Territory. Thus, it can be foreseen that, as soon as government tutorage of the colonisation projects comes to an end (i.e. when the projects are "emancipated" in the early 1980s) the colonists will suffer an irresistible barrage of seductive offers and threats which will oblige them to move on in search of new land.

If land becomes inaccessible to small farmers in Rondônia, where will they go? This is not just a rhetorical question in view of the previously-discussed closing down of the Amazonian frontier. In this connection, another related government measure which will have a decidedly negative effect on the absorption of small-scale producers is the recent decision to turn over the task of organising and implementing colonisation projects to private development companies.[1] In essence, such a measure will serve to accelerate the reproduction of the conditions prevailing in traditional agricultural areas and to bestow economic viability on the investments which have been made in Amazonia, especially during the last five years (via government subsidies).

---

[1] Ianni demonstrated that the shift to private colonisation companies began in 1974 (Ianni, 1979, Chapter 6). In retrospect however, it is clear that strong steps in this direction were announced shortly after the Figueiredo administration began in 1979.

Grosso modo, the newly created colonisation companies will be located on some of the land which was ceded to large companies during the past few years; the latter will divide part of their tracts into small plots, build roads and provide minimal infrastructure (with government subsidies) and sell it to would-be settlers at prices which although lower than in traditional areas, are outrageous by comparison to the initial capital outlay. Thus, in addition to materialising the initial expectations which motivated their penetration into the Amazon in terms of land speculation, these companies will benefit from the ready availability of cheap labour. Conversely, the prospects for stable settlement by colonists arriving in the region will be significantly reduced, since the profit motive underlying private colonisation is essentially antithetical to social development and to the creation of stable and adequate employment opportunities.

V. Final Considerations

The information discussed in this paper would seem to cast considerable doubt on the ability of colonisation projects to serve as an effective outlet for the absorption of the relative surplus rural population in Brazil. Compared to the size of the demand in the country as a whole, the impact of the projects carried out in Rondônia is relatively small. By comparison to the size of the demand constituted by those migrants who have already arrived in the Territory, the colonisation projects evidently fare somewhat better, but they are still forced to omit many more families than they can admit into the projects. Moreover, even for those families fortunate enough to obtain a plot in one of the official projects, the difficulties encountered are sizeable.

But perhaps of even greater consequence for the future of such endeavours is the consideration that, in the short time that it has been besieged by the mass influx of land-hungry migrants, Rondônia is clearly reproducing - even within the socially-oriented organisation of agricultural production - the vicissitudes of the predominant mode of organisation of agricultural production.

On the one hand, there is distinct evidence that the process of "minifundisation", or progressive parcelling of lots into smaller functional units, is already taking place within official projects as the result of a combination of the inefficient official support to colonists, the marginalisation of large numbers of families who are unable to obtain access to a piece of land, and of the unscrupulous behaviour of land grabbers sheltered by the disorganisation of institutional checks in a frontier situation. On the other hand, an overview of the land tenure situation in Rondônia reveals that, despite the recency of its settlement process, the distribution of land holdings in the Territory appears to be as skewed as in the rest of Brazil. Finally, there are signs that the abrupt rise in land values, brought on in part by the work put in by the colonists themselves and in part by the government's provision of basic infrastructure - in short, by the increasing economic viability of production in the Territory - will eventually force a sizeable proportion of those colonists who have managed to gain access to the land to move on.

Such conditions are, of course, not the product of chance nor are they peculiar to Rondônia. Indeed, the principal conclusion which can be derived from an examination of the settlement process in Rondônia is that the latter is faithfully reproducing the deficiencies of the prevailing system of agricultural production in the country as a whole. Thus, the Rondônian experience cannot be analysed independently of the nature, history, and conditions of the agrarian structure which prevail in the rest of the country, nor of the growth model which fashions the contours of the land tenure system and the organisation of production, whether in traditional agricultural areas or in frontier regions.

In this connection, it is pertinent to recall that the development of Brazilian agriculture has, throughout its history, been accomplished via the incorporation of new lands. Gifted with an enormous expanse of open lands, Brazil has perennially reacted to the problems of relative surplus population or of shortages in agricultural production - whether for domestic consumption of for export - by expanding the total area of cultivated land. The frontier is thus not external to the Brazilian model but rather simultaneously conditions and results from the prevailing agrarian structure (Graziano da Silva, 1979). As Graziano argued:

> "the existence of open lands on the frontier functions as a regulator of the intensification of capital in agriculture, thus conditioning its intensive/extensive development. Conversely, the intensification of capital in agriculture determines the rate of productive incorporation of frontier lands." (ibid., pp. 32-33).

Graziano also pointed out that frontier expansion performs a series of specific functions in Brazilian agriculture. Among these, he emphasised its role as the locus for the re-creation of peasant agriculture, as an important producer of foodstuffs - and thus as a mechanism which regulates the prices of basic staples - and as an escape valve for the social tensions which arise periodically in agricultural areas (ibid., p. 33).

In short, given the symbiotic relationship between traditional agricultural areas and frontier expansion and, in view of the prevailing model of growth - which a recently-ousted Brazilian Finance Minister repeatedly described as that of "savage capitalism" - it is hardly surprising that Rondônia is currently reproducing the deficiencies which characterise the nation's agricultural system, at the expense of small-scale farmers.

On another plane, it should be pointed out that the numerous criticisms which are directed at the official agency in charge of colonisation or at other government agencies are relatively pointless. Indeed, within the scope of its external and internal limitations, INCRA has performed creditable feats against great odds in the implementation of colonisation projects. True, its model of colonisation is overly complex, paternalistic, and expensive. In this sense, it would have been preferable to concentrate on assisting spontaneous or semi-oriented movements or to introduce support to simpler and cheaper forms of assistance to colonisation projects. Moreover, the ambiguous and limited support received by colonists in frontier areas is a mere reflection of the situation which prevails in areas of traditional agriculture. In spite of their importance for food production and for the absorption of manpower, and despite their high rates of economic productivity and efficiency, the small and medium-sized agricultural producers invariably find themselves on the periphery of institutional support.

However, the technical failings of the colonisation programmes and the lack of systematic support for small farmers are themselves consistent with the orientation of the over-all development model and with the functions assigned to government intervention in this model. Thus, the role played by INCRA and that of other agencies charged with the execution of social development policy has to be viewed within a more global context of the role played by the State in modern-day capitalist societies. In this respect, O'Connor's analysis of the authoritarian State is particularly germane to our problem (O'Connor, 1971, in Turchi, 1971, pp. 6-7). O'Connor suggests that the authoritarian State performs two fundamental and contradictory roles in the modern capitalist society. On the one hand, it propitiates conditions for the expansion of the process of accumulation through investments which permit an increase in the productivity of labour while decreasing the costs of labour force reproduction; on the other it serves to legitimise and perpetuate the existing power structure through the provision of projects and programmes destined for the lowest socio-economic groups. Such social development policies guarantee the reproduction of the labour force while relieving social tension.

These contradictory functions are particularly visible in the expansion of the agricultural frontier.[1] Thus, despite initial efforts directed to the rural poor and to small farmers, whether in projects along the Belém-Brasília and Trans-Amazon highways or in the Territory of Rondônia, the eventual outcome ultimately benefits the expansion of the prevailing modes of production and leads to the expulsion and/or proletarianisation of the original settlers.

Such considerations, in turn, lead to an indictment, not so much of colonisation itself nor of the ineffectual action of the government's social policy executors, but rather of the global process which utilises the agricultural frontier as a secular expedient with which to sidestep a re-examination of the very nature and conditions of the agrarian structure. In this sense, it is highly symptomatic that the major recent decisions announced by the government in the area (i.e. roadbuilding and preferential treatment for private colonisation companies) will inevitably favour the reproduction of the patterns of dominance which prevail in other areas. True, such measures will be instrumental in the incorporation of new regions into the national market but this will occur at the cost of minimising the possibilities for stable and satisfactory employment opportunities among low-income rural populations. The ultimate result of this situation will inevitably be the intensification of migration streams to large urban areas, with all the negative consequences which this alternative implies for social development.

---

[1] For an applied study of contradictory roles of government to colonisation on the Trans-Amazon highway, see Chaloult (1979).

References

Chaloult, N.B. (1979): "Settlement along the Trans-Amazon highway: Planning and reality", in Conference on the development of Amazonia in seven countries (Cambridge, Centre of Latin American Studies, University of Cambridge, Sep.).

Furley, P. (n.d.): "Development planning in Rondônia based on naturally-renewable resource surveys", presented at the conference on the Development of Amazonia in Seven Countries, Cambridge.

Graziano da Silva, J.F. (coord.) (1978): Estrutura agrária e produçâo de subsistência na agricultura brasileira (Sâo Paulo, Editora Hucitec).

--- (1979): "A porteira está fechando?" in Ensaios de Opiniâo (Rio de Janiero, Paz e Terra), Vol. 2, No. 9.

Ianni, O. (1979): Colonizaçâo e contrareforma agrária na Amazônia (Petrópolis, Editora Vozes).

Jatobá, J. (1979): "Dinâmica demográfica e econômica na pré-Amazônia maranhense: Fronteira de recursos e o programa de colonizaçâo do Alto Turí", in Anais do I Encontro Nacional da Associaçâo Brasileira de Estudos Populacionais.

Martine, G. (1979a): "Migraciones internas: Investigar para qué?", Notas de Población (Santiago, CELADE), Apr. Vol. 7, No. 19.

--- (1979b): "Recent colonisation experiences in Brazil: Expectations versus reality", in J. Balan (ed.): Internal migration and development, Proceedings of the CLACSO/UNESCO Symposium on migration in Cuernavaca, Mexico, 1979 (to be published).

Ministério da Agricultura, INCRA/CETRO (1979): As correntes migratórias e a colonizacâo (Vilhena, Rondônia, Aug.; mimeographed).

MINTER (1979): "Rondônia: os migrantes, seus problemas e esperanças", in Interior (Brasília), July-Aug. Vol. II, No. 2.

Mueller, C. (1979): "Recent frontier expansion in Brazil: The case of Rondônia", Conference on the Development of Amazonia in Seven Countries (Centre of Latin American Studies, University of Cambridge, Sept.).

O'Connor, J. (1971): USA: A crise do Estado capitalista (Rio de Janeiro, Paz e Terra).

de Oliveira, F. (1976): A economia brasileira: Crítica à razão dualista (São Paulo, CEBRAP/Brasiliense).

Osório, C. (1979): "Migrações recentes e desigualdades", in Anais de I encontro nacional du Associação Brasileira de Estudos Populacionais.

Paiva, J.M. (1977): Movimento (São Paulo), Vol. 21, No. 2.

Sawyer, D. (n.d.): "Colonização na Amazônia: Migração de Nordestinos para uma frente agrícola no Pará" (preliminary version, CEDEPLAR/BH; mimeographed).

de Souza Martins, J. (1975): Capitalismo e tradicionalismo (São Paulo, Pioneira).

Tavares, P., et al (1972): Colonização dirigida no Brasil: Suas possibilidades na Regiao Amazônia, Relatório de Pesquisa, No. 8 (IPEA/INPES).

Tcheyan, N. (1979): A comparative study of the administration of two Amazonian projects: Alto Turí and Ouro Preto (Washington, DC, IBRD; mimeographed).

Turchi. L.M. (1971): Colonização dirigida: Estratégia de acumulação e legitimação de um Estado autoritário, Master's thesis (University of Brasilia).

Chapter 6

INDUSTRIALISATION AND MIGRATION IN MEXICO

by Claudio Stern*

I. Introduction

This paper consists of three parts. The first presents a summary of the main features of Mexican economic development during the last century, especially as far as they have affected population movements. The second describes in a more systematic manner the main characteristics of urbanisation and interregional migration during recent decades. The third, in formulating various propositions relating development strategies to those population movements briefly evaluates State policies designed to influence urbanisation and migration patterns in Mexico.

Being a country that underwent a social revolution, from which evolved a long period of political stability and a series of relatively strong political régimes, and a country which has gone through a massive process of land distribution (much of it before the start of rapid industrialisation), Mexico provides an interesting case study for analysing the relationships between industrialisation and migration.

Are urbanisation and migration patterns in Mexico any different from those in other so-called less developed countries where a social revolution and a massive process of land distribution have not taken place? Given its long period of political stability and the persistence of a relatively strong and well legitimated State, have policies designed to influence urbanisation and migration patterns been any more successful in Mexico than in other countries?

II. Economic Development and Social Change in Mexico, 1876-1970

There is little doubt that Mexico has undergone a massive economic and social transformation in the last hundred years, and that this has had important effects in terms of the distribution of the population over the territory.

* El Colegio de México, Mexico City.

From a more or less typical export economy based on mining, cattle-breeding and commercial agriculture - enclaves surrounded by a sea of subsistence agriculture - the country has been transformed into a more integrated nation, with a more diversified economy, where the role of domestic demand has greatly increased.

During the present century the population of Mexico has more than trebled, agricultural production has increased more than sixfold, and there has been a manifold increase in industrial production. The proportion of the population working in agriculture has diminished by a third and that in manufacturing almost doubled (Reynolds, 1970, pp. 2-3). The proportion of the population living in urban locations has increased from less than 20 to more than 50 per cent, involving more than a fivefold increase in absolute terms, while the rural population has doubled over the same period (Unikel, 1976, p. 24).

There is no doubt that these and other changes have led the country to a higher level of social and economic development, but it is also clear that this process has taken place in the midst of extensive rural and urban poverty, the extinction of which is not foreseeable in the near future.

Unfortunately, no systematic attempt has yet been made to relate migration movements to economic development processes in Mexico from a historical perspective, and very little is known in terms of the concrete consequences of alternative social and economic policies on population movements.

Given, however, that migration patterns are part of the major social and economic transformations occurring in a nation, we have found it useful to include a summary of some of the most important aspects of this process during recent Mexican history.

In the summary that follows we have tried to select those aspects of social and economic development which seem to have had the greatest relevance for population movements.

1. The period 1876-1935

For long after its political independence from Spain in 1821, Mexico experienced almost uninterrupted internal political upheavals and foreign interventions, which repeatedly frustrated efforts towards industrialisation and development. It was only during the Porfiriato (i.e. the regime of Porfirio Díaz, which lasted from 1877 until 1910) that a more lasting effort at industrialisation was undertaken, through the accelerated construction of a rail system and of a certain industrial infrastructure, and through the development of modern large-scale agriculture.

During the Porfiriato the country experienced some economic growth, slow but sustained (Hansen, 1971, p. 134). This was accompanied by a substantial growth of the population, a slow increase in the rate of migration, and some redistribution of the population throughout the national territory (Reynolds, 1973, p. 20).

Mexico City, which had somewhat lost the dominant character it had during the colonial period, regained its preponderant role as the most dynamic centre and organising entity of the nation. During this period there were also important developments in mining and in the production of cotton in the northern parts of the country, as well as in sugar-cane and henequen plantations in, respectively, the Gulf of Mexico and the Yucatán Peninsula, both regions which attracted population (Moreno Toscano, 1972, p. 86; see also map 1 on the following page).

The central regions of the country suffered from more depressive effects during this period, owing to the introduction of the rail system and to the absence of agricultural investments. It soon became a region of net emigration (ibid., pp. 181-182).

Deterioration of living conditions in most rural areas in the last decade of the Porfiriato, as well as the incapacity of urban labour markets to absorb all the labour force displaced by mechanisation in the new manufacturing enterprises, provoked the first important wave of emigration to the United States (Clark, 1976, p. 52). This deterioration, together with the incapacity of the Díaz régime to provide social mobility for a growing middle class, as well as a division within the governing élite between the científicos (intellectuals) and the regional caciques (political bosses), were some of the factors which contributed to the ousting of Porfirio Díaz in 1911, as well as to the subsequent civil war, the Mexican Revolution, which lasted until the mid-1920s (Hansen, 1971, pp. 20-23).

Between 1922 and 1928 the economy of the country suffered major upheavals. The rail system was destroyed to a great extent, and both agricultural and manufacturing production was diminished, except in the case of some of the mining and oil enclaves, which remained relatively isolated from the more direct effects of the military phase of the Revolution (Reynolds, 1973, pp. 26-27).

By 1930 the greater part of commercial agricultural production, such as henequen, sugar-cane and coffee, had surpassed the levels of 1910. However, the production of maize and beans - the traditional diet of the Mexican population - had not regained previous levels. The major part of the upheaval in rural Mexico affected

MAP 1

Mexico: Division by political entities and main geo-economic regions

small-scale cereal producers and not the large commercial landholders. It was the central regions of the country which suffered the greatest pressures and consequences both of armed revolution and of the initial implementation of the agrarian reform derived from the Constitution of 1917. It was also this region where displacements from the rural areas towards urban centres occurred with the greatest intensity. Both peasants and landowners fled from the disorder which prevailed in the countryside (Reynolds, 1973, pp. 102-107).

Between 1910 and 1930 the urban population of the country (according to the census criterion which defines it as that living in communities with 2,500 inhabitants or more) increased by more than 40 per cent, while the rural population remained stable or diminished slightly, which gives an idea of the combined effect of the deaths that occurred in the countryside during the Revolution and of the rural-urban migration that took place during the period (Unikel, 1976, pp. 30-31).

Civil war also affected the regional distribution of the population throughout the country: the lowest rates of increase were in the Centre region (excluding the Federal District) and the North, which were the regions most affected by armed conflict. The population increased rapidly in the North-west, in the Gulf and in the Federal District (Reynolds, 1973, Chapter 1, footnote 14). During this period Mexico City served as a refuge for farmers and, especially, landowners fleeing from the provincial towns and cities where they lived.

In 1930 communication by paved road to Mexico City was still in its beginnings. It was formed mainly by two axes leading to the two main seaports - Acapulco in the Pacific and Veracruz in the Gulf of Mexico - and by a secondary road to the mining state of Hidalgo (Secretaría de Obras Públicas, 1975, p. 55). A substantial proportion (close to 40 per cent) of the migrants to Mexico City came from cities of a considerable size at the time (12,000 inhabitants or more) (Stern, 1977, Chapter 7). Many of them came from large urban areas in the Centre and Western regions (such as Puebla, Guadalajara, Morelia and Guanajuato). The majority of migrants with a rural origin, on the other hand, came from the immediate surroundings of Mexico City (Muñoz, de Oliveira and Stern, 1977, pp. 115-128).

Once civil peace had been restored towards the second half of the 1920s, when the nation was working hard to restore pre-revolutionary production levels and to apply the reforms contained in the Constitution of 1917, the collapse of world markets brought about by the Great Depression of 1929-33 frustrated most of the efforts undertaken. The markets for Mexican basic export products collapsed overnight and, together with them, income and internal demand. Imports and exports were reduced by half between 1929 and 1932 (Reynolds, 1973, p. 35).

To make the situation worse, the recession in the United States led to a massive repatriation of Mexicans. Between 1929 and 1937 more than 400,000 were repatriated, either voluntarily or by force (Clark, 1976, p. 54).

As a result of these factors, the socio-economic conditions of the majority of the Mexican population were not much better at the beginning of the 1930s than they had been 20 years before, at the outset of the Revolution.

2. The period 1935-54

Great changes were needed to modify the socio-economic conditions existing in the early 1930s, and the subsequent years were to witness many of them. Railroads were nationalised and the expropriation of land was accelerated during the first years of the 1930s. During the régime of President Lázaro Cárdenas, from 1934 to 1940, the role of the State in economic development was strengthened through economic and social investments (dams, roads, credit institutions, education, social security). And most importantly, the petroleum industry was nationalised in 1938 (Wilkie, 1970, pp. 71-78).

Outstanding among the structural reforms promoted by Cárdenas was the extension and intensification of agrarian reform, when close to 20 million hectares were redistributed. This performance has no parallel in any other period of Mexican history. Cárdenas distributed more than three times the amount of land that had been distributed by the previous post-Revolutionary régimes and a greater quantity than that was distributed during the 20 years following the end of his term (ibid., p. 188).

Indeed, it was only through the Cárdenas agrarian reform that the domination of the rural population by the *hacendados* (landlords) was finally broken, establishing the conditions for the development of a "free" labour market (Hansen, 1971, p. 36).

In the short term, the intensification of the agrarian reform had the effect of keeping in the countryside hundreds of thousands of peasants who would have probably emigrated to the cities, with few possibilities of finding employment there, since an intense industrialisation process had not yet begun (Reynolds, 1973, p. 183).

By increasing agricultural productivity levels and improving the diet of peasants, the *Cardenista* agrarian reform resulted in a redistribution of income and a reduction of inequality between the levels of living in the cities and in the countryside. Moreover, the great investments in rural infrastructure that took place during this period probably had as an effect a lesser degree of economic concentration throughout the national territory. Furthermore, this effort to achieve greater social justice was not to the detriment of industrial growth: by 1940 the value of manufacturing production was twice that of 1934 (Wilkie, 1970, pp. 193-197).

Without doubt, these various processes reduced the extent of migration to Mexico City (especially of migrants with rural origins), leading to a diversification of the regional origin of migrants and a diminution of inter-regional differences in the volumes of migration due to a more balanced distribution of employment opportunities throughout the national territory.

In the 1940s the Mexican economy entered a phase of accelerated growth (Reynolds, 1973, p. 39) sparked off by a sudden awakening of external demand after the beginning of the Second World War (Vernon, 1963, pp. 94-95); this was made possible by a coalition of interests that was able to maximise the benefits for the economic and political élites of the country, while minimising the social demands of peasants, workers, and broad sectors of the middle classes.

The growing demand for Mexican products, as well as the difficulties of importing industrial products during the Second World War, stimulated the rapid growth of both commercial agriculture and manufacturing, through a highly protected programme offering substantial incentives for import substitution and investments in agricultural and industrial infrastructure.

The ideological basis for rapid industrialisation of a capitalist type was strengthened during the régime of Miguel Alemán (1947-52), a period during which constitutional amendments to the agrarian law were implemented to protect private property and investments from governmental intervention. Thus protected, agricultural and livestock production increased substantially, especially in the recently irrigated zones of the north-west of the country.

Distribution of land in <u>ejidos</u> (communal lands) went on at a much slower pace and few investments were made in regions of subsistence agriculture (Solís, 1970, Chapter 4). Investments in manufacturing were made predominantly in those urban centres that had already a sufficiently developed infrastructure, especially in the city of Monterrey in the north and in Mexico City in the centre.

Densely populated states in the central regions of the country experienced a worsening of the _minifundismo_ problem (increasing subdivision of land into smaller and smaller plots), due to greater population increases derived indirectly from the _Cardenista_ agrarian reform (through better nutrition and greater access to medical and educational services) (ibid., p. 158). The absence of productive investments in these regions, where subsistence agriculture was predominant, was reflected in greater pressure on the land and on resources in general.

On the other hand, the concentration of productive investments in the sparsely populated states of the North and in the capital, as well as the institutionalisation of the _Bracero_ programme in 1942 (the agreement to provide Mexican temporary workers to the United States), offered the necessary opportunities for increasing the geographical mobility of the population (Clark, 1976, p. 54).

As far as migration during this period is concerned, it can be surmised that the capital attracted only a proportion of the migrants from the central regions of the country, since there existed important alternative destinations with the opening of irrigated land and the development of the industrial centres in the North. However, the rapid process of industrialisation of Mexico City probably attracted not only impoverished farmers from the central, southern and western regions, but also significant numbers of urban migrants from the cities of those regions, since they were not experiencing any important process of economic growth at the time.

In short, productive investment in Mexico underwent a certain decentralisation during the 1935-54 period, although the forces responsible for this phenomenon - _Cardenismo_ and _Alemanismo_ - were very different. This undoubtedly resulted in a greater capacity to retain people in their regions of origin and in a diversification of migratory flows, only part of which was towards Mexico City.

3. The period 1954-70

The outward-oriented period of economic growth, impelled by the external sector and financed by internal sources and by government deficits, came to its end when the Mexican economy suffered the consequences of the post-Korean War recession in the United States (Gollás and García Rocha, 1976, pp. 410-417).

The fall in the prices of raw materials exported by Mexico, together with a temporary government deficit caused by the efforts of a new administration to counter the effects of the recession through public expenditure, severely drained the international reserves of the country, and precipitated the devaluation of the peso from 8.50 to 12.50 to the dollar in 1954 (Solís, 1970, pp. 115-116).

This crisis was followed by a relatively long period of price stability, characterised by growing external financing, an intensification of the import substitution programme and modernisation and capitalisation of the industrial set-up. This era was marked by increased participation of external capital and especially of multinational corporations.

A sizeable reduction of public investments in agriculture was noticeable during this period, with the long-term effect of decreasing the agricultural growth rate, which for the 1960 decade barely managed to equal the rate of population growth, which had increased rapidly in the two previous decades (Bueno et al, 1977, p. 26).

The dualism between commercial agriculture and subsistence agriculture had also become more marked by the early 1950s. Better seeds and large investments in machinery and fertilisers had brought about substantial gains in productivity and in total production in the privileged areas of capitalist agriculture (especially in the North-west and the North-east of the country), while extensive areas of seasonal agriculture had been left to their own devices. This growing dualism had also increased existing regional inequalities.

At the other end of the economic spectrum, the cheaper costs of production of raw materials - and of the labour force as a result of government subsidies and credit policies - combined to favour the industrial sector, which between 1957 and 1967 grew two or three times as fast as the agricultural sector (Solís, 1970, p. 113). Moreover, industrialisation during this period was characterised by the growing use of capital-intensive methods of production; although allowing a certain improvement in the wages of a minority of privileged workers (Bueno et al, 1977, p. 24), this contributed to a general rise in unemployment and underemployment, which reached extremely high levels by the end of the period (Urquidi, 1974, pp. 141-153). The problem was aggravated in 1964 by the closing of the border for legal temporary migrants to the United States.

In these conditions, labour began to shift more rapidly from agriculture to the other sectors of the economy. The proportion of the labour force working in the primary sector, which had decreased by 9.5 per cent between 1930 and 1950, declined by 19 per cent in the following two decades. However, this relative decline was accompanied by an absolute increase in the number of farmers, since the size of the total population was growing (see table 1).

As far as migration processes are concerned, the combination of the above-mentioned factors had probably, amongst other consequences that of growing pressure on the land, especially in the densely populated regions of the Centre, West and South of the country, which resulted in higher rates of emigration, mainly into Mexico City, since the absorption capacity of regions that had previously attracted large numbers of migrants (especially the Northwest and Northeast) was virtually saturated both because smaller areas of new land were opened up for irrigation and because more advanced production techniques were used.

As a result of this, it is possible to assume a closer relationship between socio-economic regional conditions and migratory flows to Mexico City, except in those cases where the development of urban industries provided alternative centres of destination, as was the case in some regions close to the cities of Guadalajara, Monterrey, and a few others located in the central regions of the country, which experienced some development during the period referred to.

III. Redistribution of the Mexican Population in the Twentieth Century

Three phenomena characterise the redistribution of the Mexican population during the first seven decades of the twentieth century: a constant process of urbanisation, the concentration of the population in relatively few regions, and the concentration of the population in a few cities.

1. Urbanisation and urban concentration[1]

The proportion of urban to total population (the degree of urbanisation) rose from 10.5 per cent in 1900 to 44.9 per cent in 1970.[2] Two clear stages in this process of urbanisation stand out. Initially, it grew at a relatively moderate pace (at mean annual rates of 1.5 to 3.5 per cent in the different decades) but between 1940 and 1970 became more rapid growing at mean annual rates of between 5.4 to 5.9 per cent). The main factor which accounted for this change in the pace of urbanisation was

---

[1] This section is based mainly on Unikel (1977, 1976).

[2] Urban localities are here defined as those having 15,000 or more inhabitants.

Table 1: Distribution of the labour force of Mexico by industrial sector, 1930-70

Sectors and industries	Thousands			Percentages		
	1930	1950	1970	1930	1950	1970
EXTRACTIVE	3,677	4,909	5,249	71.5	62.0	43.0
Agriculture	3,626	4,819	5,103	70.5	60.8	41.8
Mining	51	95	146	1.0	1.2	1.2
PROCESSING	566	958	2,295	11.0	12.1	18.8
Food, beverages & tobacco	159	173	452	3.1	2.2	3.7
Textiles, leather & footwear	231	355	488	4.5	4.5	4.0
Wood products & furniture	72	119	208	1.4	1.5	1.7
Paper and paper products	11	24	122	0.2	0.3	1.0
Chemical products	21	40	220	0.4	0.5	1.8
Mineral products	26	48	146	0.5	0.6	1.2
Basic metals	5	24	73	0.1	0.3	0.6
Metal products & machinery	15	127	391	0.3	1.6	3.2
Utilities	15	24	49	0.3	0.3	0.4
Other	11	24	146	0.2	0.3	1.2
CONSTRUCTION	62	222	574	1.2	2.8	4.7
DISTRIBUTIVE SERVICES	375	863	1,599	7.3	10.9	13.1
Commerce	267	657	1,196	5.2	8.3	9.8
Transportation	108	206	403	2.1	2.6	3.3
PRODUCER SERVICES	5	55	269	0.1	0.7	2.2
Finance	-	31	110	-	0.4	0.9
Business	5	24	159	0.1	0.3	1.3
SOCIAL SERVICES	201	356	916	3.9	4.5	7.5
Education and health	201	158	513	3.9	2.0	4.2
Public administration	-	198	403	-	2.5	3.3
PERSONAL SERVICES	257	554	1,306	5.0	7.0	10.7
Domestic	190	308	538	3.7	3.9	4.4
Laundry	10	24	134	0.2	0.3	1.1
Repair services	31	48	195	0.6	0.6	1.6
Entertainment, hotels & restaurants	5	126	354	0.1	1.6	2.9
Other services	21	48	85	0.4	0.6	0.7
Total	5,143	7,917	12,208	100.0	100.0	100.0

Source: Adapted from Muñoz et al (1977, p. 45).

the process of industrialisation which, as noted earlier, greatly accelerated during and after the Second World War.

Another characteristic of urbanisation reflecting this latter fact was that the growth of a few large cities, and mainly the Mexico City Urban Area, accounted to a large extent for the growing degree of concentration of the urban population in Mexico as well as the pace of urbanisation. The three largest cities in the country (Mexico, Guadalajara and Puebla for 1900, and Mexico, Guadalajara and Monterrey for 1940 and 1970) accounted for 4 per cent of the total population in 1900, 8.4 per cent in 1940, and 22.4 per cent in 1970. The same three cities contained 37.6 per cent of the urban population in 1900, 41.9 per cent in 1940, and 50.3 per cent in 1970.[1] Most striking of all, the population of Mexico City grew from less than half a million in 1900 to 1.5 million in 1940 and 8.3 million in 1970, accounting for 2.5, 7.9 and 17.3 per cent of the total population of the country in the respective years.

The role of rural to urban migration was important both in terms of over-all urbanisation and of the growth of large cities. From 1940 to 1970 migration brought more than 6 million individuals to towns and cities, during which time total urban growth was approximately 16 million. It is estimated that Mexico City received more than 60 per cent of the total number of rural migrants during that period (Consejo Nacional de Población, 1970).

2. Regional redistribution of the population and main migration flows in contemporary Mexico

An analysis of the regional distribution of the Mexican population during the first 70 years of the twentieth century shows that it was increasingly concentrated in the small Metropolitan Region dominated by Mexico City (see map 1 and figure 1).

The Metropolitan region almost doubled its share of the population in the 70-year period (from 12 to 23.4 per cent; see table 2). In that period, only two other regions showed significant but much smaller increases in their share of the total population: the North-west (from 5.3 to 8 per cent) and the North-east (from 4 to 6.5 per cent).

As can be seen in figure 1 and table 2, this increasing concentration of the population in the Metropolitan Region was paralleled by substantial decreases in the

---

[1] Computed from data in Unikel (1976, tables I-A1, II-A2, II-A3, and 2-A4).

FIGURE 1

Regional re-distribution of the Mexican population, 1900-1970

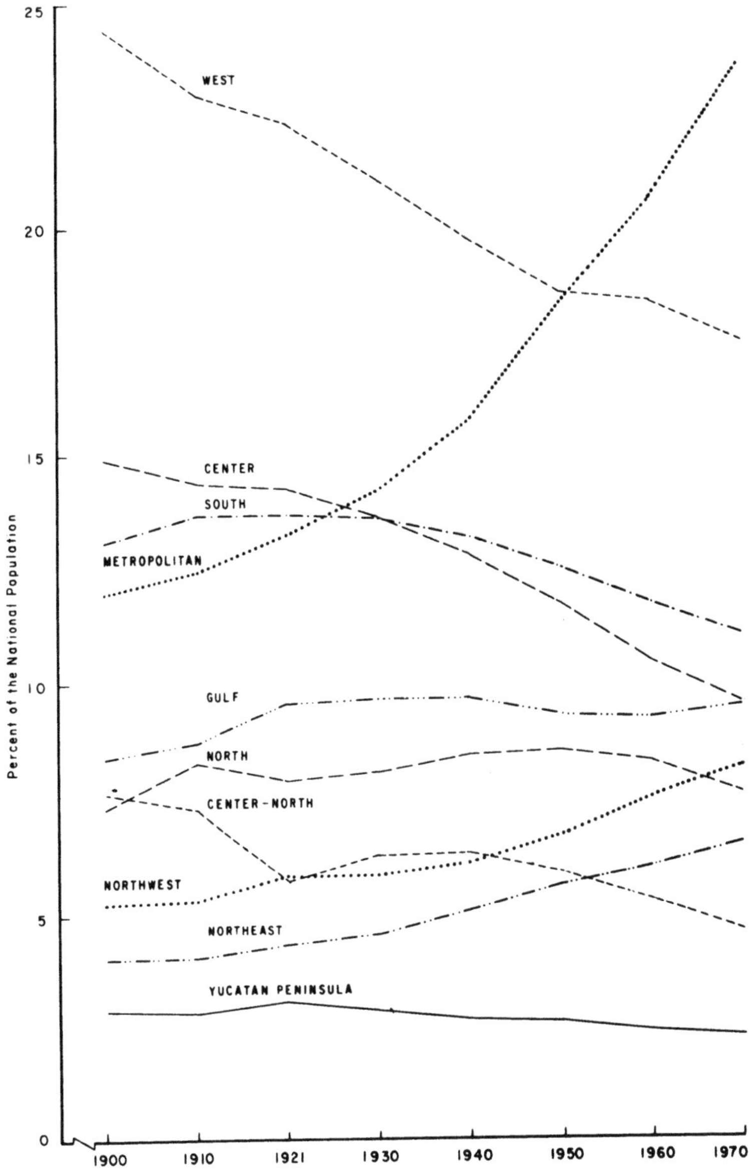

Source Table 2

Table 2: Distribution of the Mexican population by geo-economic regions 1900-70 (in percentages)

Regions		1900	1910	1921	1930	1940	1950	1960	1970
I.	Northwest	5.25	5.35	5.86	5.88	6.12	6.70	7.48	8.07
II.	North	7.31	8.26	7.90	8.05	8.43	8.52	8.29	7.57
III.	Northeast	4.02	4.06	4.35	4.60	5.09	5.66	6.02	6.51
IV.	Centre-North	7.63	7.29	5.76	6.27	6.33	5.90	5.34	4.62
	Subtotal: Northern	24.21	24.96	23.87	24.80	25.97	26.78	27.13	26.77
V.	West	24.39	22.93	22.28	21.06	19.79	18.62	18.44	17.51
VI.	Centre	14.93	14.39	14.27	13.70	12.91	11.82	10.51	8.52
VII.	Metropolitan	12.03	12.46	13.21	14.22	15.70	18.28	20.49	23.41
VIII.	Gulf	8.38	8.71	9.56	9.68	9.69	9.32	9.23	9.48
	Subtotal: Central	59.73	58.49	59.32	58.66	58.09	58.04	58.67	59.92
IX.	South	13.14	13.68	13.70	13.64	13.26	12.60	11.82	11.04
X.	Yucatán Peninsula	2.92	2.87	3.11	2.90	2.68	2.58	2.38	2.27
	Subtotal: Southern	16.06	16.55	16.81	16.54	15.94	15.18	14.20	13.31
	Total	100.00	100.00	100.00	100.00	100.00	100.00	100.00	100.00

Source: Computed from Unikel (1976, tables II-A1; II-A2; II-A3; II-A4).

MAP 2

Mexico: Trends in inter-state migration by regions, 1950-1970

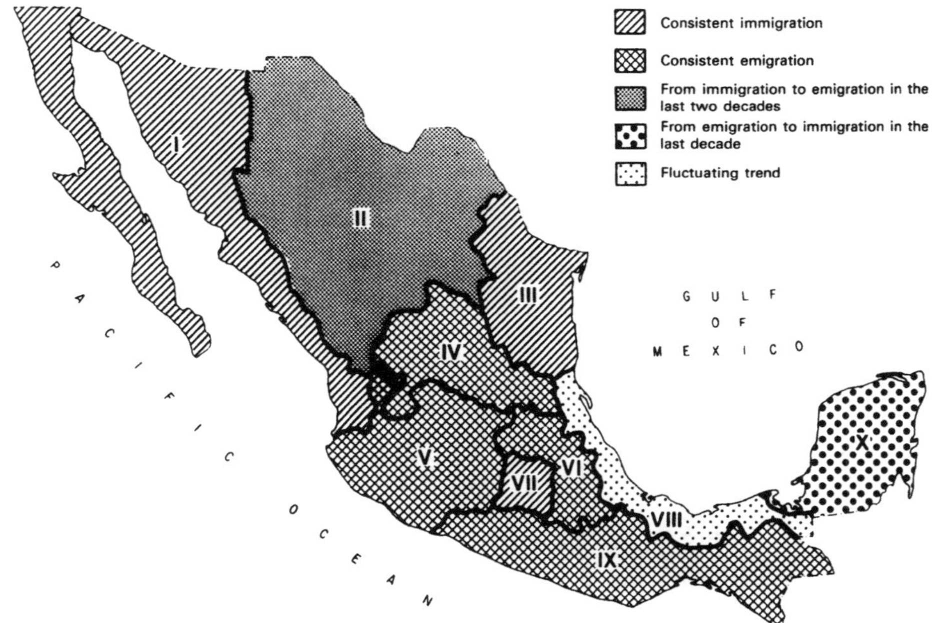

population of the regions surrounding it (West, Centre, South), both trends having accelerated after the 1930s, when the great spur towards industrialisation started.

Most of the above-mentioned changes in the distribution of the Mexican population have been the result of internal migration (Stern, 1977, Chapter 5), which have become increasingly directed into the Metropolitan Region. Lifetime migration data show that by 1950 the States comprising the Metropolitan Region had a net positive migration balance more than four times greater than that of those States comprising the north-east, which was second in importance as a pole of attraction at that time. During the 1950-60 decade the Metropolitan Region maintained its pre-eminence in terms of net immigration, and increased it considerably during 1960-70, when its net balance was almost eight times greater than that of the Northeast, still the second region in order of importance. Lifetime migration trends from 1950 to 1970 can be seen in map 2, where it can be observed that the Metropolitan Region is surrounded by regions showing a pattern of consistent emigration.

These trends become even clearer when recent migratory flows are analysed (see table 3 and maps 3 and 4). By comparing the most important interregional migration currents occurring in two periods - 1955-59 and 1959-70 - it can be seen that <u>all</u> important migration currents directed into the Metropolitan Region have increased, while many of those directed into other regions have diminished. Thus, the relative attraction exerted by the Metropolitan Region has been increasing owing both to a growing tendency to channel towards it greater proportions of migrants from most regions of out-migration and to a diminishing capacity of other growth poles to attract migrants.

IV. Development Strategy and State Policies Influencing Urbanisation and Migration Patterns

1. Strategy of development and concentration of the population in Mexico City

Internal migration patterns occurring in today's "developing nations" are a result of the interaction between the "strategy of development" they follow and the social structure on which this strategy is based. The strategy of development itself is conditioned by the relationship between the country under consideration and the world market and political order. Both the development strategy and the social structure are conditioned by their historical experience. And in order to understand, explain and evaluate internal migration processes it is

Table 3: Main inter-regional migration currents, 1955-59 and 1959-70

Regions of origin and of destination	Percentage of total migrants	
	1955-59	1959-70
II to I	2.08	2.32
V to I	6.20	5.00
IV to II	2.45	*
II to III	3.29	2.81
IV to III	4.09	4.32
V to III	1.97[a]	*
IV to V	*	2.62
VII to V	*	2.36
IV to VII	*	2.93
V to VII	15.18	16.05
VI to VII	10.99	12.31
VIII to VII	3.56	3.99
IX to VII	6.17	9.59
VI to VIII	2.26	*
IX to VIII	2.32	2.12
Total	60.56	66.42

a Figure rounded up to 2.per cent.

* Less than 2 per cent of the total migrants.

Source: Stern (1977, p. 109).

MAP 3

Mexico: Main inter-regional migration currents, 1955-1959

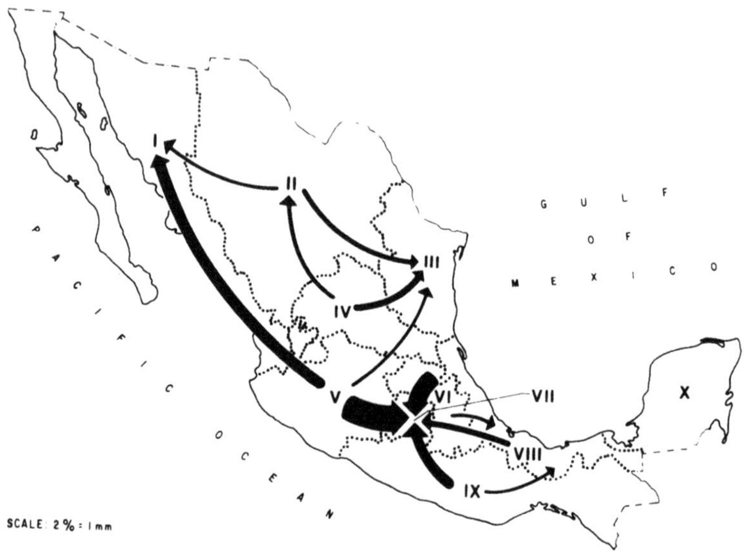

MAP 4

Mexico: Main inter-regional migration currents, 1959-1970

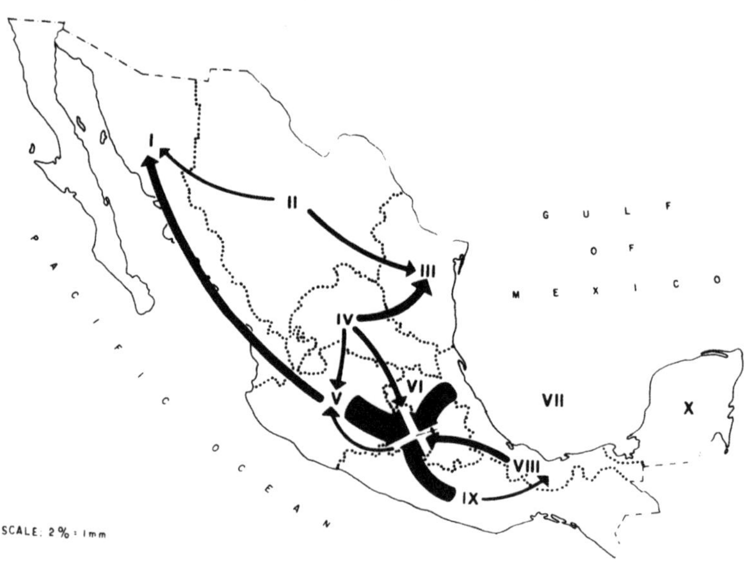

necessary to locate them within their wider structural and historical contexts.

Twentieth century Mexico can be defined, in terms of its social structure, as an agrarian and "underdeveloped" nation. Its strategy of development can be defined as dependent industrial capitalism. These are the two basic parameters under which migration processes in Mexico have taken place in the twentieth century.

The development of industrialism in an agrarian nation involves the transfer of labour from primary to secondary and tertiary activities, and implies the geographical mobility of the population from dispersed villages to urban areas. The development of industrial capitalism in an underdeveloped nation involves the concentration of capital in a few areas, with migration accordingly flowing from most rural areas of the nation towards a few dynamic urbanising centres.

The dependent character of industrial capitalism in today's world implies, among other things, the need to export the products demanded by a particular world market involved (initially raw materials, food, and other unprocessed goods), and the need to import complex labour-saving technology, as well as other manufactured goods, ill-fitted to the characteristics of the existing combination of factors of production (scarce capital and abundant labour) or to the production of goods suitable for satisfying the basic needs of the majority of the population, instead of the non-basic ones of a small minority.

The characteristics assumed by the productive system of a dependent nation are thus largely shaped by external demands and conditions, as they interact with the existing hierarchical social structure. The evolution of dependent industrial capitalism reinforces the class structure and strengthens the political domination needed for such a system to function, all of which makes it extremely difficult to change the basic conditions under which "development" takes place. Since the characteristics of migration movements depend fundamentally on the interaction between the strategy of development followed and the social structure within which it is implemented, they themselves are very difficult to change.

Other fundamental elements of the social structure determining internal migration are the characteristics of the regions of the nation involved, the historical process of the human settlement of these regions, and the distribution of the population throughout them at a given time.

In the case of Mexico, various historical factors have determined a relatively high concentration of the population in the Central Plateau, at least since the fifteenth century during the Aztec domination over most of what constitutes contemporary Mexican territory, and continuing until our own day. Difficulties in overcoming various natural elements prevented the full settlement of the southern tropical lands and the northern desert icones until quite recently. The development of the northern part of the country, mainly a facet of the relations of dependence established with the United States during the last quarter of the nineteenth century, has been the only relevant centrifugal force counteracting the centripetal one exerted by Mexico City over the whole territory.

The only period of Mexican history when the predominance of Mexico City suffered a relative decline was that during which the existence of the Mexican nation as such was in danger - during the 50 year period after its independence from Spain in 1821 (Moreno Toscano and Florescano, 1976). Under the Porfirian period, between 1876 and 1910, the predominance of the capital was re-established, and the first three decades of industrialisation after 1940 reinforced its preponderant role as the economic, political, and cultural centre of the nation. By 1970, the Metropolitan Area of Mexico City, with 17 per cent of the population, concentrated close to 50 per cent of the value of industrial production of the country, and more than 60 per cent of the federal bureaucracy, of professionals, and of students receiving higher education.

The conditions under which the industrialisation strategy was followed after the 1930s have led to a relative impoverishment of the rural population concentrated in the Central Plateau. From there growing numbers have been forced to move, seeking employment and better conditions for survival in the few places where they could find them - the capital city, the northern areas on both sides of the border and, more recently, a few other large cities such as Guadalajara.

As a result, most major migratory flows in the last 40 years have been from the impoverished states in the central and southern regions of the country towards the north and the capital city. Mexico City received an average of 40 per cent of the total number of inter-state migrants over the last three decades, and the relative magnitude of the flow increased throughout that period. Most important migratory flows into Mexico City originate in the regions surrounding it or relatively close to it. The Centre and the West have provided most of the migrants, but the importance of flows originating in the South and the Centre-North has steadily increased in the last decades.

One analysis of the regional origins of migrants to Mexico City revealed that the relative number coming from predominantly rural and agricultural regions has substantially increased throughout the last four decades, while the number coming from predominantly urban regions, and especially from regions having large cities and a diversified economic structure, has markedly declined. This analysis also revealed that the relative number of migrants coming from regions in the immediate vicinity of the capital has decreased, while the number coming from remoter regions at larger distances has risen (Stern, 1975, pp. 179-200).

What has apparently been taking place is that some of the larger cities in the vicinity of the capital have been able to absorb most of their own population growth, but that their relatively small size, as well as the specialised and dependent character of their economies, have not allowed them to absorb more of the still growing surplus rural population, which has been forced to move into Mexico City, even from relatively far away. The only exception to this seems to be Guadalajara, which has been able to absorb an increasing number of rural migrants from its vicinity during the last two decades, and which is probably becoming a counter-force to the attraction exerted by the nation's capital over the whole central and southern area of the country.

2. Decentralisation of economic, political and cultural activities

The basic reasons for the concentration of migration into Mexico City have been: (i) its preponderant economic, social and political role; (ii) the fact that it is encircled by densely populated rural areas; and (iii) the fact that no other cities in its vicinity have been able to compete with it in terms of attracting population. Let us consider what will probably happen in the near future with reference to each of these factors.

Various policies have been adopted in the last two decades to decentralise economic activities from the capital. Attractive tax exemptions have been offered to industries establishing themselves outside the Federal District; the government has invested in the infrastructure for the establishment of these industries in various places throughout the country; it has itself developed large industries in various provinces, such as Ciudad Sahagún in the state of Hidalgo, with factories assembling motor vehicles and railroad freight cars, and the Las Truchas/Lázaro Cárdenas steel manufacturing complex.

However effective these policies might have been in other ways, (growth of the GNP, for instance), they have done little to divert migration from the capital. Tax exemptions for the establishment of new industries outside the Federal District have mostly had the effect of enlarging the economic space of the nation's capital: most of these industries were established in the outskirts of the Federal District, in the adjoining municipalities of the state of Mexico, or in nearby cities such as Querétaro, Toluca, Cuernavaca, or Puebla, located at very short distances from Mexico City. The result has been the rapid enlargement of the Metropolitan Area and the slow establishment of a large conurbation of these centres, which will probably become a single megalopolis in the not too distant future. At most, what has occurred is a deconcentration of manufacturing industry from the Federal District to its periphery, but there has been no decentralisation nationally (Lavell, 1972; Unikel, 1976).

For the most part, state-owned industries have developed in isolated industrial towns, generating employment for workers from outside the regions in which they become established.

The attraction exerted by Mexico City for most industries and all kinds of business has not disappeared. Proximity to the federal bureaucracy, where most national decisions are taken, often in minute detail, is an important factor in deciding the location of almost any business in Mexico. A location close to consumers is also important; the capital consumes close to 50 per cent of the total value of manufactured goods, and as much as 80 or 90 per cent of specialised products (optics, photography, etc.) and services, such as advertising (Bataillon, 1972, Chapter V). So, even factories located outside Mexico City keep part of their administrative personnel in it. The same considerations apply to higher education, cultural activities and entertainment, which are other important factors taken into account by industrialists when they decide on their location.

Some policies have been implemented to decentralise the bureaucratic and cultural concentration in the capital. Federal budgets for state universities were substantially increased between 1970 and 1976, and new regulations were implemented restricting the admission to the National University of students from provincial cities. Nevertheless, even today more than 80 per cent of the federal budget for higher education is spent in the Metropolitan Area, and many students from the provinces still find their way into institutions of higher learning in Mexico City. Moreover, large new state-supported universities have recently been established in the capital (the Autonomous Metropolitan University, with four campuses, the Professional Schools from the National University, and various others). Policies are thus contradictory, and still seem to be motivated more by immediate political needs than by long-range planning.

Under recent presidential régimes various plans and measures directly related to migration and the spatial distribution of the population have been decreed. Since December 1976, and as part of an important administrative reform, the Ministry of Public Works was redefined as the Ministry of Human Settlements and Public Works. In 1977 this Ministry issued the National Plan for Urban Development in which important objectives for the redistribution of the population were established. A year later, the President approved a document on regional demographic policy, presented to him by the National Population Council (CONAPO), an institution established in 1974 after the promulgation of the National Population Law. The Council defined the main demographic parameters which were put forward as goals to be reached by the year 2000.[1] These goals were taken as a base for both the Urban Development Plan and the Regional Demographic Policy, to which we will now turn.

One of the central considerations of the Urban Development Plan was the irrational distribution of the population in terms of the water resources of the country. The Plan considers that probably 80 per cent of the Mexican population will live in urban localities (census definition of 2,500 inhabitants or more) by the year 2000. At present, 70 per cent of the urban population live in cities over 1,000 metres above sea level and in the Central and Northern parts of the country. On the other hand, it is estimated that more than 80 per cent of the water resources of the country are located in the southern parts of the country and below 500 metres above sea-level, making it "a zone which can receive, with great advantage, important migratory flows through the creation and development of sources of work" (Secretaría de Asentamientos y Obras Públicas, n.d., p. 26).

Consistent with its central objectives, the Plan aims also at drastically limiting the growth of the three existing multi-million metropolitan areas, and stimulating the growth of medium-sized cities and the concentration of

---

[1] The National Population Council consists of representatives of various ministries and has as its main objective the incorporation of demographic considerations and objectives into plans and programmes put forward by the ministries. Its President is a representative of the Secretaría de Gobernación (Ministry of the Interior). The goals set in the National Plan of the Health Sector for Family Planning, equivalent to a National Demographic Plan, were to reduce the annual population growth rate from approximately 3.4 per cent in the mid-1970s to 2.5 per cent in 1982 and to 1 per cent by the year 2000.

dispersed rural settlements. The goals are to have 38 per cent of the population living in the cities with 1 million or more inhabitants by the year 2000 (instead of 50 per cent if present trends were to continue), and to have 40 per cent of the population living in small and medium-sized cities (instead of 28 per cent). Mexico City would have 20 million inhabitants instead of approximately 40 million, Guadalajara would have 4 million instead of 8.4 million, and Monterrey would have 5 million instead of 7.7 million.

In regional terms, the Plan aims to reverse most existing trends. The percentage of the population in the North-west, the North-east and the Metropolitan Region, which as we have seen has been increasing for the last 50 years at least, would diminish. The proportion would increase in all regions where it has so far been diminishing (South, South-east, West and Centre-North). The Plan aims basically at greatly increasing the importance of the coastal regions in the Gulf and in the southern portion of the area bordering the Pacific.

So, an important objective of the plan is to substantially modify the spatial distribution of the populaton by changing migratory flows. The Plan says little, however, on how to reach the goals it has established. To anyone familiar with past trends and with the strength with which factors determining these trends have operated, most of the quantitative goals of the plan appear quite unrealistic, especially since, almost without exception, they imply a complete reversal of present trends.

For the Metropolitan Region, for example, whose relative population is expected to decline as early as 1982 according to the Plan, the goal would imply not only halting the current very heavy migratory flows into the region (see maps 3 and 4), but also stimulating substantial out-migration. Both of these are highly problematic, at least in the short term.

In other regions, like the North-west, whose share of the total population has been increasing uninterruptedly for the last 80 years, there appears to be no reason to stop relative growth; nor does there seem to be any point in increasing the proportion in other regions, such as the Centre-North which is extremely poor and, as far as is known, possesses few exploitable resources.

The Regional Demographic Policy defined by the National Population Council in 1978 is somewhat more realistic in its goals. As far as population movements are concerned, this policy centres on three programmes: "Retention, Redirection and Relocation". The first is aimed at retaining in their places of origin some of the potential migrants, the second at redirecting migration movements, and the third at relocating part of the personnel at present working in the federal bureaucracy in Mexico City to other cities around the country.

The Policy aims also, like the Urban Development Plan, at limiting the growth of the three largest metropolitan areas and at redirecting migratory flows into other regions. However, it takes present trends more seriously into account and does not ignore the fact that these are very difficult to change. Accordingly, its aims are much more modest than those of the Urban Development Plan, and the timing for reaching them is more gradual.

In the Regional Development Policy, aims are established for a ten-year period (1978-88), subdivided into two subperiods which correspond to the two presidential régimes, 1978-1982 and 1982-1988. The first of the subperiods was contemplated as a transitional one, during which the processes envisaged by the various programmes included in the Regional Development Policy would be gradually set in motion, and the second as a period of consolidation, after which the processes would be speeded up.

With respect to retaining the population in the states which have accounted for most out-migration into the three largest metropolitan areas, the aim was to reduce the out-migration rate by 0.5 per cent in some states and 1.0 per cent in others during the ten-year period, which would mean retaining some 800,000 to 850,000 individuals who would otherwise migrate, most of them probably to the three metropolitan areas.

The aim of the Redirection policy was to encourage migration from the West and Centre-North to the Northwest and the state of Tamaulipas, and from the Centre and South to the Gulf. The objective of this would be to slow down migration to the Metropolitan Areas and to strengthen migration to states capable of absorbing migrants. It was hoped to change the destination of 530,000 to 550,000 migrants between 1978 and 1988.

The Relocation policy concerns only the Metropolitan Area of Mexico City, where in 1975 approximately 19 per cent of the population depended directly on public employment, whereas in the rest of the country the proportion was less than 8 per cent (Consejo Nacional de Población, 1970, p. 97). The "Territoral Deconcentration Programme for the Public Administration" (incorporated into the Regional Demographic Policy) envisaged the relocation of 110,000 public employees in the 1978-82 period. If the aims on the programme were met, it would mean that 330,000 individuals would leave Mexico City during that period.

The net results of these policies would mean close to 1.3 million fewer migrants into Mexico City during the ten-year period (equivalent to the net immigration observed between 1960 and 1970); 160,000 fewer into Monterrey; 80,000 fewer into Guadalajara; and 50,000 fewer into the border cities of the state of Baja California Norte.

Added to expected reductions in the natural growth rate of the population, the effect of these policies, though not spectacular, would be quite significant. They would probably not change the basic profile of the distribution of the population in the short-term or medium-term, but they would certainly help to attenuate some of the problems of "over-concentration" which are already present and which would become much worse if recent trends continue unchecked.

A lot of questions remain about the probable effectiveness of these plans and policies, especially since the means of attaining the established goals are not defined in any detail. Their orientation is basically correct, and implicitly they tend to take account of recent developments in Mexico;[1] as such, at least in the longer run, they might bring substantial changes in the distribution of the population.

3. Agrarian reform and rural exodus

As noted, a second major reason for the concentration of population in Mexico City is the fact that it is practicaly encircled by densely populated rural areas, from which there is a steady flow of migrants. What are the prospects for reducing this migration or for rechannelling it towards other areas?

Various specialists on urbanisation have stated, somewhat optimistically and basing themselves on the experience of so-called Western countries, that they do not expect major cities in developing nations to continue growing at similar rates as in the past, partly because the levels of urbanisation they reach will limit the supply of potential migrants (Browning, 1970). Although this may be true of some cities and countries in Latin America, we fear that it is unlikely to apply generally, and perhaps least of all in the case of Mexico City.

---

[1] I am thinking of various developments derived from an increasingly "oil-centred" economy. Other programmes, like the National Industrial Development Programme and the recently approved Global Development Plan, point in the same direction.

In the regions around Mexico City there are very large numbers of peasants living in both rural and so-called urban localities (census definition of 2,500 inhabitants or more). In fact, more than 60 per cent of the nation's agricultural labour force lives in the 10 states (out of 32) from which Mexico City recruits most of its immigrants (Cauthorn and Hubbard, 1976), adding up to more than 3.2 million persons. It is most likely that a large proportion of these peasants, as well as their families and offspring, will be forced to emigrate in the next 20 years.

Contrary to the projections of Browning and other specialists, we think that in the case of Mexico City the supply of migrants will increase in the near future. Obviously, even with an increase in the level of urbanisation in a country the number of rural inhabitants can continue to grow if the population keeps increasing. To give an example, only about 30 per cent of the population of Mexico were living in so-called urban localities in the 1930s, the percentage is now probably approaching 20; however, the number of rural inhabitants is now around 25 million, more than twice what it was in 1930.

Perhaps even more important for our argument are the facts that: (i) the quantity of available land - at least in the central regions with which we are primarily concerned - has increased very little in recent decades; (ii) the quality of most of this land has deteriorated, and perhaps even more importantly (iii) most of the agricultural production on this land has become little more than marginal, given the commercial nature of the market at the present day.

However important politically and otherwise, in economic terms the Mexican agrarian reform led to an increasingly dualistic structure of agriculture through which most of the commercialised production has become concentrated in a very few regions, mostly in the northern states of Sonora and Sinaloa. These few regions produce more than 50 per cent of the total value of agricultural exports and close to 30 per cent of the value of agricultural products consumed internally (Proceso (Seminario de Información y Análisis), 1976; Bueno, 1977). As we have seen, in recent decades most agricultural investment, both public and private, including resources devoted to research and development of new seeds and methods of production (i.e. the "Green Revolution"), have gone into these areas of commercial, capitalist agriculture.

At the same time, as we have also seen, most of the rest of the agricultural land has been left to the course of nature, which has resulted in soil erosion, abandonment due to lack of credit in some regions, and overpopulation in most others. The number of landless peasants grew from 1950 to 1970 approximately from 2.3 million to more than 3.3 million, and the average number of days worked by the agricultural population diminished from approximately 194 in the 1950s to 100 in the 1960s (Hansen, 1971, p. 81; Reyes Osorio et al, 1974, pp. 425 ff). While the rural population continues to grow at a high rate (between of 1.5 and 2.0 per cent per year during the last three decades), employment in the agricultural sector is apparently beginning to diminish, which will increase the rural surplus population and thus increase the migratory potential from them in the near future.

It is from this group that most rural-urban migrants originate. Some are temporary migrants - who drift to the United States or to zones of commercial agriculture in Mexico when their labour is needed (Botey et al, 1976), or to the large cities, mostly during the "dry months" when the demand in the construction industry is high. Other are permanent migrants, usually the young with no opportunities whatever in the countryside.

It is very difficult to estimate what proportion of the potential rural migrants of the near future will end up moving permanently to the cities, but it is possible to surmise that their numbers will be even greater than in the recent past.

The remaining question, related to what was proposed as the third basic reason for the concentration of the population in the capital is: where will this potential migration be directed to? Undoubtedly, part of it will go to regions where industrial and other projects are being implemented, especially along the Gulf (Tamaulipas, Veracruz, Tabasco and Campeche) where most oil discoveries have been made recently, and along the Pacific coast, where the Las Truchas steel complex is being built, as well as the various tourist resorts to the north of it. But much of it will find its way to the Metropolitan Region, to other large cities in the Centre, and to Guadalajara.

V. Conclusion

Industrialisation in Mexico during the last 40 years has led to a highly concentrated pattern of urbanisation, made possible partly through a massive movement of rural migrants who have drifted towards a few cities that have grown at very fast rates. Some of these cities have become huge metropolitan areas, others are on the verge of doing so.

The growth of Mexico City itself during this period has produced a substantial redistribution of the national population, close to one quarter of which is now concentrated in the small territory dominated by this city, which we have called the Metropolitan Region.

Over this whole period, the Mexican Government has been concerned with regional inequalities, the uneven distribution of the country's population, the consequences of rapid urbanisation, and especially the tremendous size of Mexico City. A variety of plans to counteract some of these trends have been made, much legislation has been promulgated, and a host of programmes have been implemented (Unikel, 1976, 1977). The results have been meagre, to say the least.

Why have policy measures to influence population movement in Mexico mostly failed? A satisfactory explanation would have to include at least some of the following elements:

- Basically, population movements are affected by economic policy or what in more general terms we have called "development strategy". And this has not significantly changed in Mexico for the last 40 years. To take an example, terms of trade have been mostly unfavourable to agricultural products, urban salaries have been significantly higher than rural incomes, and both these factors have stimulated rural emigration.

- To a great extent policies to correct the maldistribution of the population have been in contradiction with these more general economic policies, or, if not contradictory, have at least been inconsistent with them.

- The Mexican Government has been structurally limited in its power to enforce legislation. It has been limited by the type of economic system legitimating it (and thus been unable to impose measures running counter to the logic of the system), and by the type of political system supporting it (so that it cannot impose measures running counter to the interests of the dominant sectors). Examples abound - while legislation prohibits the establishment of new industries within the Federal District, new industries are not only established, but representatives who speak for the interests of private enterprise have often announced that they will not comply with existing legislation.

- In formulating urbanisation and migration policies, the basic mechanisms that determine the concentration processes have generally not been seriously considered. When they have been taken into account, their force has been underestimated. This has led, as we have illustrated, to the development of plans and programmes that are highly unrealistic to anyone with some knowledge of the determinants of population movements.

There is little doubt that urbanisation trends and population movements can be changed, and that they actually have been changed in some countries. The best known example is that of Cuba, where the growth rate of Havana has been slowed since the 1960s, where the development of some provinces seems to have actually succeeded in attracting population, and where programmes aimed at concentrating the dispersed rural population seem well on their way (Acosta and Hardoy, 1972, pp. 41-67; Instituto de Planificación Física, 1975). But there is little doubt that this reorientation of urbanisation patterns and of population movements would only be possible through a drastic redefinition of national priorities and/or through profound changes in the development strategy.

References

Acosta, L. and Hardoy, J.E. (1972): "La urbanización en Cuba", in Demografía y Economía, Vol. VI, No. 1.

Bataillon, C. (1972): La ciudad y el campo en el México central (Mexico, Siglo XXI).

Botey, E.C., et al (1976): Los jornaleros agrícolas migratorios, una solución organizativa, research progress report presented to the Consejo Nacional de Ciencia y Tecnología, México.

Browning, H.L. (1970): "Primacy variation in Latin America during the twentieth century", Actas y Memorias del XXXIX Congreso Internacional de Americanistas (Lima).

Bueno, G., et al (1977): Opciones de política económica en México (Mexico, Editorial Tecnos SA).

Cauthorn, R.C. and Hubbard, G.P. (1976): "Economic factors in Mexican migration" in T. Weaver and T.E. Downing: Mexican migration (Arizona, The University of Arizone Press).

Clark, M.B. (1976): "Mexican migration to the United States", in T. Weaver and T.E. Downing (eds.): Mexican migration (Arizona, The University of Arizona).

Consejo Nacional de Población (1970): Política demográfica regional (Mexico City).

Gollás, M. and García Rocha, A. (1976): "El desarrollo económico reciente en México", in J.W. Wilkie: Contemporary Mexico (Berkeley, University of California).

Hansen, R.D. (1971): The politics of Mexican development (Baltimore, Johns Hopkins Press).

Instituto de Planificación Física (1975): Migraciones internas, 1943-1970 (Cuba).

Lavell, A.M. (1976): "Regional industrialisation in Mexico: Some policy considerations", in Regional Studies, Vol. 6, No. 3.

Moreno Toscano, A. (1972): "Cambios en los patrones de urbanización en México, 1910-1910", in Historia mexicana, Vol. XXII, No. 2.

Moreno Toscano, A. and Florescano, E. (1976): "El sector externo y la organización espacial y regional de México (1521-1910)", in J.W. Wilkie: Contemporary Mexico (Berkeley, University of California).

Muñoz, H., de Oliveira, O. and Stern, C. (eds.) (1977): Migración y desigualdad social en la ciudad de México (México, UNAM and El Colegio de México).

Proceso (Seminario de Información y Análisis) (1976): "Sonora-Sinaloa, las tierras de la ira" and "Valle de Yaqui: el emporio agrícola" (Mexico City, Nov.).

Reyes Osorio, S., et al (1974): Estructura agraria y desarrollo agrícola en México (México, Fondo de Cultura Económia).

Reynolds, C.W. (1970): The Mexican economy, twentieth century: Structure and growth (New Haven, Yale University Press).

Secretaría de Asentamientos y Obras Públicas, Comisión Nacional de Desarrollo Urbano (n.d.): Plan nacional de desarrollo urbano (Mexico City).

Secretaría de Obras Públicas (1975): Caminos y desarrollo, 1925-1975 (Mexico City).

Solís, L. (1970): La realidad económica mexicana: Retrovisión y perspectivas (México,, Siglo XXI).

Stern, C. (1975): "Migraciones a la ciudad de México: Cambios en los volúmenes de migrantes provenientes de distintas zonas geo-económicas", in Cahiers des Ameriques Latines, special number.

--- (1977): The growth of Mexico City: Varying sources of its migrant inflow, 1900-1970, unpublished Ph.D. dissertation (St. Louis, Missouri, Washington University).

Unikel, L. (1976): El desarrollo urbano de México (México, El Colegio de México).

--- (1977): "El problema urbanoregional en México" in Gaceta UNAM, Cuarta Epoca, Vol. III, 9 August supplement.

Urquidi, V.L. (1974): "Empleo y explosión demográfica" in Demografía y Economía, Vol. VIII, No. 2.

Vernon, R. (1963): The dilemma of Mexico's development (Cambridge, Harvard University Press).

Wilkie, J.W. (1970): The Mexican Revolution: Federal expenditure and social change since 1910 (Berkeley, University of California; 2nd edition).

Chapter 7

INDUSTRIALISATION AND URBANISATION IN COLOMBIA

by Alan Simmons and Carol Vlassoff*

I. Introduction

Colombia has recently experienced extremely rapid rural-urban population transfer. Two-thirds of the nation's population now live in towns and cities, compared with only one-third 40 years ago.[1] The sprawl of low-income housing within and around the large cities is a testimony to the speed of recent city growth and to the poverty of many rural-urban migrants. The objective of our paper is to analyse how this massive rural-urban population movement came about and how national development strategies accelerated the urbanisation process. Three types of development policies are considered: policies for industrial expansion, policies for agricultural growth, and policies for regional and intermediate city development.

Our approach to studying urbanisation in Colombia is based on a broad political-economic framework which may be applied to a number of Third World nations. This framework includes the following features common to many developing countries: technological dependency (i.e. a reliance on unprocessed mineral and agricultural export earnings to purchase industrial goods and machinery), the dominant role of national élites in the formulation of agricultural and industrial policies beneficial to their own class interests, and the relatively marginal political and economic status of peasants and low-income urban workers. These features define the context in which Colombia's rapid urbanisation has taken place, and in our view also provide the basic variables for explaining the process itself. The specific mechanisms which motivate

---

* International Development Research Council, Ottawa.

[1] The causes and consequences of this migration have been extensively documented and analysed by SENALDE (Ministry of Labour) in collaboration with the UNDP/ILO project COL/72/027. This study partly relies on the work carried out under this project.

rural-urban migrants, such as lack of access to farm lands, high rural unemployment and the hope of finding a job in the city, are best understood within this broader institutional framework.

We may outline the major elements of our analytic approach to urbanisation in Colombia as follows:

State policies	Distribution of employment and income opportunities	Urbanisation and sectoral transformation of the labour force
a) Agricultural	a) Rural areas	Migration
b) Industrial	b) Urban areas	
c) Regional and urban		

Stated briefly, this approach views urbanisation as a geographical perspective on an economic transformation, in which a large proportion of the labour force leaves agriculture and moves into the urban economy. We argue that this transformation is strongly determined in the Colombian case by state policies influencing the distribution of private investments, employment, incomes and technological choice in agriculture and industry in rural and urban areas. Peasants are expelled from rural areas largely as a result of state policies which favour land consolidation and mechanised agriculture. Migrants take refuge in low-income urban service and commercial employment opportunities which are created by industrialisation policies favouring the concentration of economic investment in cities. The research problems in this paper concern the identification of the state policies which have contributed to this process, and the assessment of their impact on rural labour markets, urban labour markets, and migration. Our model leaves aside the broader issues of Colombian class structure, political organisation, and international market forces which determine the formulation of state policies. These are important issues, but they fall outside the framework of our more focused study.

Given that our analysis is based on a national case study, it is important at the outset to note several features which distinguish Colombia from other nations.[1]

---

[1] Statistical data supporting most points in this paragraph may be found in World Bank (1979, pp. 118-173). For a recent review of the Colombian economy, see Berry (1980).

Colombia is the third most populous nation in Latin America (after Brazil and Mexico). Its urbanisation level is similar to Latin America as a whole, that is, two times the level typical of Africa and South Asia. Average income per capita in Colombia is near the middle of the range for Latin American nations. As in Latin America generally, average income is a very inadequate measure of living standards among the masses, since national wealth is highly concentrated in a minority of élite families. Colombia is heavily dependent for foreign earnings on exports of a single primary commodity (coffee). Foreign exchange for these exports has been sufficient over recent decades to permit Colombia to import manufacturing technology, and the country is now emerging as one of several "intermediate" industrialised nations in the Third World. Within the international system Colombia may be classified as a "dependent" nation in so far as its economy continues to rely heavily on imported technology and earnings from primary exports, but it is clearly less dependent than are poorer nations in Latin America. The entrepreneurial élites of Colombia own a rather high proportion of national industrial and agricultural wealth; direct foreign ownership has been increasing but is still probably low by Third World standards.

This analysis proceeds in three steps. The first section of the chapter describes the process we wish to explain: urbanisation patterns and the associated sectoral transformation of the labour force from agriculture to urban industry and commerce. The second section represents the first step in our explanatory analysis. It examines various state policies which have influenced urbanisation trends, and their associated impact on agricultural and industrial investments. The third section completes the explanatory analysis by examining the shifts in rural and urban employment opportunities and migration patterns associated with the over-all thrust of various state policies.

II. Urbanisation and Sectoral Transformation

1. Urbanisation

Up to the middle of the present century the population of Colombia was predominantly rural. Table 1 shows that in 1938 less than one-third of the population lived in urban areas: by 1951 this proportion had risen to nearly 39 per cent. Only by 1954 did it rise above 50 per cent and by 1973 almost two-thirds of the population was urban.

Urbanisation in Colombia took place under exceedingly high rates of natural population growth (see table 1).

Table 1: Population growth and distribution: Colombia, 1938-73

	1938	1951	1964	1973
Total national population (in 000's)[a]	8,850	11,548	17,485	22,360
Average annual growth in intercensal period (%)	-	2.2	3.2	2.1
Rate of natural increase (%)[b]	-	3.2	3.4	3.2
Crude birth rate[c]	30.9	36.9	45.0	34.0
Crude death rate[d]	16.2	13.2	10.6	9.5
% urban[e]	30.9	38.7	52.8	63.1
% in Bogotá[f]	4.0	6.2	9.8	14.1
Average annual rates of growth (%):				
All urban[g]	4.2	4.0	5.7	4.8
Bogotá[h]	5.4	6.8	6.2	
Medellin[h]	6.1	6.0	4.5	
Cali[h]	8.3	6.3	4.3	
Barranquilla[h]		4.8	4.5	3.6
Other cities over 100,000 population at beginning of intercensal period[h]			5.4	3.6
Cities under 100,000 population at beginning of intercensal period[h]			6.3	2.5
All rural[i]	0.9	2.2	1.2	0.0

Sources to table 1:

[a] 1938 data from Schultz (1969, p. 3); 1951 and 1964 data from Centro de Estudios Urbanos y Regionales (1976); 1973 data from DANE (1977), tables 1-7.

[b] 1951 and 1954 data from Ruddle and Odermann (1972); 1973 data from United Nations, *Statistical Yearbook*, 1973, p. 69.

[c] 1938 and 1951 data from Ruddle and Odermann (1972). Note that 1938 data is based on civil registration and is of dubious reliability. 1964 data from United Nations: *Statistical Yearbook*, 1973, p. 69; 1973 data from United Nations: *Demographic Yearbook*, 1978.

[d] 1938 and 1951 data from Ruddle and Odermann (1972); 1964 data from United Nations: *Statistical Yearbook*, 1973, p. 69; 1973 data from United Nations: *Demographic Yearbook*, 1978.

[e] 1938, 1951 and 1964 estimates based on DANE: *Censo nacional de población*, 1964; 1973 estimates based on DANE (1977), table A.

[f] 1938 data based on Schultz (1969, p. 3); 1951, 1964 and 1973 data from Gilbert (1978, p. 89).

[g] 1938 data from Schultz (1969, p. 3); 1951, 1964 and 1973 estimates based on DANE: *Censo nacional de población*, 1964.

[h] Based on figures in Gilbert (1975, p. 249).

[i] 1938 data from Schultz (1969, p. 3); 1951, 1964 and 1973 estimates based on DANE: *Censo nacional de población*, 1964.

Death rates fell dramatically after the Second World War due to public health measures (vaccination and other related programmes), while fertility remained high or even increased. Throughout this period, the rapid growth of the largest cities came about principally through rural to urban migration. For example, migrants contributed directly to about one-third of the population growth in Bogotá, and indirectly (through their fertility) to an additional one-third (Cardona and Simmons, 1977, p. 82). The remaining third was caused by the natural growth of the native-born urban population.

The migrants moved primarily to existing urban areas, particularly the largest centres. As table 1 shows, the four largest cities of the country - Bogotá, Medellín, Cali and Barranquilla - have been growing very quickly; smaller urban areas have been growing, on average, less quickly. (Not shown in the table is the fact that some smaller cities have been growing faster than the largest ones.) The rural population has been growing least quickly, and in the most recent period, 1964-1973, the rural population remained stable in absolute terms. In recent years, some rural areas have experienced numerical decline in population (Williams and Griffin, 1978). Since the natural increase in rural areas has been at least as high as that for the country as a whole (urban birth rates have been lower, especially since 1964),[1] the difference between national population growth rates and rural population growth rates may be taken as rough indicators of the rate of rural out-migration. By this reckoning, rural out-migration rates have increased and were at their highest level in 1964-1973.

Figure 1 shows how migration toward the largest centres has influenced population distribution in Colombia between 1951 and 1973. The departamentos where the four largest cities are located were, from the beginning, the most densely populated, reflecting historical patterns of colonisation and economic growth. As a result of migration trends, these departamentos experienced accelerated population growth, such that they are now politically, socially and economically more dominant in the national structure than previously. For example, Bogotá's share of the total national population rose from 4 per cent in 1938 to 12 per cent in 1973.

---

[1] World Fertility Survey data indicate that women have an average of 3.9 children, compared to 5.0 children for rural women. The survey also notes a "considerable decline in fertility" in the last 16 years (Corporación Centro Regional de Población, 1979).

FIGURE 1

Population distribution in Colombia

(Scale: equals 50,000 inhabitants)

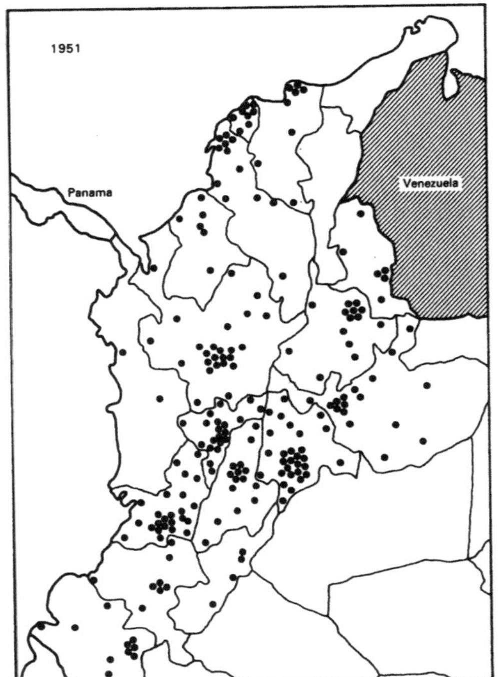

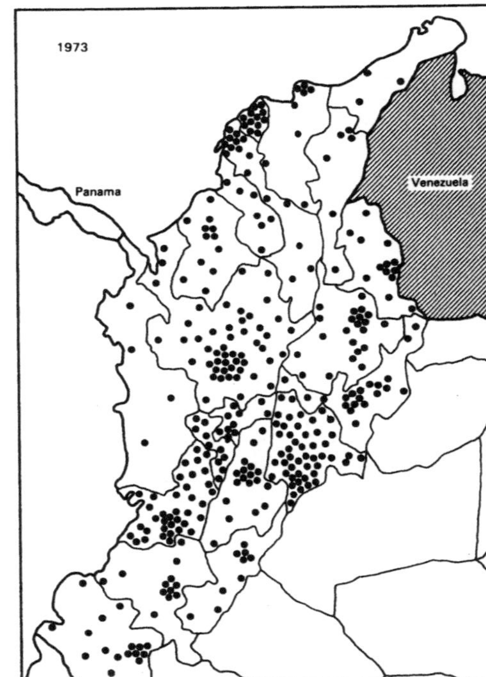

Prior to initiating our analysis of the influence of economic transformation and state policies on urbanisation in Colombia, we may ask: "Is urbanisation in Colombia distinct from other developing nations, particularly those in Latin America?" The following two features do indeed partially distinguish Colombia's urbanisation: (1) Colombia is unusual among Latin American countries in that it has several large cities and an articulated system of intermediate towns and cities. Bogotá, with about 20 per cent of the nation's urban population, is clearly dominant, but not as dominant as are the largest cities in other Latin American countries. Colombia's urban primacy index (a measure of population concentration in a single city) is the lowest among all countries in Latin America except Brazil.[1] (2) Colombia has rather high levels of industrial employment and national income. Generally, countries with higher levels of industrial employment and faster rates of economic growth have higher levels of urbanisation. For most nations one can predict urbanisation quite accurately from a knowledge of levels of industrial employment. If we define IW as the proportion of the total labour force active in the industrial sector and URB as the proportion of the total population living in urban areas, then IW and URB are typically related in the proportion 1:2. That is, a 1 per cent increase in IW is roughly associated with a 2 per cent increase in URB (Preston, 1979, p. 203).

The typical relationship between industrial employment and urbanisation does not hold equally well for all regions of the world. Preston notes that the Latin American pattern deviates considerably in that cities in this region are growing faster than would be predicted on the basis of a 1:2 ratio. To illustrate this point, figure 2 plots IW against URB for selected countries and regions of the world. The nations chosen for comparison in figure 2 are ones which have industrial employment levels similar to those found in Colombia over the period 1950-1970. For most of the developed and developing countries shown, the expected 1:2 ratio is apparent. Some nations which had slightly deviant patterns for 1960 had moved toward the more typical relationship by 1970 (see Republic of Korea and Pakistan). Latin America as a whole has demonstrated a somewhat unusual pattern, with higher than predicted urbanisation levels in 1960 and 1970.

---

[1] The primacy index is the ratio of the population of the nation's largest city to the total urban population of the nation. For national comparison in Latin America, see Renaud (1979, p. 31).

FIGURE 2

Relation between percent urban and percent labour force in industry,
Colombia and select countries with similar levels of industrial employment, 1950-1970.

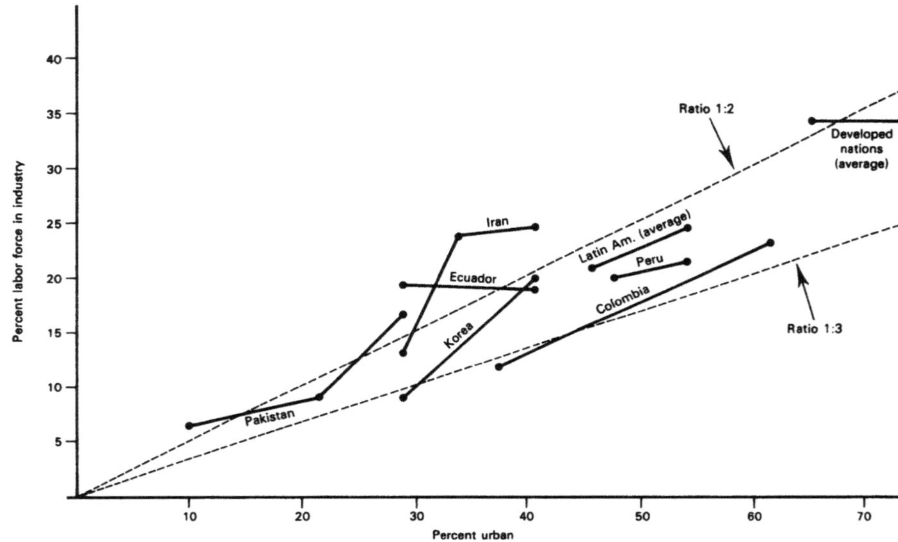

Note: 1) Lines connect points for 1950, 1960 and 1970 for each country or region. Where there are 3 dots the left dot represents 1950, the middle dot, 1960, and the right dot, 1970. Where there are only 2 dots, the dates represented are 1960 and 1970. First dot for Iran represents 1955.

2) Percent labor force in industry differs somewhat from percentages in Table 2 because the present figures refer only to the manufacturing component of the industrial sector.

Sources: Data are from World Bank Tables, (1971): Table 2) and (1976): Tables 2) and 3).

The industrial employment to urban ratio is quite distinct for Colombia in all three periods, 1950, 1960 and 1970. In each case the ratio is approximately 1:3. Ecuador and Peru, two neighbouring Andean nations, show similar patterns but are less extreme. Colombia is therefore unusual, not only in the context of the developed and developing countries outside Latin America, but also within its own region.

Industrial employment and per capita income are generally closely and positively associated in the development process. Nevertheless, it is known that Latin American nations derive a high proportion of their incomes from the export and sale of agricultural goods, forestry products and mineral resources. These primary export sectors have been able to attract large amounts of capital, and labour inputs are often low relative to over-all production. This raises the possibility that high urbanisation in Latin America may be a function of over-all level of per capita income, a large part of which is derived from primary production rather than from manufacturing.

Figure 3 shows that urbanisation levels in Latin America as a whole are higher, at each level of per capita income, than those in other regions of the world. The differences are striking. An increase of $1,000 in GNP per capita is associated with the following percentage increases in urbanisation: 2.9 per cent in developed countries considered together; 5.2 per cent in Africa; 7.4 per cent in Asia; and 17.6 per cent in Latin America as a whole. Since the regression line for Latin America is based on rather divergent national patterns, the association between income and urbanisation in 1978 is shown for a number of individual countries. From this analysis it is apparent that Colombia is one of several Latin American nations with very high levels of urbanisation relative to per capita income. Some of these countries grew economically and urbanised early in the century and subsequently experienced low rates of economic growth (Uruguay and Argentina). Among countries near Colombia's stage of development, only Peru has a similar level of urbanisation; Ecuador and Paraguay have much lower levels.

2. Sectoral transformation

Prior to 1938 economic investment and growth patterns had little impact on industrial and commerical employment, or on urbanisation, since investments were almost entirely in the primary sector (principally agriculture). The first major foreign investment in Colombia in the post-Independence period was during and just after the First World War. Colombia and other countries in

FIGURE 3

Relation between percent urban and GNP/capita

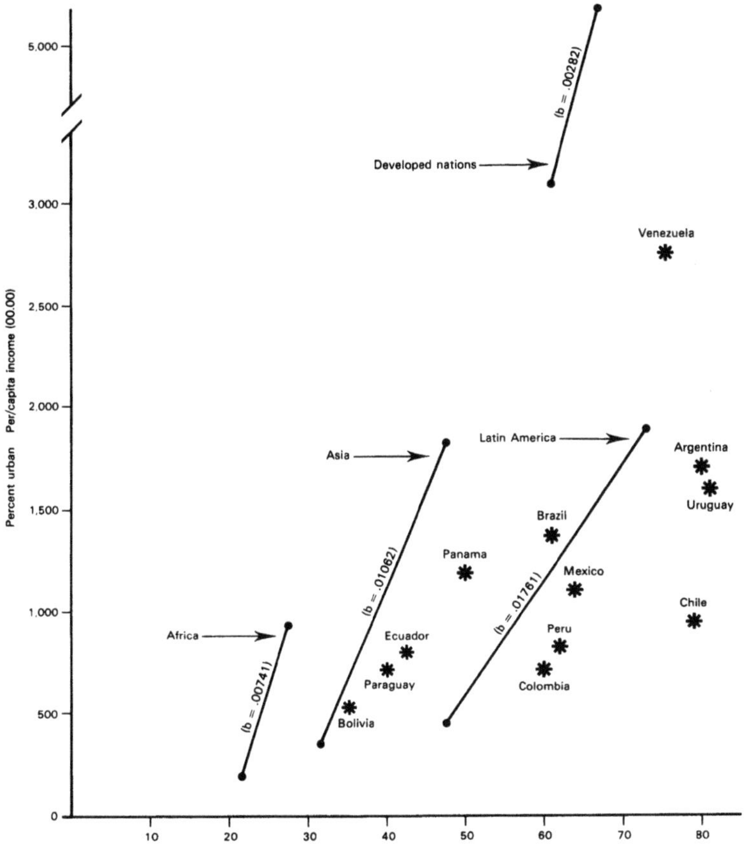

Sources: ENP/capita taken from U.N., Statistical Yearbook, 1978: 749.
Percent living in urban areas from U.N., Demographic Yearbook, 1977: 65-181.
The figures refer to most recent information available, usually mid 1970's.

Table 2: Sectoral shares of labour force, production and productivity: Colombia, 1925-73

	1925	1938	1951	1964	1973
Labour force distribution (%)					
Primary (agriculture)[a]	67.1	65.0	59.0	50.5	30.9
Secondary (manufacturing)[b]	15.7	17.3	16.9	17.7	17.1
Tertiary (services)[c]	17.2	14.6	24.1	31.8	52.0
Total labour force	100.0	100.0	100.0	100.0	100.0
Gross domestic product (%)					
Primary (agriculture)	-	-	38.2	31.6	26.2
Secondary (manufacturing)	-	-	14.8	21.4	24.6
Tertiary (services)	-	-	47.0	47.0	49.2
Total GDP			100.0	100.0	100.0
GDP/worker (index)					
Primary (agriculture)	-	-	.64	.62	.84
Secondary (manufacturing)	-	-	.87	1.20	1.44
Tertiary (services)	-	-	1.94	1.65	.98
Total = Average GDP/worker/all sectors together			100.0	100.0	100.0

Notes to table 2:

(a) The primary sector includes extractive enterprises (mining and forestry) in addition to agriculture, but more than 98 per cent of the labour force within the primary sector is engaged in agriculture (1973 data).

(b) The secondary data includes construction in addition to manufacturing, but in 1973, 77 per cent of all labour engaged in the secondary sector was located within the manufacturing or industrial component.

(c) The tertiary sector is composed of commerce, finance, electricity and gas production, the armed forces, transportation and communications, the liberal professions and domestic services. In 1973 the three largest sub-components of the service sector employment were: commerce and finance together (18 per cent), government (15 per cent), and domestic service (12 per cent). Further details may be found in the sources cited below.

Sources: Labour force data from 1925 to 1964 are from Berry (1978, p. 223); and for 1973 are from World Bank (1976, p. 514). Gross domestic product data are from DANE (1977, table II).

the region experienced an unprecedented demand for raw materials and received considerable external financing to exploit these resources. The proportional increase in the influx of US financial capital between 1913 and 1928 was greater for Colombia than for any other Latin American country (Rippy, 1931, p. 161).

The composition of the Colombian economy showed rather dramatic change during and immediately following the beginning of the Second World War. Table 2 documents the timing and nature of this transformation by examining percentage shares of agriculture, industry and service employment and production over the period 1925 to 1973. The following observations emerge from an analysis of data on these sectoral shares.

(1) In the period 1925-1938, the Colombian economy continued to be dominated by the agricultural sector. The primary sector share of the labour force declined only slightly over the period, from 67.1 per cent in 1925 to 65.0 per cent in 1938. Subsequently, the labour force structure changed dramatically: the proportion in agriculture dropped to 59.0 per cent by 1951 and to 50.0 per cent by 1964. The largest decline has been in the most recent period. By 1973 the proportion of the labour force in agriculture was only 30.9 per cent or less than half of what it had been 35 years earlier.

(2) The rapid decline in the share of agricultural labour since 1938 is matched by an almost identical increase in the share of service sector employment. By 1973 one-half of the national labour force was employed in services. This is an exceptionally high level for a developing nation with a low to moderate per capita income (US$ 710 in 1978). In fact it is higher than levels found in many developed countries: Great Britain in 1961 had 41 per cent of its labour force in the service sector, Canada in 1965 had 49 per cent, and Japan in 1964 had 35 per cent (Kuznets, 1971, pp. 250-253).

(3) In sharp contrast to the rapidly changing sectoral labour force shares of agriculture and services, the share of the secondary sector (mostly composed of manufacturing) has remained constant over time. For the entire period 1925-1973, the proportion of labour in the secondary sector has been in the range of 15 to 17 per cent. Within this sector a progressive shift has taken place from production in small artisan shops to production in larger enterprises. For example, "factory" employment as a proportion of all workers involved in manufacturing may have been as low as 18 per cent in 1938, probably rose to about 40 per cent in 1951, and may have been as high as 49 per cent in 1964.[1] The

[1] These estimates are taken from Berry (1978, pp. 223-224).

capital intensive nature of factory enterprise has led to an expansion of the manufacturing share of the total domestic product which did not require a proportional labour force expansion.

(4) Production per worker has shown divergent trends in the three sectors. Since 1951 production per worker in agriculture has clearly risen, the most notable change taking place in the most recent period.

(5) In recent decades there have been systematic and dramatic increases in the productivity of industrial workers, compared to the productivity in all other sectors. By 1973, the average industrial worker was almost 70 per cent more productive than the average service worker.

(6) Productivity in the service sector has declined rapidly relative to other sectors: in 1973 it was only half of what it had been in 1951. Productivity in services was very high in 1951 relative to both agriculture and industry, with a productivity level almost twice the national average and more than twice that in manufacturing. By 1973 it was only slightly greater than that in agriculture and much below that in manufacturing.

The above trends are consistent with our general understanding of the transformation of the Colombian economy and urbanisation. In earlier periods the service sector was composed of a relatively small number of urban workers, many of whom were involved in established commerce, government and the professions. This relatively small, well paid, urban-based group provided administrative, business and professional services to the nation as a whole. However, around 1951 the service sector began to undergo a fundamental internal transformation. Agricultural workers drifting into the cities were unable to secure employment in the manufacturing sector; hence the majority were obliged to sustain themselves by providing "informal" services (domestic work, transportation, traditional "artisanal" industry, petty commerce, and so on). Average income (as reflected in average productivity) in the service sector plunged as its composition changed.

The changing sectoral composition of the Colombian economy clearly correlates with urbanisation over time, yet does not fully explain it. The driving forces behind these two interdependent processes were international markets and the way in which the state in Colombia responded to them, favouring particular kinds of agricultural and industrial production. In the following sections we focus on the role of state policies in this process.

III. State Policies

We may broadly distinguish three historical periods of policy formulation in Colombia.[1] The "early" period began in 1819 and ended around 1930. During this period Colombia established the framework of an élite-dominated capitalist development which set the stage for subsequent patterns of sectoral change and urbanisation. The "middle" or "transition" period, from 1930 to 1960, was characterised by a continuing consolidation of élite-controlled free enterprise, and by increasing direct government promotion of programmes to encourage particular kinds of technological innovation in private industry and agriculture. These policies accelerated sectoral transformation and urbanisation processes. The strongest policy initiatives were introduced after 1960, and it is this "recent" period which is of primary concern in our analysis. A brief introduction to the over-all development strategy emerging in the early and transition periods will clarify the context in which these recent policies were developed.

1. Over-all development strategy

Colombia's political economy has been uncompromisingly structured around the principles of private property and a "free" competitive marketplace. Elements of Colombia's colonial heritage, particularly the overwhelming concentration of power in the hands of two competing

---

[1] These time periods ignore the colonial era (up to 1819 when Colombia broke from Spain) and the immediate post-colonial era (1819 to 1849) when the internal economic structure remained largely unchanged. Kline fixes 1849 as the date in which Liberal and Conservative Parties were formed, and the starting point for a series of legislative reforms designed to integrate Colombia into the international capitalist economy (Kline, 1980, p. 60). From the perspective of political history, the next key date was 1902, when the "Thousand Days War" ended and Liberals and Conservatives began to restrict disagreements to the political sphere. From an economic view, however, the next significant stage began in the 1930s and 1940s when the state began to intervene more directly in fostering technical innovations favourable to an élite-dominated capitalist growth strategy. The next major political and economic watershed was 1958 when Conservatives and Liberals began open, full co-operation to devise and implement agricultural and industrial growth strategies.

élites, strongly influenced how these principles came to be applied. After breaking with Spanish rule, Colombia initiated a series of legislative reforms designed to "free" land, labour and capital from the constraints of the colonial economy. These reforms included the elimination of censos (church monopolies on the control and rent of lands), the abolition of resguardos (reservations where an Indian poor pool was held and made accessible to a limited clientele), and the cancellation of a complex web of taxes which had been central to the survival of the colonial system but which tended to greatly restrict the flow of goods and services.[1] These reforms were not brought about easily. Colombian history up to the "Thousand Days War", which ended in 1902, was structured around the often violent conflict between conservative and liberal élites. The conservatives were largely tied to land and church, and threatened by free trade and urban commercial development. The liberals favoured free trade and urban commerce, while they simultaneously sought to limit the powers of the church and the landed classes.

After 1902 the conflict between conservatives and liberals was largely restricted to the political arena. Over time the divergence in political perspective was diminished, as élites in both political parties began to share a wider range of common economic and class interests. Faced with insurgency and populist political movements in the 1950s, the conservatives and liberals formed a series of four "United Front" governments (from 1958 to 1974) in which power was shared and the presidency was rotated from one party to the other at four year intervals (Kline, 1980; Dix, 1967). As a result of this political evolution, Colombia has exhibited a distinctive approach to economic planning and state intervention in development. It is capitalistic in nature, and favours the economic interests of a national élite which shares agricultural and urban-commercial property interests and which has been able to largely retain political and economic power for itself.

Colombia's development strategy broadly explains several key features of its sectoral transformation and urbanisation since 1930. Over this period, the élite did not seek to create intermediate-sized "family farms", and modernise them in order to raise agricultural productivity. This would have required a redistribution of land and capital. Instead, pursuing their self interest in a capitalist economy where they controlled investment, the élites modernised and expanded their large farms. Similarly,

---

[1] See Tirado-Mejia (1972) and McGreevey (1971) for the evolution of the early Colombian economy.

in the field of manufacturing, national entrepreneurs saw the disadvantages of using their capital (and loans from abroad) to import technologically efficient industrial machinery capable of competing in international markets and locally, with only modest protective tariffs. Agricultural investments, in the context of rapid population growth, created a large rural labour surplus; related industrial investment led to "spin-off" demand for construction, transportation and commercial services such that a large portion of rural labour transferred to towns and cities. Since labour productivity in these services was low and labour plentiful, wages for unskilled migrant labour remained low. These aspects of Colombia's urban history are shared by a large number of countries in Latin America, and may be repeating themselves elsewhere in the Third World.

Our focus in this chapter is on specific state policies which since about 1960 have accelerated the urbanisation process. These specific policies may be considered as logical extensions of the nation's development strategy. These policies are to be found in three planning sectors: industrial, agricultural, and regional development.

2. Industrial development

The first two National Front governments (1958-1962; 1962-1966) were faced with a series of economic development problems stemming from the low world price for coffee and the shortage of foreign earnings with which to import capital goods for industrial growth to meet consumer demand. Several policies established in this period were designed to overcome these barriers to economic growth by encouraging national production of manufactured goods, and thereby gradually reducing the need for imports. Among the steps taken were the following (see Poveda-Ramos, 1979; Rocha and Arboleda, 1979):

(1) The Instituto de Fomento Industrial (IFI), which had been created in 1941, was given substantially increased financial support to extend credit to entrepreneurs wishing to purchase new industrial technology. Total credits extended by the IFI rose from $35 million in 1958 to $2,157 million in 1969, and $5,935 million in 1972.

(2) Faced with inadequate national funds for investment, the government began to seek loans from international banking sources. In the 1960s Colombia had one of the highest levels of foreign assistance in per capita terms in the world. More than US$ 200 million flowed into Colombia annually. The most important part of this aid was infrastructure and capital investment beneficial to industrial development. Credit from the World Bank and

the United States Agency for International Development were intended to make Colombia one of the showcases for the Alliance for Progress.

(3) In 1959, Decree 1345 provided increased tariff protection for industrial capital goods and intermediate manufactured goods produced in Colombia. The protections applied to the manufacture of paper, iron, glass, electrical equipment, fertilisers, synthetic fibres and other high technology products. Duties were adjusted periodically. A World Bank review at the end of the 1960s observed that "tariffs for Colombian manufacturing are relatively high" (World Bank, 1972, p. 13). Duties on intermediate industrial goods averaged 28 per cent, while those on consumer durables averaged 50 per cent.

(4) Probably the most important instrument for effecting technological change in Colombian manufacturing was Law 81 of 1960 (Poveda-Ramos, 1979, p. 103). It gave industrial tax exemptions and write-offs for up to 10 years for investments in a wide variety of heavy and high technology industries (iron, petrochemicals, synthetic resins, acids, machine tools, electrical equipment, etc.). It also provided tax incentives for exports of these products. The intent of the policy was to expand import substitution beyond consumer durables to include "intermediate" industrial products which served as inputs to the manufacture of consumer goods.

(5) The above policies were reinforced by efforts to stabilise international exchange rates and thereby assist exporters; to provide information, reduced credit and facilitate international financing for exports (the creation of the Export Promotion Fund, PROEXPO, in 1967); to protect high technology manufacturing (Decree 3168 of 1965); to open up industrial trade with neighbouring countries (the Cartagena Agreement of 1969 and the formation of the Andean Pact). Thus, two sets of policies were pursued at the same time: those that would protect national industry (and reduce imports), and those that would promote exports. The common objective was to improve Colombia's balance of payments, and to reduce the need to borrow foreign capital.

(6) A number of relatively minor programmes were established to provide credit to smaller, more labour-intensive industries (Rocha and Arboleda, 1979, Part V). Some of the IFI funds, particularly those advanced from the Inter-American Development Bank after 1969, were specified for small and intermediate-sized manufacturing plants. Another initiative was the establishment in 1967 of the Corporación Financiera Popular (CFP) with a credit line to the central bank. Its stated criteria for granting credit included its potential impact on employment, import substitution and exports. The latter two objectives are

often in conflict with the first. Industries which are sufficiently productive to compete with international markets or to replace imports are frequently equipped with the most modern technology available and hence have only a modest impact on employment. Not surprisingly, in the early and mid-1970s the CFP granted in excess of 80 per cent of its credit to high technology manufacturing in textiles, metal products and related areas (ibid.)

The vigour and orientation of the industrial development policies described above had a strong influence on manufacturing structure and growth in Colombia. There was considerable product diversification during the 1960s and 1970s. Growth of over-all industrial production, however, remained linked to world coffee prices and the state of the Colombian economy in general.[1] As a result, industrial production grew slowly during the early 1960s when coffee prices were low, and increased in the late 1960s when coffee prices rose. Further growth took place in the early 1970s and was carried even further by the "bonanza" in world coffee prices in 1975 resulting from frost in Brazil and the destruction of its harvest. Over the 1960-1977 period, Colombia's total production (GNP) grew rapidly, at around 5.7 per cent per year - a level roughly comparable with other "middle income" countries in the world which for the most part also experienced rapid economic growth (World Bank, 1979, p. 128). From 1970 to 1977 manufacturing grew at 7.5 per cent annually. This level of growth was approximately two times greater than that experienced by the industrialised nations over the same period, but was again not exceptional among "middle income", industrialising nations in the Third World.

The over-all thrust of industrial policy in Colombia in the past two decades has unequivocally given strong support to larger, capital intensive enterprises relying on high technology and low labour inputs. This is evident, for example, in the growth of output in different sized firms between 1960 and 1967 (World Bank, 1972, p. 106):

Size of firm	Annual growth rate (%)
5-15 workers	3.2
15-29 workers	4.7
100-199 workers	6.7
200 or more workers	7.0

[1] Over the past two decades, coffee has accounted for about one-third of Colombia's agricultural production and two-thirds of its merchandise exports. For a recent study of the effects of changing world coffee prices on inflation and economic growth in Colombia, see Ridler (1980, pp. 1-16).

Over the same period high technology manufacturing grew very quickly in comparison with low technology manufacturing. Food processing (low technology) grew at 5.2 per cent annually while pharmaceuticals grew at 10.5 per cent, electrical appliances at 12.5 per cent, paper products at 14 per cent, and chemical products at 21 per cent (ibid., p. 108).

The growth of high technology, large-scale manufacturing has tended to reinforce élite prosperity interests in Colombia. This can be inferred in part from the lower labour absorption of these industries and from patterns of industrial ownership. A capital-intensive enterprise by definition gives a higher return to those who own or control the machinery (in terms of interests on loans or return on investment) and a lower return to labour (wages constitute a small part of production costs). Of the 10,803 manufacturing establishments in Colombia in 1967, nearly 80 per cent were small, employing less than 20 workers each. These were concentrated in low productivity industries such as furniture, food and clothing, and were owned by individuals (owner-managers). It may be assumed that these owners had modest incomes. In contrast, only 10 per cent of the firms were large, employing 50 workers or more. These included the high technology industries, most of which were controlled by corporations, whose profits flowed back to wealthy investors capable of financing up to 50 per cent of new investments from internal profits. The smaller firms, by contrast, were forced to borrow nearly all their new capital (ibid., p. 113).

3. Agricultural development

After 1960 the Colombian Government gave somewhat greater attention to supporting agriculture. Total government supports to agriculture averaged about 1.5 per cent of the national budget during the 1950s and subsequently rose to about twice this level (Berry, Hellman and Soloun, 1980). This is a rather modest expenditure for a nation which obtains 80 per cent of its foreign exchange from coffee. Similarly, the various policy initiatives to support agriculture were less vigorous in this period than policies to support industry.

There are two possible reasons for this less intensive activity. Firstly, total Colombian earnings from coffee sales have depended more on variations (often very wide) in the world price than in the quantity produced. This has been especially true in recent years where the amount Colombia can sell is fixed by international agreement between producing countries. Colombia has had no difficulty producing its limit. Secondly, international and local market forces operating within the framework of Colombia's free enterprise economy have been expanding and diversifying the production of a number of important commercial crops. Credit through private banking sources has seemed generally adequate.

New government agricultural policies implemented in the 1960s, and still in effect in rural areas, were partially concerned with assisting the growth of commercial agriculture. However, they were equally concerned about the political and social implications of rural poverty and stagnant or declining economic prospects for small farmers. Upon taking office in 1958 the first National Front government faced a list of agrarian problems rather typical of the Latin American region. Land concentration was increasing, the average size of peasant holdings was declining, significant tracts of productive land on large holdings and in frontier areas were not being farmed, the pool of landless rural labour was growing, and productivity on peasant holdings was low. These trends were regarded as threatening to the stability of the political system and, indirectly, as a cause of the wave of political and class violence which swept Colombia from 1948 through the mid-1950s. Several steps were taken to counter these trends:[1]

(1) In 1961 the government established INCORA, a national agrarian reform institute, and assigned it the task of assisting the farm sector by adjudicating land claims, purchasing and expropriating land, redistributing land, providing technical extension services to farms, co-ordinating agricultural infrastructure (electrification, irrigation) and facilitating credit to small farmers.

(2) In the same year, the government established the Caja Agraria, a major rural credit institution, with the specific purpose of making credit available to small farmers who did not qualify for commercial bank loans. These initial efforts were later supplemented by policies to encourage private agricultural investment (e.g. Law 5 of 1973 gave tax deductions to encourage select kinds of investment). The central bank also requires that commercial banks advance a certain proportion of their overall credit to agriculture. For example, 15 per cent of all commercial bank credit was to go to livestock production. This actually created an excess of credit in the primary sector, and some funds normally borrowed for agricultural investment were apparently diverted into higher-interest urban construction and manufacturing.

---

[1] For previous and more detailed documentation in agrarian policies in Colombia, see Havens, Flinn and Cornhill (1980); World Bank (1972, Chapters 7 and 18); and Junquito et al (1975).

(3) During the 1960s a number of overlapping policies were introduced to encourage agricultural exports and national self-sufficiency in food. These were part of a broad policy designed to overcome balance of payment problems through a combination of measures affecting both agriculture and industry. Many elements in this strategy are summarised in Decree 444 of 1967. In addition to the credits, market information and tax breaks (available to agricultural exporters as well as industrial exporters), Colombia curtailed the imports of both processed and unprocessed foodstuffs.

Taken together, these agrarian policies have undoubtedly accelerated farm modernisation in Colombia. However, they did not reverse many of the trends which initially prompted action: land concentration continued, the proportion of landless labour continued to rise, and peasant productivity and technical innovation remained low. Larger farmers and agro-business continued to consolidate their positions. The reforms intended to benefit small farmers were not sufficiently strong; they were implemented in ways that benefited larger farmers as much or more than they benefited small farmers.

Consider these specific points:[1]

(1) The more radical features of INCORA's mandate, namely land expropriation and redistribution, failed due to lack of broad political support and strong opposition by landowners. As a result of these problems, less than 2 per cent of the land INCORA has acquired since its creation has come through expropriation. By 1970, after almost 10 years of INCORA effort, only between 1 and 2 per cent of all farm families in Colombia were resident on lands received from INCORA.

(2) The Caja's loans to the small landowners have been frequently used to manage short-term deficits for household consumption rather than for improved technology.

(3) Technical choice in agriculture fostered by INCORA and funded by the Caja seems to have benefited small farmers, but it may have benefited large-scale farmers even more, since they had the "risk capital" to try innovations.

(4) Tax incentive legislation appears to have solely benefited large commercial producers, in part because the legislation required large investment in order to be eligible for tax deductions.

---

[1] The following points summarise observations from previous reviews, described in footnote 1 on page 228.

We may conclude that the agricultural development legislation introduced since 1960 has had a very mixed effect on income opportunities for small farmers. The major determinants of land consolidation and technical innovation in farming which displaced rural labour were well underway prior to 1960 as an outgrowth of Colombia's broader development strategy; they continued after the specific agricultural development legislation was introduced. One can only conjecture about the net effect of the legislation. Our judgement, based on the evidence we have reviewed, suggests that it accelerated rural land concentration and out-migration.

4. Urban and regional policies

Approximately 80 per cent of manufacturing in Colombia is found within or adjacent to the nation's four largest cities: Bogotá, Medellin, Cali, and Barranquilla (Gilbert, 1974, pp. 425-467; idem, 1975, pp. 241-71). The nation's skilled labour force, industrial infrastructure, and credit and banking facilities are also concentrated in these cities. In the 1960s and 1970s, concern over the high concentration of national wealth in a few cities and widespread poverty and economic stagnation elsewhere, led to the formulation of various policies intended to encourage industrial decentralisation as a key to more balanced regional development and intermediate city growth. The government also invested heavily in communications and transport infrastructure in less developed regions of the nation. One stated objective in national planning was to encourage a reduction in population concentration and congestion in the largest cities (ibid.)

A simple reading of the policies formulated might lead one to believe that vigorous action in favour of urban decentralisation was in progress. A more careful reading, however, leads to a different conclusion: some decentralisation policies had major loopholes which limited their effectiveness; others had an urban concentration bias; and many were weakly implemented. The following points outline problems with the major regional policies.

(1) In 1968 the central bank created the Fondo Financiero Industrial (FFI) to finance small and medium-sized industry and decentralise credit to smaller cities. An 80 per cent discount was given to small manufacturing investments in cities of less than 900,000 inhabitants, and a 65 per cent discount to similar industries in larger cities. The small discount difference between small and large urban locations was not great enough to influence investors, and nearly all the FFI's funds went to high technology manufacturing, predominantly in the large cities.

(2) During the Michelsen presidency (1974-1978) import licences for machinery and intermediate industrial goods were controlled to favour companies which showed a willingness to invest in increased production outside major cities (Rocha and Arboleda, 1972, p. 147, table 22). However, the legislators exempted industries which exported at least 50 per cent of their production and those which would face high transportation costs if they were located away from their major urban markets. Industrial establishments falling into the two exempt classes constituted only 13 per cent of all firms, yet these were the very largest firms, contributing 80 per cent of all value added in industry. In 1977, one year after the legislation was enacted, the Import Licencing Board approved 136 projects for a value of US$ 210 million in order to permit industries to import new machinery. Of this 71 per cent went to the three departments in which Colombia's largest cities (Bogotá, Cali, Medellin) are located (Gilbert, 1975, p. 262).

(3) During the Pastrana presidency (1970-1974) a series of inter-related development goals were proposed under the title "the four strategies" (Lubell and McCallum, 1978, pp. 13-17). The plan recognised the necessity of slowing rural out-migration through agricultural reform, and the need for encouraging intermediate city development. But it also argued that the national economy could be stimulated by providing increased credit for urban housing construction. This strategy was to have three major benefits: it would stimulate a demand for a wide range of construction materials and services; it would create employment for less skilled workers; and by upgrading over-all housing levels it would make improved habitats available for the poor. The plan was implemented and did have a significant impact on urban housing construction, particularly in Bogotá, for about two years. However, it was also judged to have contributed to high inflation and the programme was cut back after 1974. If it had any effect on urbanisation at all, it probably favoured increased concentration in Bogotá. Other strategies in the programme designed to hold farmers on the land and direct migrants to intermediate cities were weakly implemented and had no measurable effects.

(4) Toward the end of the 1960s, the Colombian government shifted its own spending on social and economic infrastructure to favour less developed regions. From 1964 to 1969, there was a tendency for the wealthier departments to receive higher per capita government grants. But from 1969 to 1974 less developed regions received more.[1] This was particularly reflected in supports to industrial and commercial infrastructure.

However, it is not entirely clear what the impact of investments in roads, electricity systems, communications and related infrastructure has been on urban concentration. On the one hand, such investments increase the possibility of employment generating enterprises in the poor regions. On the other, they integrate poor regions into a national market, facilitating the further concentration of industry in the largest cities.

The above discussion indicates that government policy has indeed been conscious of urbanisation pressures in Colombia. None the less, the major policies have focused on the development of manufacturing and construction in existing cities, and on infrastructure and credit to benefit large-scale farmers. The net effects have been to reinforce existing trends towards greater population and economic concentration, in spite of stated objectives to slow these processes.

IV. Employment and Income Opportunities

This section briefly analyses the socio-economic linkages between state policies and urbanisation. Our assumption is that agricultural, industrial and regional policies were instrumental in creating a gap between rural and urban areas with regard to income and employment opportunities. Since the various state policies which helped create this gap were operating simultaneously and had overlapping impacts, it is not possible to precisely separate the effects of each policy. We therefore focus on the available evidence concerning the structure of the rural labour and urban labour markets as they responded to various state policies, investment patterns and the migration of workers from rural to urban areas. We also examine very briefly the relationship between shifting patterns of regional economic opportunity associated with urbanisation and inter-regional migration patterns.

1. Rural labour markets

Our concern here is with the impact of agricultural policies on income and employment opportunities for peasants, small farmers and landless rural labour. As we have noted in the policy analysis section, Colombia's over-all development strategy facilitated the expansion of

---

[1] See Leon and Richter (1979, pp. 2197-2208). Unfortunately, their findings are based on an analysis in which they were able to identify the region of destination for only about two-thirds of government expenditure, hence their findings require further verification.

large-scale commercial farming, and specific agricultural "reform" policies introduced in the past two decades seem to have had little or no impact in moderating the negative effects of this expansion on peasants and small farmers. Large numbers of workers consequently left rural areas. We may therefore ask: "Did those small farmers, peasants and workers who remained in rural areas suffer declines in economic opportunity? Or did out-migration of surplus labour and rising productivity on larger farms keep incomes stable or even rising among these poor rural classes?"

Unfortunately, there are no adequate data on rural unemployment and incomes in Colombia over time: there are only partial data on land tenure and wage levels in rural areas. We have therefore made a review of the evolution of the rural labour market on the basis of partial information.

From 1950 to 1960 modern large scale agriculture was expanding, particularly in some regions (Valle de Cauca, Tolima, etc.) and in relation to some crops (sugar, rice, cotton). The encroachment of large commercial farms on land and production, formerly in peasant hands, has been well documented in several regional case studies. For example, Taussig notes that between 1950 and 1958 in the Cauca Valley, cocoa production fell by 80 per cent and sugar production increased dramatically (Taussig, 1978, pp. 62-90). Cocoa is largely a labour-intensive peasant crop, while sugar is a large-scale commercial farm crop, utilising modern machinery and seasonal wage labour. Over this period, the rural population continued to grow (natural population increase was greater than out-migration), and the twin processes of land consolidation and population growth led to a continuing decline in the size of the average small farm.

In Colombia as a whole, the average small farm size declined from 1.84 hectares in 1954 to 1.64 hectares in 1960. In specific areas such as the Cauca Valley, the declines appear to have been much greater. In this period, the landless labour force (i.e. workers dependent entirely on wages) was small, but presumably increasing rapidly. Most of the labour on large farms was provided by peasant households whose incomes were derived from a combination of seasonal wage employment, cash crop farming and subsistence production. No precise data on the total income and level of unemployment for these peasant families are available. Presumably, increasing wage labour opportunities compensated in part for loss of land and income from subsistence and market production. But the over-all impression is that rural peasant and small farm incomes were stagnant; they may have decreased, and they almost certainly did not increase.

In the 1960s rural labour markets underwent significant changes. Out-migration became so great that the rural population as a whole stopped growing.[1] It appears that the further subdivision of marginal peasant holdings came to an end, such that average small farm size (already very reduced) did not change (Junquito et al, 1975, table 1-4). Most significantly, however, a much larger proportion of the rural labour force became landless, hence dependent entirely on wage labour. From 1960 to 1970 the number of landless farm families increased from 85,000 to 190,000, despite the fact that there was massive out-migration (ibid.). Rural wages appear to have changed very little over this period, suggesting that over-all incomes in rural areas also remained largely constant for the peasants and small farmers, whose seasonal wage labour continued to be important on the commercial farms. The following figures show estimates of average agricultural wages in this period (World Bank, 1972, p. 30):

Year	Real wages in agriculture (1960 = 100)
1960	100.0
1961	103.3
1962	113.1
1963	112.3
1964	115.0
1965	115.8
1966	114.3
1967	111.3

We may provisionally conclude that from 1950 to the present there was an enormous contraction in economic opportunity for small farmers, peasants and landless labour in rural areas. The extent to which incomes of peasants, small farmers and landless workers declined in this process is difficult to evaluate with the evidence at hand. The partial evidence available suggests that incomes in these groups, already very low, did not fall. Rather they remained stable. This can only be explained by the high and sustained out-migration of labour from the rural sector over this period. Faced with almost certain income declines, this "excess" rural labour moved to urban areas. In so doing, it prevented forced declines in average small farm size, and rural wages remained low but stable. Thus, the evolution of

---

1 See table 1 of this chapter.

the urban labour market which permitted the exodus becomes a central element in understanding the over-all process.

2. The urban labour market

We turn now to the impact of industrial and urban-regional policies on urban labour markets. As we have noted in the policy analysis section, Colombia's industrial policy and even several important elements of urban and regional policy have tended to strongly reinforce the growth of high-technology, large-scale manufacturing in the largest cities of the country. We may therefore ask: "Did urban wages fall as large numbers of migrants moved to the cities and were unable to find employment in high-productivity enterprise? Or did modern industry provide sufficient "spin-off" employment in the service sector to keep wages from falling and unemployment from rising?"

There is no doubt that capital-intensive industry directly benefited the workers and salaried employees in this sector. Consider the following estimates of increases in real wages for workers in its industrial sector over the 1960s (ibid.).

	Real wages in industry (1960 = 100)	
Year	Employees (salaries)	Workers (wages)
1960	100.0	100.0
1961	123.0	120.9
1962	129.2	133.2
1963	127.7	145.4
1964	125.7	140.6
1965	129.8	145.7
1966	127.2	142.0
1967	130.8	145.0
1968	134.9	148.9

While agricultural workers' wages improved by at most 11.3 per cent[1] over the period (see previous chart), industrial workers' salaries increased by almost 50 per cent.

There are no adequate time-trend data on the evolution of urban incomes for workers in all sectors, but the situation in 1973 is perhaps representative of wage differentials by skill level. The modal category of educational achievement in rural areas is "some primary schooling completed". This is probably also the modal

1 See the data in previous subsection.

educational category for urban service workers. Rural workers with this level of schooling earned only about half as much as urban workers with the same level of schooling. Less pronounced but still significant differences were evident for other skill levels, as the following data indicate.

Worker incomes, 1972

Mean monthly income in 1973 pesos

Education	Rural	Urban	Difference (%)
None	463	688	48
Primary	543	1053	93
Secondary	1066	2158	50
Higher	5330	6520	22

Source: Fields and Schultz (1980), table 2.

Rural income in the previous table is undoubtedly underestimated because the data shown do not take into account the value of food and other goods which rural households produce for their own consumption. More precise data indicate that real income differentials between rural and urban areas in Colombia have been closer to 15 to 20 per cent for unskilled workers over the period of our analysis. For example, a comparison of the basic agricultural wage in the regions adjacent to Bogotá with the wages for unskilled construction workers in Bogotá over time reveals that since the 1950s the urban workers have benefited from salaries up to 20 per cent higher, although in some years the differences were less.

A number of studies have shown that low-income urban workers, the majority of whom are of rural origin, tend to improve their incomes over time in Colombia. While there is relatively little mobility in Colombia from manual to non-manual jobs, there is a tendency for greater experience to be associated with an increase in responsibilities and skill levels within the manual category (Cardona and Simmons, 1977, Chapter 5). Income levels also rise over time as these workers gain more experience (Kugler, Reyes and de Gomez, 1979).

Unemployment data in Colombia are available only for the larger urban centres. These data may be briefly summarised as follows:[1]

---

[1] The findings reported below are extracted from fuller documentation in Lubell and McCallum (1978, Chapter 7); Mohan (1979, Chapter V); and World Bank (1972, p. 7).

(1) Open unemployment (defined as individuals of working age without a job and looking for work) has been relatively high in Colombian cities, ranging between 7.1 per cent and 12.2 per cent (average annual rates) between 1963 and 1976.

(2) Unemployment rates for males are generally about 20 per cent lower than those for females, and rates are much higher for young workers. A 1974 survey found that among men in the prime working ages (25 to 64 years) open unemployment was less than 5 per cent.

(3) "Underemployment" (defined as individuals working less than 32 hours per week who would like to work more) in urban areas has generally been low, in the range of 2 per cent.

(4) While not all surveys provide the same picture, the largest city in the nation (Bogotá), where industrial growth has been most heavily concentrated, generally has had lower rates of unemployment than other cities such as Medellín and Cali. From 1973 to 1977, unemployment in Bogotá was in the range of 6.3 to 8.3 per cent, while in Medellín the rates were between 13.7 and 13.9 per cent.

(5) Finally, a 1977 survey indicated that a disproportionately large number of the underemployed were professional and technical workers. In fact about 30 per cent of the underemployed were found in these groups, even though they represented a far smaller proportion of the total labour force (about 8.2 per cent). The poor, by contrast, have had to find additional work, even if poorly paid.

(6) The above data ignore, of course, "disguised unemployment" (defined as unemployed workers who are not looking for work, but who would do so if jobs were available or if salaries were higher). It is simply too difficult to estimate levels of disguised unemployment. We can only guess that in Bogotá it is not particularly important among male workers over age 25, since extremely high proportions of those in this group who are eligible to work are actually employed. It may be a more important problem for younger workers and for women, as the following data indicate:

Proportions in employment, by age and sex: Bogotá, 1977

Age group	Per cent of the age group who are employed: Males	Females
15-19	39	37
20-24	68	59
25-29	93	62
30-34	98	53
35-39	98	43
40-44	97	18
45-49	97	39
50-54	95	33
55-59	82	16
60-64	71	16

Source: Lubell and McCallum (1978), table 3.17.

A recent detailed analysis of the urban labour market in Colombia concludes that the major source of widespread urban poverty is not unemployment, or even under-employment, but very low wages among those who are working. Moreover, the low wages are not restricted to people with truly marginal occupations (such as street-corner vendors) who in any case represent only a small proportion of the total labour force. Rather, they predominate in the major categories of employment, in services, small "traditional" manufacturing, and commerce. For example, about one-quarter of all workers are involved in manufacturing, and these are among the lower-paid groups. "The only groups paid significantly less than production workers are construction workers and domestic servants. Among women, even maids are paid higher than production workers. Sales workers earn almost one and a half times as much as production workers." (Mohan, 1979, p. 90). The low wages are a product, in part, of low productivity. But low productivity results from a distribution of income and investments favouring very high-technology enterprises which neglect the improvement of productivity in sectors where a larger number of workers might benefit.

We can tentatively conclude from the above that in the Colombian case, industrial and commercial development strategies have been sufficiently effective in urban job creation to prevent wages from falling, even during recent periods of exceedingly rapid rural-urban migration. In fact, urban wages appear to have risen slightly:

migrants who have spent longer in the city appear to have benefited from some upward mobility. State policies which pursued industrial development with greater labour force participation in high productivity enterprises would have spread the income effects of economic growth much more. However, existing policies at least did not lead to a deterioration of economic circumstances among the poor.

V. Migration

The final question concerns the relationship between labour markets and migration. Are rural-urban wage and employment differentials important determinants of rural-urban migration? To what extent do other factors, particularly land concentration, also contribute to this process?

At least for recent years it would appear that migration patterns in Colombia are closely correlated with regional differences in wages and unemployment. Land tenure patterns also appear to be significant, at least for the period prior to 1964. Support for these assertions is partial, resting on the results from previous studies and a re-analysis of census data for 1964 and 1973.

Fields noted that lifetime migration rates calculated for each of the departments of Colombia (using 1973 census data) are positively correlated with average income per capita levels in these departments (Fields, 1979, pp. 247-265). High income levels explain 48 per cent of the variance in lifetime migration rates. Unemployment rates and average income levels of departments in Colombia explain 54 per cent of the variance in lifetime migration. The departments with higher income levels were of course those with large cities, and most interdepartmental lifetime migrants in these departments resided in urban areas.

Shaw has taken a different approach to migration in Colombia. He hypothesised that out-migration rates for each of Colombia's departamentos over the period 1951-1964 would be associated with land tenure structure (Shaw, 1976, pp. 98-99). He found that when population growth and land concentration together reduced the amount of land available to an average small farmer, out-migration rates were higher. While the number of departments in this early analysis is small (nine cases) his simple regression explains 62 per cent of the variance in departamento out-migration rates over this period.

Fields' and Shaw's results are not necessarily contradictory. Land tenure patterns may be an important determinant of low income and high unemployment in a given department. Also, Shaw's results refer exclusively to the period 1951-1964, while Fields' study incorporated a larger time span, including the numerically significant migration for the period 1964-1973. Given that industrial production has become more significant in Colombia in recent years, it is possible that large differences in wealth between regions resulting from industrial expansion have only become significant determinants of out-migration relatively recently. Previously, land tenure patterns may have had a more decisive role to play. We were not able to test this hypothesis directly, but the following indirect evidence from a re-analysis of available census data is at least consistent with this hypothesis.

Rural-urban migration may be regarded as a function of three sets of variables: rising industrial and urban commercial activity, increased income, and a number of social-institutional factors, such as farm land availability. We sought to measure these variables and examine recent temporal changes in the prediction of rural-urban migration. For this purpose rural-urban migration was measured indirectly by the level of urbanisation in each department of the nation. The growth of urban commerce and industry was measured by the sectoral share of each department, and institutional and other determinants of migration were measured indirectly through net lifetime migration into or out of the department. This proxy variable for institutional and other unmeasured determinants of the repulsive or attractive character of a department was entered into a regression analysis after the effects of the previous variables had been accounted for. The results are shown in table 3.

Our model is tested cross-sectionally with data at two points in time: 1964 and 1973. The over-all variance explained is equally good for both periods, but the proportion of variance accounted for by specific variables shifts dramatically. In 1964, the economic variables themselves (sectoral share of GDP and GDP/capita) predict only a small part of the variation in urbanisation levels between departments. One would interpret this as an indication that institutional and other unmeasured economic factors, summarised by the proxy measure, were especially important in encouraging urbanisation prior to 1964. Since this preceded significant urban industrial growth, urbanisation in this period was possibly heavily influenced by land concentration and population pressure in rural areas. In 1973, the picture had changed substantially. By this later date the sectoral transformation and income levels per capita provide a strong prediction of urbanisation levels. Industry had grown rapidly in the latter half of the 1960s and the early 1970s and was closely associated with higher levels of urbanisation. Our analysis would benefit from more precise measures of various institutional variables, particularly land tenure

Table 3: Multiple regression analysis of the percentage urban population in Colombia's departments, 1964 and 1973

Dependent variable		Independent variables					
% Urban	C	% GDP Ag.***	% GDP Ind.***	% GDP Serv.***	GDP/ capita**	% Immigration	R^2
1964							
Unstandardised b's (F to enter)	.394	-.413 (4.35)*	.349 (2.07)	.158 (1.49)	.038 (1.41)	.704 (34.27)*	.90
1973							
Unstandardised b's (F to enter)	.26	-.199 (33.21)*	.292 (15.85)*	.372 (11.54)*	.092 (13.27)*	.53 (7.27)*	.91

* Significant at .05 level (d.f. = 5.18)
** 000's pesos/year
*** 000,000's pesos

patterns and rural employment levels. It suggests, however, that the determinants of migration have changed as industry and urban commerce have grown in Colombia.

VI. Discussion

What conclusions can be reached concerning the relationship between state policies and urbanisation in Colombia? We have argued that Colombia is very highly urbanised relative to its level of industrial employment and that the growth and distribution of the urban population can be only partly explained in terms of industrial development and growth. Up to the early 1970s, other factors such as the rapid natural increase of Colombia's rural population, land concentration and mechanisation in agriculture created pressures for peasants to migrate to metropolitan areas in search of employment opportunities. Meanwhile industries concentrated to a growing extent in the largest cities, leading to a small demand for skilled and professional workers, and generating a wide range of employment opportunities in construction, commerce and services. Although the great majority of these jobs provided only low incomes, they served as an "escape valve" for hard-pressed landless labourers and small farmers. It is this combination of circumstances which explains the very heavy rural-urban migration during a period when the demand for labour in the modern urban industrial sector increased very slowly.

State policies in Colombia undoubtedly tended to accelerate the urbanisation process in the country. The basic and most profound influence stems from a national development strategy favouring a capitalistic approach to economic growth, in which élite classes (the owners of capital) invested in imported technology which favoured their interests and largely ignored the interests of the working classes. In the 1960s and 1970s specific state industrial, agricultural and urban development policies were introduced which accelerated labour expulsion in rural areas and which also supported the even greater concentration of modern industrial investments in urban areas. Among these policies were several which explicitly sought to stem urbanisation by improving rural economic and employment conditions and by relocating industry in smaller centres but these were weakly formulated or poorly implemented, such that they either had no effect, or even reinforced urbanisation trends. Rural land concentration and out-migration continued in response to relatively more attractive urban opportunities. While incomes among rural migrants, most of whom are employed in services and commerce, are low in comparison with those employed in the high productivity industrial sector, their social and economic circumstances at least have not deteriorated. They remain exceedingly poor in absolute terms, and in relative terms. They have experienced some income growth as the economy has expanded, but at best they have retained only the same small share of total income that they previously obtained.

Against this background we may ask how the Colombian case may update and improve current models of Third World urbanisation. These may be summarised as follows:

(1) The urban economy. Previous efforts to explain high rates of rural-urban migration and unexpectedly high levels of urbanisation in Latin America have been largely directed toward analysis of what is happening in rural areas.[1] Investigators have focused on the high and growing concentration of agricultural property in the hands of wealthy owners and agro-business, and on the way in which peasants have been "pushed out", with little alternative but to migrate, usually to an urban area. The rural side of this analysis is clearly correct for many nations and can be further substantiated in Colombia. But the analysis is incomplete. The Colombian case reveals how a more complete explanation of recent massive rural-urban migration can be achieved by considering determining forces in both urban and rural areas. The extent to which large numbers of rural out-migrants choose urban destinations and are able to remain and survive in them is determined by the political economy and labour markets of towns and cities.

(2) Industrial development. A number of Latin American nations like Colombia have recently experienced significant industrial growth. It has been widely observed in previous studies that the new industries are technologically sophisticated and tend to directly employ only a relatively small number of workers. This has given rise to a concern for the "marginal" status of large numbers of unskilled workers.[2] Migrants who have

---

1 See Peek (1978) for a comparative study of land concentration and rural out-migration in Latin America. Shaw (1976), analyses the relationship of land tenure and rural exodus in four Latin American nations in greater detail. Both studies include Colombia. See the chapter on Ecuador in the present volume, which examines these processes for that country.

2 For example, Ducoff concluded: "In Latin America, the rate and volume of rural-urban migration far exceeds the current absorptive capacity of the principal cities, thus creating widespread underemployment and

flooded into the cities from rural areas cannot even be considered an "industrial reserve" of labour, since industry does not need them. But the "marginality" of unskilled workers needs to be critically examined and qualified. At least in some Third World countries industrial growth appears to have produced a substantial "spin-off" demand for construction labour, transportation services and other unskilled work. The workers are poorly paid, but only in this restricted sense do they seem marginal to the economy. The Colombian case has illustrated this point.

(3) Policy contradictions. Previous research on urban concentration has led to the hypothesis that agricultural and industrial development policies are often the major determinants of large city growth, and that urban decentralisation and regional development programmes have been inadequate to withstand the momentum created by these other policies.[1] However, detailed case studies are lacking. Colombia provides an example of the over-riding urban emphasis of sectoral economic policies, and the consequent ineffectiveness of urban decentralisation and intermediate city development efforts. Most interesting in the Colombian situation is the way in which several aspects of regional development policies themselves have tended to reinforce urban concentration.

---

serious housing, education, and other social problems" (Ducoff, 1965, p. 205). Since "underemployment" is difficult to measure, many empirical studies of "marginality" among migrants have tended to focus on measures such as "incomes under the legal minimum wage". See, for example, Muñoz, de Oliveira and Stern (1973); or they have emphasised a web of poverty, poor housing and low political power (Quijano, 1971).

[1] In Latin America this approach was first advanced in the context of the over-all "dependency" of Latin American nations with respect to capitalist industrial nations, and the consequences of this dependency on agricultural and industrial policies and on urbanisation (see Quijano, 1971; and Castells, 1977, Chapter 3). Lipton argued a variation of this viewpoint, focusing not on trade and capital dependency in developing countries, but on class structure and competing interests between powerful urban interest groups and weaker rural interest groups inside the Third World nations themselves (Lipton, 1978). There are, however, few detailed case studies. Turner's article provides an outline of issues and some evidence for Peru (Turner, 1977, pp. 189-203).

We can only speculate about the significance of Colombia's experience for other developing nations, or for the future of Colombia itself. The broad constellation of world market forces, a political and economic structure favouring élite interests in determining national response to these forces, and the relatively weak power of the working class to generate investment and technological choice policies more in their own interest, are common features of the Third World. These factors help us understand the current trends in urbanisation in many countries. But the specific circumstances in each are distinct. The evidence that rural-urban migrants in Colombia have at least held their own and perhaps improved their economic circumstances as the sectoral transformation, pushed by state policies, took place may be duplicated in few other instances.

Even in Colombia, it is not clear that past trends will continue. Should coffee prices fall or some other event slow over-all economic growth, the "spin-off" income from high industrial investment and construction would quickly dry up, leaving the service and construction workers in a precarious position. Earlier migrants have possibly benefited from the continued high urban growth rates, which expanded the market demand for housing, construction interests, furniture, various small industry products, and services. With rapidly declining national fertility and a growing emphasis on decentralisation, the growth of urban areas can be expected to slow. The emerging impact on the urban poor constitutes an important topic for future research.

References

Berry, A. (1978): A positive interpretation of the expansion of urban services in Latin America, with some Colombian evidence", in Journal of Development Studies, Jan., Vol. 14, No. 2.

--- (1980): "The national front and Colombia's economic development", in A. Berry, R. Hellman and M. Soloun: Politics of compromise: Coalition government in Colombia (New Brunswick (NH), Transactions Books, 1980).

Berry, A., Hellman, R. and Soloun, M. (1980): Politics of compromise: Coalition government in Colombia (New Brunswick, NH, Transactions Books).

Cardona, R. and Simmons, A.B. (1977): Destino la metrópoli (Bogotá, CCRP).

Castells, M. (1973): Imperialismo y urbanización en América Latina (Barcelona, Editorial Gustavo Gili).

--- (1977): The urban question: A Marxist approach (London, Edward Arnold Ltd.).

Corporación Centro Regional de Población (1979): Encuesta Nacional de Fecundidad, Colombia, 1976 (Bogotá).

DANE (1964): Censo Nacional de Población (Bogota).

--- (1977): Encuesta nacional de fecundidad, Colombia, 1976: Resultados generales, prepared in collaboration with the Ministry of Health, Bogota.

Departamento Nacional de Planeación (1977): Cuentas regionales de Colombia, 1960-1975 (Bogota).

Dix, R.H. (1967): Colombia: The political dimensions of change (New Haven and London, Yale University Press).

Ducoff, J.L. (1965): "The role of migration in the demographic development of Latin America", in Milbank Memorial Fund Quarterly, Vol. 43.

Fields, G.S. (1979): "Lifetime migration in Colombia, tests of the expected income hypothesis", in Population and Development Review, Vol. 5, No. 2.

Fields, G.S. and Schultz, T.P. (1980): "Regional inequality and other sources of income variation in Colombia", in Economic Development and Cultural Change, Apr., Vol. 28, No. 3.

Gilbert, A.B. (1974): "Urban growth and industrial development: The Colombian case", in Proceedings of the Commission on Regional Aspects of Development of the International Geographical Union, Vol. 1.

--- (1975): "Urban and regional development programs in Colombia since 1951", in Latin American Urban Research, Vol. 5, No. 11.

--- (1978): "Bogotá: Policies, planning and the crisis of lost opportunities", in Latin American Urban Research, Vol. 6, No. 3.

Havens, A.E., Flinn, W.L. and Cornhill, S.L. (1980): "Agrarian reform and the Colombian national front: A class analysis", in A. Berry, R. Hellman and M. Soloun: Politics of compromise: Coalition government in Colombia (New Brunswick, Transactions Books, 1980).

Junquito, R., et al (1975): La política agraria en Colombia: 1950-1975 (Bogotá, FEDESARROLLO).

Kline, H. (1980): "The national front: Historical perspective and overview", in A. Berry, R. Hellman and M. Soloun: Politics of compromise: Coalition government in Colombia (New Brunswick, Transactions Books, 1980).

Kugler, B., Reyes, A. and de Gomez, M.I. (1979): "Educación y mercado de trabajo urbano en Colombia: Una comparación entre sectores moderno y no moderno" (Bogotá, CCRP).

Kuznets, S. (1971): Economic growth of nations (London, Oxford University Press).

Leon, A. and Richter, C. (1979): "Inversión pública y desarrollo regional: El caso de Colombia, 1970-1974", in Desarrollo y sociedad (Bogotá).

Lipton, M. (1978): Why poor people stay poor: Urban bias in world development (London, Temple Smith).

Lubell, H. and McCallum, D. (1978): Bogotá: Urban development and unemployment (Geneva, ILO).

McGreevey, W.P. (1971): An economic history of Colombia, 1845-1930 (Cambridge, Cambridge University Press).

Mohan, R. (1979): Population, income and employment in a developing metropolis: A spatial analysis of Bogotá, Colombia (Washington DC, Urban and Regional Economics Division, IBRD; mimeographed, Chapter V).

Muñoz, H., de Oliveira, O. and Stern, C. (1973): "Migración y marginalidad ocupacional en la ciudad de México", in Espaces et Sociétés, Vol. 3 (Paris).

Peek, P. (1978): Agrarian change and rural emigration in Latin America (Geneva, ILO; mimeographed World Employment Programme research working paper; restricted).

Poveda-Ramos, G. (1979): Políticas económicas, desarrollo industrial y tecnología en Colombia, 1925-1975 (Bogotá, COLCIENCIAS).

Preston, S.H. (1979): "Urban growth in developing countries: A demographic reappraisal", in Population and Development Review, Vol. 5, No. 2.

Quijano, A. (1971): "La formación de un universo marginal en las ciudades de América Latina", in Espaces et sociétés, Vol. 3 (Paris), reprinted in Castells, 1973, pp. 141-66.

Renaud, B. (1979): National urbanization policies in developing countries, World Bank Staff working paper No. 347 (Washington, DC).

Ridler, N.B. (1980): "Windfall gains: A paradox", in North-South (Journal of the Canadian Association of Latin American Studies), Vol. V, No. 10.

Rippy, F. (1931): The capitalists and Colombia (New York, Vanguard).

Rocha, G. and Arboleda, H. (1979): Política industrial y distribución territorial de la populación (Bogotá; mimeographed), Part V.

Ruddle, K. and Odermann, D. (1972): Statistical Abstract of Latin America, 1971, 15th ed. (Los Angeles, Latin American Center).

Schultz, T.P. (1969): Internal migration: A quantitative study of rural-urban migration in Colombia (Santa Monica, Rand Corporation).

Shaw, R.P. (1976): Land tenure and the rural exodus in Chile, Colombia, Costa Rica and Peru (Gainesville, University of Florida Press).

Taussig, M. (1978): "Peasants, capital accumulation and rural underdevelopment", in Latin American Perspectives, Part I, Vol. 5, No. 3.

Tirado-Mejia, A. (1971): Introducción a la historia económica de Colombia (Bogotá, Universidad Nacional de Colombia, Dirección de Dilvulgación Cultural).

Turner, F.C. (1977): "The rush to cities in Latin America: Government policies have more effect than we recognise", in Habitat, Vol. 2, Nos. 1/2.

United Nations (1973): Statistical Yearbook, 1973 (New York).

--- (1977): Demographic Yearbook, 1977 (New York).

--- (1978): Statistical Yearbook, 1978 (New York).

Williams, L.C. and Griffin, E.C. (1978): "Rural and small town depopulation in Colombia", in Geographical Review, Vol. 68, No. 1, pp. 13-30.

World Bank (1972): Economic growth of Colombia: Problems and prospects (Baltimore, Johns Hopkins University Press).

--- (1976): World tables, 1976 (Baltimore and London, Johns Hopkins University Press).

--- (1979): World development report (New York, Oxford University Press, 1979), Annex.

Chapter 8

CONTRIVED STAGNATION, MIGRATION AND THE STATE IN GUYANA

by Guy Standing

I. Introduction*

The pattern of population mobility in Guyana has reflected changing social and material relations of production and the effect of state policies associated with the changing nature of the social formation. Less abstractly, migration in Guyana has to be explained in terms of the changing needs and power of the plantations, the colonial authorities, and the mining companies that until recently dominated Guyanese society.

For much of the country's history the predominant productive relations could be aptly described as semi-feudal. This term is controversial, but the essential characteristic is that the producers face a combination of forms of exploitation, the transfer of surplus being effected by wage labour and by other mechanisms such as feudal rent, usury, and extra-economic coercion. With semi-feudal relations workers are not fully divorced from the means of production, but are expected to provide part of their subsistence needs from work on plots of land they own or rent from landlord-employers. This typically implies the wage is less than the cost of reproducing labour power.

Under semi-feudalism, landlords, capitalist farmers or a plantocracy normally seek to inhibit rural-urban migration and bind peasants and estate workers to the rural areas under their control.[1] Two conditions favour the establishment of semi-feudal relations rather than purely capitalist relations of production. The first is a low population density in rural areas. In those circumstances reliance on "free" wage labour would be costly, given the labour scarcity and the high opportunity cost of wage labour for peasants with the alternative of cultivating land for themselves. Accordingly,

---

* Thanks to Ajit Ghose, Peter Peek, Gerry Rodgers and René Wéry for comments.

1 The rationale for this practice is discussed elsewhere (see Standing, 1981).

landlords or commercial plantations would attempt to secure control of the land to force the peasants to provide wage labour at low wage rates. But where the land available is substantial relative to the population, that process is likely to be protracted and hard to achieve. The second condition favouring semi-feudal relations is a low level of development of productive forces on the land. Because co-ordinating production would not raise total product substantially, the landlords or estates would be relatively disinterested in cultivating the maximum amount of land in their possession. Rather they would attempt to get the peasants to produce at least part of their subsistence requirements on small plots with primitive techniques of production. Land, in other words, would be used to entice workers into estate employment as well as to drive them into it, and then to influence the level and pattern of migration.

To the extent semi-feudal relations entail policies binding workers to specific rural areas and systematically restricting their purchasing power or subsistence income, an inherent conflict exists between the estates and nascent industrial and commercial capital. The latter rely on an expanding domestic market for means of production and consumption, and on the existence of a low-cost and mobile labour force. Thus alongside the conflict between peasants and landlords, or plantations, is a conflict between landlords and industrial and commercial capitalist interests. These conflicts have to be resolved in the political sphere, for just as landlords use the state apparatus to secure a subordinated peasantry and require policies restricting population mobility, so the commercial and industrial classes need a contrary set of policies.

In much of the following the focus is on the actions and objectives of the planter class, or the plantocracy. Within that category we must include not only the plantation owners and later the management of the multinational sugar-based companies but the colonial and other administrative officials who were concerned with ensuring the continued flow of surplus to shareholders in London and elsewhere, as well as the various groups whose profits depended on the prosperity of the sugar industry. It was this composite class which was dominant politically for most of Guyana's history, at least up to 1966.

The theme of the following analysis is that the plantocracy and latterly the mining companies relied on a combination of economic mechanisms and government policies to secure a pliant labour force. In effect, the economic and political tactics were based on two objectives: the need for a rural proletariat and the need for a peasantry providing an adequate supply of means of subsistence to allow very low money wages. Given the emphasis on sugar as an export crop, these twin needs involved an inherent conflict, for they required a delicate balance of a labour-supplying and a food-producing peasantry. To have squeezed the peasantry excessively would have entailed rising food costs and thus a rising cost of reproducing labour power, which would have reduced the rate of exploitation. To have allowed the unchecked growth of petty commodity production would have meant a loss of labour as the opportunity cost of wage employment rose, and would have produced a sector competing with the estates for scarce labour power. This fundamental dilemma dominated the development and underdevelopment of productive forces in Guyana from 1838 to at least 1966, and continued to influence the pattern of development after Independence.

Essentially, to maintain profit levels the estates needed to partially dissolve the petty commodity producers' economic base. It was in their interest to restrict the so-called peasantry only partially, because they needed to tie workers to the estate-dominated areas and reduce the necessary efficiency wage.[1] In other words, the estates needed to allow the partial reproduction of the petty commodity economic formation, in doing so ensuring that it remained what Althusser has called a subordinated mode in the economic structure, facilitating capitalist accumulation. What the estates could not allow was the emergence of alternative forms of production in competition with them for labour, purchasing power, and ultimately political control. The consequence was what will be characterised as "contrived stagnation".

Retention of a rural workforce was essential; if the peasantry was squeezed excessively, their ties to the soil would have been loosened and their propensity to leave estate-dominated rural areas increased. But to the extent productive forces developed outside the estate and mining sectors, there was likely to be a process of class differentiation, primary capital accumulation, and land consolidation. All those are normally associated with the creation of a landless population liable to migrate out of rural areas.

Given the complexity of maintaining the necessary balance, and the growing political conflict associated with the socio-economic changes taking place, it was scarcely

---

[1] The actual wage reflects the level of bargaining power (the state of class struggle etc.) as well as the cost of reproducing labour power. The greater the non-wage economic support available to wage-workers the greater their bargaining power.

surprising that rural out-migration was always a major obstacle to estate production. But what is particularly fascinating is the range of economic and political mechanisms adopted to control migration and the long-term impact of those policies on the underdevelopment of the Guyanese economy.

Schematically, although relations of production on the plantations and in the mining enterprises became increasingly capitalistic (if always retaining semi-feudal elements), the dependent nature of the economy blocked capitalist industrialisation. Since the development of productive forces was for long controlled by absentee planters and subsequently by a small group of non-competing multinationals, there was no substantial accumulation in rural areas, despite the "super-exploitation" of the rural labour force through low wages and complementary mechanisms for depriving the workers of surplus.[1] In the long run that accumulation might have raised working-class living standards by stimulating a demand for labour in an industrially diversifying economy. But that only occurred to a small extent. Even accumulation in urban-industrial areas, which in most countries has accompanied the growth of agrarian capital, was checked by the external domination, basically because the surplus was taken out of the country in the form of repatriated profits. Thus the impoverishment of the peasantry was matched by a stagnant urban economy, which grew as the surplus population migrated out of rural areas and became part of a growing body of urban unemployed.

---

[1] If exploitation through wage labour is defined as the rate of surplus value in the classic sense, then super-exploitation arises if the wage falls below the cost of reproducing labour power. It would be foolish to pretend there are no difficulties in the notion of exploitation, since there are subjective as well as objective elements involved. Nevertheless where one class appropriates the surplus product of the direct producers one would be much more foolish not to make exploitation the fulcrum of analysis.

II. Guyana in Historical Perspective: Emancipation and the Aftermath (1800-1864)

For most of its history, Guyana was an agricultural colony geared to sugar production on plantations located in the narrow, flat coastal region.[1] Consisting of some 83,000 square miles, the country has always been extremely sparsely populated. But with an interior savannah region separated from the coast by a thick belt of tropical forest and connected to it by vast rivers and a web of navigable streams, it is the coastal region which has always been the main area of inhabitation and cultivation. Reflecting a situation that had changed little in the previous 150 years, the 1970 Census indicated that more than nine out of every ten people lived in that coastal region, where the population density was some 30 times as great as in the remainder of the country (table 1).

Table 1: Population density of Guyana: 1960 and 1970

Regions	% of country's population	Density (per sq. m.) 1960	1970	Rate of increase (p.a.)	Population distribution 1960	1970
Coastal	31.5	20.2	25.2	2.3	93.8	93.8
Interior	28.5	0.6	0.8	2.1	6.2	6.2
Guyana		6.8	8.5	2.2		

Source: Population census reports.

Ecologically, the peculiarity of the coastal region is that it is not only flat but mostly below sea level, which has meant that over many generations a great amount of expenditure and human energy has been required to maintain effective systems of drainage and irrigation. As such, much of the most fertile land has relied on empoldering to be cultivable, involving a system of dams, canals, and irrigation channels.

[1] Throughout the text the name Guyana will be used, although between 1831 and 1966 the country was known as British Guiana. The territory was captured from the Dutch in 1803 and formally ceded to Britain in 1814.

It was in the coastal region that in the eighteenth and early nineteenth centuries cotton, coffee, and sugar plantations were first established. The European settlers found the indigenous Indians an inadequate source of labour and relied on slave labour imported from Africa. As such the early estates had a captive if not entirely reliable labour supply. But in Guyana the slave mode of production possessed particularly pronounced deficiencies that hastened its demise. Slavery involved considerable costs for the planters; slave mortality was high, productivity was low, and with escape into the vast interior always possible costs of supervision were high.[1] The costs of reproducing labour power were borne by the estates and to ensure a surplus required keeping slaves at a low level of subsistence, which only intensified the problem of mortality. Moreover to reproduce the labour force, it was necessary to maintain workers who were not themselves productive labour, which lowered the over-all rate of exploitation. So any decline in sugar prices left the estates little leeway to extract more surplus from the labour force.

After the abolition of the slave trade in the British Empire in 1807 production costs rose sharply, for once the estates had to reproduce all their labour force internally, they had to raise the level of subsistence to reduce mortality. They attempted to make the slaves bear part of the cost of reproducing labour power by providing them with small plots on which to produce "ground provisions". But the surplus the estates could extract continued to be small, partly because low incomes due to a low world price for sugar and an unhealthy ecological environment meant they continued to suffer a loss of slaves through high mortality and escape. Thus with the various costs that included costs of coercion and the corresponding risks of relaxation, the slave mode gave way without much struggle.

In 1838 slave labour was abolished after a four-year transition period known as Apprenticeship. What happened then is remarkable. The planters' main objection to abolition was the fear that the freed slaves would promptly migrate into the interior of the country, thus attaining a level of subsistence that would enable them to avoid having to work on the estates. As the plantations were on the relatively fertile coastal strip, this meant that the potential labour force would move away from the estates and be unavailable even on a

---

[1] Roberts estimated that in the period immediately before Emancipation the life expectancy of slaves was only 22.8 years (Roberts, 1952).

part-time or seasonal basis.

Given the scarcity of labour power, the existence of vast stretches of cultivable land, and the sensitivity of marginal plantations to declines in profitability, the plantocracy campaigned to retain some form of direct control over the labour force. This was done in almost open conflict with the Colonial Office in London which advocated a rapid move to a "free" labour market consistent with the capitalist laissez-faire doctrines in vogue in Britain. Between 1834 and the early 1860s this divergence of view persisted and was only resolved, in the planters' favour, after a protracted period of stagnation within the plantation society.

In the years immediately following 1838 the planters' worst fears were realised, though not in the way they had anticipated. There was indeed a massive expansion of the peasantry as the ex-slaves acquired land. But this took place in or near the coastal area, for several reasons. First, that was where land was most fertile and accessible; second, there was land available there; and third, that was where the population could have access to (imported) consumer goods. These circumstances arose because in the period preceding and during the abolition of slavery - partly in anticipation of subsequent labour shortages and partly as a result of them - many of the marginal, relatively inefficient plantations were abandoned. Moreover, in the quarter of a century after 1838, when the move to free trade in the British Empire was at its height and when imperial protection was reduced, the sugar industry suffered one of its periodic slumps due to low sugar prices in the United Kingdom. Consequently much land was cheaply available, so that many ex-slaves were able to acquire small plots with a few months' saving from wage labour. Others resorted to squatting, while in many cases groups combined to purchase large tracts of land, which were then parcelled out or worked on rudimentary co-operative principles. Important as this was for the subsequent pattern of rural development, and the ideological direction it encouraged Guyanese governments to take more than a century later, this came to be called "the village movement". It is remarkable for its rapidity, the extent of its expansion, and its initial success.

Yet neither the plantocracy nor an increasingly alarmed Colonial Office could allow it to flourish, for it threatened the very foundation of the colonial economy in Guyana. Indeed it was the movement's effect on plantation profitability which forced the Colonial Office to make concessions to the plantocracy, gradually inducing it to support attempts to check the migration from the estates so as to secure an adequate supply of wage labour.

With that convergence of views the ambivalence of state policies, which characterised the period between 1834 and about 1860, declined. That period of transition reflected a struggle over the most appropriate form of the capitalist mode of production, a struggle which concluded with the acceptance of semi-feudal controls. With images of a flourishing yeomanry, the colonial authorities initially insisted on a more complete transition to a "free" wage-labour market, whereas the planters realised that with such vast stretches of available land and the odium associated with plantation labour, that would mean a steep rise in wages which few estates could afford. In their turn the colonial authorities realised that colonial income was based on the profitability of the plantations, so that in the wake of intense lobbying by West Indian merchants in the UK, the advent of a free labour market was postponed.

To increase the labour supply to the estates the plantocracy pursued a double-edged strategy. They set out to severely restrict access to the land while securing an additional source of "unfree" labour through indentured immigration.

1. Access to the land

At the time of Emancipation most of the country, including all the vast interior, was designated Crown land. The large group of plantations of various sizes, including some that had recently been abandoned, were concentrated in the coastal areas. In addition there was a relatively small amount of land, mostly attached to estates, which had been set aside as small plots for peasant farming of ground provisions. On Emancipation, the plantocracy set out to retain control of the land. As early as 1838 Governor Light expressed the determination to restrict land settlement, asserting ominously, "If persons without capital will consider themselves entitled to demand land, let them not possess it without such restrictions as shall induce them to pause before they quit the more densely peopled regions for the interior." (Farley, 1953-54, p. 97).

With the subsequent growth of the peasantry in the 1840s the planters' immediate objective was the disruption of the village movement, and in particular the "communal" villages, which were formed by groups of ex-slaves who collectively bought tracts of land, often whole abandoned estates. For the estates, there was less cause for alarm with what have been called "proprietary" villages, those that were virtually attached to estates and which were a convenient means of tying workers to those estates (Young, 1958). It was communal villages which were the threat, as they contained the germs of economically and socially viable independent communities.[1] It was these initiatives the estates and the colonial officials set out to destroy.

At first they were singularly unsuccessful and by 1852 most of the population owned or had settled on land. However by that time the plantocracy's offensive was gathering momentum, and in fact the village movement peaked in 1848. The onslaught included both legal and extra-legal measures. To deter settlement in the interior, the authorities stipulated that crown land - i.e. most land not owned by estates - could only be purchased in minimum parcels of 100 acres. Later this was raised to 500 acres. And although much of the crown land was located in the undeveloped and only partially accessible interior, the price of crown land was fixed well above that of other land, much of which was clearly more fertile. Indeed, in the 1840s consistent with the official reluctance to see ex-slaves acquire crown land, the peasants had to pay on average about 25 times as much as the planters, according to one planter's calculations (Adamson, 1972, p. 164). By the 1860s the price of crown land was set at about five times that of land being sold elsewhere in Guyana.

Communal villages were curbed more directly when an Ordinance in 1853 prohibited the joint purchase of land by groups of more than 20 persons; this was reduced to ten in 1856. Another ordinance converted communal villages into individually owned plots, the law stipulating that if a group of more than ten persons owned land it had to be partitioned and levied for maintenance rates. This led to a pattern of land fragmentation that had a lasting effect on the underdevelopment of productive forces in non-estate agriculture, for in the partition of co-operative villages individual peasants were allocated small strips of "good", "fair", and "poor" land, according to their share in the co-operative village; often the parts of the composite plot were at different ends of the village.

Other measures included efforts to stop peasants purchasing land near estates, the intention being to force them to work as wage labourers on the estates. Yet that had the effect of forcing many to move into the interior (ibid., p. 35). The plantations even organised

---

[1] A major reason for this was that the land in the coastal region required systematic drainage and irrigation schemes which relied on communal organisation and which were relatively unlikely in villages consisting of individualistic small-scale farmers.

the destruction of fruit trees, provision grounds, and fishing areas, as part of the general strategy of making peasants reliant on wage-labour earnings for their subsistence. For their part, the colonial authorities, pressed to do so by the planters, forcibly evicted squatters from abandoned estates or unsettled crown land, and when peasants tried to establish settlements away from the estates in what has been called "the creek-and-river movement" the authorities pilloried them by sending raiding parties to burn stores and ruin crops (Farley, 1953-54). These heavy-handed methods helped achieve the planters' objective. The interior was not extensively settled, and the great majority of the peasants were forced to stay in villages near the estates on fragmented landholdings that were insufficient to provide more than the barest of subsistence incomes. Faced with additional demands, such as rent and taxes, and an inability to develop the infrastructure essential for productive land utilisation in the ecological conditions of Guyana, the peasants faced a stagnation that was truly contrived and became dependent on wage labour to realise something approaching an adequate subsistence income.

Having disrupted the communal village economy and created the basis of a dependent peasantry, the plantocracy further increased their control of the land. The purpose was partly to increase estate production, but this was scarcely the main reason, for as their ownership and control of land expanded the proportion devoted to sugar cane or other estate crops declined. The increased control had two other objectives: to ensure an adequate labour supply, and to increase the rate of exploitation by squeezing the peasants on to a smaller amount of land, thereby facilitating higher rents and lower wages, which increased the surplus accruing to the estates. However, the means by which peasants were denied access to land and prevented from developing the forces of production should be seen as one part of the two-sided strategy adopted by the plantocracy to obtain a low-cost labour supply. The other tactic involved increasing the supply through indentured labour.

2. Indentured labour

In the immediate aftermath of Emancipation the Guyanese planters were prevented by Imperial rule from enacting vagrancy and "located labourers" laws binding ex-slaves to the estates. At the time bourgeois freedoms were being created in Britain - the Poor Law of 1834 had just replaced the Speenhamland System - and the Colonial Office, for a short time and never wholly consistently, was more concerned "with the establishment of personal and political freedom for the emancipated class than with the preservation of economic prosperity" in Guyana.[1] It took extensive lobbying by West Indian merchants and a slump in the sugar industry to induce a reassertion of labour controls, by which internal migration was to be severely restricted.

The system of indentured labour was established between 1840 and 1854 as pressure on the Colonial Office gradually prevailed. By the early 1860s it had become the mainstay of the plantation economy (Lawrence, 1965, pp. 9-27). Although Chinese, Portuguese, and other nationalities were also imported as part of a calculated policy to create a racially diverse and thus divided labour force, most indentured workers came from the Indian subcontinent. The adoption of an indentured labour system can be seen as having been the most effective mode of appropriating surplus. At the time "free" wage labour was incompatible with high profits because of the labour scarcity and the availability of land, despite the planters' on-going attempts to restrict access to land. Reverting to some form of feudal mode of production based on peasant production and a transfer of surplus primarily through rent was impracticable because of the relatively high productivity that could be attained through large-scale estate production based on a concentration of workers and a fairly developed division of labour. Indentured labour represented an appropriate compromise.[2]

The costs of importing indentured workers were partly borne by those planters hiring them and partly by the government, which subsidised the costs through the fiscal system, thereby placing part of the costs on the non-estate population. The indentured workers were obliged to work 12 hours a day, were entitled to some welfare protection, and by statutory regulation were paid a wage determined by the wage paid to non-indentured workers doing similar work. But of course the very existence of indentured workers lowered the wage necessary to secure "free" wage labour. One consequence was that "creoles", the ex-slaves, were not hired for many estate jobs, because their virtual exclusion meant that wages of indentured workers could be kept low.

---

[1] See Green (1969, p. 65). On the significance of the Speenhamland system, see Standing (1981).

[2] Between the 1860s and 1891 immigrants accounted for the whole increase in the labour force. During that period there was probably a natural decrease in population (Roberts and Johnson, 1974, p. 74).

During the period the immigrants had to serve as indentured labour (usually five years) the estates attempted to ensure (usually successfully) that they had to remain as estate workers at the end of the period. This was because of the initial cost of hiring and because the regulations specified that the estates had to pay the return passage to India or whatever the country of origin. Consequently the estates manipulated the conditions of indenture to prolong the period of obliged employment or offered inducements to reindenture or, later, to settle as peasant farmers. The manipulations were diverse, sometimes ingenious, often callous. Most frequently the workers were forced into chronic debt. Thus as they were paid on a task-work basis, variations in sugar prices or the cost of acquiring fresh labour power led to a tightening of work conditions and a lowering of net income, which forced them to take advances to cover costs of subsistence. Workers were fined for allegedly unsatisfactory work or for being unable to meet output requirements set at unrealistically high levels, while the estates could extend the indenture period if work was deemed unsatisfactory. And despite token protection provided by the colonial authorities there was little check on the estates' power. As the Attorney-General himself admitted in 1877, the government was "quite in the dark" as to how justice was administered outside the main urban areas of Georgetown and New Amsterdam (Adamson, 1972, p. 145).[1] In such circumstances, indentured workers were abused and demoralised, and compelled by debt to reindenture, a tendency further encouraged by the payment of a bonus to those reindenturing, a bonus just large enough to enable them to buy a cow or hold out the hope of acquiring sufficient savings to buy their independence as a peasant farmer later.

III. The Transition to "Free" Labour (1864-1917)

By about 1864 the plantocracy had reasserted effective political and economic control, helped by rising sugar prices. The following period was one of consolidation characterised by a growing monopolisation. In 1838 there were 308 sugar estates; fifteen years later, after the long crisis in the sugar industry and during the transition to the new mode of production, there were 173;

---

[1] A typical feature of feudalism identified by Dobb in his classic study of the transition of feudalism to capitalism was "the possession by a lord of judicial or quasi-judicial functions in relation to the dependent population" (Dobb, 1963, p. 37).

by 1884, by when a new crisis had struck the industry, there were 105; and by 1904 there were only 46. In 1900 the sugar and shipping company, Booker McConnell, came into existence, subsequently to become so hegemonic that many Guyanese would refer to their country as "Booker's Guyana".[1]

The amalgamation of adjoining estates in the late nineteenth century largely reflected a process by which the larger plantations absorbed the smaller, the demise of marginal estates being reflected in the fact that between 1852 and 1884 the average size grew from 256 to 757 acres (Adamson, 1972, p. 202). The consolidation reflected a development of productive forces, for the introduction of machinery, especially after 1880, and the erection of large central factories involved economies of scale that undermined the ability of smaller estates to compete. In 1849 there were 180 factories scattered across the coastal region; by 1896 there were 64 (Government of British Guiana).

This process was facilitated by the plantocracy's success in securing a source of unfree labour and controlling the use of land. And as monopolistic control increased, so did the underutilisation of the land controlled by the plantations. By 1884, it was estimated that about 43 per cent of empoldered land belonging to the sugar estates was kept idle (Adamson, 1972, p. 259).

Yet in this period the needs of the estates changed. Most particularly, from the 1870s onwards the necessity of indentured labour was increasingly questioned, in part because land monopolisation, population growth and contrived stagnation had resulted in a growing relative surplus population and in part because technological innovations had made employment in the sugar industry mostly seasonal. Instead of a fairly steady requirement throughout the year, labour was mostly required for reaping and grinding. The maintenance of indentured labour throughout the year became unnecessarily costly, the use of casual labour relatively less so. But the abolition of indentured labour could only be countenanced by the plantocracy if they could be sure of obtaining "free" labour at the appropriate time at an appropriately low wage to allow high rates of profit.

If the 1870s was a period of technological innovation in the sugar industry, following a period of rising sugar

---

[1] Links between Booker Brothers and McConnell (a plantation owner) started in the 1840s. When the company was formally established in 1900 it operated one-quarter of the colony's sugar estates (Booker McConnell Ltd., 1955).

prices and costs, the innovations themselves contributed to a reduction in employment and wages. Their fall was greatly accelerated by the slump in sugar prices in the mid-1880s. And because other workers were then resigned to accept less than the statutory minimum wage set for indentured labour, the latter were often under-employed. Thus, just as the relative inefficiency of the slave mode of production had accelerated its collapse half a century earlier, it was the relative inefficiency of the indentured labour system which led to its replacement by a free wage-labour system. Partly because of resentment by some estates, the practice of "reindenture" came to an end in the 1870s.[1] Thereafter the growth of the rural surplus population reduced the relative costs of free wage labour, so that by 1917 the abolition of indentured labour was scarcely resisted.[2]

At the same time efforts to reduce labour costs led to a shift in land policy from outright restriction to controlled and strictly limited release of land. Initially reflecting their desire to retain an adequate labour supply and to avoid the costs of return voyages, the plantocracy encouraged immigrant workers to settle in Guyana once their period of indentured labour had been completed. But the most important reasons were the desire to reduce the costs of workers' subsistence and the need to absorb the growing surplus population. Thus efforts to encourage the settlement of immigrants led to an expansion of a peasantry growing food for sale to estate workers who would otherwise have had to spend time working on provision grounds rather than devoting their labour to sugar production. As the leading planter of the day, William Russell, commented, "In reality, what has resulted from the discontinuance of reindenture is rather a division of labour than an actual withdrawal of labour from the estates." (quoted in Adamson, 1972, p. 134). In other words, it resulted in an expansion of food production and thus lower prices, which lowered the cost of reproducing labour power, while increasing the available labour of those working in estate employment.

---

[1] Its prohibition partly represented an oligopsonistic recognition of a competitive tendency for reindenture "bonus" payments to rise. Resentment was due to a few estates being able to entice workers from others through higher bonuses.

[2] Indentured labour formally ended in 1921, when the last group of workers concluded their term of contract.

The most significant expression of a change in policy was the release of crown land for the purpose of establishing "Indian villages" to absorb the growing number of immigrants off estates (table 2). These set the precedent of land settlements that became a preoccupation of the authorities throughout the twentieth century. The initial schemes were unsuccessful, partly because plots were too small and conditions of membership too restrictive.[1] However, the impetus to village settlements was boosted in the 1880s when the estates became increasingly cost-conscious as their competitive position in the world market was further threatened and as growing seasonality of estate labour and mechanisation greatly reduced the potential labour input of marginal workers, notably women and children. With the need to reduce wages as a result of a slump in sugar prices, the estates were keen to make workers produce a larger proportion of their subsistence needs.

So, from the 1880s, really starting with an Ordinance in 1882 which permitted greater acquisition of crown land, land previously locked up was slowly released to a growing peasant population. But given the small plots granted to the Indian immigrants and the location of the villages close to the estates, it was clear the authorities were preoccupied with maintaining a situation of contrived stagnation, obliging the peasantry to rely on wage income from estate employment, almost regardless of the wage level. The objective was to maintain and expand the rural population, resisting migration by binding semi-proletarianised workers to estate areas.

Table 2: Distribution of Asian immigrant population in Guyana, 1861-1881

Year	Estates	Villages and settlements	Urban	Rural	Percentage non-estate
1861	23,401	533	700	24,704	5.2
1871	50,420	3,215	1,466	55,101	8.4
1881	64,326	17,441	3,396	85,163	24.2

Source: Census of British Guiana, 1861, 1871, 1881.

1 The first attempt was made as early as 1871; the first Indian village to be settled was in 1880, when East Indian families were granted small cultivation plots for which they paid a small annual tax. It proved unsuccessful.

Apart from the village settlements, some land was released by a Crown Lands Ordinance of 1887, but the price and conditions of purchase were put beyond the reach of peasants, significantly except for land within 10 miles of the public road connecting the estates along the coast. A more liberal land policy was introduced in 1894, largely reflecting the growing political strength of the merchant interests and despite fierce opposition of the planters. Finally in 1903, a Crown Lands Ordinance formalised the system of land tenure. It was to remain the basis of land law in the country, with lasting consequences on rural stagnation and thus patterns of migration.[1]

The changing land policy coincided with a shift in official attitudes on agricultural production. It was at this time that rice first became an important "peasant crop". When the British acquired Guyana it produced more cotton than anywhere else in the world and was the largest grower of coffee in the British Empire. Yet thereafter sugar displaced other export crops, and during the nineteenth century agricultural specialisation increased until cotton, coffee, and cocoa, all once major crops, were unimportant.[2] Off the estates the peasants might have diversified to encompass a wide range of cash crops. Had they been able to do so, primary accumulation almost certainly would have led to some form of agricultural capitalism, with class differentiation and the growth of a sector in competition with the estates for labour power. This the estates prevented. It was in their interest to force peasants to produce subsistence crops that would reduce the cost of reproducing labour power while forcing them to rely on estate employment.

In the mid-nineteenth century the peasants were induced to concentrate on the farming of "ground provisions" and sugar cane by a combination of official restrictions on the production of certain cash crops, a lack of markets, the presence of cheap imported food, the land tenure system, and fragmentation of peasant landholdings.[3] Ironically, rice, which was to be farmed

---

[1] As its effects were mainly in the following periods the details are discussed in the next section.

[2] In 1828 there were 174 plantations growing cotton and coffee; by 1849 there were only 16, and subsequently these also failed.

[3] The market was small partly because plantation labourers had their own gardens, and the towns were small, and there were no export market opportunities (Smith, 1964, p. 308).

more extensively than any other crop in the twentieth century, was banned, even though it was imported from India and Burma (Masefield, 1950). However, in the late nineteenth century the plantocracy realised that rice production would serve their interests, peasant rice cultivation being an ideal means of reducing the cost of subsistence and thereby the necessary wage on the estates, while producing a source of income and employment that was not competitive with the estates. There were several reasons for the plantocracy to favour rice. First, rice was suited to the flat, low-lying land in the villages and to peasant farming; the income from rice-farming was low, and crops other than rice needed considerable infrastructural investment, notably communal drainage facilities. Second, rice was both a subsistence crop and required labour inputs that were seasonally complementary with those of the sugar estates. It was thus a highly appropriate crop for the estates to encourage as a means of lowering wages and maintaining the supply of rural labour. As an official report in 1949 noted,

> "The provision plot and the rice plot are closely connected in the economy of the estate worker...the demands of sugar and rice conflict only in the autumn reaping season, when the estates, faced with a labour shortage spread over three weeks, plan their cutting and grinding accordingly." (Commission of Inquiry into the Sugar Industry of British Guiana, 1949, p. 139).

The petty cultivation of rice expanded dramatically at the end of the nineteenth century. The area under rice jumped from about 2,500 acres in 1888 to 15,020 in 1903, and 61,200 by 1919 (Smith, 1957, p. 502). Stimulated by the emerging merchant class, it was first exported in 1903. As a means of retaining a peasant population, it proved initially successful but its expansion was to have a lasting effect on the rural economy, exacerbating rural emigration and labour underutilisation.

IV. Contrived Stagnation and State Policy in the Twentieth Century (1917-1977)

By 1917 the economic contours of Guyana had been established. Sugar and rice were the main crops, there was a chronic underutilisation of land, a surplus population existed, and relations of production maintained a state of contrived stagnation off the estates, supported by legislative and administrative machinery. The population was concentrated in the coastal region, from which there was insignificant migration into the remainder of the country. Only Georgetown and New Amsterdam, both on the coast, received a substantial flow of migrants, drawn from the growing surplus population.

However, the proportion living in urban areas had not risen in the past half century, and the most notable change in the distribution of the population was the shift from the estates to villages and land settlements, which by the turn of the twentieth century accounted for more than half the total population (table 3). The sharp drop in the estate population reflected the shrinking labour requirements and the associated growth of a rural surplus population.

Table 3: The distribution of population by place of residence, Guyana, 1851-1970[a]

Year	Urban and sub-urban (%)	Estates (%)	Villages, farms, settlements
1851	23.6	30.8	45.6
1861	22.8	37.2	40.0
1871	21.7	35.1	43.2
1881	21.0	34.5	44.6
1891	22.9	33.2	43.9
1911	22.4	24.0	53.7
1921	22.8	24.0	54.9
1931	25.0	21.7[b]	50.5
1970	26.0	-[c]	-[c]

[a] Rounding accounts for deviations from 100.0 per cent.

[b] This refers to sugar estates; a further 2.9 per cent not included elsewhere were the rice and coconut estate population.

[c] The proportion on estates and special areas, including land settlements and all incorporated local authorities, was 34.9 per cent. The remaining 39.2 per cent were the remainder of the rural population.

Source: Census Reports 1851-1970. Singh (1977, p. 50).

Even so, the monopolisation and underutilisation of land continued to grow. The plantations were consolidated into two multinationals (Booker McConnell, which by the 1950s controlled about 90 per cent of the country's sugar production, and Jessels). Between them they owned vast expanses of the country and rented large areas from the state at tiny "peppercorn" rentals. Correspondingly, the number of factories shrunk steadily, until by the 1970s there were only 11 in operation. Meanwhile land utilisation declined. By the 1930s, according to one estimate, about half the plantations' land was idle (Thomas, 1977). In 1949 an official estimate suggested that of the 155,000 acres owned by the 21 sugar estates only about 60,000 acres were under cane (Commission of Inquiry into the Sugar Industry of British Guiana, 1949, p. 6). Subsequently, the figure rose somewhat, but continued to represent only a modest proportion of the total land under the estates' control.

Moreover, by the twentieth century the plantations were no longer the only large landlords. The major new factor was the emergence of huge mining conglomerates, which had acquired rights to large areas of the country towards the end of the nineteenth century. After 1917 vast stretches of land were acquired by multinational bauxite companies. The two North American companies concerned obtained rights to land which gave them exclusive permission for exploration. But the area they acquired was always out of all proportion to the companies' production. Indeed, in 1969 it was estimated that it would take one company at least 30 years to mine its existing reserves (Senate of Canada, 1969, p. 21). In the same year it was estimated that various companies held about 2.6 million acres for possible exploration, mostly held by the bauxite companies but some for exploration for diamonds and other minerals; a further 21,700 square miles were held for oil prospecting and 10,585 square miles for radioactive minerals (Co-operative Republic of Guyana, 1971, p. 8). Those figures have to be seen in the context of an estimate made in the same report that about 900 square miles were devoted to cultivation, and that although much of the idle land owned by the multinational companies was unsuitable for cultivation, especially near the bauxite town of MacKenzie, large areas were classified as suitable for a wide range of crops.

A second and, in terms of quantity of land involved, more important means by which peasants were denied access to land was the state regulations which restricted access to crown land and hindered its development. The Ordinances of the 1850s had severely impeded the peasants' ability to settle on crown land, some of which was released by Ordinances introduced in the late nineteenth century. But it was the 1903 Crown Lands Ordinance which helped perpetuate the rural stagnation off the estates, thereby contributing to the urban drift in the twentieth century.

The details of the 1903 Ordinance need not detain us, but the salient points are that it delineated five types of tenure - absolute grants, provisional grants, leases, licences, and permissions - and that the state retained control over crown land in a way that contributed to its continuing underdevelopment. Very few absolute grants were ever made, and these were the only type which placed no restrictions on the purchaser. With provisional grants the grantees had to occupy the land "beneficially" during the period in which the purchase price was being paid; in other words, the land had to be worked immediately and it was left to government discretion whether or not the land was forfeited. That meant the purchasers faced a prolonged period of uncertainty, especially as before 1917 leasehold rights were not recognised by the Roman-Dutch law in operation, thus meaning that lessees could not enforce personal rights against the Crown. A clause in all crown land leases stressed the necessity of beneficial occupation, but investment in land improvements was also discouraged by the shortness of many leases. Even so, such leases were superior to licences, which were merely issued "subject to the pleasure of the licensor", and to permissions, which were of short and restricted duration.

The law relating to crown land was thus thoroughly unsatisfactory from the peasants' point of view. But that raises a more general malaise, which is that throughout the history of Guyana rural development has been hindered by the fact that titles to most land have been unclear due to the absence of effective machinery for registration. For a long time this served the plantations' interests. For the absence of secure titles discouraged land settlement and, perhaps more importantly, discouraged investments that would have raised the productivity of the land, discouraged the planting of long-term or permanent high-yielding crops, and made it difficult for small farmers to obtain investment loans because of the lack of effective collateral.

At the end of the nineteenth century it was estimated that 400,000 acres of privately owned land could not be properly settled because of uncertainty of title (Adamson, 1972, p. 259). Reflecting the growing pressure of commercial groups, in 1897 a Tax Ordinance was passed to tax "ruinate" land so as to stimulate cultivation and terminate claims by those without title. However, no effective machinery for collection was set up, and it was repealed in 1900. In 1897 the Chairman of the West Indian Royal Commission was told by the Head of the Crown Lands Department,

> "Private land is not so easy to obtain on account of much of it being locked up, and also on account of the titles of land on the river banks are not being satisfactorily settled. Titles are not defined."

Over 70 years later, a committee appointed by the government to survey the pattern of land use noted that "much private lands still remain locked up for various reasons." (Co-operative Republic of Guyana, 1970, Vol. I, p. 1). In 1971, when the committee completed its review, possibly 60 per cent of all private land lacked a registered title, or was subject to squatting, wrongful occupation, or more than one claim (ibid., 1970, Vol. II, pp. 2-3). The report concluded that the situation constituted a major obstacle to intensive farming.

With uncertain titles, and unable to gain access to much of the fertile land in the coastal region, the peasants were faced with a persistent land shortage. In the nineteenth century land fragmentation had been a major consequence of the village movement. As those villages had little room for expansion, subsequent population growth merely accentuated the fragmentation. This was further accentuated by the establishment of the immigrant villages, with their small plots and restrictions on land transfer. It was even further accentuated by subsequent resettlement schemes, which will be considered later and which merely transferred some of the surplus population onto small plots, thereby institutionalising the process of fragmentation.

Unfortunately, as in most countries, official statistics provide little or no clue to the extent of fragmentation, let alone of trends. Data on size of landholdings are also sparse, but surveys conducted towards the end of the period, in 1970 and 1971, indicated that most farmers had plots of less than five acres, and that the situation had deteriorated since the 1953 agricultural census, when 55 per cent of farms had less than five acres (Lewars, 1977, p. 13). The 1971 survey suggested that in several regions of the country over 70 per cent of farmers had fewer than five acres, and tiny proportions had more than 20 acres (table 4).

In the same year the Government's Land Use Survey estimated that a somewhat larger proportion of all landholders in the country had fewer than five acres, the figure being some 75 to 80 per cent depending on the district surveyed; this category of farmer possessed between 3.5 and about 9 per cent of the total area under

Table 4: Size distribution of farms by districts, Guyana, 1971

	Size of holdings in acres (proportion of total)				
	Less than 1	1-5	5-10	10-20	20+
West Coast Demerara	18.4	35.5	17.1	23.7	5.3
West Bank Demerara	38.7	53.2	0.0	4.8	3.2
North West District	4.8	57.1	19.0	14.3	4.8
East Bank Demerara	33.3	33.3	27.8	5.6	0.0
Essequibo Coast	11.5	35.4	26.0	24.0	3.1
Essequibo Islands	0.0	68.0	20.0	12.0	0.0
East Coast Demerara	42.3	31.7	10.6	8.9	6.5
East Berbice	18.4	35.5	17.1	23.7	5.3

Note: It was not stated whether or not estates were encompassed by the survey, but it must be presumed they were excluded.

Source: Lewars (1977, p. 13).

cultivation (Co-operative Republic of Guyana, 1971). Further evidence was provided by a 1971 Food and Nutrition Survey, for which some data on land ownership were collected. These suggested that over 80 per cent of farms were of ten acres or less and a further 16 per cent were of between 11 and 25 acres (Pan American Health Organisation, WHO, 1976, p. 49).[1] The data from these various sources differ, but not to the extent of challenging the basic picture of a rural land structure consisting predominantly of smallholders on very small parcels of land. At the same time, it appeared that about 96 per cent of the total land area was still undeveloped; that about 90 per cent of total gross and net production was obtained from less than 2 per cent of the land, and that almost all that production took place within 100 miles or so of Georgetown (Ministry of Economic

[1] There is some inconsistency between these figures and those given on the previous page of the report which suggested a somewhat smaller proportion of farms under 10 acres in size.

Development, 1975, p. 13).[1] As can be seen from the accompanying map, based on information for 1976, there was considerable land that could have been used. Indeed, the miniscule amount cultivated by smallholders is eloquent testimony to the success of the estates' strategies in preceding generations.

This picture of land fragmentation and under-utilisation was in part a legacy of the nineteenth century tactics of the plantocracy. But it also reflected the struggle of the multinationals and the colonial authorities to retain control as "contradictions" became increasingly acute. This has to be considered from three angles. The first is the structure of production the authorities encouraged and the adaptive responses of the working population; the second is the contrived stagnation preserved by state policies at least until Independence; the third is the prevailing labour relations, notably the paternalistic nature of the estate and bauxite communities. Each has a bearing on the pattern of population mobility, and rural out-migration in particular.

1. The structure of rural production

Towards the end of the nineteenth century, as estate employment began to decline, Indian immigrants settled in large numbers in villages near the estates. By 1921 less than half the working population of adult males were classified as agricultural labourers (British Guiana Census Commissioner's Office, 1921). And in contrast to the negligible and in many years negative rates of natural increase in the nineteenth century, at least by 1921 (and possibly before that census year) the natural rate of population growth was positive and had begun to accelerate. The very high levels of mortality observed in the nineteenth century had fallen, and the low levels of fertility had begun to increase.[2] But the settlement of large numbers of Indians in villages was done as a means of regulating the seasonal supply of labour to the estates. Efforts by the authorities to stimulate and diversify production were, at least in the early part of the twentieth century, negligible. Only rice and sugar cane were actively encouraged.

---

1 In 1968 an FAO study estimated that 2.8 million hectares of good soil could be cultivated if drained and/or irrigated and that a further 3.6 million hectares were suitable for development and livestock-raising.

2 The causes of the mortality decline have received considerable attention. See, inter alia, Mandle (1970, pp. 301-15); Newman (1965).

MAP I:

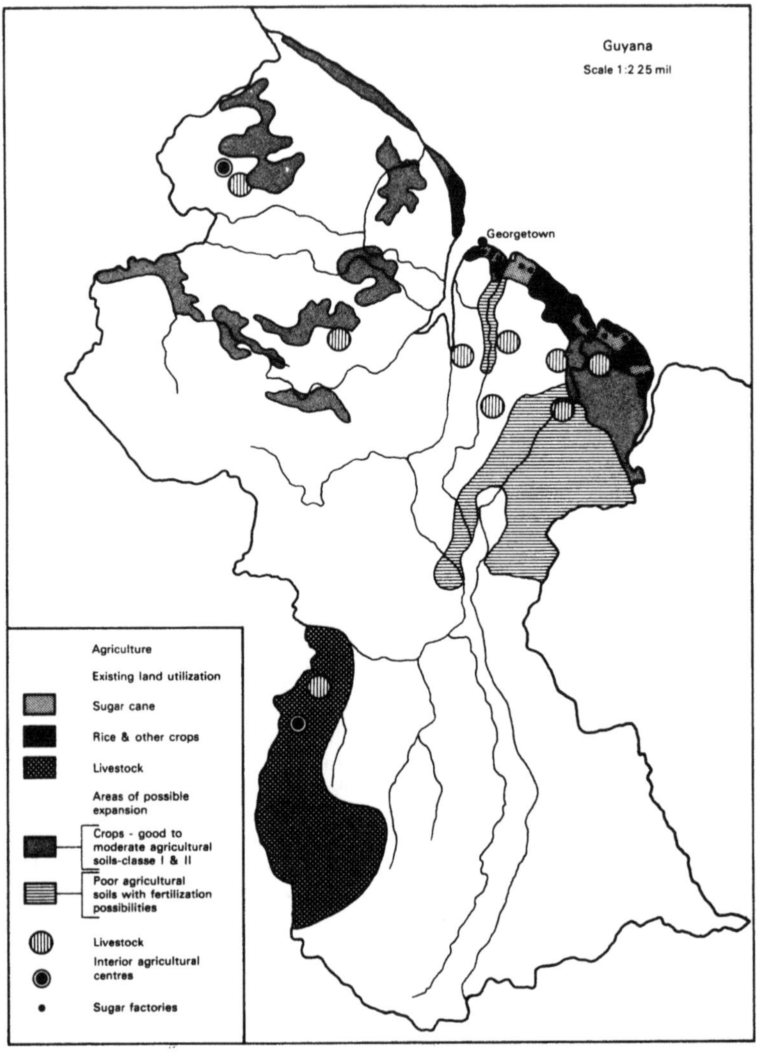
Guyana
Scale 1:2 25 mil
Georgetown
Agriculture
Existing land utilization
Sugar cane
Rice & other crops
Livestock
Areas of possible expansion
Crops - good to moderate agricultural soils-classe I & II
Poor agricultural soils with fertilization possibilities
Livestock
Interior agricultural centres
Sugar factories

The growing peasant population were discouraged from cultivating other cash crops by a combination of state policies and structural impediments to diversification which will be considered later and which shaped the pattern of population mobility. However, from the inception of the village movement crops for plantation production had a higher market return than others, and the authorities encouraged the peasant production of cane. Thus Governor Light in 1840 urged local magistrates to advise villagers to secure contracts for supplying cane to the estates (Smith, 1962, p. 63). Many did grow cane as their principal cash crop, placing themselves in a position of dependence and allowing the estates to appropriate economic surplus. Once induced to grow cane, they had to sell it to the plantations in the absence of any alternative, and therefore had to take the price offered. They were also more tied to wage labour on the estates than if they had been producing subsistence or other cash crops, both in the sense that the estates could refuse to purchase their small amount of cane unless they accepted wage employment and because they were forced to depend on the wage income even if the price of cane and estate wage rates were low. Gradually these petty cane-producers were more intensely exploited by being forced to rely on the estates for credit and by being obliged to purchase fertilisers from them.

Government policies were also geared to induce semi-proletarianised rural workers to grow cane for the estates. Various schemes were introduced in the 1950s including a so-called co-operative and settlement project known as Belle Vue, which forced farmers to produce cane under the direction of the estates, to whom they were required to sell the cane. Such schemes merely rationalised the structure of production into which the plantocracy had locked the rural economy. The political state of mind that induced was reflected in the continued espousal of cane-oriented settlement schemes, aptly summarised by a statement in 1963 by the Chief Agricultural Officer who said, with reference to one settlement scheme (ironically named the Garden of Eden):

> "By putting this area into sugar cane the income of the settlers will be improved greatly. Every ton of cane a settler produces he can sell. At present he is planting citrus, and there is no organised market for his crop." (Benn, 1963, p. 79).

Such statements highlight the constraints, dependence and contrived stagnation under which smallholders traditionally had to operate.

Until 1964, rice production was also very actively encouraged by the State, first as a means of absorbing the surplus population and reducing the necessary subsistence wage while being a seasonally complementary crop for cane, and latterly because rice farmers became a dominant group in the population and the principal source of support for the dominant political party in the 1950s, the PPP.

Although the export of rice was banned for a time in 1917 its production expanded rapidly in the 1920s, and from 1931 onwards more acres were devoted to rice than to sugar cane. The biggest expansion occurred during the Second World War, at a time when sugar production declined due to labour shortages, inadequate fertilisers and shipping difficulties, and when the import of rice was not possible. A central Rice Marketing Board was set up in 1939 to regulate prices and exports during the war, and this became the sole authorised exporter of rice. Subsequently all rice except that used for family consumption had to be sold to that authority. And through the 1950s huge investments by the government and its agencies were made in the rice industry, despite the relatively low yield. Thus it was estimated that in 1957, for example, some 81,000 acres were devoted to sugar cane, producing a crop with a market value of $58 million, while some 22,000 rice farmers with about 137,000 acres of padi produced a crop worth only $17 million (Smith, 1962, p. 63). After 1957 the acreage under rice further expanded, reaching a peak of 394,000 acres in 1964, declining somewhat thereafter but remaining easily the largest user of land (Department of Agriculture, various dates). Rice farming also received the bulk of commercial bank loans to agriculture (table 5). Yet despite mechanisation - or perhaps partly because of it - yields continued to decline. Remarkably, average yield per acre declined from 17.2 bags (140 pounds) in 1899 to 13.4 bags in 1964 (Ramgopal, 1964, p. 16). In 1969 it fell to a mere 9.8 bags per acre, and though that was lower than in subsequent years, productivity scarcely improved despite the planting of improved varieties and more intensive use of fertilisers and technological inputs. The low yields can be explained in part by the inadequate drainage and irrigation. In 1964 it was estimated that less than 40 per cent of the land under rice was drained and irrigated (ibid., p. 17; see also, Caffey and Effenson, 1965, p. 12). Another reason was the persistence of poor farming practices, shown by inadequate land preparation, infrequent weeding, and the lack of crop rotation. According to at least one analysis, those practices worsened in the post-1945 era, and certainly, given changed technologies and seed varieties, their

Table 5: Sectoral distribution of loans to agriculture by commercial banks (G$ '000)

	1967		1970	
	G$	%	G$	%
Sugar cane	50	1.3	559	8.7
Padi	3,072	78.7	2,908	45.5
Livestock	166	4.3	670	10.5
Forestry	145	3.7	128	2.0
Shrimp and fisheries	294	7.5	1,737	27.2
Other agriculture	174	4.5	390	6.1
Total	3,901	100.0	6,392	100.0

Source: Bank of Guyana Annual Report, 1971.

Table 6: Cultivated area of principal crops, Guyana, 1972

Crop	Acres	Square miles
Sugar cane*	130,421	204
Rice and maize	199,919	312
Other crops	54,615	85
Total	384,955	601

* This excludes the 15-20 per cent of sugar estate land left fallow.

Source: Ministry of Economic Development

adverse effect on productivity increased (Madramootoo, 1970).

As rice was unlikely to provide the peasants with a high standard of living, the emphasis placed on it must be seen as reflecting the continuing influence and needs of sugar estates. While rice provided a base for the subsistence of the rural workforce, much of the rice was exported, and in many years exports accounted for about three-quarters of total sales (O'Loughlin, 1958, p. 116). As such, it was an important source of foreign exchange that helped pay for the import of consumer and capital goods. It is also significant that the mechanisation in rice farming in the 1950s and 1960s involved equipment imported through agencies owned by the two multinational sugar companies (Hanley, 1975, p. 134). In other words, the expansion of rice production also directly benefited the estates.

In sum, the emergence of rice as the prime "peasant" crop was the outcome of the encouragement of merchants, the estates, and a government eager to see the absorption of a growing surplus population as well as the continued profitability of the plantation economy. Rice production was a means of lowering the cost of reproducing labour power - both in terms of reducing the cost of subsistence and the necessary wage - while retaining a large labour force in rural areas. Rice fitted into an economic structure based on semi-feudal productive relations, facilitating a higher rate of exploitation and the appropriation of economic surplus. As such, it was certainly not the crop to provide the basis for a structural transformation of the rural economy.

2. Impediments to crop diversification and rural accumulation

The specialisation on rice and sugar cane was the dominant feature of the contrived rural stagnation in twentieth century Guyana. Other crops were neglected or their development discouraged. And among the resources chronically underdeveloped for generations were the forests with their vast array of woods. Indeed the 1953 World Bank Report on Guyana noted that softwoods were imported and could be replaced by domestic woods (World Bank, 1953, p. 14). The underdevelopment of the lumber industry can be simply explained - it would have allowed an outlet for labour power away from the estates near the coast. However, it was the land tenure system and the nature of land fragmentation which were the most pervasive barriers to agricultural development.

As most villages suffered from periodic flooding, and as the small and fragmented plots were generally contiguous, land productivity depended crucially on the drainage provisions of surrounding plots as well as on the landholder's own efforts. This was a major impediment to efficient, innovative farming. A second was that from the beginning the size of the plots was such that the workers were inclined to treat them as a supplementary and not primary source of income. Both these factors discouraged investment or the planting of long-term crops, which of course restricted the range of crops cultivated.

A third impediment was what has been called "praedial larceny" of crops. This was encouraged by a negligible administrative structure in most villages and, crucially, by the fragmented system of landholding by which the farmer's dwelling was often a long way from the cultivated land. This discouraged citrus growing in particular and was cited by the Ministry of Agriculture and National Resources as a major reason for the long-term decline in the cultivation of coconuts (Ministry of Agriculture and National Resources, 1967, p. II.26).[1]

Another impediment to cash-crop farming was the lack of a marketing network, except around Georgetown. Moreover domestic food crops had to compete with imports. Somewhat paradoxically, because the transport (road-and-railway) network was geared to the needs of the plantations, distribution of imports was probably easier and cheaper. On some food items there were import duties, but for many there were none, and as a consequence the growth of food imports long outstripped the growth of domestic food production.[2]

The development of domestic markets was hindered by the isolation of most villages due to poor roads and an inadequate transport system, which the authorities made little attempt to alter. But a further barrier to effective land utilisation, and thus to the development of commercial, capitalist farming, was the widespread lack of registered land titles. As noted earlier, the authorities allowed that to persist. For smallholders, the associated uncertainty discouraged investment in long-term or permanent crops. It also contributed to soil erosion, in that farmers could be expected to have taken less care of

---

[1] From being an exporter of coconuts, Guyana became an importer.

[2] Even towards the end of the period under review this was true. For instance, between 1960 and 1970 imports grew at an annual average of 5 per cent while domestic food production grew by only 1 per cent annually (Ministry of Agriculture, various dates).

the land than if they had been sure of ownership or right of possession. Furthermore, a lack of satisfactory title excluded many farmers from credit or loans, simply because they had no security in the form of land title to offer.

Lack of credit is a severe impediment to the growth of a subclass of capitalist farmers, and in that context two further factors restricted distribution of the type of credit that would have facilitated capital accumulation. The first was that for much of Guyana's history savings that might have been channelled through financial intermediaries into agriculture were mainly invested abroad, largely because of the dominance of commercial banking by two foreign banks (World Bank, 1953, p. 14). These generally lent money locally only for short-term purposes and, consistent with a conservative risk-averting policy, were disinclined to make loans for relatively high-risk agricultural projects (Smith, 1962, p. 79).[1] The World Bank in 1953, for instance, noted that there had never been any credit institution granting medium or long-term credit, except mortgages, and discussed the role of agricultural co-operative banks as being small and oriented to "mortgage rather than productive credits" (World Bank, 1953, p. 37).

In 1954, as part of a general strategy to defuse unrest following the suppression in 1953 of the popularly elected PPP Government of Cheddi Jagan, the Guyana Credit Corporation was established to provide medium- and long-term credit. However, this concentrated on providing small short-term loans, and surprisingly mostly for non-agricultural uses. Indeed the proportion going to agriculture declined, and in 1969 agricultural loans accounted for under 13 per cent of the total value of loans granted and 26 per cent of the total number of loans supplied (Lewars, 1977, p. 43). This pattern of lending was related to the second major reason discouraging the institutional provision of credit for small-scale agriculture, the dislocation of the village economy. With insecure land titles making it hard for credit institutions to get effective collateral, agricultural loans were made even more risky by the land fragmentation, generally bad irrigation and drainage, and related factors. Reflecting the longstanding situation, the Land Use Study concluded in 1970:

---

[1] In 1966, to take a fairly typical year, only 6 per cent of the commercial banks' loans and advances to the "private sector" went to non-plantation agriculture (Bourne, 1974, p. 106).

> "In Guyana it is nearly impossible to obtain credit because the recognised finance institutions associate too high a degree of risk with agriculture. Such operations as land levelling, the development of long-term maturing crops and livestock require credit which must be extended over many years. There is at present no institution private or government which caters primarily for these long- and short-term demands for credit."

Informal credit mechanisms and rural credit unions developed, but interest rates and the precarious nature of agricultural production meant that smallholders generally resorted to loans only out of dire necessity rather than as a means to expand production.

3. The role of rent and usury

Another impediment to agricultural development was the dependent nature of many smallholdings. Rent can be capitalist ground rent or feudal rent, and in Guyana it more closely resembled the latter. Theoretically, the importance of the distinction lies in its impact on the development of forces of production and thus the general process of accumulation. Given the plantocracy's need for contrived stagnation, rent was one means of mopping up surplus; it was also a convenient mechanism for controlling labour supply and population mobility.

Even before indentured labour was established, the estates attempted to bind workers by renting out plots to those prepared to be wage labourers. But during a strike in the early 1840s, the planters overplayed their hand by trying to force workers back to work by threatening to stop tenants from reaping and retaining ground provisions raised on the rented land. Although the planters capitulated in 1842, granting higher wages than intended, many labourers deserted the rented plots once the insecurity of their tenure had been shown. They were demonstrably mere tenants-at-will, while the law had been shown to be on the planters' side (Young, 1958, p. 16). Even so, this early conflict had a long-term significance, for it demonstrated the moral limit of the labour relation, the desertion demoralising planters, who were forced to recognise their precarious control. If rents were pushed too high, workers would desert the estates.

Subsequently, indentured labourers were required to produce part of their subsistence on small rented plots. And even after 1917 that remained an institutional feature of the rural labour market. As an official report in 1949 noted, "Generally speaking, workers are given half an acre or more of estate land, just enough to keep them and their families in rice." (Report, 1949, p. 139). This induced them to work on the estates, since they required the cash to pay the rent and could be evicted if they did not work on the estates (Reubens and Reubens, 1962). And it made wage cuts easier, because of the tie to the land and the reliance on it for at least part of the family subsistence.

The planters, the state, merchants and the multinational companies all rented out land to workers. But although such "semi-proletarianised" workers were not completely divorced from means of production, and were thus motivated to develop the forces of production on the land they possessed, there was an inherent restriction on accumulation, as any surplus was likely to go in higher rents.

Rent was by no means the only mechanism for mopping up non-estate surplus. Indeed, the estates became "patrons-in-capital" as well as "patrons-in-land". As machinery and fertilisers were introduced into the rural economy - encouraged by the development of productive forces on the estates and by the growth of a merchant class - smallholders were obliged to rent equipment, so that any surplus generated by higher productivity largely went to rentiers, often the estates.

In the twentieth century the estates were no longer the only major group impeding rural development. The land tenure structure maintained a basically peasant population, in that reproduction rather than accumulation dictated the behaviour of the great majority of smallholders. But some class differentiation was apparent, though it was basically associated with the prevalence of usury. As a mode of exploitation usury restricted the development of productive forces on the land in so far as the profits went to professional moneylenders, merchants, and others not directly involved in agricultural production.

Theoretically, usury has no clear effect on the development of forces and social relations of production. Some have seen it as essentially progressive in that it reflects and accentuates differentiation, accelerates the formation of a capitalist class, and by contributing to primary accumulation fosters a proletariat dispossessed of the means of production (Dobb, 1963). However, there would be no justification for assuming that usury leads to a transition to capitalism. As Marx noted,

> "Usury has a revolutionary effect in all pre-capitalist modes of production only in so far as it destroys and dissolves those forms of

property on whose solid foundations and continual reproduction in the same form the political organisation is based...usury can continue a long time, without producing anything more than economic decay and political corruption. Only where and when the other prerequisites of capitalist production are present does usury become one of the means assisting in establishment of the new mode of production." (Marx, 1967, p. 597).

In Guyana usury continued for a long time without strongly stimulating the development of productive forces. It was both a mode of exploitation and of control. As used by the estates it helped appropriate remnants of "peasant" surplus not taken by rent and helped tie indentured workers to the estates, thereby restricting migration. As used by merchants and moneylenders it merely dissipated surplus without contributing much to the transformation of the rural economy, primarily because the rural stagnation encouraged the use of surplus revenue in consumption and display, often involving the import of items of conspicuous consumption.

The estates traditionally provided workers with loans or advances for building or improving their housing, even though workers only benefited from improvements as long as they remained in estate employment. They also rented out equipment and provided consumption loans that were often needed to meet a shortfall in income due to inadequate wages or work opportunities on the estates themselves or because a crop failure forced them to purchase additional food. The estates also had company shops from which workers were obliged to buy items of common consumption, giving the estates monopolist profits while contributing to the workers' endemic indebtedness.[1]

Indebtedness to other groups was partly a consequence of the peasants' poverty and insecurity, which forced them to apply for loans at the slightest misfortune and to borrow at exorbitant rates of interest. Indebtedness inflicted most villages and led to widespread alienation of land to speculators, shopkeepers, mill-owners and others living outside the village, who then rented out

---

[1] In general company stores are also a convenient means of limiting the workers' consumption aspirations. If items on sale are limited, workers are less likely to perceive the depth of their deprivation, and are less likely to be drawn into the "money economy" and migration.

the land to its previous owners. For rice-farmers mill-owners were a major source of loans, and as there were only a small number of millers they had a lucrative business as commercial capitalists, purchasing padi from farmers and processing their grain, charging fees for transporting the padi and for milling it into rice. Often millers were also rice farmers, owned land which they operated, rented out other land, owned transport facilities, operated a store, rented out farm equipment and, from the proceeds, and as a mechanism for securing greater leverage for exploitation, indulged in money-lending (O'Loughlin, 1958, p. 120). They thus represented a growing commercial class, extracting surplus from the peasantry and contributing to rural class differentiation.[1] But their numbers always remained small and the scope for accumulation was limited by the low level of productive forces, the contrived stagnation, the various social obligations attendant on relative wealth, and the appeal of conspicuous consumption.

4. The functions of paternalism

Paternalism is a somewhat loose term encompassing a wide range of practices by which employers or landlords look after the interests of their workers in the interest of raising the rate of exploitation. It involves the establishment of ostensibly personal bonds which tend to create "structured reciprocity", a network of informal rights and obligations and, to some extent, a set of constraints to the behaviour of both the dominant and subservient groups. Paternalism may conceal exploitation or indeed reduce it in the interest of creating a dependable labour force, but is a means of maintaining existing modes of exploitation.

Paternalism was always a feature of the sugar industry. Slave-owners provided slaves with a modicum of welfare to cajole them to work, and employers of indentured labour introduced a wide variety of non-wage fringe benefits. In both cases - and also for non-indentured labourers - provision of part of the wage in non-monetary form was both a means of preventing workers from saving to become independent farmers and a

---

[1] One feature hard to investigate was that the absence of reliable titles to much of the land made it hard for moneylenders to turn the peasant off the land by selling to recover the debt. Understandably, potential purchasers would have been reluctant to buy land in such circumstances, which would have meant a lower market value than if title had been secure.

way of ensuring that payment went to reproducing labour power. Above all, supplementing money wages by non-wage benefits was designed to ensure a reasonably efficient labour force.

The paternalism extended from the provision of poor housing and small plots of land to assurances of minimal medical care and basic schooling, all conditional on reliable employment. As early as 1853 every estate was required by ordinance to have an estate "hospital", staffed by a qualified medical practitioner (Young, 1958, p. 75; Lawrence, 1964, pp. 59-67). At various times additional items were added. Thus by the 1950s welfare expenditure for sugar workers included the provision of community centres, clinics, crèches, housing loans, co-operative shops, and courses in "home economics" (Smith, 1962, p. 85). The estates also provided institutional means for settling disputes, long resisting the formation and recognition of unions by the convenient device of making the Colonial Office in London and the Governor in Georgetown responsible for worker protection. Partly as a result of paternalistic labour laws it was not until long after the abolition of the indenture system that trade unions started to represent the Indian immigrants (Chase, 1964; Nath, 1950, Chapter V).[1]

These tactics did not fundamentally alter the real relations. While ostensibly protecting them, the colonial authorities prohibited indentured workers from striking (Adamson, 1972, p. 154). While allowed to make improvements to their rented dwellings - many of which were justly described as "barracks" - with loans provided by the employers, the workers were left in no doubt about their insecure livelihood. This was vividly brought to light by a Commission which reported in 1949 that many men worked all their working lives on the estates to retire still classified as temporary workers (Report, 1949).

A third objective of paternalistic labour relations, which became increasingly important after the Second World War, was the need to placate political pressure for

---

[1] The principal means of ameliorating the grievances of indentured immigrants was the Migration Agent-General, an official appointed by the colonial authorities as protector of labourers' rights. One occupant of the post, James Crosby, became a revered figure in Guyanese folklore. The first union to represent estate workers was the Manpower Citizens Association, established in 1937 and recognised in 1939. It became identified as a company union and was superseded by the unrecognised Guiana Industrial Workers' Union, formed in 1946.

nationalisation by a potentially revolutionary working-class movement. In that context Bookers greatly expanded its welfare paternalism, resettling workers in extra-nuclear housing areas and even drafting a programme for local government.

One outcome of paying part of the wage in non-monetary form was that the correspondingly low money wages prevented workers from acquiring savings to purchase land or means of production, and made it much more likely that the workers would be pushed into debt, which of course could be used to restrict their movement away from the estates. In sum, paternalism was designed to preserve a semi-proletarianised workforce, keeping money wages below the cost of reproducing labour power and tying workers to estate employment.

The dependent insecurity associated with paternalism intensified the odium associated with estate labour, for workers recognised that the limited benefits were merely a means of locking them into the estate areas. It was also recognised that the benefits could be used as a stick as well as a carrot. In the mid-nineteenth century many planters reacted to the reluctance to do estate labour by evicting workers, in the hope that deprivation of lodgings and plots of land would force them back to estate employment. The widespread resentment this caused and the subsequent labour shortage made planters reluctant to repeat this practice, but although more subtle tactics prevailed subsequently, eviction remained a threat to recalcitrant workers (Riviere, 1972, p. 5).

In the twentieth century paternalistic relations of production were also fostered by the state, particularly on land settlement schemes. As discussed later, in the 1950s and 1960s several of these were set up with the objective of encouraging peasant cane-farming under the direction of the estates, which provided housing, drainage, and irrigation, specified the acreage to be planted, and supplied fertilisers and machines for ploughing, at a fee (Thomas, 1977, p. 148).

The paternalism exercised by the bauxite companies was equally pervasive. The two multinationals created "company towns" in which they extracted surplus in one way or another from almost the whole resident population as well as from many living outside them. This was so even though only a small proportion were directly employed by the firms - never more than about 6,000 people, or about 4 per cent of the country's workforce. According to an estimate made in 1968, in the bauxite community of Christianburg-Wismar-MacKenzie only 15 per cent of the resident population were employed by Demba

(Alcan's Guyanese subsidiary) (Grant, 1971, p. 52).[1] The company owned the land on which workers and others rented housing and it prohibited the construction of private accommodation, thus extracting surplus through rent as well as securing a dependent labour force.[2]

Established in 1920, Linden became an area of migrants, and, after a number of ugly racial conflicts, essentially an area of migrants of African origin. In 1960 in the Upper Demerara district, which encompasses the bauxite mining community, only 38 per cent of the population were born in the area, according to the 1960 census. A survey in the mid-1950s suggested that only 11.4 per cent of the adult population in Mackenzie were born in the Mackenzie-Wismar area, and only 7.7 per cent of the Mackenzie-Wismar adult population had been born there (Roback, 1969). According to the 1970 census no less than 46.5 per cent of Linden's population were migrants, nearly two-thirds of whom had arrived in the 1961-70 decade. One factor in the migration was the relatively high wages earned by manual workers in the bauxite industry, even for unskilled workers.[3] But the company's paternalism, used primarily to secure a dependable, efficient labour force, also made the area attractive to many holding out little or no hope of employment in the bauxite industry. This was because the company developed a social infrastructure which, however rudimentary, contrasted favourably with the contrived stagnation in most rural areas. Until the 1960s Demba provided all the rudimentary social services available which included public sanitation, health services, schools, roads, and housing. In doing so it attracted a rapidly growing population, which initially served the company's

---

[1] The community is now known as Linden (or Linden-Mackenzie).

[2] Tenants were made highly insecure by the leases they were required to sign: "That I will vacate the house on request of the Company without any notice and in the event of any failing to leave, the Company shall have the right to take possession and eject me without recourse to law." (cited in M. St. Pierre, 1975, p. 487).

[3] A survey of wages prevailing at the end of 1973 reported that unskilled male wage rates in the bauxite firms were two-and-a-third times those paid to adult male field workers in the sugar industry and two-and-three-quarter times those paid to adult male labourers in the rice industry. Fringe benefits were also much greater (Ministry of Labour and Social Security, 1977).

purposes in that it gave it a sizeable labour reserve. But as this surplus population grew the costs of supporting the community escalated. In particular, despite company attempts to control in-migration by a pass system and restrictions on entry to South Mackenzie, a large "squatter" population emerged, whose poverty represented a health hazard to the authorities. Thus the company provided not only fringe benefits and various forms of credit for its workers, but had to ensure a sufficient development of social services to prevent a dangerous deterioration in public health.

As this obligation intensified Demba attempted to reduce its paternalistic role in the area. In 1964 it set up a trust to operate as a development bank with responsibility to develop housing, improve community facilities, and attract new industrial enterprises. Then in 1965 tentative steps were taken to phase in local government. But the community remained an extension of the bauxite industry; it was not until 1968 that a road was built to connect the isolated community to the coastal area and its position scarcely encouraged industrial diversification. Demba continued to direct community affairs through its financial and technical contribution to the fledgling village council. In 1968 the company revealed that community expenditure accounted for 30 per cent of its industrial payroll (Grant, 1971, p. 65). By that time unions and a new nationalist government, whose political power was based on the support of the Linden workforce, made it impractical for Demba to shed its paternalistic role or avoid a vicious circle into which that role had placed it. The more people who migrated to the township the greater the company's social service costs, and the more it spent on the community to safeguard public health and pacify local and national discontent, the more people were likely to migrate from the rural areas where even such basic amenities as found in Linden were absent. But the effect this situation had on rural underdevelopment cannot be estimated, for Linden sucked many of the relatively skilled workers out of the rural areas. Considering that this occurred at a time of increasing agricultural mechanisation, particularly in the rice sector, the loss of mechanics may have contributed substantially to the declining productivity that accompanied rural mechanisation (Madramootoo, 1970).[1] Whatever the exact effect, there can be scarcely any doubt that the lure of Linden, and indeed the relative availability of social amenities in the more "developed" sugar estates, contributed to the stagnation of other rural areas.

---

[1] See the earlier discussion.

5. The role of the State

As long as the estates were politically and economically dominant it was to be expected that the full machinery of government would be geared to facilitate their profitability. In the main, until Independence in 1966 that was true. But between 1838 and 1966 the power of the plantocracy greatly fluctuated and in some respects at least waned. Very briefly, the plantocracy suffered reverses in the 1840s, until indentured labour was established, but from then until the 1870s the estates were dominant. Electoral reforms in 1891 extended the franchise and reflected the emergence of a merchant class, whose role was both reactionary - restricting accumulation in the industrial sphere (the merchants in Georgetown dealt mainly with import/export trade, helping the accumulation process abroad) - and progressive, in that the merchants were opposed to the dominance of the estates.[1]

The merchants were implicitly opposed to the estates because the latter relied on the restriction of the purchasing power of the working population and on their retention in rural areas. To increase that purchasing power was the *sine qua non* of the merchants. As such they acted as the vanguard of the class opposition to the essentially semi-feudal form of production. But the merchants had only limited potential for political action because the class base for effective opposition was too narrow and weak, given the underdevelopment of industrial capital which was an outcome of the contrived stagnation.

Nevertheless, the 1891 reforms gave the vital political class struggle the necessary impetus. Further constitutional reforms followed in 1909 and 1927 and although the latter were followed swiftly by a period of retrenchment by the estates with the introduction of Crown Colony status in 1928, whereby much of the political control was transferred to the colonial authorities, the plantocracy were by then firmly on the defensive. Their major difficulty was that the economic stagnation they had contrived had produced widespread impoverishment and, with population growth and shrinking labour requirements on the estates, a rapidly growing surplus population. The poverty and unemployment precipitated social unrest, and after a protracted period of strife in the 1930s, set in abeyance by the Second

---

[1] The Constitutional Reform of 1891 extended the vote to those with property other than land and slightly lowered the income qualifications for voting rights.

World War, and reiterated in the general strike at Mackenzie in 1947 and in the Enmore riots of 1948, a national general election based on universal adult suffrage was held in 1953. The elected, avowedly Marxist government of Cheddi Jagan and the PPP was quickly crushed by the British and Americans, partly as a result of the PPP's inexperience and maladroitness but largely because Jagan was vehemently opposed to multinational capital in the country. But just as the riots of the unemployed in Jamaica in 1938 set in train a series of reformist policies for the whole of the British West Indies (epitomised by the Moyne Commission) so the riots of the late 1940s and the events of 1953 accelerated the process in Guyana.

After 1953 state policy, restored to colonial control, was concerned with rapidly ameliorating the worst consequences of the rural stagnation; by this means the authorities hoped to defuse the discontent which had given the PPP such an overwhelming mandate (Grant, 1965, p. 181). Rural stagnation was exacerbated by the continual decline in agricultural employment, the "decasualisation" of estate labour forces which occurred in the 1950s, increasing seasonality of employment, and a reduction in family income due to a reduction of "secondary" jobs and a long-term displacement of women workers on the estates (tables 7 and 8). Open unemployment by the 1950s had become an endemic feature of the economy, and was to remain so (tables 9 and 10).

After 1953 the authorities attempted to stimulate "peasant" production, hoping to retain the rural population in the villages and draw some of the surplus population away from urban and semi-urban areas where they had concentrated and were regarded as politically explosive. But whereas the World Bank Mission in early 1953 recommended a five-year programme (1954-58) heavily concentrated on "directly productive" investment, the government continued to emphasise social welfare expenditure as a means of raising real living standards. The underlying economic structure was not radically affected.

In 1957 new elections were allowed and again won by the PPP. With limited powers, the PPP was committed to agricultural investment and in particular to the interests of the basically Indian rice farmers, who comprised the PPP's principal constituency. This highlights a legacy of the plantocracy's strategy, for the existence of a large rice farming population pressured the nationalistic government to safeguard their incomes and expand rice production, despite its low economic return and the unbalanced nature of rural production.

Table 7: Agricultural employment and female employment in agriculture, Guyana, 1911-1970

Year	Total agricultural employment	% of working population in agriculture*	Female agricultural employment	Female as % of total
1911	106,514	56	43,421	41
1921	84,970	47	32,751	39
1931	74,603	51	24,442	33
1946	61,125	46	15,989	26
1960	59,790	37	9,456	16
1970	46,201	29	3,868	8

* These figures are only approximately comparable, since labour force definitions varied from one census to another.

Source: Population censuses.

Finally, whereas the PPP had a "rural bias" or an essentially "peasant bias", the People's National Congress party which came to power in 1964 was based on the support of the urban working and middle class, and in particular on the African segment of the population. This was a crucial development, for not only did the urban population find their interests better represented but the rice farmers experienced declining incomes and investment in their industry, which was associated with the fall in production noted earlier. Increasingly, the central government was alienated from the mainly Indian rural population and this placed considerable constraints on rural development, which Burnham's government has been unable to overcome. The country became formally a Co-operative Republic in February 1970, and during the next decade the PNC placed much rhetorical emphasis on "co-operativism" as the means of overcoming rural under-development.

Clearly the objectives of the state changed dramatically in the course of the twentieth century. But considering their impact on migration patterns and the geographical distribution of the population - it is worth focusing on four crucial areas of state action - the structure and functions of local government, government fiscal policy, land settlement schemes, and "co-operatives".

Table 8: Weekly employees in sugar industry (field and factory workers) 1950-1970

Year	Total	Field	Factory
1950	28,235	21,641	6,594
1960	20,479	16,001	4,478
1970	17,380	14,212	3,168

Note: These figures exclude administrative and miscellaneous staff and are based on annual returns submitted by the Guyana Sugar Producer's Association to various tribunals of enquiry. The figures represent an estimate of the average number working in the industry each week and are based on weekly records averaged over the whole year. As few workers were employed for anything like a full year the number of workers employed in the sugar industry was very much greater than implied by these figures. Seasonality has been such that, for example, the number of man-days worked in the seasonally peak month was between two and three times the number of workers in slack months. Even in the 1970s an estimated 150,000 persons (i.e. sugar workers and their dependents) relied on earnings in the sugar industry as their principal means of livelihood (Thomas, 1977, p. 51).

Table 9: Unemployment rates by sex, Guyana, 1956 1960, 1965, 1970 (%)

Unemployment	July 1956	April 1960	March 1965*	March 1965+	April 1970
Male	13.8	9.8	7.7	18.4	15.0
Female	25.1	13.7	27.0	27.8	19.6
Total	18.0	10.9	14.1	20.9	15.9

Notes: In 1960 the age limits were 10 years old and over; in the other years the range was 14 years and over. In the 1965 survey two unemployment rates were estimated: * refers to the rate based on the past 12 months; + gives the rate based on the survey week in April 1965, which corresponds to the 1956 figures. The 1970 figures are based on main activity in the past 12 months; the unemployed were those seeking their first job, others seeking work, and those who wanted and were available for work. All figures refer only to those not attending primary or secondary school.

Sources: Population census, 1960, 1970; Labour force surveys, 1956, 1965.

Table 10: Unemployment rates by area and sex, 1977

	Both sexes		Male		Female	
	U_1	U_2	U_1	U_2	U_1	U_2
Guyana	6.6	17.5	5.6	12.0	9.3	30.2
Urban	7.8	19.0	7.1	13.3	9.0	19.4
Rural	6.0	16.9	5.1	11.6	9.4	32.4

Source: Caesar and Standing (1978, p. 18); two definitions of unemployment were used: U_1 is a highly restrictive definition, based on jobseekers in past week; U_2 is a more realistic measure based on availability and need for work. See the source for fuller discussion of the concepts.

(a) The structure of local government

Population mobility is clearly affected by the organisation of community development and local government, since they determine the unevenness of regional and subregional development, the distribution of social amenities, and to some extent the geographical pattern of economic opportunities and incomes. This has been notably true in Guyana, with its peculiar terrain and a coastal region largely below sea level.

The local government system had its roots in the village movement of the 1840s. The liquidation of that movement and the Crown Land regulations concentrated the population on the narrow stretch of coastal land. To flourish, the resultant village economy required comprehensive investments in sea defences, drainage, irrigation, transport and related infrastructure. That required community organisation and local government machinery empowered to collect and organise the use of funds, to allocate tasks to various groups, and to administer infrastructural investments.

The system encouraged by the plantocracy and the colonial authorities was highly decentralised, in that local government was based on the village unit and on the local mobilisation of community labour. However, village councils never had much power and, most particularly before reforms in 1970, were too small to mobilise sufficient resources to be effective or to avoid control from central government, which retained fiscal, technical, and administrative power. This was epitomised by the government-appointed District Commissioners, who emerged in the wake of the 1928 change to Crown Colony status and who were seen by the Governor at that time as "the iron hand in the velvet glove". These officials tended to represent the interests of the plantocracy and have been described as "stifling local initiative" (Grant, 1967, p. 71).

To make matters worse, many villages were never incorporated in the local government network and the sugar estates were conspicuously excluded from its jurisdiction. Indeed the Marshall Report on Local Government estimated that only 54.3 per cent of the rural coastal population came within the ambit of local government (Marshall, 1955). This was largely rectified only in 1970, but by then the party rivalry of the PPP and PNC ruled out effective local government elections, from which the PPP withdrew. Thus the dislocated system of local government persisted.

From its inception, local government raised revenue primarily from rates levied on all landholding villagers. This placed the tax burden on the villagers rather than the estates, which were the only bodies that could have contributed sufficient resources for local infrastructural development. The estates of course were automatically excluded from rate paying by being outside the local government network.

Moreover, as local authorities had little financial power and severely limited statutory functions they tended to avoid tax increases. According to one analyst they "failed to pay loan charges, curtailed services, neglected essential maintenance, and deprived employees of overdue increase in salaries or even of a decent rate of remuneration" (Singh, 1976, p. 73). Indeed, in rural areas the proportion of rates actually collected declined from a low 70.8 per cent in 1962 to 60 per cent in 1964 and 55.8 per cent in 1968 (ibid., p. 81). This exacerbated an already severe shortage of funds and it is scarcely surprising that local government revenue usually accounted for less than 2 per cent of GNP (Odle, 1976, table 4.8, p. 94).

Not only was the revenue always inadequate for village needs, but paradoxically the chief beneficiaries of public expenditure were the estates rather than the villages. And to the extent the villages did benefit from local government, those that benefited most were those nearest the estates. The first means by which the estates benefited was through the receipt of substantial subsidies to meet the "costs" of indentured labour. Even at the end of the nineteenth century, by when there was a recognised labour surplus, the Colonial Office rationalised the continuation of public subsidies on the grounds that further immigration would keep down wages and maintain a plentiful supply of labour (Adamson, 1972, pp. 148-149). Those subsidies were phased out in the early twentieth century, but other subsidies were boosted. For instance, although estates were initially responsible for the construction and maintenance of estate roads and for part of the costs of the medical service provided to estate workers, from the end of the nineteenth century financial and administrative responsibilities for both were transferred to the central government, which acquired the funds mainly from villagers through taxation (ibid., pp. 196, 199).

So local government not only lacked the independence to mobilise village initiatives to stimulate rural development but proved unequipped to raise and allocate funds. All efforts to reform the system were stillborn and after the bitter political experience following the 1970 reforms little improvement can be anticipated in the near future.

(b) Government fiscal-monetary policy

Central government financial policies have also had a pronounced impact on the geographical, sectoral and class distribution of income, wealth and production, and as such have greatly influenced the pattern of population mobility.

Perhaps the major feature has been the inability of the agricultural population to obtain access to government loans and credit facilities. After Independence that was less true, but the pattern scarcely changed. Historically, the large estates had access to extensive credit facilities and were provided with medium and long-term loans, whereas those outside the ambit of the estates received little in either credit or loans and were often faced with censure of land or other assets if they did not pay off debts rapidly. One consequence was that most small cultivators gave up attempting to get government loans, fearing that either they would not be able to pay promptly or some arbitrary government or judicial action would result in loss of land or equipment. From the late nineteenth century onwards insecurity of tenure was such that villagers refused government drainage loans, even when their land was lying under water, fearing their property would be sold at execution if the loans could not be repaid (ibid., p. 88). As noted earlier, no financial institutions provided long-term loans for relatively risky agricultural development, and this was true of government as well as private institutions. Even the British Guiana Credit Corporation, set up in 1954 to fulfil that role, failed to do so.[1] The Guyana Credit Corporation (formerly the BGCC) channelled most of its loans to non-agricultural uses and seems to have been even less "liberal" in extending credit to farmers than commercial banks (Lewars, 1977, p. 51).

Also like commercial banks, at least up to the era of Independence, government financial institutions deprived the rural population of investible surplus by channelling their savings abroad rather than back into the rural economy. For instance, the Post Office Savings Bank, established in 1899 and designed to accommodate small savers, sent most of its deposits abroad. As the World Bank Report of 1953 concluded:

---

1 For a critique of the BGCC, see Thomas (1965, pp. 156-166).

"Although existing regulations provide that up to one third of the total deposits may be invested locally, the funds of the Bank are invested, except for very small holdings of British Guiana securities, in issues of the Dominions and of other colonies." (World Bank, 1953, p. 45).

Similarly, the government's Sugar Price Stabilisation Fund was mostly invested abroad. So one way or another rural areas and the small-scale agricultural sector in particular were deprived of investible funds. The performance of the Guyana National Co-operative Bank, set up in 1970 partly to rectify that situation, will be examined later.

Historically, the impact of taxation was also generally deleterious to rural development, not only channelling surplus from the village population to the estates but increasing labour supply to the estates. Thus the estates received subsidies derived from general taxation, most from indirect taxes but also from rates as well as income taxes.[1] The rationale for using taxes to stimulate labour supply was that the need for cash to pay the taxes reduced the discretionary nature of wage labour force participation. This issue preoccupied colonial administrators. At various times attempts were made to stimulate "tastes" for imported consumer goods. But this was not really satisfactory for the estates' purposes, as it implied commercial growth and was difficult as many estate villages were cut off from contact with urban areas, where living standards were more dominated by such items of consumption. The introduction of non-basic consumer goods increased dissatisfaction with estate life and the low level of subsistence.

In contrast, taxes not only stimulated wage labour force participation but helped increase crop specialisation. From the nineteenth century onwards the plantocracy used fiscal policy to compel peasant farmers to concentrate on sugar cane (Adamson, 1972, p. 257). Cane had sales potential and cash was required to pay for heavily taxed basic commodities.

Government public expenditure policies also had an impact on the geographical and sectoral distribution of income and thus on the pattern of population mobility. In the nineteenth and early twentieth centuries the provision of subsidies to the estates and the emphasis on social welfare spending rather than directly productive

---

1 Traditionally well over half of central government revenue came from indirect taxation (Odle, 1976, p. 202).

investment meant that public expenditure was geared to the needs of the plantocracy and subsequently to ameliorating the consequences for living standards of the contrived stagnation. After the events of 1953 the emphasis began to change but, particularly between 1957 and 1964, most directly productive investment went to bolster rice production. Public investment became heavily biased in favour of housing and the provision of overheads for rice production (Thomas, 1965, pp. 11-12). The latter should be seen in a context of an estimated capital-output ratio of 6:1 in rice production, much higher than that prevailing in other industrial and agricultural sectors (Newman, 1960, p. 275). Indeed the impact of public expenditure on rural development and rural employment could easily be exaggerated, as part of it went to subsidise labour-displacing mechanisation in rice production (Madramootoo, 1970). Perhaps the greatest boost to mechanisation was the Mahaicony-Abary Rice Development Scheme launched by the government in 1942 as a large-scale mechanised rice estate. The scheme was expanded in the 1950s, even though yields were less than in other rice-growing areas and even though "the alternative of using the land and credits for small-scale farming would bring greater soil productivity and increased employment" (World Bank, 1953, p. 157). Rice continued to be heavily subsidised through the provision of marketing depots, extension services and price guarantee schemes.

After the PNC acquired power government resources were shifted away from rice, and government controlled padi prices were allowed to decline. But the adverse effect on rural areas was not compensated by investment in other forms of agriculture. The Guyana Development Plan 1966-1970 shifted public investment to urban areas, where most of the PNC supporters happened to live; this was maintained in the 1972-1976 Plan.[1] As with the PPP, the PNC found themselves struggling to overcome the legacy of contrived stagnation and to some extent their policies could be seen as political expediency. The most immediate consequence was that incomes stagnated, while unemployment grew as the artificially structured rice-growing rural population suffered from declining yields, incomes, employment and prospects.

---

[1] For a discussion of the shift in the pattern of public expenditure, see Standing (1979).

(c) Land settlement schemes

Land settlement schemes in Guyana have not been marginal experiments in attempting to alter population distribution and the structure of production, but for different reasons integral parts of the over-all strategy of successive governments. They had their roots in the communal village movement of the 1840s but really started with the Indian villages set up at the end of the nineteenth century.

The main objective of the early schemes, starting with the Huist Dieven scheme in 1880, was to absorb the emerging surplus population. In effect the schemes were an attempt to alter the social division of labour, encouraging part of the peasantry to produce means of subsistence for themselves and for estate workers, though many of those settled also did seasonal estate labour. By getting settlers to produce their subsistence needs, estate wage rates could be subsidised and reduced. But as can be seen from their location, illustrated in map 2, it is striking that all the early settlements were set up near the estates, which were thereby able to obtain seasonal labour from the settlers.

The early schemes were little more than palliatives to absorb the surplus rural population. Between 1880 and 1930, every one was situated in areas in which the natural vegetation could be characterised as mangrove-marsh-swamp. And though some of those schemes lingered for years, all but one ceased to function. Fundamentally, the cause of their failure lay in the implicit objective of the state policy-makers, who were not really concerned with generating rural development, rising income levels, or agricultural diversification.

Despite the lack of success of the early schemes two new schemes were set up after the Second World War and then after 1953, as part of the effort to defuse social unrest following the political upheavals, there was a spate of settlements. A Department of Land Settlements was established in 1954, and redesigned as a Land Development Department in 1959. In 1960 the largest settlement of all was created, the Black Bush Polder scheme.

It is notable that the second group of settlements, beginning with Anna Regina, were slightly more dispersed. The rationale for settlements after 1953 was to absorb the surplus population and stimulate rural production, but still most of the new settlements were located near the sugar estates. It was not until the 1960s that settlements were established away from that small area. This was the first time settlement schemes were used to open up other areas of potential agricultural production, a tendency subsequently extended with the siting of three

MAP 2

Early land settlement schemes 1880-1930

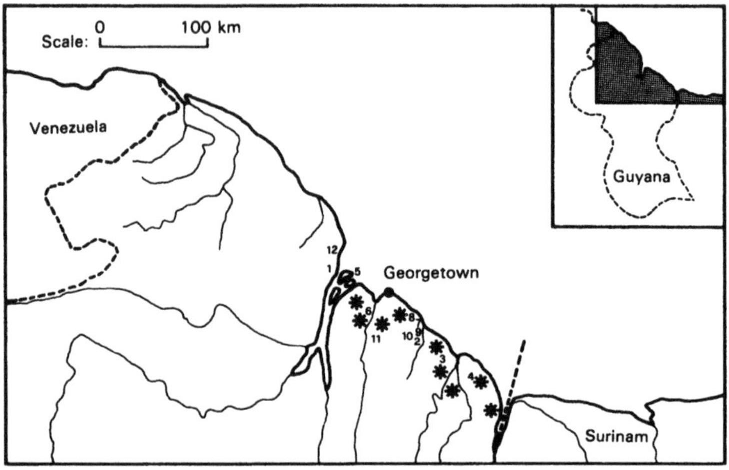

MAP 3

Later land settlement schemes 1940-1968

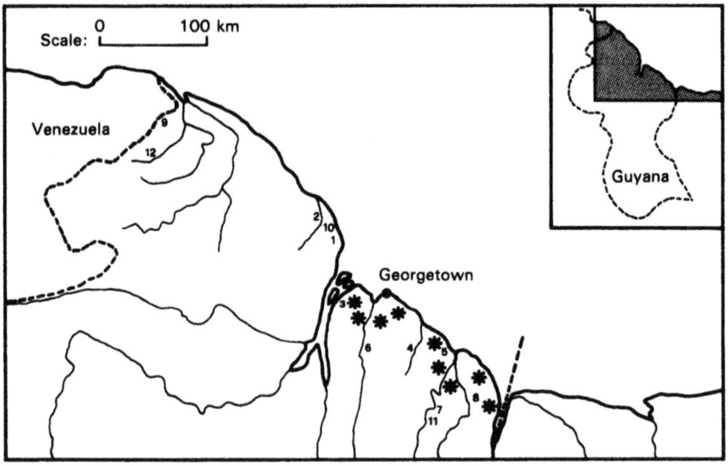

Note: Numbers indicate land settlement schemes in order of establishment. For code see Table 10.
* Indicates main sugar estates in 1970.

national service camps as quasi-military land-clearing settlements in the interior savannah region. As can be seen from table 11 the later settlement schemes were also far more varied in the type of natural vegetation found on the selected sites.

The reasons for the failure of most of the early schemes, and for the very limited success of the later schemes, can be split into two types. The first was the general objective of the schemes which did not place primary emphasis on productive aspects but concentrated rather on the social and political needs of the government and plantocracy. The second type were the more technical reasons, though they were a reflection of the first. There was little formal planning, sites were often poorly selected, and in none of the 17 schemes established before 1956 did the government organise or even subsidise any land clearing, that being left to settlers equipped with primitive implements (Vining, 1976, pp. 86-97). With the exception of the one surviving scheme, all the early settlements suffered from an absence of water control, which the government would have had to organise. In some schemes settlers had to travel miles for well water, while roads were left in a state of disrepair, and no government assistance was available for housebuilding. It was scarcely surprising that settlers drifted away.

Other factors afflicting the schemes were the size of plots, the conditions attached to membership, and the settlers' apparent reluctance to respond as expected. In many ways the problems encountered in the largest scheme of all were typical. Though other settlements involved variants of the arrangements at Black Bush Polder, the main features were similar. Each settler family was provided with a two and a half acre homestead area and a 15 acre plot on which rice had to be grown (or in a few cases a 7 acre plot for permanent crops). Initially, some attempt was made to encourage co-operative production, but this token gesture was soon abandoned. Ostensibly, no land transfers or consolidation were permitted, and responsibility for infrastructure and assistance rested with the government authorities.

The size of plots in Black Bush and in other settlements was loosely based on the expected subsistence needs and work capacity of the typical peasant family. But the schemes rarely succeeded in reducing malnutrition or rural poverty, most failing to live up to even modest official expectations. In Black Bush Polder ambitious drainage, irrigation and other infrastructural projects were launched, but the settlement was never a success, either in generating agricultural development or in retaining the settler population. Reasons for the failure,

Table 11: Land settlement schemes, Guyana, 1880-1968[+]

Map No.	Scheme	Date opened	Natural vegetation	Vegetation at start of scheme	Water control
1	Huist Dieven*	1880	MSM	PC	Poor
2	Helena*	1897	MSM	UM	Poor
3	Bush Lot (W. Berbice)*	1897	MSM	UM	Poor
4	Whim*	1899	MSM	UM	Poor
5	Maria's Pleasure*	1902	MSM	UM	Poor
6	Government estates	1910-13	MSM	PC	Very good
7	Clonbrook*	1913	MSM	UM	Poor
8	Triumph*	1913	MSM	UM	Poor
9	Unity*	1914	MSM	PC	Unknown
10	Lancaster*	1914	MSM	PC	Unknown
11	Craig*	1915	MSM	UM	Unknown
12	Bush Lot (Essequibo)	1930	MSM	SL	Poor
1	Anna Regina	1940s	MSM	SL	Poor; good after 1964
2	Charity Amazon	1944	MS	UH	Fair
3	Vergenoegen	1946	MSM	UL	Good
4	Cane Grove	1947	MSM	UL	Poor
5	Onverwagt	1955	MSM	PC	Poor
6	Garden of Eden	1956	MS	DS	Good
7	Mara	1957	EF	DS	Poor
8	Black Bush Polder	1960	HS	HS	Good
9	Wauna-Yarakita	1964	TR	TR	Good

10	Tapakuma	1964	MSM	DS	Good
11	Brandwagt-Sari	1964	EF	EF	Fair
12	Matthew's Ridge - Arakaka-Kaituma	1968	TR	TR	Good

Note: The classification of initial vegetation and subsequent state of water control are based on data from the National Archives of Guyana and field work carried out by James Vining.

+ Notation:

MSM	: mangrove-swamp-marsh	UH	: unknown, but probably heavy undergrowth
MS	: marsh-swamp	UL	: unknown, but probably light undergrowth
EF	: evergreen forest	SL	: scattered light secondary growth
TR	: tropical rainforest	DS	: dense secondary growth
PC	: predominantly cleared	HS	: herbaceous swamp
UM	: unknown, but probably light to moderate undergrowth		

* Indicates that scheme is defunct.

there as elsewhere, included inefficient administration, the criteria used for homestead allocation, the settling of non-farmers with limited incentives for farming, lack of access to credit, and a persistent lack of supporting services. One reason for the abandonment of holdings was that roads were so bad that they were often impassable in the rainy seasons and impeded communications and the transport of crops.

Another factor was that many settlers had little experience or commitment to independent small-scale farming. This reflected the fact that the settlements were primarily designed to defuse unrest and lower unemployment; many settlers were previously unemployed or displaced wage labourers. In allocating holdings preference was given to those who (a) had large families; (b) were unemployed or in low-paid jobs; and (c) had little or no property. Consequently, settlers tended to be relatively uneducated, to lack work experience or skills, and to have little or no funds for investment. These were scarcely the required ingredients for a successful settler. It was not surprising that absentee farming became widespread, or that in Black Bush Polder, for instance, yields were below the national average despite the rich soil and, far from picking up as the settlement became more established, actually declined. However, it would be a mistake to overemphasise the selection procedures, for that could be misconstrued as suggesting that if only the right individuals had been chosen, the schemes would have flourished. There were more fundamental problems.

At least until Independence, one feature of the settlements was that they tended to reproduce the narrow crop specialisation of the rural economy. This can be seen from the cropping patterns of schemes started after 1953, as shown in table 12. Most schemes were mainly rice settlements and indeed following an official policy decision in 1957 rice schemes were the only type on which the government helped clear the land (ibid., p. 90). The authorities also subsidised mechanisation, mills and related facilities, besides giving price supports to rice.

It was clear that the size of plots was inadequate to provide satisfactory incomes and full-time employment, especially in the wake of the subsidised mechanisation from the 1950s onwards. In 1963, at a fairly early stage of mechanisation of rice farming, it was estimated that a 15 acre plot devoted to padi required about 38 man-days of work per year (Dumont, 1963). For the great majority of settlers rice farming held out the prospect of a low and static income, and this contributed to the widespread absentee farming, which in turn contributed to the declining rice yields and was reflected in seasonal

Table 12: Establishment of land development schemes, 1950-1971

Scheme	Date started	Acreage	Size of holdings	Main crops (initially)
Onverwagt	1955	5,401	5 or 10 acres	Rice
Garden of Eden[1]	1956	1,000	7 (mostly) acres	Citrus, dairy cattle
Mara[2]	1957	3,870	25 acres	Rice and food crops
Black Bush Polder	1960	31,000	17.1/2 acres, 10 acres	Rice mainly. Permanent crops
Tapakuma	1961-62	3,100 1,000	5 or 10 acres Communal	Rice mainly Dairy cattle
Brandwagt/Sari	1963	11,800	Co-operative[3]	Vegetables, permanent crops and dairy cattle
Wauna/Yarakita	1964	1,500	15, 25 or 50 acres[4]	Food, mostly permanent crops
Kurukururu	1970	5,867	10 acres	Permanent crops

Notes:

1 Garden of Eden became an essentially cane-farming area.

2 Mara was a total failure, neither attracting many settlers nor retaining many of those who did take plots.

3 The co-operative failed.

4 The large landholdings were for dairy farming.

Sources: British Guiana Annual Reports of the Director of Agriculture, 1960, 1961, 1965; Ministry of Agriculture and National Resources, Guyana Annual Report, 1969, 1970.

and longer-term migration out of the settlement areas.[1]

Several features of the country's chaotic land tenure system were reproduced rather than ameliorated by the settlements. First, as the World Bank recognised, they were not "real settlements, but rather a form of organised settlements. The farmers are tenants of the government." (World Bank, 1953, p. 208). Second, the disarray surrounding land titles was intensified by the almost clandestine transfer of property that such schemes encouraged. In theory, holdings were only leased to selected occupiers who had no right to transfer their occupancy. But these regulations were widely abused, due in part to indebtedness which was always likely given the narrow margin on which the farmers operated. Many farmers ceased to operate though retaining their land, while others expanded not only by acquiring land from outside the schemes (often from adjacent unoccupied government-owned land) but from disaffected or indebted settlers, making land transfers fairly common. As one observer concluded about one scheme on an ex-estate, Windsor Forest:

> "In theory each occupier...should hold a 99 year lease issued by the government. In practice there has been a good deal of buying and selling of rights, "exchanging" of pieces of land, inheritance and gifts of rights without proper notification and transfer of leases." (Smith, 1957, p. 506).

Such expediency contributed to disorganisation and stagnation on the settlements. A third factor was that rigid institutionalisation of land parcelling accentuated the fragmentation of landholdings, as had inheritance practices. In some instances fragmentation was deliberately created, typically in the interests of "equity". For instance, in Cane Grove, a settlement formed in the late 1940s following the closure of a sugar estate, ex-estate workers were allocated several strips of land of different quality.

Fragmentation became almost as common on land settlements as elsewhere, and as in villages was not necessarily restricted by any relationship between plot

---

[1] A survey of five villages conducted in 1967-68 reported that over half the rice growers had a wage job as well, and that only 4.5 per cent depended solely on rice for a livelihood. For the great majority an extra-village job represented an integral part of his livelihood (Richardson, 1975, pp. 205-224).

size and output. It was argued that fragmentation would be checked at "a certain minimum size beyond which a farm cannot provide a worthwhile return" (ibid.). But that view neglects behavioural responses ranging from poor husbandry to lack of crop rotation leading to soil erosion, and the misutilisation of heavily subsidised mechanised methods, which relied on more intensive labour inputs to raise yields than traditional methods of cultivation (Madramootoo, 1970). With rising production costs, declines in the rice terms of trade in the 1960s and 1970s and the potential economies of scale that mechanisation offered, there was a rise in the size of farm needed to ensure a reasonable standard of living ("worthwhile return"). A small plot that provided a family with an adequate income in 1960 was less likely to do so in the 1970s. That greatly contributed to the increase in part-time farming and absentee landholding, as settlers sought urban employment or were forced to return to seasonal estate labour.

So, settlements failed to overcome the structural inadequacies of the rural economy, perpetuating inefficient husbandry, underutilisation of cultivable land, seasonality of employment, and rural unemployment. They scarcely checked rural out-migration or caused a substantial shift of population away from the suburban and urban centres, as was one of their objectives.

(d) Co-operativism

Guyana became the Co-operative Republic of Guyana in February 1970. Institutional reform is often regarded as the means of overcoming rural underdevelopment and as essential if rural-urban migration is to be reduced without resort to repressive controls.[1] In Guyana its advocates have always seen "co-operativism" as a social vehicle for doing both, by transforming the material base and social relations of production stimulating agricultural and industrial diversification and a more balanced distribution of the population.

The PNC régime has stumbled from crisis to crisis preaching the virtues of co-operativism, or "co-operative socialism". According to the rolled-over 1972-1976 Development Plan:

---

[1] Significantly, the only country in Latin America in which the urban population has grown slower than the total in recent years is Cuba (see Landstreet and Mundigo, 1978).

"The attraction of Co-operativism lies in its propensity to promote egalitarianism, in its ability to create self-reliance and, as a result, greater self-employment opportunities, and its capacity to promote national unity since various groups can live and work together in the Co-operative Unit."

The appeal of co-operativism stemmed from the post-1838 village movement, the belief being that similar forms of co-operatives would flourish in rural Guyana if incentives and political encouragement were provided. The post-Independence government emphasised the voluntary nature of co-operatives and made no attempt to impose a specific set of rules and procedures for the evolution of partial into full co-operatives. This is important, for the "voluntaristic" principles of the Co-operative Republic were not set in 1970 let alone in the mid-nineteenth century, but in a Co-operative Societies Act of 1948, when the colonial authorities were certainly not intent on securing a transition to socialism. More probably they saw co-operatives as a means of alleviating poverty and inequality and thereby placating an increasingly rebellious population. Therefore, it seems strange for post-Independence planners to hope that such defensive mechanisms would transform themselves into a vehicle of a socialist transformation.

A lack of useful data makes it difficult to assess the impact of co-operativism on rural production. However, there are at least four reasons for believing they have increased inequality and class differentiation.[1] First, with the emphasis on voluntary participation and acceptance of partially co-operative enterprises, there has been a powerful tendency for co-operatives to be little more than loose alliances of farmers or other groups, alliances which at most have enabled the more efficient or active members to secure credit or other resources or a market for their products, while often enabling them to exploit the remainder. Worker recognitition of this tendency led to widespread alienation from co-operatives. On land settlement schemes, to give the most dramatic example, attempts to foster co-operative production were abandoned, as in Black Bush Polder and Brandwagt/Sari (table 12). It is significant that nowhere have "peasant" communities voluntarily transformed themselves into

---

[1] For a more extended discussion of the issues mentioned in this section, see Standing and Szal (1979, pp. 70-6).

quasi-socialist organisations.[1]

The second reason for believing co-operatives have increased rather than reduced inequalities and class differentiation is that the main form of co-operatives has been the so-called savings-and-thrift society. Many such societies have been formed, including a large number in primary and secondary schools, so that children have contributed to the generation and mobilisation of small surpluses for investment. However, beneficiaries have been generally those with the means of production to make use of credit, so that in practice the societies have been a vehicle by which relatively affluent and powerful members of communities have acquired the small savings of the poor and have thereby strengthened their relative income, wealth and status. Moreover, though it is not possible to estimate the sectoral distribution, it is likely that much of the savings have been channelled into urban and semi-urban enterprises and away from relatively backward villages, for the same reasons that commercial banks and other financial intermediaries have traditionally done so.

Third, even "co-operatives" formed to purchase land have had little impact on rural development. Some of these have been formed as investment schemes for urban-based speculators - including civil servants - with the purpose of purchasing land to be farmed on an absentee basis or left idle as a speculative holding. Where land co-operatives have been formed to enable groups of farmers to purchase a reasonably large tract of land, the extent of joint farming was limited, often lasting only as long as it took to establish rudimentary drainage and irrigation facilities or for individual farmers to acquire sufficient savings to risk farming independently. According to the government's Chief Co-operative Officer, in such cases the less successful or active have drifted away or remained only if they could get the land divided into separate freehold plots (Hoyte, 1977, p. 7). Recognising such tendencies, officials resorted to the

---

1 Throughout the world the immediate aspirations of peasants and petty commodity producers have been individualistic by virtue of their class experience. Conditioned to struggling to retain some tiny plot or minimal quantity of some other means of production, they have identified their immediate objectives as marginal improvements in those terms, their daily and lifetime struggle defining their subjective and objective horizons. Conceiving of a new social structure has only rarely and momentarily inspired the collective consciousness of the poor.

argument that this reaction would decline as the commitment to co-operatives evolved. But there is no evidence or reason to believe either the commitment or reaction has changed.

Fourth, key co-operative institutions failed to help transform the economic structure or substantially reduce various inequalities, because they existed in competition with non-cooperative enterprises, and adopted the principles of those organisations in an attempt to match their efficiency. The most notable is the Guyana National Co-operative Bank, set up in 1970. The GNCB should have helped reduce the flow of surplus out of rural areas. Commercial banks had retarded over-all deposit growth in Guyana, as they were urban-based and thus inaccessible to the rural majority of the population; it was hardly economical for the banks to set up branches in villages where there were few income earners (Bourne, 1974, p. 111). In contrast, anybody could make a deposit with the GNCB through the Post Office Savings Bank, which did have a widely dispersed branch network.

Ostensibly, the GNCB was established to aid co-operatives, notably in agriculture. In practice, to the extent it mobilised any extra savings for investment it tended to be a vehicle by which funds flowed from small-scale, mainly rural savers to business and commercial enterprises. Indeed, in 1971, for example, only 5.2 per cent of its loans went to agriculture (compared with 8.9 per cent in the case of the foreign-owned commercial banks) (ibid., p. 115). The inability of the GNCB to change the pattern of lending was largely because it was in competition with the private banks and, in adopting traditional banking principles, lent mostly to the most creditworthy, requiring collateral and preferring larger, established enterprises to supposedly more risky smaller enterprises.[1] Even though it made concessions to co-operatives in terms of lower interest rates and less collateral, the traditional banking practices (enunciated most forthrightly in the GNCB's Annual Reports by the chairman) meant that the GNCB often lent to private firms more readily than to co-operatives. It was scarcely encouraged to change its practices by the government's failure in the late 1970s to reimburse the GNCB for bad debts reasonably promptly or to cover risky investments. In short, it seems the GNCB did not reduce inequalities or contribute substantially to the efforts of rural producers to overcome low incomes and stagnation. There is no reason to think that co-operatives have been well

---

[1] In discussions with GNCB officials in 1978 this tendency was candidly admitted.

conceived or developed in Guyana, or that they have induced a more balanced distribution of the population.

V. Conclusions

Until very nearly the end of the nineteenth century the plantocracy and colonial authorities were intent on restricting migration. Thenceforth governments have tried to redirect the migration that was occurring, and their efforts offset to some extent the underlying pattern of rural emigration. Indeed for that reason it is extremely difficult to estimate the extent or changing levels of migration, for the limited data available only indicate net movements. However, certain features emerge quite clearly.

The most striking is the racial or ethnic problem. It is tempting to analyse most social phenomena in Guyana in racial terms, and it is implicit in this paper that that would be a mistake. Nevertheless, the geographical and sectoral distributions of the various races are such that it is clear that there is a racial division of labour. The explanation is straightforward. After emancipation the ex-slaves moved away from the estates to form "African villages" and in some cases to become artisans in urban areas. From the mid-nineteenth century Portuguese and Chinese immigrant labourers were displaced on the estates by indentured East Indian "coolie" labour; they then became the nucleus of a merchant class, many becoming small shopkeepers (Lawrence, 1965, pp. 50-74).[1]. Able to charge high prices because of their monopolistic control of local marketing, Portuguese shopkeepers were attacked as early as 1856, in the "Gabriel riots". Racially identifiable, their role in the village economy was long resented, especially as they were often important local moneylenders. It is significant to note the authorities' reaction to the exploitation, by which mark-ups on basic foodstuffs such as saltfish, flour, and rice were as high as 60 per cent, and sometimes up to 300 per cent. Numerous reports show officials knew of the exploitation, but no restrictive policy was formulated (Bourne, 1975, p. 519). Almost certainly, this can be attributed to the planters' desire to weaken and control the African population, who had to work more to acquire money to pay the inflated prices.

---

[1] The Chinese were never very numerous but soon settled in urban areas despite efforts to establish "Chinese villages" at the end of the nineteenth century (Young, 1958, p. 152).

The East Indians came to predominate in the sugar estate areas and then in the "Indian villages" near the estates. By 1891 over three-quarters of all those occupied in agriculture were East Indians, at a time when they accounted for only 38 per cent of the total population. Subsequently, in the 1950s and early 1960s a large proportion of the plots on settlements were allocated to East Indians, the land mostly being given to landless workers.[1] Conversely, the bauxite community of Linden became a predominantly Afro-Guyanese area, especially after racial violence in the early 1960s, during which many Indians fled the area. And Georgetown and New Amsterdam have always had a disproportionately large number of Afro-Guyanese. In sum, the racial distribution of the population has continued to display the social division of labour created by the plantocracy.

For most of Guyana's history, population distribution and the pattern of migration reflected the efforts of the plantations and mining companies to secure a pliant, low-cost labour supply. Given the sparse population and the concern of the plantations, colonial authorities and multinational capital to limit accumulation in the country, state policies helped concentrate the population around the major estates. But the more successful those policies the more their inherent contradictions induced social instability, in the wake of population growth, labour-displacing mechanisation, rising urban unemployment, and worsening poverty. It was then that the state resorted to such palliatives as land settlement schemes and subsidised rice cultivation.

The legacy of the contrived stagnation was pervasive, for despite the slight possibility of a revolutionary transformation in 1953, the inertia built into the social formation proved remarkably resilient. For instance, paternalistic labour relations induced a sense of dependent insecurity among workers. The lack of a tradition of commercial farming and independent enterprise partly explain the failure of settlement schemes and the more recent apparent failure of costly national service agricultural ventures. Once rural producers are even semi-proletarianised, the process is unlikely to be reversed.

Similarly, while a chaotic land tenure situation was being allowed to develop, a legal system was being moulded in Georgetown making it extremely difficult to untangle the land laws, with individual rights and claims being the subject of almost interminable litigation.

---

[1] Despres documented that tendency for Black Bush Polder (Despres, 1967, p. 248).

Likewise, once political institutions had been established in a way that impeded rural development, attempts at local government reform, as in the widely-approved Marshall Plan of 1955, proved practically stillborn. The political superstructure had been created as a highly centralised system whereby economic surplus could be appropriated from the village population and redistributed to the estates and urban élite. This was facilitated by the ineffectual and highly fragmented system of local government that prevented villages from achieving the co-ordination and resource mobilisation essential to arrest rural stagnation. Correspondingly, government fiscal, monetary and expenditure policies channelled funds from the labouring population to the estates and to some extent to urban areas. For many years sanitation, health and educational facilities were concentrated in urban, suburban and estate areas, so that, for example, malaria control was neglected in other, rural areas.

Clearly the plantocracy did ensure the under-development of productive forces off the estates and by repatriating profits impeded internal accumulation and industrialisation. This persisted even after the emergence of a surplus labour population, which could have migrated to areas of urban-industrial growth to provide a low-cost proletariat. Even in the 1950s attempts to set up an Industrial Development Department were effectively resisted, while efforts to extend hydro-electrification to rural areas were prevented by the bauxite companies, which had the capacity to extend it.[1] Without substantial accumulation, rural poverty, insecurity and unemployment became endemic, and contributed to high levels of urban unemployment.

The resort to land settlements was designed to defuse social unrest, absorb the surplus population, and alter the pattern of migration which had concentrated the population in and around Georgetown. But because of the conflict between the social welfare role of such schemes and the need to increase production, they were mostly ineffectual on both grounds. The schemes did have some impact on population movements in that there were settlers, but many of those came to spend much of their time away from the schemes, while others have left altogether - often leaving their land virtually idle. The schemes have had only a small impact on the concentration of the population in the coastal region, and if the settlement model as used in the 1950s and 1960s is used to try to open up the interior, the prospects of doing so are bleak indeed.

---

[1] For revealing anecdotes from a former government official, see Thorne (1963, pp. 210-218).

References

Adamson, A.H. (1972): Sugar without slaves: The political economy of British Guiana, 1838-1904 (New Haven, Yale University Press).

Benn, B.H. (1963): Extracts from seminar on land development, held under the auspices of the Hon. B.H. Benn, Minister of Agriculture, Forests and Lands (Georgetown, Government Printers, Dec.).

Booker McConnell Ltd. (1955): Booker's sugar (London, Thomas and Newman Ltd.).

Bourne, C. (1974): "The political economy of indigenous commercial banking in Guyana", in Social and Economic Studies, Mar., Vol. 23, No. 1.

--- (1975): "Review article: The plantation economy of Guyana", in Social and Economic Studies, Dec., Vol. 24, No. 4.

British Guiana Census Commissioner's Office (1921): Report of the results of the census of population, (Georgetown, Argosy Co., 1922).

Caesar, N. and Standing, G. (1977): The labour force in Guyana: A preliminary report (Geneva, ILO; mimeographed World Employment Programme research working paper; restricted).

Caffey, H.R. and Effenson, J.N. (1965): An appraisal of rice production and marketing problems in British Guiana (Georgetown, Government Printers).

Chase, A. (1964): A history of trade unionism in Guyana, 1900-1961 (Demerara, Guyana, New Guyana Company Ltd.).

Commission of Inquiry into the Sugar Industry of British Guiana (1949): Report (London, HMSO).

Co-operative Republic of Guyana (1970): Land use study (Georgetown, Nov.), Vol. I.

Co-operative Republic of Guyana (1971): Land use study (Georgetown, Government Printers), Vol. III.

Department of Agriculture: Annual reports (Georgetown, various dates).

Despres, L. (1967): Cultural pluralism and national politics in British Guiana (Chicago, Rand McNally and Co.).

Dobb, M.H. (1963): Studies in the development of capitalism (London, Routledge and Kegan Paul).

Dumont, R. (1963): Report to the Government of Guyana of planning agricultural development (Rome, FAO).

Farley, R. (1953-54): "The rise of the peasantry in British Guiana", in Social and Economic Studies, Vol. 2, No. 4.

Government of British Guiana: Annual reports of the Government of British Guiana (Georgetown).

Grant, C.H. (1965): "The politics of community development in British Guiana, 1954-1957", in Social and Economic Studies, June Vol. 14, No. 2.

--- (1967): "Rural local government in Guyana and British Honduras", in Social and Economic Studies, Mar., Vol. 16, No. 1.

--- (1971): "Company towns in the Caribbean: A preliminary analysis of Christianburg-Wismar-Mackenzie", in Caribbean Studies, Apr., Vol. II, No. 1.

Green, W.A. (1969): "The apprenticeship in British Guiana, 1834-1838", in Caribbean Studies, July, Vol. 9, No. 2.

Hanley, E.R. (1975): "Rice, politics and development in Guyana", in I. Oxaal, T. Barnett and D. Booth (eds.): Beyond the sociology of development: Economy and society in Latin America and Africa (London, Routledge and Kegan Paul).

Hoyte, G. (1977): Co-operatives: the Guyana experience (Georgetown, Ministry of Co-operatives and Community Development; mimeographed).

Landstreet, B. and Mundigo. A.I. (1978): Development policies and demographic change in socialist Cuba, paper presented at the annual meeting of the Population Association of America, Atlanta, 13-15 April 1978.

Lawrence, K.O. (1964): "The development of medical services in British Guiana and Trinidad, 1841-1873", in The Jamaican Historical Review, Vol. IV.

Lawrence, K.O. (1965): "The establishment of the Portuguese community in British Guiana", in The Jamaican Historical Review, Nov., Vol. V, No. 2.

--- (1965): "The evolution of long-term labour contracts in Trinidad and British Guiana, 1834-1863", in The Jamaican Historical Review, May, Vol. V.

Lewars, G. (1977): Small farm financing in Guyana, 1968-1970 (Mona, Institute of Social and Economic Research, University of the West Indies).

Madramootoo, H. (1970): Declining paddy yields, or the rice farmer and his machine (Georgetown, Guyana Rice Corporation, Oct.).

Mandle, J. (1970): "The decline in mortality in British Guiana, 1911-1960", in Demography, Aug., Vol. 7.

Marshall, A.H. (1955): Report on local government in British Guiana (Georgetown, Argosy Co. Ltd., May).

Marx, K. (1967): Capital (New York, International Publishers), Vol. III.

Masefield, G.B. (1950): A short history of agriculture in the British colonies (Oxford, Oxford University Press).

Ministry of Agriculture and National Resources (1967): Annual report of Agricultural and Land Development Departments (Georgetown, 1967).

Ministry of Agriculture: Annual reports (Georgetown, various dates).

Ministry of Economic Development (1975): National transport plan (Georgetown).

Ministry of Labour and Social Security (1977): Annual report for the year 1973 (Georgetown, Government Printers), Appendix I, table V.

Nath, D. (1950): A history of Indians in British Guiana (London, Nelson and Sons).

Newman, P. (1960): "The economic future of British Guiana", in Social and Economic Studies, Sep., Vol. 9, No. 3.

--- (1965): Malaria eradication and population growth (Ann Arbor, University of Michigan, School of Public Health).

Odle, M. (1976): The evolution of public expenditure: The case of a structurally dependent economy: Guyana (Mona, ISER).

O'Loughlin, C. (1958): "The rice sector in the economy of British Guiana", in Social and Economic Studies, June, Vol. 7, No. 2.

Pan American Health Organisation (1976): National food and nutrition survey of Guyana (Washington DC, WHO).

Ramgopal, L. (1964): Our rice industry (Georgetown, Rice Producers' Association).

Reubens, E.P. and Reubens, G.B. (1962): Labour displacement in a labour surplus economy: The sugar industry of British Guiana (Mona, ISER, University of the West Indies).

Richardson, B.C. (1975): "Plantation infrastructure and labour mobility in Guyana and Trinidad", in H. Safa and B. du Toit (eds.): Migration and development: Implications for ethnic identity and political conflict (The Hague, Mouton Publishers).

Riviere, W.E. (1972): "Labour shortage in the British West Indies after emancipation", in Journal of Caribbean History, May, Vol. 4.

Roback, J. (1969): Bases of social differentiation in a Guyanese mining community, unpublished M.A. dissertation (Department of Sociology, McGill University).

Roberts, G.W. (1952): "A life table for a West Indian slave population", in Population Studies, Vol. V, No. 3.

Roberts, G.W. and Johnson, M.A. (1974): "Factors involved in immigration and movements in the working force of British Guiana in the 19th century", in Social and Economic Studies, Mar., Vol. 23, No. 1.

Senate of Canada (1969): Proceedings of the Senate Standing Committee on Foreign Affairs Respecting the Caribbean area, Second Session, 28th Parliament, 25 November, No. 3 (Ottawa).

Singh, P. (1976): "The politics of local government reform, 1930-1970", in H. Lutchman, P. Mars and H. Addo (eds.): Selected issues in Guyanese politics (Georgetown, University of Guyana).

Singh, S. (1977): The demography of social change in Guyana, unpublished Ph.D. dissertation (Berkeley, University of California).

Smith, R.T. (1957): "Economic aspects of rice production in an East Indian community in British Guiana", in Social and Economic Studies, Vol. 6, No. 4.

--- (1957): "Rice production in an East Indian community in British Guiana", in Social and Economic Studies, Dec., Vol. 6, No. 4.

--- (1962): British Guiana (Oxford, Oxford University Press).

--- (1964): "Ethnic difference and peasant economy in British Guiana", in R. Firth and B.S. Yamey (eds.): Capital, saving and credit in peasant societies (London, Allen and Unwin).

Standing, G. (1979): "Socialism and basic needs in Guyana", in G. Standing and R. Szal: Poverty and basic needs (Geneva, ILO, 1979).

--- (1981): "Migration and modes of exploitation: The social origins of immobility and mobility", in Journal of Peasant Studies, Jan., Vol. 8, No. 2.

Standing, G. and Szal, R. (1979): Poverty and basic needs (Geneva, ILO).

St. Pierre, M. (1975): "Race, the political factor and the nationalisation of the Demerara Bauxite Company", in Social and Economic Studies, Dec., Vol. 24, No. 4.

Thomas, C.Y. (1965): Monetary and financial arrangements in a dependent monetary economy (Mona, ISER).

--- (1977): Plantations, peasantry and the state (Georgetown, University of Guyana, Institute of Development Studies; mimeographed).

Thorne, A.P. (1963): "Some reflections on British Guiana", in Social and Economic Studies, June, Vol. 12, No. 2.

Vining, J.W. (1976): "Site development and settlement scheme failure in Guyana", in Journal of Tropical Geography, June Vol. 42.

World Bank (1953): *The economic development of British Guiana* (Baltimore, Johns Hopkins Press).

Young, A. (1958): *Approaches to local self-government in British Guiana* (London, Longmans).

Chapter 9

AGRARIAN STRUCTURE, MIGRATION AND THE STATE IN CUBA

by David Lehmann*

I. Introduction and Summary

Many underdeveloped countries are experiencing rapid rates of economic growth without those changes in social structure predicted by Marxist theories of capitalist development or sociological theories of modernisation. Where one might expect a decline in the number of smallholders, one often finds an increase; where one expects an increasing proportion of wage-earning proletarians in the labour force, one finds scarcely any increase at all, in town or country, and where one expects a decline in the kinship-based organisation of production and distribution it seems to survive and even expand from the countryside into the towns (Goodman, 1977, pp. 3-32). Of course, these trends are not universal, but are frequent (in the north-east of Brazil, for example) and probably more frequent than cases which conform to a "conventionally" expected pattern. In analysing the occupational structure of such countries social scientists might seek to explain how expected changes in social structure have "failed" to follow observed economic changes (though explaining an absence is not easy). In this study of Cuba the most general question is the reverse: how has the social structure been able to change so drastically while the structure of material production has remained largely unchanged and its volume increased but erratically, especially during the 1960s.

This paper will concentrate on two major features of the transformation of Cuban society, and indeed of the mode of production prevailing within it: the place of private agricultural production in a centrally planned economy, the changing balance between private agricultural producers and the rural proletariat, and patterns of migration and urban growth. In all these areas Cuba exhibits characteristics which differ radically from those we have come to expect in underdeveloped capitalist countries undergoing rapid transformation. It could be said that in these countries the peasantry fills two crucial

* University of Cambridge.

roles: it reproduces its own labour force at little or no cost either to the state or to corporate capital, and it contributes to the reproduction of the labour force as a whole through the production of wage goods, especially food, more cheaply than capitalist producers would produce them. The reasons for this are explained at the beginning of section III.2, and it is necessary to state here that this contention remains controversial (for a review of some of the issues see Lehmann, 1980a, 1980b), but assuming that the thesis has some validity, it is indirectly supported by the Cuban case which, as a socialist model of development, offers a radically different picture: in Cuba, the private sector of agriculture is, from the point of view of capital accumulation, probably "not exploited enough": this point is developed in section III.2.

Similarly, Cuba offers a strong contrast to the processes of proliferation and fragmentation of small-scale agriculture and to the increase in seasonal rural employment, and parallel decline of the permanent agricultural wage labour force which is observed in the more dynamic capitalist countries of Latin America.[1] In Cuba we find a probable growth, and certainly a stabilisation of the permanently employed rural proletariat, and a reduction of seasonal labour migration, together with a slow reduction of private holdings and an expansion of their average size.

These differences can be explained in the most general terms by the obvious point that Cuba has embarked on a socialist path of development. But more specifically, it is also worth pointing out that this causal mechanism has been mediated by the administrative (or planned) character of the economy, and in particular of the labour market, and also by the well-known difficulties arising from the trade boycott imposed by the US and Latin American countries, which has only partially been lifted in recent years as some Latin American countries have resumed trade with the island. The process and structure of growth in Cuba is conditioned by three major factors: the island's continuing and extreme dependence on export of one single crop, sugar, the already mentioned boycott, and the inevitable - and necessary - dislocations produced by any revolutionary transformation, and in particular by the radical redistribution of income which has occurred in Cuba. Thus it would not be true to say either that the differences between Cuba and capitalist societies in Latin America arise from the socialist

---

[1] Some of these tendencies are summarised in Lehmann (1981).

model alone, nor would it be correct to say that they arise from the differences in growth processes.

Although research on Cuba is hampered by a scarcity of statistical data, especially on the state sector of agriculture and its use of labour, the themes of this paper can be approached in a most interesting and relevant fashion by "entering" through seasonal labour and private agricultural production - both issues which are closely related to the question of migration. The following paragraphs offer a summary of some of the main points.

Although seasonal labour seems to have increased during the 1960s, and was made visible by large-scale mobilisations of urban workers for agricultural work, the long-term trend has been a reduction of such seasonal movements and an apparently large increase in the numbers of permanently employed agricultural workers on state farms whose precise numbers remain unknown. Initially the private sector of agriculture experienced a substantial growth in number and area of farms, but subsequently this growth was reversed, though it continues to account for an important portion of agricultural activity and the private farmers are in no way an underprivileged stratum of Cuban society. Private farmers have a right to the same rations as all other groups, plus their own subsistence production, although they have less access to common services such as electricity and housing. The latter, however, is in desperate shortage among all social groups.

Private sector farming is ceasing to be a family-based system of production, since the state has gradually displaced the family from crucial decisions in the allocation of labour and capital and, to a lesser extent, land. I have called this a process of structural differentiation (see section V). It is directly related to penetration and control by the state apparatus, and embodies a broad process of bureaucratisation of social relationships. That is, they become more single-stranded, more impersonal, and subject to bounded authority structures.

It emerges that although smallholders have sustained reasonable levels of consumption, their production has not risen, and may have fallen; the national diet remains highly dependent on imports, despite notable advances in rice, egg and milk production, and political and managerial efforts are largely oriented to the export sector in agriculture. Economic growth has been erratic: table 1 shows that after the violent fluctuations in the 1960s, 1970 was a year in which sugar spurted ahead, at the expense of other sectors (hence the contrast in that year between Industrial Product, which includes the refining of cane into sugar, and GMP). Thereafter,

Table 1: Indicators of economic growth rates, 1962-78 (1962-66 at constant prices; 1967-68 at current prices)

	Global social product		Gross material product	Industrial product
1962				
1963	-1.1		1.0	-1.7
1964	7.3		9.0	4.2
1965	4.9		1.5	3.5
1966	-1.0		-3.7	-1.9
1967	n.a		n.a	n.a
1968	1.6		7.2	-1.8
1969	-1.3		-4.5	1.5
1970	15.4		0.6	25.9
1971	7.4		14.7	4.4
1972	16.2		25.3	6.7
1973	14.4		11.1	11.9
1974	12.5		10.5	8.1
1975	12.1			11.4
1976			4.0	
1977				
1978	7.4	(GNP)		
1979	4.5-5.0	(GNP)		
1980 (planned)	3.0	(GNP)		

Sources: To 1975, Mesa-Lago (1978, p. 57). Also, reports of Chief of Planning Board to People's Assembly, in Granma Weekly Review, 21 January 1979 and 6 January 1980. Data are not available for 1967, a year of deep crisis and of important changes in economic management and organisation, but the indications are that it was a year of zero, and probably negative, growth. For 1978-80, the source spoke of GNP, not GSP.

high growth rates reflect the recuperation of non-sugar sectors and the high world price of sugar in the early mid- 1970s. From 1975 onwards, the world sugar price declined and, although data are missing for several years, the over-all rate of growth seems to have declined gradually after 1975. But the society has been transformed by an extraordinary improvement in services, especially health and education, and by the development of numerous complex forms of political participation. The major expansion of employment opportunities has occurred in state-run services, not in the informal sector or in manufacturing (table 3), and since services in Cuba do go to where the people live, this is not entirely surprising. Hence the paradox: modernisation without - or with fitful - growth.

Thus there has been a process of modernisation in the sense of a growing importance of formalised relationships in production and distribution and in decision-making, of the development of a truly national state apparatus, of the centralisation of political authority;[1] but this has not been accompanied by a process of rapid or even substantial industrialisation, or by a reduction in Cuba's extreme dependence on a single export crop, or indeed by a steady process of economic growth. Rather, as table 1 suggests, although production has grown over the long term, this growth was marked, no doubt inevitably in the aftermath of a revolution, by violent fluctuations which reflect above all changes in the country's trading partners as a result of blockades and boycotts, in sugar price, policy and production, as well as in the over-all organisation of production itself. According to Ritter (1974, p. 208), gross material product fell in 1967 back to its 1962 level, and although 1970 produced a record sugar harvest, this was at the expense of major losses in almost all other sectors (United States Congress, Joint Economic Committee, 1979), so that the high growth in subsequent years was in part a recuperation of losses incurred then, and in part a result of a rising world sugar price. But again, the record in the 1970s shows notable fluctuations. The modernisation process would certainly not have been possible without Soviet assistance, which, according to the US Department of Commerce, constituted some 25 per cent of Cuba's national income at the end of the 1970s (ibid.)

The main trend analysed in this paper in migratory patterns between provinces is the over-all decline in non-seasonal migration since the Revolution. This is

---

[1] For the development of this point in a comparative context, see Skocpol (1979).

Table 2: Sugar production in millions of tons

1957	5.67
1958	5.78
1959	5.96
1960	5.86
1961	6.77
1962	4.82
1963	3.82
1964	4.40
1965	6.05
1966	4.46
1967	6.13
1968	5.31
1969	4.35
1970	8.53
1971	5.92
1972	4.32
1973	5.25
1974	5.92
1975	6.31
1976	n.a
1977	n.a
1978	7.30
1979	8.00 "almost"

Sources: Until 1970, Ritter (1974); for 1971 to 1975, *Anuario Estadístico*, 1975; for 1978 and 1979, Chief of Planning Board: speeches to People's Assembly.

attributed to the character of the labour market, which operates on an administrative (or planned) rather than a market basis. A similar change can be detected in the seasonal labour market, where the state now regulates a flow of urban workers to the cane fields and annually establishes their rates of pay. This is in marked contrast both to pre-Revolutionary labour markets and to the labour mobilisation of the late 1960s, which officials now criticise as examples of unplanned, spontaneous resource allocation.

The apparent reduction in over-all migration since the Revolution may be due to low economic growth, to the relatively even distribution of real consumption across the island, to technological changes in cane production, or to the rigidities of a largely administered labour market. Besides the pattern of migration, the paper will also

Table 3: Cuba: Economically active population in 1943 and 1970

	1943			1970	
	No.	%		No.	%
Agriculture	630,256	41.4	Agriculture	790,258	30.0
Industry	400,513	26.3	Industry	533,258	20.2
Trade	146,572	9.6	Construction	157,182	6.0
Services (personal and domestic)	73,963	4.9	Transport	146,133	5.6
Government	70,763	4.0	Trade	305,958	11.6
Other	198,784	13.8	Communications	15,155	0.5
			Social services	621,957	23.6
			Other activities	63,220	2.4
TOTAL	1,520,851			2,633,309	

Source: Population Censuses, 1943 and 1970.

briefly consider city growth, and concludes that although the process of urbanisation, which declined during the 1960s, revived during the 1970s, growth has become less concentrated in La Habana and Santiago de Cuba, while smaller towns have been growing particularly fast in recent years. Thus recent trends do not point to "rural bias" - nor is this the intention of the government, which speaks of the "urbanisation of the countryside", involving a more equilibrated urban growth than in the past.

The paper contains a brief summary of the agrarian reform process in section II, and in sections V and VI the macro-economic context of the changes discussed is outlined, including a short account of the various changes in development strategy which have taken place since the Revolution.

II. Agrarian Reform and Seasonal Employment in the Early Years

As the appendix to this paper shows, the agricultural labour market in pre-Revolutionary Cuba was an extreme case of seasonality, utterly dominated by the labour needs of sugar cane, but accentuated by the coincident requirements of other crops, such as tobacco and coffee. These labour needs were satisfied because of the high rates of unemployment and underemployment.

To survive, the Revolution could not restrict itself to the removal of the social class and institutions which had most benefited from the previous sytem; it also had to create a new system. In the early years, the seasonal supply of labour was bound to be disrupted by land reform, by the expansion of employment opportunities in construction and public works, and by the growth of the education system and the state administrative apparatus. The establishment of a centrally controlled economic structure combined with foreign trade dislocations arising from embargoes and boycotts were also bound to have long-term effects. I shall enumerate these briefly, beginning with land reform.

Although the over-all process of land redistribution remains largely unchronicled,[1] Gutelman's data indicate that after the first agrarian reform, there were 150,210 holders under 5 caballerías (67.1 hectares), owning 3.5 million hectares (Gutelman, 1967, p. 64). This number rose further, as shown by the existence of almost 230,000 "self-employed" in agriculture in 1970 (table 4) and the 213,000 members of the Small Farmers' Association in 1975

---

[1] There is a partial, qualitative account in Martinez Alier (1970).

Table 4: Cuba: Economically active population in agriculture by employment status, 1953 and 1970*

		Pinar del Rio	Habana**	Matanzas	Las Villas	Camagüey	Oriente	CUBA	
Wage labour	1953	43,700	44,300	43,200	107,200	91,100	173,400	503,000	
	1970	35,222	81,426	34,519	95,789	64,513	209,871	521,340	[519,212]
Non-wage labour	1953	12,700	3,500	3,700	15,700	4,100	29,400	69,100	
	1970	7,712	2,044	1,243	7,158	1,865	15,212	34,334	[34,289]
Self-employed	1953	34,200	15,100	10,500	59,400	22,200	94,000	235,500	
	1970	26,446	15,062	12,126	52,311	19,847	103,364	229,156	[236,801]
Total	1953	90,700	62,900	57,400	182,300	117,400	296,800	807,600	
	1970	69,380	98,532	47,888	155,258	86,225	328,447	784,830	[790,396]
		[77,365]	[97,657]	[47,889]	[155,263]	[86,228]	[328,466]	[792,868]	
Annual increase (%)		-1.6	2.6	-1.1	-0.9	-1.8	0.6	-0.2	

* Figures in square brackets denote "totals" as given by 1970 Census, which diverge from actual totals for unknown reasons.

** To take account of the removal of Artemisa from Pinar del Rio to Habana province, 5,000 persons should be deducted from the former and added to the latter for 1953. The annual increase for Pinar del Rio would then be -1.2 per cent, while the increase for Habana would decline to 2.2 per cent.

Source: Population Censuses, 1953 and 1970.

(table 5). In contrast there were only 32,000 holders of farms under 50 hectares in the 1945 Agricultural Census (Appendix, table 1), and these accounted for 1.8 million hectares; by 1961, according to Gutelman, they occupied 2.5 million hectares, but by 1975 the area of the private sector of farming, whose maximum size of holding was 67.1 hectares, had declined to just under 2 million hectares (table 5).

Although the initial increase and subsequent decline may not have been as violent as Gutelman's data suggest, that general trend is consistent with agricultural policy. The number of holdings under 5 caballerias rose during the implementation of the first and second Land Reforms (the second dates from 1962), and then must have declined, despite the régime's scrupulous respect for the rights of remaining landholders. The initial increase arose from the policy of conferring property rights on tenants and providing landless workers with small holdings of about 27 hectares, though the numbers involved are unknown (ibid.).[1] Pollitt gives evidence of a growth in plots conceded to agricultural workers by apprehensive members of the agrarian bourgeoisie and of extra-legal land distributions by soldiers and officials implementing the agrarian reform in the early years (Pollitt, 1979). The subsequent gradual fall arose from the state policy of purchasing any farm offered, paying the seller a life-long monthly pension, or from occasional compulsory purchase where, according to officials, health considerations made it desirable to acquire land for particular crops or ranching activities.[2]

After the first agrarian reform small farmers had less need of a supplementary income from wage labour, for often their holdings were increased in size and rental payments abolished. Furthermore, a substantial number of semi-peasants or semi-proletarians and even full proletarians became relatively self-sufficient due to land redistribution.[3] In 1959-61, the 6 per cent annual economic growth rate must have created employment for some people who otherwise would have worked in the cane harvest. Yet the harvest of 1961 was the second highest

---

[1] Gutelman suggested the figure of 27 hectares.

[2] These health considerations arise, for example, where there is large-scale spraying of insecticides on state rice farms, thus necessitating the removal of smallholdings surviving in their midst.

[3] Pollitt indicates this in his sample survey of rural households in 1966 (Pollitt, 1971).

Table 5: Total area of private holdings and number of ANAP members in 1975 compared with number and area of holdings under 50 hectares in 1945 (thousands of hectares)

		1945	1975
Pinar del Rio	no.	21,301	37,145
	area	251.9	206.7
La Habana	no.	12,553	18,829
	area	215.1	118.7
Matanzas	no.	9,811	11,459
	area	174.7	113.8
Las Villas	no.	33,835	51,102
	area	601.1	216.4
Camagüey	no.	12,645	17,841
	area	270.1	308.6
Oriente	no.	45,034	76,659
	area	303.8	1007.3
CUBA	no.	135,179	213,035
	area	1,816.7	1,971.5

Note: The number of ANAP members exceeds the number of smallholders, since farm families may have more than one member. ANAP sources were estimating the number of farm-owners at 158,000 in 1978 (Brian Pollitt, personal communication) while the Association's Congress Resolutions of 1971 spoke of 202,000 small farms with 2.4 million hectares: there would seem to have been, therefore, a steady erosion of the private sector since 1970, amounting to a loss of 21 per cent of farms up to 1978 and 18 per cent of land up to 1975. Source: Resoluciones del Congreso de la Asociación Nacional de Agricultores Pequeños, 29 December 1971, reproduced by ICIRA, Santiago de Chile, 1972.

Source: Agricultural Census, 1946; Anuario Estadístico, 1975, p.53; Comité Estatal de Estadísticas: Resumen estadístico: Sector campesino, May 1977 (table 2.8: members of ANAP).

in Cuban history, even though there is no indication of a mass mobilisation of urban or volunteer labour for that year. So initially it seems the labour supply was sufficient for a large harvest, although many competing sources of activity, such as education and social services, still had to develop on a large scale, and despite the Bay of Pigs invasion, and the US refusal to buy Cuban sugar.

At first, the government created cane co-operatives on expropriated sugar estates. Their membership seems to have been restricted mainly to previously permanent employees, so that they continued to employ seasonal labour.[1] However, these co-operatives were soon turned into state farms (granjas del pueblo) and thus protected from some market pressures. Because state farms came under the Agrarian Reform Institute's administrative budget, they could employ far more permanent workers than co-operatives who, at least in principle, were under more urgent pressures to make ends meet. This increasing security of employment was paralleled in urban areas, at least in enterprises managed by the state, and reinforced from about 1967 - when monetary transactions between enterprises ceased and a policy of "moral incentives" was adopted.[2] These trends presumably made workers less inclined to do seasonal labour, as did the decline of the urban informal sector which, with its inevitably insecure labour force, was an important source of such labour before 1959. In 1943, the census had found 427,656 persons working in urban areas either in "unclassified industry and trade" or of "unknown employment status". The 1970 census gives only 27,381 persons in "ill-specified activities" in urban areas. Although this reflects procedural and definitional changes, it also reflects the demise of the informal sector and the often unstable employment it offers; such informal activities as still existed were "moonlighting", implying that those involved also had a stable job.

The government thus came to step up the mobilisation of volunteer workers for the cane harvest. The number of urban volunteers working for prolonged period in the zafra (harvest) grew from 58,000 in 1965 to 71,000 in 1966 and 170,000 in the massive harvest of 1970

---

[1] Personal communication from Brian Pollitt.

[2] See Fidel Castro's Report to the First Congress of the Cuban Communist Party, 1975.

(Mesa-Lago, 1978, p. 50).[1] After 1970 mechanisation and rationalisation of production increased, but labour mobilisation proved difficult. By 1974, according to Mesa-Lago, the number of urban volunteers working for most of the harvest was down to 20,000.

The number of workers mobilised in the 1960s according to these figures fell far short of the number of "hard-core" seasonally unemployed in 1945 (see appendix), even though they probably do not include people who worked in agriculture voluntarily on commemorative days, weekends, and the like. This is evidence that the replacement of a system based on income insecurity by one guaranteeing workers a minimum level of consumption and a secure job posed major difficulties for an ambitious programme of increasing agricultural and in particular sugar production. The problem was intensified by the fact that Cuba could not make major labour-saving investments in cane-cutting or the processing of cane into sugar at that time. Subsequently, however, that situation improved - by 1979-80 some 40 per cent of cane-cutting was mechanised - and we may presume that seasonal flows of labour declined considerably. As the economy became more of an administered system, so permanent employment in formally defined and designated positions became more widespread even though productivity, in this economically and politically turbulent period, probably did not rise. We thus find a structural change in the rural wage labour force, as a mass of temporary workers acquired permanent agricultural jobs, while others dropped out of the seasonal labour market once their expanded private holdings or their "rise" from tenancy to ownership ensured them a livelihood. This structural change would not have affected the supply of labour at any particular time of the year, since the agricultural wage-labour force remained virtually stable. But the mobility of labour was reduced. Indeed if urban workers supplied seasonal labour in agriculture prior to the Revolution, some of those workers must have shifted to a rural base: otherwise from where would all these permanent wage-workers have come, at a time when smallholder numbers and self-sufficiency were increasing and when rural infrastructure projects were increasing labour needs?

Urban volunteer labour emerged as a prolongation of earlier pre-Revolutionary seasonal movements, in a

---

[1] The 1970 harvest aimed to produce 10 million tons of sugar: enough cane was harvested, but the target was not met, due to insufficient, inadequate or simply antiquated milling equipment.

radically different institutional context. It rose to a peak in 1970 as the productive effort rose, falling off thereafter for a number of reasons. One reason was the substitution of low productivity volunteers by seasonal wage-earners paid on a piece-rate basis in the wake of economic reforms after 1970. By 1978, between 120,000 and 130,000 workers worked in the cane harvest. This compares with some 360,000 in the early 1960s, and a similar figure in 1970. In the late 1970s production was slightly higher than in the 1960s, so there were gains in productivity (for sugar, see table 2), though there have been no workforce statistics since 1970. A second reason was the mechanisation of cane-lifting and then cane-cutting (Auroi, 1975, pp. 169-171).[1] These two changes and the apparently very large increase in permanent wage-earners in agriculture reduced the need for seasonal workers. This was partially compensated by the decline in non-wage employment in holdings under 67 hectares, but a comparison of the 1970 census with either its 1953 counterpart (table 4) or with the 1945 Agricultural Census shows that this decline was small. What was this increased permanent workforce doing? Perhaps they were engaged in clearing land for cultivation and pasture. According to the 1975 Anuario Estadístico, cultivated land rose from 1,376,400 hectares in 1962 to just over three million in 1970 and 3,791,300 hectares in 1975. But this was not reflected in large-scale productive increases, except in rice which accounted for only 107,500 hectares of land in 1975. Many state farm workers had private plots, but these were small. Pollitt identified numerous private plots in state farms in the mid-1960s (Pollitt, 1971). In his sample there were 367 state farm workers of whom 179 (48.8 per cent) had plots on those farms. Among the 158 classified as "other workers" - essentially private-sector wage-earners - 67.7 per cent had such plots. Plot size was small on state farms, for only 15.4 per cent of those who had them declared a plot of more than one hectare, and 47.2 per cent reported one of less than a quarter of a hectare. The possibility of access to land would have been one minor attraction of secure jobs on state farms, especially in the pre-1970 period of shortages and rationing - and it might also have reduced the effort devoted to activities directed by the state farm itself.

---

[1] Auroi says that in 1970 only 2 per cent of the cane was cut mechanically but according to Pollitt (in a personal communication) this had reached some 40 per cent by 1970-80.

In sum, though the number of private farmers with holdings below the ceiling initially expanded, the longer-term trend involved an increase in permanent wage labour on state farms, and a reduction both of the number of private farmers and of seasonal labour migration, despite spurts of such migration in the late 1960s. Whether that was a consequence of a "maximum of ruralism and a minimum of urbanism" (Gugler, 1980, pp. 516-534) rather than of a slow improvement in levels of agricultural land and labour productivity in a context of an administered labour market offering substantial job security, is a matter for controversy.

III. The Private Sector of Agriculture

The previous section noted trends in agricultural wage employment in the state sector. This section gives an account of the private sector to assess how far it "held back" labour on the farm and avoided the pressures on peasant economies which elsewhere produce high rates of urban migration. It also discusses the role of the private sector in the reproduction of labour and in food production, which have an indirect bearing on the pattern of migration. The various themes link up in so far as both trends in migration (seasonal and permanent) and the current features of the private sector are explained by processes of bureaucratisation and structural differentiation in Cuban society. These processes have two aspects: one is the creation of an apparatus of administered production and distribution, the other is the specialisation of roles and the reduction of kin-based control of production, largely achieved by massive educational expansion.

1. Its role in the economy

The availability of unpaid family labour declined by more than 50 per cent between 1953 and 1970 (table 4) even though the area and number of farms which one might expect to use such labour remained stable or perhaps grew.[1] So it is hardly surprising that wage labour persists in the private sector, and may even be in

---

[1] Note that (a) in 1945 some 15 per cent of non-wage employment was on farms over 50 hectares, and 9 per cent on farms over 75 hectares, according to the 1945 Agricultural Census; and (b) the post-Revolutionary landholding ceiling has been, formally, 67.1 hectares. So the statement needs slight, but only slight, modification if like is to be compared with like.

short supply. The massive expansion in education and formal employment that occurred in the 1960s removed children from domestic production, while hired labour was available to private farmers at a very low or even zero price, though not in unlimited quantities. From the late 1960s, it seems the state provided seasonal labour, based in state farms or urban areas, free of charge to private producers in cane, coffee, tobacco and citrus crops. Only from around 1977 did the government begin to charge for this labour.[1] But one may suppose that during the whole period private farmers hired wage labour directly and semi-legally. Pollitt's 1966 survey showed that private farmers were net hirers of labour, and in 1978 ANAP estimated that there were 26,000 permanent wage-earners in the private sector - only 8,000 less than the number of non-wage workers given in the 1970 Census (Pollitt, personal communication).

What is the role of this private sector in the economy as a whole? If the Cuban private farmers do feed themselves - thus saving the state the cost of their subsistence and keeping down the demand for marketed food as well as their own seasonal wages - they do not thereby forego government rations, which are formally the same as for any rural wage-earner or urban worker. There is no self-financing mechanism on state farms forcing workers to reproduce themselves as peasants by subtracting wages from their production valued at low prices, as was the case for many years in Soviet collective farming (Nove, 1965). There is little trace of "community" labour being used as essentially free labour in infrastructure projects.[2] Indeed, when in vogue in

---

[1] The information received on this was vague, though it was clear that in 1978 they were paying for hired labour. On a "special plan", near Ciego de Avila, which I visited in April 1978, the smallholders were certainly not paying for outside labour, which was supplied without charge through the state. It should be added that, at that time microplans were in the way of being "vanguards" in a process of integration, with each other and with state-controlled production being promoted among smallholders. For a similar comment, see Dumont (1970, pp. 90-93).

[2] The only Cuban institution remotely resembling a cheap labour public works programme was the "microbrigada" system for urban housing. Discontinued in 1979, this was an arrangement whereby workers would be "seconded" from a work centre to build houses for themselves or their colleagues, on the understanding that

the late 1960s, large scale mobilisations drew on urban labour and did not save the state money; workers drew wages from their habitual place of work, or if away for long periods, were paid as agricultural workers. Of course, private farmers do work seasonally for wages, but the extent of this phenomenon is unknown.

One region of Cuba where one undoubtedly found a peasant ownership structure with limited access to land, and therefore the conditions of an exploited peasantry, is the province of Oriente. In 1945 this province contained one-third of all units of production under 50 hectares, but only 16.7 per cent of the land in such units; their average size was 6.7 hectares (Agricultural Census, 1945).[1] But in 1970 the size of the average private holding was between 9.7 and 13.1 hectares, depending on one's estimate of the number of smallholders.[2] In 1978, Oriente had between 36 per cent and 45 per cent of the country's smallholders, and some 51 per cent of private sector land. Between 1953 and 1970 the province's population grew faster than that of any other, including Habana, at just over 3 per cent a year compared with the national rate of 2.3 per cent, even though more people probably left the province than entered it (see below, section III.3). In Oriente in 1975 there were 25.2 births per thousand, compared with a national rate of 20.7 per thousand. The only sign of relative poverty - which might be related to a large peasant sector - was that Oriente (with Camagüey) had a disproportionately large increase in infant mortality in the late 1960s, at a time when the rate was also rising nationally. But this has declined substantially since 1969 (Anuario Estadístico, 1975, p. 30). Had conditions in Oriente 35 years ago

---

production would be maintained. Other workers would contribute in their spare time. But this could also (perhaps unfairly) be viewed as a subsidy to low-productivity work centres with labour to spare.

[1] This average is probably an overestimate since the census may well have understated the number of squatters.

[2] Source for amount of land in private sector: Anuario Estadístico (1975, p. 53). The low estimate of smallholders is from the number of small farmers in the 1970 Population Census; the high estimate is equal to the members of the National Small Farmers' Association (ANAP) in 1977 (see Comité Estatal de Estadisticas, 1977) and table 5 above. For further relevant data, see section III.3 below.

remained one might have expected a very different pattern: fragmentation of smallholdings, increasing use of family labour, uncontrolled urbanisation, the growth of shanty towns, and, even if production increased, increasing poverty and inequality. In Oriente, production has not increased very substantially; coffee marketing, for example, in this Cuba's main producer province, was still below its 1966-69 levels in 1975. Urbanisation and proletarianisation are proceeding rapidly. But consolidation rather than fragmentation is taking place, and the indications of poverty show a rapid improvement since 1970, in tune with the rest of the country.[1]

---

[1] Despite its initial disadvantage, Oriente does not yield a different trend from the island as a whole. The situation of the peasantry, in terms of pressure on the land, has been relieved but, though the agricultural labour force grew by 0.6 per cent a year from 1953 to 1970, this may conceal a massive increase in permanent rural wage labour. However, in general, the bias of Cuban agricultural investment has been labour-saving. And government has not taken strenuous measures to intensify peasant production of traditional labour-intensive food-crops, such as tubers and root crops. The two characteristically peasant products actively encouraged are tobacco and coffee. Peasant sector credit for tobacco production has apparently exceeded credit for cane production: between 1972 and 1976, 37.1 per cent of its total credit was for tobacco, 16.6 per cent for coffee, and 31 per cent for cane, although this may be distorted by the non-accounting of free wage labour in cane before about 1975. Some 15.6 per cent of total credit was for capital investment, but 55 per cent of this was for planting coffee trees, again reflecting a policy of encouraging coffee production, which was given a further impulse in 1978 by a decree writing off all outstanding debts for coffee production (Gaceta Oficial, 18 February 1978). This was so even though the private sector had far more land under cane (208,000 hectares) than under either coffee (85,000) or tobacco (32,000). Unfortunately, neither tobacco nor coffee production have experienced significant growth since 1966, despite large-scale planting of coffee, probably on state farms, in the Escambray mountains of Las Villas province in 1967. One reason for this relative stagnation may have been the absence of "self-exploiting" family labour and the priority assigned to cane in the mobilisation of seasonal labour from the cities.

2. The costs of private sector prosperity and of the redistribution of consumption

It is often claimed that in underdeveloped capitalist countries the peasantry plays two crucial roles: it reproduces its own labour force at little or no cost and it contributes to the reproduction of the labour force as a whole by producing wage goods more cheaply than capitalist producers would, especially food. The reason for the cheapness of the food is to be found in the kinship-based organisation of production which functions without, or with little, wage payment. In a socialist country one would expect these relationships to change: either the cheapness of labour is reduced by income redistribution, or the structural basis of the relationship between the peasantry and capital is modified by the reorganisation of peasant production. In Cuba both processes can be observed. Indeed, there is perhaps a case for saying that private producers have not been exploited enough, either by themselves or by the state, so that they have obtained relatively high levels of private consumption without substantial increases in production, marketed or otherwise, and without using their land intensively. The reasons for this include the lack of incentives for food production, in the form of prices, credit or technical assistance; the costs can be seen in the country's massive food import bill.

In that context, it is noteworthy that in an interview with three peasant producers in the municipality of Candelaria, Pinar del Río, in September 1978, I found that while one of them owned 52.8 hectares, and the others 13 and 19.5 hectares, the first did not sell more coffee or food on the market than the others. Total sales were equivalent respectively to 16, 24 and 13 monthly wages at the lowest standard wage rate, and in addition they all worked 45 days for wages in the coffee harvest on a nearby state farm, earning an average of 182 pesos per month, which was more than double the minimum of 85 pesos (though if piece work were accounted for and weekend work excluded from the 45 days it might be similar). The three producers cultivated 6.5, 2 and 2.5 hectares respectively, and seemed to have little incentive to cultivate food crops more intensively, although they were receiving credit and technical assistance to plant new coffee trees. Tables 6 and 7 may or may not illustrate this, as the note to table 6 indicates. One may suppose the crops mentioned in those tables, with the exception of rice, are characteristic of smallholder production, and constituted the staple diet in pre-Revolutionary times (table 8). Much of the wheat to make bread was imported, and much of the corn as well.

Table 6: Marketed production of selected food crops, 1958-1975 (three-year averages except for 1975, in thousands of tons)

		Potatoes	Yuca	Boniato	Malanga	Beans	Rice
1958		82.6	207.8	168.1	185.6	19.8	218.9
1963		87.1	108.7	117.3	49.5	29.2	185.7
1968	Private	46.7	23.1	26.7	22.5	3.5	14.9
	State	59.6	23.4	48.5	17.5	6.6	107.1
	Total	106.3	46.5	75.2	40.0	10.1	122.0
1973	Private	25.2	34.5	32.0	17.3	2.5	12.4
	State	47.9	34.8	47.5	6.4	1.7	249.2
	Total	73.1	69.3	79.5	23.7	4.2	261.6
1975	Private	36.9	44.5	34.9	23.5	3.0	21.9
	State	79.9	40.3	56.9	9.0	2.0	316.1
	Total	116.8	84.8	91.7	32.5	5.0	338.0

Sources: For 1958 and 1973, Ritter (1974, p. 188); Anuario Estadístico, 1975, p. 81. The two sources are compatible and give the same figures for years when they overlap. Ritter mistakenly heads his table "Production" whereas, with the exception of 1958, the source he uses is clearly "Acopio" - that is, quantities sold to the state purchasing agencies, or, at least, when private trade was still allowed, to "formal sector" buyers. Note that the averages in this table conceal precipitous declines in "acopio" in 1969, after the abolition of private trade, in all these products except rice, which by then was predominantly grown on state farms. Pollitt has pointed out to me that there has been a decline in total private sector area recorded in official statistics since 1969. This presumably reflects the microplans and such like arrangements integrating the organisation and marketing of the private sector with the state, though without necessarily removing holdings from private owners. Pollitt says that much production previously in the private sector then began to show up in the state sector. If this is an indication of the general case, then this table shows precisely the opposite of what it appears to show: the private sector would be maintaining its production despite losses of land, while the state sector does not increase it despite increases of land.

Table 7: Comparison of production and marketing (acopio) of selected food crops in the private sector, 1970-1976 (thousands of tons)

		Potatoes		Beans		Yuca		Platano		Malanga	
		Volume	Per cent marketed	Volume	Per cent marketed	Volume	Per cent marketed	Volume	Per cent marketed	Volume	Per cent marketed
1972	Prod.	35.1		10.1		45.8		107.3		43.0	
	Mark.	29.7	84.6	3.8	37.6	32.6	71.2	74.4	69.3	16.8	39.1
1973	Prod.	23.2		7.9		49.6		105.7		41.5	
	Mark.	17.8	76.4	1.5	19.0	37.4	75.4	72.2	68.3	15.1	36.4
1974	Prod.	30.9		7.8		40.1		84.6		47.3	
	Mark.	28.0	90.6	2.0	25.6	33.6	83.6	63.5	75.1	20.0	42.3
1975	Prod.	40.9		8.5		45.7		76.0		48.9	
	Mark.	36.9	90.2	3.0	35.3	44.5	97.4	51.6	67.9	23.5	48.1
1976	Prod.	49.1		8.1		52.2		92.6		62.2	
	Mark.	44.3	90.2	1.8	22.2	51.6	98.9	65.6	71.3	34.2	55.0

Source: Comite Estatal de Estadísticas (1977, tables 14 and 17).

Table 8: Farm household per capita food consumption in Cuba, 1945-46

Banana	456 lb.
Vegetables	355 lb.
Rice	194 lb.
Corn meal	93 lb.
Beans	92 lb.
Pork	86 lb.
Bread	86 lb.
Lard	78 lb.
Chicken	20 lb.

Source: Nelson (1950, p. 211).

Table 9: Distribution of agricultural land between state and private sectors and proportion in each of natural pasture or uncultivated land, 1974 and 1975 (in percentages)

		State	"Privado vinculado"	"Privado disperso"
Agricultural land	1974	72.7	17.9	6.1
	1975	75.8	15.1	6.1
Proportion uncultivated, including natural pastures	1974	42.3	45.9	72.7
	1975	41.5	40.5	74.4

Note: The definitions of "vinculado" and "disperso" are not given, but presumably refer to producers who respectively are and are not co-operating with state planning agencies. The figures do not add up to 100 per cent due to discrepancies between partial and total figures in the source.

Source: Anuario Estadístico (1975, p. 53).

Table 10: Cane yields, 1965-1975 (tons per hectare)

	State	Private
1965	48.2	47.3
1966	37.7	37.4
1967	49.2	48.2
1968	41.3	45.7
1969	43.8	49.6
1970	54.5	58.6
1971	40.2	42.3
1972	37.2	38.4
1973	43.3	47.0
1974	43.5	51.1
Average harvested area (hectares):	913,231.7	257,917.3

Source: Comité Estatal de Estadísticas: Resumen Estadístico, Sector Campesino (May 1977).

Table 9 suggests that the private sector cultivates no more or less intensively than the state sector, so long as it is linked ("vinculado") to the planning apparatus, though cane yields (table 10) have clearly been better in the private sector.

A paradox of the Revolution is that while it has scrupulously respected the property rights of smallholders it has not given them incentives to produce efficiently or simply to make full use of their land. Though malnutrition has declined dramatically,[1] this has been achieved at a higher cost in foreign exchange than *prima facie* seems necessary.

---

[1] Average mortality per 1,000 children under one year: 1953-1960, 34.5; 1961-70, 39.8; 1971-75, 29.3. The 1953-60 figure is based on data for 1953, 1958, 1959 and 1960 only (source: Anuario Estadístico). Note that, for unknown reasons, there was a leap in infant mortality in 1969, after which the rate has declined steadily, from 48.2 to 27.3 per thousand. The mortality from diarrhoetic diseases has declined from 57.3 in 1972 to 6.0 in 1976, per 100,000 inhabitants (Vargas and Amador, undated). The 1975 Anuario Estadístico (p. 238) shows a two-thirds drop (from 1,640 to 507) in the number of deaths of children under one year caused by enteritis and other diarrhoetic diseases between 1969 and 1975.

Table 8 shows average per capita food consumption from a survey of 734 farm families including 173 landless workers, carried out in 1945-46. They may overstate the position somewhat because the sample seemed to under-represent the smaller landholders and landless workers in relation to the 1945 Agricultural Census. Also, as Nelson noted, the 1943 Population Census showed lower per capita consumption of rice (110 lb.) and beans (35 lb.). Furthermore, average figures for nutrition are misleading since they do not reflect decreasing marginal utility of food consumption at higher income levels. None the less, in the absence of direct nutrition data, a comparison with post-Revolutionary rations is instructive: in 1978 each Cuban received only 72 lb. of rice and 3 lb. of beans per annum, but 120 lb. of bread (with fairly easy access to extra amounts through the normal distribution system), and 26 lb. of chicken or 13 lb. of beef. These are not averages, but more or less guaranteed per capita rations for persons of all ages in town and country. One litre of milk was available per day for all children under 6, for each man over 60 and woman over 55. The Anuario Estadístico shows a wholesale distribution of 174 eggs per capita per year for the years 1971-1975, assuming a population of 9 million; according to Nelson, in the 1940s they were not commonly eaten in the farmhouse (Nelson, 1950, p. 209). Not imported, eggs have been produced almost exclusively on state farms and have been abundant at very low prices (like all other food) since about 1973. As for milk, also largely produced on state farms, between 1970 and 1975 there was an average shortfall of 217,000 tons, which may have been made up by some 52,480 tons of powdered milk imported per annum.[1] Table 12 gives import figures compared to internal wholesale distribution, and the Anuario Estadísticos for 1974 and 1975 show that between 1970 and 1975 Cuba spent 23 per cent of her export earnings, in peso terms, on food imports, almost the same as the 21.7 per cent for 1958 (O'Connor, 1970, pp. 33, 80). These rationing data do not reflect total consumption because school children and working adults eat at least one meal a day at school or work, while primary school children and all those between 12 and 15 attending rural secondary schools as weekly boarders, receive

---

[1] Figures reached by calculating difference between average annual wholesale distribution of milk for 1971-1975 (557,800 tons) and average domestic production (340,142 tons) for 1970-1975 (Anuario Estadístico, 1975, pp. 88, 150). For imports, see, ibid., p. 166.

more.[1] Furthermore, one may suppose that the milk for children and the elderly is also consumed by other members of the family. Thus real consumption is well above rations. In short, those who would not have been able to afford chicken in the ancien régime, as Nelson noted (p. 210), and who would have been undernourished, especially in protein terms, are now properly fed. However, changes in diet seem related to import dependence and the apparently disappointing performance of "under-exploited" private producers, and are certainly not explained by crop substitutions in the private sector. Since 1970, the sector's area under cane has fallen from 338,000 hectares to 224,000 in 1975, presumably reflecting a net decline in over-all area of the private sector (Anuario Estadístico, 1975, p. 59). It did not reflect substitution of crops. Indeed, though the data in table 6 are rough approximations, as the note to the table explains, the trends strongly suggest that marketed production of basic food crops collapsed in the early 1960s, after the first and second land reforms.

Table 7 shows that since 1972 an increasing proportion of potato, yuca and malanga produced in the private sector has been marketed, though it is impossible to tell whether this reflects a decline in self-consumption or in "parallel" distribution networks, improved input distribution, or changes in relative prices. Consumption of beans has long been heavily dependent on imports (table 12), domestic production having been almost wiped out by pests. Rice production, overwhelmingly concentrated in state farms, doubled between 1957 and 1975, but consumption of this staple food also remains heavily dependent on imports.

The private sector, therefore, does not seem to be making the expected contribution to the nation's food consumption. Tables 6 and 7 do not hint at any large-scale transfer of land to the state, but the observed fluctuations may reflect temporary changes, such as the "microplans", in which the state may have sought greater control of the sector, while its production may have been recorded in the state sector. This may explain the decline in land under cane, and the collapse of cattle sales by almost a half between 1972 and 1976, from 685,600 head to 371,900 (Comité Estatal de Estadisticas, 1977, p. 45). The one food product which has been rising in the private sector is eggs, from 688,600 in 1972 to 1,648,900 in 1976, representing a small but rising

---

[1] Families do not have their rations reduced, except in respect of meat, when children are away at boarding school.

Table 11: Wage and non-wage labour in Cuban agriculture, 1945 and 1953

	Pinar del Rio		La Habana		Matanzas		Las Villas	
	Wage	Non-wage	Wage	Non-wage	Wage	Non-wage	Wage	Non-wage
1945	40,117	48,854	37,827	30,622	44,094	27,063	90,289	89,913
1953	43,700	46,900	44,300	18,600	43,200	14,200	107,200	75,100

	Camagüey		Oriente		CUBA	
	Wage	Non-wage	Wage	Non-wage	Wage	Non-wage
1945	112,277	33,124	152,809	123,709	477,383	352,285
1953	91,100	26,300	173,400	123,400	503,000	304,600

Sources: Agricultural Census, 1946, table 19; and Population Census, 1953, as reported by Pollitt, 1971. See comments in Appendix I on the comparability of the data.

Table 12: Average annual imports and wholesale distribution of selected food products, 1970-1975 (in tons)

	Imports	Wholesale distribution
Cereals	1,289,495	
Beans	90,276	90,373
Potatoes	27,543	98,041
Rice*	235,339	389,364

* Included in cereals.

Note: Wholesale distribution presumably does not include goods distributed for consumption at work places or at school. The figures do not refer to total consumption.

Source: Anuario Estadístico (1974, p. 177), and Anuario Estadístico (1975, pp. 149, 166).

proportion of national egg production. So it seems the Cuban diet has also been changing, as food supplies from the smaller farms have been replaced by imports, moving away from domestic high-carbohydrate tubers and beans towards imported wheat and wheat derivatives. Rice has remained a constant factor, now produced domestically in much greater quantities than before the Revolution, on state farms, but the island is still also dependent on imported rice (table 12).

Nevertheless, there are indications that, in relative terms, the private sector has achieved higher yields than state farms (tables 10 and 13). Table 9 shows the distribution of uncultivated land between the state, the "privado vinculado" sector and the remainder of the private sector, as a proportion of each one's agricultural land. The difference between these two sub-divisions of the private sector is not defined in the Anuario, but we may presume that the "vinculado" sector consists of units with production contracts with a state agency, whereas the remainder do not. Although the "vinculado" private sector cultivates much the same proportion of its land as the state farms, and has higher yields in cane and several annual crops it probably has a less than

Table 13: Marketed product per hectare of sown area in state and private sectors, 1974 and 1975 (tons)[1]

		Sown area[2]		Acopio (tons)		Yields	
		1974	1975	1974	1975	1974	1975
Rice	State	194,310	169,583	293,493	316,148	1.51	1.86
	Private	9,334	8,617	15,755	21,882	1.68	2.54
Beans	State	6,560	8,379	1,149	1,955	0.18	0.23
	Private	2,702	3,123	1,999	3,005	0.74	0.96
Tubers and roots[1]	State	43,717	43,435	154,754	187,335	3.54	4.31
	Private	14,443	15,631	117,866	145,092	8.16	9.28
Vegetables[3]	State	37,603	45,781	185,332	196,600	4.93	4.27
	Private	20,015	25,172	207,991	253,243	10.39	10.06
Tobacco	State	14,488	16,535	8,497	7,352	0.59	0.44
	Private	55,430	52,734	36,188	34,078	0.65	0.65

1 Figures for yields given in the Resumen Estadistíco for the sector campesino (May 1977) do not correspond to production or marketed production divided by sown area in that publication. I have therefore used the Anuario Estadístico.

2 This includes potatoes, boniato, malanga, yuca, name.

3 This includes pumpkins.

Source: Anuarios Estadísticos, 1974 and 1975.

proportionate number of cattle, though it is hard to be sure as since 1968 published statistics have not distinguished between state and private sector sales of cattle to state agencies. In 1968, the private sector accounted for only 1.5 per cent of such sales, since when total sales have declined, by 36.9 per cent, and the number of live cattle declined by 19.6 per cent between 1969 and 1974 (Anuario Estadístico, 1974, pp. 71, 100). The private sector's minimal share in cattle sales compares with its 34.6 per cent share of "uncultivated pasture" in 1974. Thus though the private sector seems to use its pasture less intensively than the state sector, the yields of its crops are higher, as one might expect from smaller units.[1]

The effects of rationing and of providing security of tenure to private holders should be kept distinct from those of the Agrarian Reforms of 1959 and 1962. Those reforms turned many semi-peasants into peasants, and pure rural proletarians into semi-proletarians or full-time farmers (Pollitt, 1971, 1979). This is a case of sudden structural change in land tenure and occupations rather than one of migration related to longer-term processes. Once established the new system of production and distribution was not one which forced household units of production of any size to send people away to earn wages to satisfy their minimum consumption requirements. If anything, they sent fewer people away, apart from children in school, becoming net hirers of labour. Seasonal wage labour by small farmers and their families has probably declined, which may be a factor in the frantic efforts to mobilise urban workers in the 1960s, despite mechanisation, and may also explain the absence of substantial improvements in production from 1961 until 1970. But of course there has been some permanent migration, both to permanent jobs on state farms and to the cities. Otherwise the numbers of self-employed shown in table 4 would have grown more rapidly. The following sections go into this question in more detail, but the evidence shows that, while pre-Revolutionary social trends were massively reversed in terms of seasonal migration and wage-dependence, private farmers have been cushioned from the shocks which usually accompany modernisation. This is illustrated by their secure tenure and consumption levels and the absence of strong pressure to produce a surplus, however defined.

---

[1] Of course, production for the black market may be truly enormous, but one had the impression that it is unorganised and largely restricted to sales of pig meat.

3. Bureaucratisation and the division of labour

The policies of the Revolution have encouraged neither the expansion nor the "involution" of peasant agriculture; most conspicuously, attempts to encourage coffee and tobacco production have been held back by a policy of labour allocation giving preference to cane, as well as by education and social mobility prospects drawing people away from the farm. But what has happened to the workers whom we might have expected to contribute to the growth of the peasantry?

It is difficult to trace areas of major occupational growth because the 1970 Population Census contains, in its tables of occupations, a vast undifferentiated "social services" category, accounting in 1970 for 28 per cent of the urban, and 15 per cent of the rural labour force. The 622,000 people in social services in 1970 included some 88,000 teachers at all levels, quite apart from the administrative personnel in the education system; they also included some 33,000 medical personnel, again not counting administrators and unskilled support staff (Anuario Estadístico, 1975, pp. 206, 231). This ill-defined sector must have absorbed many rural workers who might have joined either the rural semi-proletariat of part-peasant, part-workers, or the urban sub-proletariat of unstably employed - two categories which, as we have seen, may well have overlapped in pre-Revolutionary days. Some 23.9 per cent of those in social services lived in rural areas - a proportion hardly conceivable in pre-Revolutionary Cuba, and indicating that the massive increase in this sector does not imply a parallel massive increase in urban jobs. What it does imply is an increase in the formal organisation of work, for besides education and health, and other unspecified subsectors, the sector contains the entire state administrative apparatus - which in 1943 had accounted for only 4 per cent of the labour force. There is no direct evidence to allow us to trace the destiny of those who would otherwise have become peasants, or part-peasants, but the educational expansion not only opened up opportunities for the younger generation but must have enabled many rural people, especially women, to become teachers.[1]

Apart from a shift out of agriculture, there has probably been a shift out of the private sector into state farms. In table 4 the figures for 1953 overstate the

---

[1] Teacher training begins in secondary school, after 8th grade; students begin to teach primary school in their fourth year of training.

number of wage labourers (if these are assumed to be permanent) and understate the number of "self-employed" or peasants and farmers (see appendix). We may therefore assume that whether or not there has been an increase in days worked by agricultural labourers, there has been a growth in the number of permanent wage-earners in the agricultural labour system.[1] This increasing proportion of wage-earners has been most pronounced in Habana and Oriente provinces. In Habana it may have been fed by migration from the capital. But in Oriente, the province where tenure was most fragmented, there has been a substantial labour transfer out of the peasant sector. According to table 6 of the 1945 Agricultural Census in this province units under 5 hectares were 29 per cent of all units yet controlled only 1.5 per cent of the land. In 1974 the private sector in Oriente controlled 33.2 per cent of the land (Anuario Estadístico, 1974, pp. 48-49) compared with the 11.7 per cent controlled by units of less than 25 hectares in 1945, yet its share of permanent labour in 1974 was 36 per cent compared with at least 40 per cent in 1945.[2]

The bureaucratisation - in a neutral sense - of rural labour, and indeed of urban labour, has important social effects. One feature of the informal sector in underdeveloped countries is that workers, peasants and smaller entrepreneurs lack access to many institutions and benefits because - or apparently because - they lack proper documentation, which is an essential feature of bureaucratisation in any society. Survival depends on a network of "contacts" and personal obligations; to maintain this network, an individual must expend an enormous amount of energy, frequently changing jobs and even sectors. In a bureaucratised system social status is more closely tied to an occupational role, which entails a fairly well-defined set of impersonal rights, obligations

---

[1] It may be incorrect to call it a labour market, even though there are market mechanisms, such as the attractions or dislike of piece-work in the sugar harvest.

[2] Some might object that it would be preferable to compare the contemplatory private sector with pre-Revolutionary units under 50 hectares, since the Agrarian Reform ceiling is 67 hectares. In this case the share in land would be seen to have declined in relation to the 50 per cent of land held by these farms in 1945. However, I have reduced the "smallholder" ceiling for 1945 to reflect the number of hired workers per farm and the greater fragmentation of units there compared with other provinces.

and tasks. In Cuba, bureaucratisation has penetrated, in different ways, both the peasantry and the rural proletariat. The state has replaced the family in the education and, to a large extent, even the feeding of children (through school meals, boarding and rationing); state farm workers, but not peasants, rely on their "work centre" for housing and electricity. It is not surprising that wage-earners have been incorporated into the division of labour, but so has the peasantry, through production contracts which embody credit requirements and are drawn up in collaboration with local branches of ANAP, local planners, the party and the bank. Labour is provided through official organs, though I noticed that in tobacco production, where work is quite skilled, a producer often asks for a particular person, whose "secondment" from a work centre is arranged by state agencies. In cane the labour process is largely centralised by the state, even on peasant farms. For a smallholder, the personal risk in innovation - as in the planting of new types of coffee - is minimal, for credit is heavily subsidised.[1] Informal credit is non-existent. As land cannot be transferred between individuals except by inheritance, a peasant cannot "accumulate" or even amass wealth except by selling his land to the state, and the proceeds cannot be invested. In theory, wage labour and credit are not available except for planned and approved production - and in practice this means for cane, tobacco and above all coffee. Although these limitations might allow peasants to earn relatively large incomes, they are constricted by the lack of wage labour for any but "contracted" crops and they can do little with money except buy certain consumer durables, unless there is a flourishing black market.[2] They cannot build houses unless the state makes materials available, which it does only for its own projects.

---

[1] Although Dominguez speaks of a 6 per cent interest charged to smallholders in 1966, the group with whom I spoke in La Candelaria, Pinar del Rio (see above, section II.2), said their credits carried no interest and, in the case of coffee, required no repayment until the trees began to bear fruit (Dominguez, 1978, p. 450).

[2] In 1980 the government began to establish peasant markets, along the pattern of the Soviet "Kolkhoz market", in order to improve distribution of peasant products. This would indicate that there has been a black market, and that it has been decided to legalise some of those activities.

Thus the bureaucratic division of labour has also penetrated private farming, restricting the "multi-activity" so characteristic of peasant production and trade elsewhere, and placing direct and indirect controls on production. Land rent does not exist, incomes being directly proportional to labour input, nor has there been a process of differentiation. But the price is low levels of production of traditional peasant crops, which the state could encourage only through a more flexible pricing and credit policy.[1]

On an unknown scale, two alternative mechanisms of production and exchange exist: the exchange of labour and private sales of agricultural produce. The first might fill gaps for which labour is necessary but unavailable; for this to occur on a large scale, landholdings would have to be much more equally distributed, so that those providing exchange labour could use their partner's labour in return. In a meeting with private farmers in Candelaria it was stated that their base, that is their ANAP branch, organises labour exchange, or mutual aid, only in "cases of emergency".

Such practices are characteristic of peasant societies in capitalist underdeveloped countries, and it is not surprising that they are absent in Cuba. But their absence is symptomatic of the absence, or at least gradual disappearance, of the breach between the nature of urban and rural social relations, in general and in production - just as the disappearance of the urban informal sector paved the way for increasing homogeneity in social relations within the urban context itself. Furthermore, there is in Cuba no process whereby migrants to cities recreate "peasant-like" mechanisms of labour allocation and control. Nor are the determinants of migration the same as in a capitalist society: in the highland Andes, for example, migration from country to town is a venture in which the individual's chances of success (i.e. economic improvement) depend very much on the capital he or she can start out with, as well as on the "capital" represented by contacts with kin and friends. Furthermore, for rural people, upward social mobility is scarcely possible without urban migration even if they return intermittently, or in later years, to their villages of origin. In Cuba, by contrast, it is often, though not always, possible to achieve some mobility in rural areas and small towns by becoming a teacher or an official, and it is also to some extent possible to join the "mainstream" of urban

---

1 According to the group of peasants to whom I spoke, there is no credit for "frutas menores", mostly root crops and vegetables.

lifestyles by remaining there. Thus migration is to a certain degree separated from upward mobility.

The obverse of this picture is the observation that, while smallholding agriculture persists in form, its content, the mechanisms of control and allocation of labour, land and other resources on which it is based, is utterly "unpeasant-like". Above all, perhaps, the uncertainties which generally dominate peasant forms of production have been drastically reduced, to the accompaniment of decreased dependence on kinship and friendship relations. This in turn must mean that in so far as insecurity constitutes a migratory stimulus, it has been reduced (as has inter-provincial migration in general - see section IV below). Fidel Castro's speech to the ANAP Congress in 1977 (see section III.4) refers to the desire of people living in remote areas to leave them, apparently in search of a more varied, attractive life-style, not for economic reasons of survival. This observation would support my view that these, rather than economic necessity or the impossibility of social mobility within rural areas, are the determinants of migration. Of course, as explained below, the job market is rigid, but that is a different consideration from the lifetime prospects of mobility for younger people, who may rise within an institution or may improve their social status by education as adolescents or, later, as adults.

4. Co-operatives, the new system of economic management and movements of labour

Viewed against this background, current policy with respect to the formation of agricultural production co-operatives is quite unique in comparison to almost any other socialist country. The private producers seem better off than the rural proletariat working on state farms, who are implicitly acknowledged by officials to be the lowest income group. They also benefit from a net transfer of resources from other sectors, although they suffer from a paucity of infrastructural investments, especially housing and electricity, and from the impossibility of purchasing machinery. It is government policy to make such investments only once small farmers have ceased living in dispersed settlements. But that requires investment in housing, which in turn would increase the likelihood of other amenities such as child-minding or nursery schools, more accessible communal buildings, shopping facilities, cinemas, and the like.

In that context, Fidel Castro's closing speech to the ANAP Congress in May 1977 inaugurated the official policy of moving towards agricultural production co-operatives, that is collective farming. By September 1978, only 269 had been created, with 7,426 members, compared to the 213,000 members of ANAP. There are two possible explanations for this slow growth: either smallholders resisted pooling their land or the government lacked the required resources. My experience in Cuba leads me to believe that, even if there was resistance, the latter explanation is the better one. The policy's objectives are many. The most general is modernisation and mechanisation of agricultural production, but that may not be the most important. The President, in his 1977 ANAP speech, referred to the need to make rural life and work more attractive for young people, children of peasants and rural workers who have acquired technical and professional skills and knowledge and who do not want to return to a small plot. He also said it was not the peasants' desire to retain their land which caused difficulties but rather their desire to leave, especially in isolated mountain areas.

I visited one agricultural co-operative (named after Julio Antonio Mella) in the province of Pinar del Río. Here a group of 30 smallholders pooled their land and "sold" it to a co-operative of 93 members, consisting of themselves, members of their families, and 11 local landless workers. The price of the land was fixed by a commission of members. The co-operative obtained finance by making a production contract with the state bringing interest-bearing credit which paid for inputs and members' wages. Production brigades had been formed by the members under the direction of one of their elected leaders, and payment was based on work norms fixed by the members and not by outside experts, as in state enterprises. The president of the co-operative indicated that some other co-operatives were not applying these norms, or had only been persuaded to do so with difficulty, thus presumably affecting production. This co-operative, founded in October 1977, was already obtaining a monetary surplus which easily financed daily wages. Some 10 per cent of the remaining monetary surplus went into a fund to finance capital purchases ("medios basicos"), 25 per cent towards the purchase of the land (that is, a direct payment to those members who had "pooled" their own land), and 50 per cent to the members, according to the number of days worked and perhaps other factors. The co-operative did not hire outside wage labour, but was able to obtain unpaid volunteers at peak periods. On the basis of figures given to me, an average of 300 pesos was distributed over and above wages after the co-operative's first eight months, by when total income per capita was 1,180 pesos, or 148 pesos per month.

In itself, that was a respectable money wage in Cuba, roughly 50 per cent above the minimum, but it does not count income in kind. The co-operative kept 119 quintals of rice out of a production of 225 quintals, and 90 quintals of maize out of 210 for consumption by the members and their families. Of the current year's production of "one caballeria"[1] of rice they expected to sell 500 quintals to the state, which on the basis of 2 tons per hectare, comes to about 18 per cent of production. Crops retained for consumption were sold to members according to size of family at the price paid by the state to producers, which were substantially less than those charged in the shops (a difference of 35 per cent in the case of beans). The co-operative cultivated 12.5 caballerias, 3.5 in tomatoes and pimento for export, with very high yields according to its president, 3 caballerias of mango and 1 each of malanga, yams, rice, corn and beans.

This co-operative was living up to the model; in conversation others were mentioned which had made losses and resisted work norms. Others had obtained social investments, such as housing, for which this co-operative was pressing. Thus it is not enough to make "profits"; some resources simply cannot be purchased. Indeed, the Julio Antonio Mella co-operative members seemed to be working hard not only to pay for land and maintain a respectable living standard, but also to show what they could do, as practitioners of socialist emulation, so as perhaps to attract funds for social investment. One gathered some co-operatives were more heavily subsidised (this one had three tractors, but 25 pairs of oxen), yet produced less intensively.

If current plans for economic decentralisation (see below, section V) are put into effect, it is to be expected that more co-operatives would be created, since the possibilities of distributing surpluses to members implies more in-built incentives to efficient production as conceived in these plans than on state farms. However, as the reforms would also liberate the labour market, it is questionable whether co-operatives would attract young skilled workers, technicians and professionals back to the land, especially as the Cuban labour force, produced by a remarkably advanced education system for an underdeveloped country, is concentrating increasingly on skill and technical expertise. One hypothesis is that under the arrangements prevailing in 1978 - when the reforms were in an experimental stage - urban and industrial

---

[1] This standard Cuban measure is equal to 13.5 hectares.

units of production were "hoarding" labour, especially skilled workers, so that even the reforms' moderate market pressures might force them to shed labour.[1] Whether or not those workers would go to the countryside, and to agriculture, would depend on the available housing and the level of capital investment. According to the Centro de Estudios y de Control de la Vivienda (CECONDEVI) there were 266 new, post-Revolutionary rural communities in Cuba in 1978, with 105,000 inhabitants, or just under 400 each.[2] The largest were in Pinar del Río, where 26 communities contained an average of 1,250 persons. In the former province of Oriente there were 64 with an average of 690 inhabitants. The communities accounted for 3 per cent of Cuba's rural population, but were model settlements offering an "urban" lifestyle to people working in agriculture. In an interview in Bohemia in early 1979, the head of the Planning Commission (JUCEPLAN) spoke of plans to build 30,000 houses per year, but most of these would presumably replace the depleted urban housing stock and create homes in the new industrial centres - Cienfuegos, Nuevitas, and Moa, the nickel project in Oriente. In fact, according to the head of National Planning, only 16,700 housing units were built in 1978, and some 20,000 in 1979.[3] It seems that it was difficult to attract young people in higher education into agriculture, since medicine and economic planning and management offered more prestigious, pleasant, or perhaps powerful opportunities. This will surely change, as more graduates fill the available jobs. Nevertheless, substantial resources must be channelled into infrastructure and capital for agriculture as a whole - and no longer overwhelmingly into cane - if the co-operatives, or even the state farms, are to attract skilled and professional youth. Even so, the retention of those workers would depend on a mechanisation process which itself would displace labour, thus

---

[1] According to Booth, a 1971 survey of 584 work centres carried out by the Communist party revealed that real labour requirements were 16 per cent of management estimates (Booth, 1973).

[2] These are the figures given to me at the Centro in September 1978. An earlier paper by the Centro's Director, Nisia Aguero, gives slightly higher figures for 1975: 282 communities or pueblos, with 127 inhabitants each (Aguero, 1977).

[3] Speeches to the People's Assembly, Granma Weekly Review, 21 January 1979 and 6 January 1980.

probably more than offsetting any contemplated inflow of population. So, as industrialisation is so difficult in Cuba, the broadly-defined services sector is likely to remain the main absorber of labour force expansion, even if - perhaps especially if - the establishment of co-operatives is accelerated.

IV. The Physical Distribution of Population

Despite its fragmentary nature, the evidence indicates that the factors determining rural-urban migration have behaved in a radically different fashion in Cuba compared with other countries in Central and South America. In this section, again on the basis of fragmentary evidence, we examine the outcome - the actual rates and levels of urban growth and internal migration.

1. The pattern of urban and rural growth

Between 1943 and 1970, the total urban population of Cuba rose from 2.6 million to 5.2 million, while the rural population rose from 2.2 million to 3.4 million. The Anuario Estadístico, 1975 estimated that in 1975 the urban population was 6 million and the rural 3.5 million.[1] Therefore, the growth of the rural population had levelled off, while the rate of population increase had fallen rapidly. The urban proportion of the population grew from 49.4 per cent in 1943 to 51.4 per cent in 1953, 60.3 per cent in 1970, and 63.3 per cent in 1975. That urban population remains heavily concentrated in the former Habana province, but since 1943 its share has declined, while that of Oriente and, to a lesser extent, Camagüey, has increased.[2]

---

[1] The exact figures are as follows:

1943	urban:	2,607,490	rural:	2,171,093
1953	urban:	3,324,628	rural:	2,504,401
1970	urban:	5,169,420	rural:	3,399,701
1975	urban:	5,950,768	rural:	3,454,131

The censuses in 1943 and 1953 use a far broader definition of "urban" than the 1970 Census, and the rate of urbanisation is therefore underestimated. In 1953 "urban" was defined as localities with 150 persons, plus "specific conditions such as electrification and medical services".

[2] This refers to the now defunct provinces of Pinar del Río, La Habana, Matanzas, Las Villas, Camagüey and Oriente.

The Cuban Physical Planning Institute (IPF) has published two studies of migration. One, Población de los municipios actuales en 1943 y 1953 (1972), reconstructs the 1943 and 1953 Censuses in terms of the municipal boundaries in 1970. The other, Cuba: Migraciones internas (1972), is an attempt to interpret rural-urban migration in terms of the changes brought about in areas dominated by different agricultural activities in the early years of the Revolution. Both studies seem to use preliminary results of the 1970 census. The procedure adopted is to estimate a natural population increase and to calculate the deviation of actual increase from the estimation. The population in 1958 is estimated at half-way between that given by the extrapolated growth rates of 1943-1953 and the growth rate of 1953-1970.

In crude terms, the pace of urban migration was the same before and after the Revolution. Some 650,000 people moved to cities between 1943 and 1958, and some 800,000 between 1958 and 1970; about 300,000 in the second, net internal emigration from rural areas as a whole totalling 2.0 per cent in the first period and 2.5 per cent in the second (Migraciones internas, 1972, p. 20). Although this study represents a remarkable effort at statistical systematisation given the absence of data, it is not easy to use here because it seeks to explain migration in terms of structural changes at the time of the Revolution, whereas I am seeking to explain later trends, using more recent data, in terms of the economic system which arose in the wake of those changes. On my census-based calculations, the growth of La Habana Metropolitan regions (Centro Habana, Cuanabacoa, Marianao, Plaza, Diez de Octubre and Boyeros) seems to have declined slightly from an annual average of 2.61 per cent in 1954-1953 to 2.19 per cent in 1953-1970. The JUCEPLAN estimate in 1961 (to the nearest 100,000) would, however, indicate a sudden upsurge in the years preceding 1961, and then a slowdown, with annual growth running at only 1.55 per cent between 1961 and 1970. When foreign emigration is taken into account the decline is less dramatic, and the IPF study estimated a stable rate of urban growth in general.

Net external migration from the province of Habana alone from 1960 to 1969 was just over 420,000 out of a national total of 450,000. Thus, the province which accounted for one-third of the urban population in 1970 accounted for over 90 per cent of emigration abroad - and emigrants were overwhelmingly from urban areas. Had Metropolitan La Habana grown at 2.61 per cent (the 1943-1953 average) per year throughout the 1954-1970 period, its population in 1970 would have been 1,861,829, whereas it was 1,751,216; if the capital city's share of emigration abroad from the province had been the same as its share of its population (and presumably it was greater) it would have lost 220,176 people, whereas it lost many more. It would seem, therefore, that discounting emigration, growth between 1953 and 1970 was marginally higher than in the earlier period.

Other data suggest a declining growth rate for Habana since the Revolution, and that the above figures are bloated by the initial massive migration. The Anuario Estadístico, 1975, indicates that the capital's population only grew by 1.35 per cent a year from 1970 to 1975, using an estimate of the 1975 population; Cuba's over-all population growth for these five years was very low, but nevertheless higher than 1.86 per cent per year. Thus though a declining over-all demographic growth rate helped slow the growth of the capital, the city's population (discounting emigration from Cuba) was still growing at a slower pace than the country as a whole for the first time since between 1899 and 1931 (the first inter-censal period for comparison). Some further evidence can be deduced from the Anuario Estadístico's annual estimates of the population between 1965 and 1975. Simple calculations suggest that migration to the province of La Habana has been steadily declining in absolute terms (table 14). These figures are only available at provincial level, but they are a good indicator of trends in the capital itself. If we set these data against those quoted above for longer-term trends, the suspicion that the capital's growth lurched forward in the immediate post-Revolutionary years and then fell back receives further support. The government has tried to reduce the attraction of La Habana city and only allows people to move from jobs elsewhere to new jobs there with a minister's permission.[1] Has this had any effect on migration patterns? If so, one would expect a reduction in the proportion and perhaps the number of migrants to Habana province, even if over-all out-migration from other provinces was increasing.

Unfortunately, available migration data are given only at provincial level, but this does not make much difference for Habana province, where 73.5 per cent of the population live in the metropolis. In the case of Oriente the proportion of out-migrants going to Habana province declined after 1966, a trend which continued even when, after 1971, total out-migration from the

---

[1] Ministry of Labour, Law 1225, 29 August 1969, and Resolution 459, 31 August 1969, reaffirmed by Resolution 93, 21 February 1978.

Table 14: Population of province of La Habana

	Net increase	Foreign emigration	Live births	Deaths	Internal migration
1960-65	194,173	121,562	232,658	88,070	113,026
1965-70	94,003	170,016	266,914	87,731	85,836
1970-75	183,753	39,661	243,110	86,688	66,792
Total	372,929	331,239	832,682	262,489	265,834

Source: Anuarios Estadísticos, 1965-1975.

Table 15: Annual percentage growth rate of 13 cities, in order of their population in 1975

	1943-1953	1953-1970	1970-1975
Havana	2.7	2.5	1.3
Santiago	3.2	3.1	2.8
Camagüey	3.2	3.4	2.5
Holguin	4.9	4.7	3.1
Guantanamo	4.2	4.1	3.1
Santa Clara	3.6	3.1	2.6
Matanzas	1.5	1.8	2.2
Cienfuegos	0.9	1.9	2.3
Pinar del Rio	3.9	3.8	2.9
Bayamo	4.8	5.9	3.3
Sancti Spiritus	2.9	2.5	2.7
Ciego de Avila	3.9	2.9	2.3
Victoria de las Tunas	4.7	5.7	3.0
Total urban population	3.1	3.2	2.8
Total rural population	1.0	1.1	0.3

Note: Figures for 1975 are estimates, whereas other years are from censuses.

Source: Anuario Estadístico, 1975.

province increased. After 1972, when the number of migrants from Oriente increased again, they continued to decline as a proportion of total migrants from Oriente. Thus the policy of restricting migration to the capital may have had some effect.

What of the growth of the other large cities? The 1975 Anuario Estadístico gleaned their size from the censuses of 1943, 1953 and 1970, and estimated it for 1975. The implied growth rates show that the cities of Oriente grew fastest throughout the period, that only five of the 13 cities grew faster in the 1953-70 period than in the 1943-1953 period, and that every one except Matanzas grew more slowly in the 1970-75 period than before, with the growth rate of the capital slowing down most of all (table 15). Bayamo, Holguín, Guantanamo and Victoria de las Tunas have been the fastest-growing cities, before as well as after the Revolution, although after 1970 their rate of growth seems to have declined along with that of other cities. Oriente's largest city, and the country's second largest, Santiago de Cuba, was not growing as fast as these smaller cities and so Oriente's share of the increase in Cuban urban population remained stable, even though its share of total population has risen since 1953.[1] A further factor was the relatively high fertility in Oriente, though fertility was declining in the country generally.

Oriente offers a test case for hypotheses about the causes of migration, since it had the greatest absolute and relative concentration of minifundia before the Revolution, and now has a relatively high average size of private farm.[2] That is so even though its land-labour

---

[1] Oriente's share of total urban population growth was 29.8 per cent in 1953-70 and 29.9 per cent in 1975. Its share of total population was 30.8 per cent in 1953, 35.1 per cent in 1970, and 35.5 per cent in 1975.

[2] Taking the area of the private sector given in table 5 for 1970 we obtain a national average holding of either 9.3 hectares (on the basis of that table) of 8.6 hectares (on the basis of the self-employed agricultural labour force in the 1970 Census, reported in table 4). The average in Oriente was, on the same basis, between 9.7 and 13.1 hectares. In addition to data previously given, we may note that in the 1945 Agricultural Census Oriente had 14,922 out of a national total of 32,195 farms under 5 hectares, and that these were 29 per cent of farms in the province compared with a national total of 20 per cent, itself heavily biased upwards by the weight of Oriente's size and population.

ratio remains the least favourable in the island (table 16) if the agricultural sector is taken as a whole.

The IPF study mentioned above shows that, on the basis of extrapolations and contrary to expectations, Oriente had by far the lowest net loss of rural population of any province in the 1943-58 period, losing 1.1 per cent of its rural population per year. This rate rose dramatically in the 1958-1970 period to 2.9 per cent, placing the province second behind Camagüey in rates of rural exodus. It seems little can be said about these figures because, as noted already, they reflect structural changes concentrated in the early 1960s, when large numbers of revolutionaries left Oriente for the capital.

After the early Revolutionary period there are no comparable urban migration data, but inter-provincial migration data are available almost annually, and we find that, between 1965 and 1975, although Oriente had the highest rate of population growth (3.1 per cent compared with 2.2 per cent in Pinar del Río, the next fastest province) the highest fertility,[1] and by far the highest rural population growth (47.5 per cent compared with a national average of 20.0 per cent), its share of gross inter-provincial out-migration (28.6 per cent) was below its share of the population, while its share of in-migration was much lower.[2]

Thus after 1965 the province with the least land per member of the agricultural labour force also had both a relatively high average size of private-sector farm and a relatively low share of gross out-migration. The province is also, with Habana, the only one in which the agricultural labour force increased between 1953 and 1970 (table 4). With an over-all growth of 10.7 per cent, the

---

[1] Live births in general declined from a high point of 35.0 per thousand in 1964 to 20.7 in 1975, and the rate in Oriente declined from 39.8 to 25.2 in the same period.

[2] Data were not available for 1968, 1970, and 1973, so the figure given is an average of the eight remaining years. Average in-migration to Oriente province over the period was 27,835 per year, though this declined after 1967, while out-migration oscillated around 32,839 (sources: Boletine and Anuario Estadístico, and for 1967, Compendio Estadístico, 1968). The tables are based on the Register of Consumers which gives access to ration cards. See also table 18 below. Of course, the low share of in-migration indicates that the province did not attract people from elsewhere as much as other provinces, even while it did not "expel" people as much as they did.

Table 16: Hectares of agricultural land per member of the agricultural labour force in 1970, and hectares of operated area in 1945 per member of the agricultural labour force in 1953*

	Pinar del Río	La Habana	Matanzas	Las Villas	Camagüey	Oriente
1970	4.6	5.4	6.2	6.8	13.6	4.9
1953	10.7	10.5	11.4	11.2	18.4	8.7

Note: The figures for 1953 should not be read in absolute terms. They are presented merely to show the relations between densities in different provinces.

Sources: For 1970: Population Census, 1970; Anuario Estadístico,1974. For 1953: Agricultural Census, 1945 (for "operated land") and table 2 above.

Table 17: Migration from and to Oriente and to Habana province, 1965-1975

	A Out of Oriente	B Into Oriente	C From Oriente to Habana	D Migrants from Oriente as proportion of total inter-provincial migration (%)	$\frac{C}{A}$ per cent
1965	28,645	24,562	21,159	26.3	73.9
1966	33,156	27,905	23,484	28.1	70.8
1967	32,605	38,421	24,989	25.1	76.6
1969	42,733	35,985	31,914	31.8	74.7
1971	25,955	36,723	19,550	23.1	75.3
1972	30,841	22,386	16,693	22.9	70.2
1974	33,245	18,566	22,467	34.5	67.6
1975	35,537	18,133	21,811	37.0	61.4
Total	262,717	222,681	182,067		
Mean	37,839	27,835	27,758	28.6	71.3

Source: Aguero (1977).

wage labour force in agriculture grew by 21 per cent and the self-employed by 10 per cent.[1] The implication is that many members of smallholder families shifted into permanent wage employment on state farms and in social services rather than migrating to urban areas or to other parts of the country, though no doubt some did migrate in those directions. This pattern is in striking contrast with capitalist countries in Latin America, for there agricultural modernisation has typically brought about an increase in employment on smallholdings and a decrease in permanent agricultural wage employment (Lehmann, 1980c; Klein, 1980). In Cuba the opposite is the case. True, technological modernisation has proceeded less rapidly in Cuba than elsewhere, but in many ways the society has been modernising more rapidly, as evidenced by the growing division of labour and educational development. It is possible that there is some underemployment, implicit in the slow growth of agricultural productivity and perhaps in the absorptive role of the wide-ranging category defined in the census as social services. According to the 1970 census, in Oriente the latter accounted for 21.3 per cent of rural and 16.4 per cent of urban employment, and 23.6 per cent of total national employment (table 3).

These data also suggest that most of the retention of rural population noted at a national level actually occurred in Oriente, whose size and population weigh heavily in national totals (table 16). While the rural population of Oriente grew by 47.5 per cent between 1953 and 1970, the rural population of Cuba grew by 20.0 per cent, Oriente accounting for 41.9 per cent of the total rural population in 1953 and 51.1 per cent in 1970. Rural population grew slowly in Pinar del Río and Las Villas and declined in all three other provinces (Anuario Estadístico, 1975). According to the estimates in the 1975 Anuario Estadístico Oriente's share of the rural population had grown yet again to 53.4 per cent.

The main region of rural retention in Cuba has also experienced the most rapid rates of growth of total and urban population (see table 18). So the conclusion must be that, once the early structural changes wrought by the Revolution had produced a new system, there was an over-all fall in migration, as measured by inter-provincial movements, and it is to this theme that we now turn.

---

[1] The disparity between rural population growth (45.7 per cent) and the growth of the agricultural labour force between 1953 and 1970 may be explained by the age structure of a fast-growing region and also by the growing importance of rural non-agricultural employment, especially in social services (see below).

2. Over-all population movements

Looking at the broader picture of inter-provincial migration, as recorded by the Register of Consumers, we again see fluctuations in migration to and from Habana province, with even net out-migration in 1967 and 1971 (table 19). But over the period there was above all a decline in inter-provincial migration as a whole, and in that context Habana province remained a net recipient of migrants and ceased to be a net source of migrants. Ironically, this may have been on account of increasing agricultural employment in the province of Habana. The agricultural labour force increased between the 1953 and 1970 censuses only in Habana and Oriente, and rose much faster in Habana (table 4). The rural population of Habana rose by 6.6 per cent between 1953 and 1970, faster than in any other province except Oriente; in the 1970-1975 period, however, the rural population declined in all provinces except Oriente, which continued to increase, though at a much slower rate (5.5. per cent). The one province which clearly increased its share of in-migration was Camagüey, the only province to have steadily increased its share since 1971.

On the whole, increasing urbanisation has been accompanied by a gradual reduction in geographical mobility. Urbanisation has taken two forms: migration to cities, and the acquisition of "urban status" by smaller settlements, as services and some infrastructure reached them. Despite the very generous definitions of "urban" in the 1943 and 1953 censuses, the proportion of the urban population living in the 13 largest cities declined very slowly, from 64.2 per cent in 1943 to 60.0 per cent in 1970. Yet by 1975 it had declined to 57.4 per cent. The pace of urbanisation may, therefore, have quickened in the 1970s, as new settlements acquired urban status, or smaller cities and towns accounted for a growing proportion of the urban population. In order to pursue this notion of a reduced concentration we can compare major city growth with the over-all growth of each province (table 20) to see whether the divergence between the two has changed. This table shows that, on average, these cities grew at 1.9 times the rate of their respective provinces between 1943 and 1953, and that this ratio was reduced to 1.4 in both the 1953-70 and 1970-75 periods. The striking points are: (i) that the cities with the highest divergences in 1943-53 (Pinar, Sta. Clara, and Sancti Spiritus) had these radically reduced in subsequent periods; (ii) that the divergence increased in only five cities in the second period and six in the third; and (iii) that only in one case did the divergence increase in both the second and third periods.

Table 18: Percentage distribution of urban population, by province, 1943-1975

	Pinar del Rio	La Habana	Matanzas	Las Villas	Camagüey	Oriente
1943	3.6	47.0	7.3	15.5	8.0	18.5
1953	3.9	45.8	6.4	14.5	9.1	20.5
1970	4.0	41.6	6.0	14.3	9.6	24.3
1975	4.3	40.4	5.9	14.3	10.0	25.1

Source: Anuario Estadístico (1975).

Table 19: Internal migration to and from Havana as percentage of total inter-provincial migration, 1965-1975

	Total	To Havana	%	From Havana	%
1965	108,729	43,878	40.0	38,904	35.8
1966	118,037	45,219	38.3	42,435	36.0
1967	129,900	46,802	36.0	51,863	39.9
1969	134,355	54,167	40.3	49,443	36.8
1971	112,337	36,216	32.2	47,457	42.2
1972	100,274	40,222	40.1	33,131	33.0
1974	96,379	41,551	43.1	27,825	28.9
1975	95,989	39,130	40.8	26,752	27.9

Source: Aguero (1977).

Table 20: Comparison of growth rates of major cities and of their provinces, 1943-1975

	1943-1953	1953-170	1970-1975
Pinar del Río	1.2	2.2	2.1
Pinar	3.9	3.8	2.9
La Habana	2.5	2.1	1.8
Habana	2.7	2.5	1.3
Matanzas	1.0	1.5	1.6
Matanzas	1.5	1.8	2.2
Las Villas	0.9	1.7	1.4
Santa Clara	3.6	3.1	2.6
Cienfuegos	0.9	1.9	2.3
Sancto Spiritus	2.9	2.5	2.7
Camagüey	2.4	1.6	2.1
Camagüey	3.2	3.4	2.5
Ciego	3.9	2.9	2.3
Oriente	2.9	3.1	2.1
Santiago	3.2	3.1	2.8
Holguín	4.9	4.7	3.1
Guantanamo	4.2	4.1	3.1
Bayamo	4.8	5.9	3.3
Victoria	4.7	5.7	3.0

Source: Anuario Estadístico, 1975, and censuses.

The table is restricted to 13 cities, of which the smallest had grown from 12,754 inhabitants in 1943 to 62,372 in 1975. It therefore seems that smaller cities are growing faster, though the relationships are a further indicatation that - assuming stable rural-urban fertility differentials - geographical mobility has decreased since the Revolution, and most likely since the late 1960s.

One factor which may explain the reduced mobility - apart from the restrictions on changing one's job to metropolitan Habana - is the absence of a labour market or, to put it another way, the lack of price competition between firms for labour. The only "unemployed" in Cuba are workers who, in the current process of economic reform (see below, section V, and also Lehmann, 1979, pp. 319-326) have been placed en disponibilidad, that is looking for a job. These may perhaps be counted only in tens of thousands. We know that, in early 1971, as a result of the law against vagancia (or "loafing", as officially translated) some 100,000 people were channelled towards productive labour.[1] We also know from official declarations that enterprises have not on the whole been under much financial pressure to shed surplus labour, and that they have tended to hoard labour in the expectation of future production goals. The difficulties of changing jobs increase with the degree of skill of the individual; even if a professional obtains permission to change jobs, he or she may have to find a replacement before being able to do so. Under the new system of economic management this could change. For unskilled workers, in contrast, one suspects that the labour market offers fewer opportunities, even though they could be released quite easily, for new investments tend to require skilled workers and to be relatively capital-intensive (as in the nickel project at Moa, and in cement production, though less so, presumably, in the construction of the new port at Nuevitas). The reduction of the labour force in sugar, especially in lifting and cutting cane, has clearly reduced unskilled job openings in that sector. So, job immobility has most likely contributed to the geographical mobility.

---

1 Quoting Cuban publications, Booth stated that the law had been discussed in 115,000 Assemblies in the first three months of 1971, and by the time it came into effect of 1 April, 101,000 persons had registered for employment (Booth, 1973).

V. Institutionalisation

The explanation of social change in underdeveloped capitalist societies has in recent years relied upon an ultimately economic image of a machine of accumulation, located somewhere in the world economy, an original source of dynamism and change. Correct or incorrect, this approach is pervasive. But in analysing Cuban society one cannot have recourse to such an image for although the capitalist accumulation system most certainly affects Cuban society, its effect is not dynamic - rather the contrary. Nor is it realistic to identify the Cuban pre-Revolutionary social structure as the single most important constraint on the achievement of a clear set of goals by the Revolutionary leadership; those goals have changed frequently since 1959, and the class structure has not proved nearly so resistant as it was, say, in the Soviet Union or China. In comparison with other revolutions, it was not difficult to remove the former political élite from power, nor was it difficult to wrest control of the economic structure from the landowners and foreign capitalists; the nation responded with remarkable unity to the major and minor external aggressions to which the island was subjected in the 1960s. The response to calls for voluntary labour was remarkable, if not universal, in the process leading up to the "10 million tons" sugar harvest of 1970. The formation and development of mass organisations, such as Committees for the Defence of the Revolution and the Federation of Cuban Women, have demonstrated how the state could mobilise civil society, indeed penetrate its interstices, in order to achieve Revolutionary goals, in particular those concerning security and social welfare. If the health care system functions smoothly, with few difficulties of access for the citizen, this is due not only to administrative efficiency, but to the role of these organisations as mediators between bureaucracy and citizenry.

Yet the stark facts of life have made the search for a viable model of development a very difficult one; writing in the early 1970s, John Dunn described the Cuban Revolution as "wildly patriotic and very much for the masses, but still more than a little uncertain over how to solve the problems of really significantly increasing production ... even a triumphant patriotism is not enough to make the position of a sugar island in the world economy an easy road to a Socialist commonwealth" (Dunn, 1972, p. 225). The series of radical changes in development strategy are well known: from the early pursuit of industrialisation, through the return to concentration on sugar leading up to the 1970 harvest, to the current slightly more moderate dependence on sugar with the hope of more diversified exports, including trained manpower. In economic organisation, the early demand-led boom allowed much play for the market, but when combined with the trade boycott by the US laid the way for a siege economy, attempts at extreme centralisation of control of production, a remarkably egalitarian distribution of real consumption by wage and salary-earners, the abolition of enterprise budgets, and a brake on the application of work norms. Then, in 1970 there began an agonising reappraisal, in the shadow of the failure to produce 10 million tons of sugar, and this in turn paved the way for political and economic reorganisation and for a resumption of growth in non-sugar sectors. By 1977 the Party had been completely reorganised (growing from 100,000 to 203,000 between 1970 and 1975; in the elections leading up to the 1975 Party Congress more than 6,000 new people acquired positions of leadership) (Castro, 1975, pp. 206, 208), and the creation of a new system of economic management was announced. Its main features are the establishment of enterprise accounts and the obligation on enterprises to achieve a monetary surplus over the year, some "freeing" of the labour market and an institutionalisation of consultation procedures within units of production. A corresponding overhaul of the price system also started.

Throughout this period of occasionally drastic changes - such as the abolition of all private trade and non-agricultural private production in 1968 when 58,000 private concerns were nationalised - there has been one constant: the search for a viable combination of administrative structure, popular mobilisation, and organisation of production. The problem might be stated in this way: in a centrally-planned economy suffering from an extreme shortage of foreign exchange, ultra-dependent on sugar exports, and where a rationing system distorts the effects of wage and productivity differentials on real consumption, how can one ensure a rational use of labour, capital and land?

The economy was subjected to formidable shocks during the early, crisis-ridden years; rationing was forced on the government by desperate shortages of consumption goods, and the impact of boycott and blockade would have provoked hyperinflation if the government had not extended administrative controls to industrial and agricultural inputs, the supply of which was disrupted with equal severity. The central administrative control of the production process itself was another inevitable step, since units could hardly be expected to function at all in response to repressed hyperinflation. Had Cuba been a large country with a mass of peasants, things might have been different.

But it was a small island desperately dependent on a dwindling supply of imports. According to Ritter, gross material product rose by 12 per cent between 1962 and 1965, only to decline thereafter to a level in 1967 below that of 1962 (Ritter, 1974, p. 208). In this context one can understand how the leadership, bereft of consumer goods, opted for a highly egalitarian policy known as "moral incentives" and fell into a vicious circle of administrative control, which Isaac Joshua described as the co-existence of "anarchic decentralisation and authoritarian centralisation".[1] It was a period in which central agencies were forced by circumstances to control all movements of goods.

However, a corollary of this phase - which officials now denigrate - was the growing need for citizens to register with a variety of government agencies in order to obtain food, employment, housing, health care, education, and so on. As individuals gradually had to adapt to a variety of impersonal "pigeon-holes", their primary relationships - patron-clientage, kinship, friendship - were less useful in their daily lives, even though the need to find a way through the bureaucracy ensured the survival (encapsulated in the word resolver) of networks of personal contacts within the bureaucratic and impersonal shell. We have seen how the kinship basis of organisation of smallholding production has been eroded by the intervention of the state in the production process, as well as by educational opportunity and social mobility.

We can now grasp how the necessary centralisation of control of production in general created a workforce at once more stable than before the Revolution and more specialised. The stability has developed in a society once characterised by pervasive instability and "multi-employment", by activities such as prostitution and multifarious services in which personal networks and dependency mediated the effects of market forces. The greater work-place stability, which should not be confused with growing specialisation, arose when enterprises "hoarded" labour during the period of over-centralisation, physical controls, absent budgets, and administered prices. The specialisation is a result of bureaucratisation, while the demand for skilled and professional personnel derived from a growing administrative apparatus and was supplied by a burgeoning educational system.

---

1 Joshua (1967). On the background to "moral incentives", see Silverman (1971). On the reasons for this decision, see Lehmann (1971, pp. 203-14).

This is a society where education has become something of a popular cult; workers are encouraged to study, get time off to do so, and are rewarded for it in the points system administered by trade union branches. They are able, through the Facultad Obrero-Campesina, to qualify for university at a mature age. Of course, this has encouraged the process by which individual identities are linked more to skill and qualification than to birth or even race. It may not be a society with completely equal opportunities, and indeed the rate of social mobility can be expected to decline after the initial post-Revolutionary upheavals and replacement of the self-exiled middle classes and entrepreneurs. But opportunities are surely more equally distributed than elsewhere in Latin America, or indeed in Western Europe.

Apart from the specialisation of productive and administrative roles, a process of structural differentiation can be observed in other features of the society.[1] Many of the functions of kinship units and relationships, and of networks of patron-clientage, have been taken over, regularised and systematised by institutions such as the block-by-block Committees for the Defence of the Revolution (CDR), the Women's Federation - with its two million members - nurseries, and schools. Indeed, one of the most striking features of the society is the multiple membership of individuals in mass organisations. Apart from those mentioned there is the agricultural smallholders' association (ANAP), with 230,000 members, and the trade unions, with two million members, which are once again present in all state-owned units of production, after a period in which they were considered "unnecessary". There are also institutions of a more restricted membership, such as Works Councils (Consejos de Trabajo) and the municipal, provincial and national organs of Poder Popular, which are elective. And finally, there is the Party, to which members are

---

[1] I find myself here, quite consciously, using a structural-functionalist vocabulary which might seem outmoded and out of place in the study of underdeveloped capitalist societies. Yet it seems the most suitable terminology for describing Cuban society today. For one of the most coherent applications, see Smelser (1959). What this framework fails to do is explain the social dynamics in Cuba before, during or after the Revolution. For Smelser, structural differentiation means "the establishment of more specialised or more autonomous structural units", or "the evolution from a multi-functional role structure to several more specialised role structures" (Smelser, 1963, pp. 102, 106).

appointed. Apart from the Party, these institutions do not have much power, and membership figures (taken from Fidel Castro's report to the 1975 Party Congress) are unlikely to reflect the extent of active participation. But they do carry out tasks at the level of street block, locality and work-place, and in doing so they recruit individuals for particular tasks in a social division of labour, operating within guidelines laid down, ultimately, by the higher echelons of the Communist party. In the case of the CDRs, their tasks include security, keeping order, ensuring children go to school, and providing a channel between health care agencies and the community. The unions administer a complex bonus scheme within units of production, and there are signs of negotiation with the government over conditions of work. Their other principal tasks are to encourage punctuality, the growth of productivity, health and safety at work,[1] and part-time study.

All these institutions, with their local-level committees and subcommittees, ensure centralised control of many social activities which in comparable capitalist countries are left to the vagaries of primary relationships and networks. They also promote impersonal, bureaucratised and differentiated structures throughout the society. Overlaying these structures, and penetrating them, is the Communist Party, a highly flexible organisation in which relations of authority are less norm-restricted than are administrative relationships. The Party is one body which might correct the rigidities arising from centralised control of production and distribution. It also co-ordinates and supervises the work of the various mass organisations, which without any doubt constitute a check on the bureaucratisation of the relation between state agencies and the public. Certainly the latter's existence has ensured that access to services is not marked by the barriers and queues observed elsewhere.

Inevitably, the administrative control of such a wide range of activities by government leaves gaps. Noteworthy among these are housing repair and maintenance, for there is no regular institutionalised system whereby people can obtain, at any price, the necessary materials

---

[1] See Juventud Rebelde, 18 September 1978, announcing the training by the Central de Trabajadores Cubanos (CTC) of 45,000 lay inspectors of health and safety in three-month courses. Punctuality and study are specifically rewarded by bonus schemes, and the bonuses are awarded in meetings of all the workers in a unit.

to work on their dwellings. Recently, the government (in Decree Law No. 14 of 22 August 1978) has allowed persons to work on their own account, to a limited extent, outside their work hours in a state-owned unit of production. This might enable people to work in such activities as house repair, but there is a shortage of materials. One therefore expects that such activities will continue extra-legally with materials being obtained directly or indirectly, openly or covertly, from the state sector. Compared with some Eastern European countries, where such extra-legal activities are widespread, they appear to be relatively limited in Cuba. Nevertheless this highlights the inflexibilities which arise in a system where control over resources and labour is so thoroughly centralised and conducted on an administrative basis; the "interstices", which are occasionally so essential and which in poor capitalist countries are filled by the "informal sector", remain unoccupied or under-occupied.

VI. Concluding Remarks

As far as the pattern of migration is concerned, it would seem that the declining inter-provincial migration partly reflects the scarcity of resources (especially urban housing),[1] the bureaucratic character of the labour market, and the egalitarian distribution of income, though it is also characteristic of a society in which a wide variety of formal relationships, identities, and activities effectively "anchor" individuals in specific areas for long periods. The formality of these relationships should not be denigrated, for they confer on individuals a social status which they might not wish to renounce. We can also interpret declining fertility in terms of the declining importance of family ties in the daily lives of people who have built up numerous non-familial rights, obligations and relationships.[2] Other factors influencing migration include urban housing shortages and severe restrictions on the construction of shanty-towns (even if materials could be obtained) - though difficult material conditions and overcrowding have not stopped urban migration in other countries. And even though urban families in Cuba often, if not usually, live three generations to a household, family ties continue to be weakened by the

[1] As recognised by the head of JUCEPLAN, Humberto Pérez, in an interview in Bohemia, early 1979.

[2] Births per thousand declined from a high point of 35.1 in 1963 to 20.7 in 1975 (Anuario Estadístico, 1975, p. 32).

diversification of single-stranded social relationships in which people participate as citizens, voters, decision-makers, workers, _dirigentes_, and so on.

If one wanted a simple phrase to sum up these points one would describe it as "modernisation with fitful growth". Readers will interpret that in divergent ways, but there is no doubt that bureaucracy, and the accompanying structural differentiation, have gone deep in Cuba, far deeper than in the "informal sectors", "peasant economies" and elaborate networks of patron-clientage which capitalist development preserves and often foments in social formations on or near the periphery of the world capitalist system. In short, the Revolution has created a national state apparatus where before there existed but a shadowy bureaucracy and a corrupt and violent network of coercion.[1]

---

[1] For a theoretical and comparative elaboration of this theme, see Skocpol (1979).

Appendix

Seasonal Labour and Unemployment before the Revolution

There are numerous difficulties with the available data on the occupational structure of Cuban agriculture before the Revolution, as Pollitt has frequently pointed out (Pollitt, 1971, 1972, 1977, 1979). The two main sources are the Agricultural Census of 1946, giving data for 1945, and the Population Census of 1953.[1] These are not strictly comparable, since agricultural censuses inquire into employment by unit of production, on the basis of responses from owners or managers of those units, whereas population censuses rely on information from heads of households. So the former generally indicate employment *opportunities*, the latter the structure of the labour force, by employment status or sector of employment. Accordingly, agricultural censuses produce higher "labour force" figures, if one chooses to interpret them as such. Many workers change employers during the agricultural cycle, and are double counted in agricultural censuses.

The 1946 census for Cuba indicates that agricultural employment opportunities totalled just under 830,000 while the 1953 census gives an agricultural labour force of 807,000. Even allowing for labour force growth in the intervening eight years, this is not a large difference. The important feature of both censuses, for present purposes, is that they show a predominance of wage over non-wage employment. This should be compared with more recent data from Mexico and Brazil: in Mexico, only 43.8 per cent of the agricultural labour force in 1970 were classified as "day workers and field hands", while 48.4 per cent were self-employed, *ejidatarios* (smallholders in *ejido* tenure) or unpaid family workers. In Brazil, in 1960, an average of 66.4 per cent of those employed on agricultural units of production in the five regions were "farm family labour", and this had risen to 81 per cent in the 1970 Agricultural Census. If we take the Mexican Agricultural Census we find that in 1970 the "producer and members of his family" provided 67.6 per cent of

---

1 Unfortunately, I have only had access to an apparently abridged version of the 1953 census, and have drawn the data in table 21 from Pollitt's 1977 article. The version of the 1953 census I have seen is in the library of the London School of Economics.

agricultural labour.[1] These comparisons, crude as they may be, are so remarkable that they tell us either that both Cuban censuses grossly underestimated family labour, or that in Cuba, as a society far more dominated by plantations, wage labour provided more employment than family units of production. This cannot be explained simply by reference to plantations, since north-east Brazil was also a plantation society.

According to the 1946 Agricultural Census of Cuba, non-wage employment accounted for 42.5 per cent of the total, whereas according to the 1953 Population Census it accounted for 37.7 per cent of the labour force in agriculture. Presuming Pollitt's reproduction of the figures to be correct, there were then only 69,100 family workers for 235,000 self-employed persons in agriculture. However, that both censuses show a minority of non-wage workers indicates that dependence on wage-employment was a dominant feature of the Cuban rural population, even among smallholders. That is the safest way to put it. Table 11 also shows that this dominance prevailed in both censuses in all provinces except Pinar del Río.

In the 1946 Agricultural Census employers were asked to report the number of months worked by their employees; anyone working less than ten months was counted a "temporary worker". It is therefore not surprising that 423,690 out of the recorded 477,383 wage workers (88.8 per cent) were classified as "temporary workers", working on average 4.1 months in the year; as that figure was calculated per worker per farm, not per worker, it is likely that most workers, moving from farm to farm, probably worked a little longer on average.[2] It is more surprising to learn that farms under 50 hectares accounted for 104,906 of those temporary workers (24.8 per cent). In itself this is remarkable, considering that the upper limit of tenure after the Second Land Reform of 1962 was 67.1 hectares, for it means 22 per cent of the labour <u>needs</u> of these smaller holdings consisted of temporary wage labour. Therefore it was a highly monetised agriculture, a far cry from the "peasant family economy" even among the smaller holdings, except those of less than one hectare.

In Cuba in 1945, only 20 per cent (32,195) of <u>fincas</u> (holdings) were under 5 hectares and they employed 51,785 non-wage workers, or 1.6 each (table 21). That

---

1 This is analysed elsewhere (Lehmann, 1979).

2 According to Ritter, the harvest lasted 111 days, that is less than four months, in the period 1947-1950 (Ritter, 1974, p. 22.)

Table 21: Distribution of land among fincas, by size, 1945

Hectares	Pinar del Río				La Habana				Matanzas			
	Fincas	%	Hectares	%	Fincas	%	Hectares	%	Fincas	%	Hectares	%
0-4.9	4,182	18.2	13,049.7	1.3	1,291	9.0	3,644.2	0.5	1,080	8.6	3,193.3	0.5
5-49.9	17,119	74.3	238,925.6	24.7	11,262	78.9	211,544.9	32.1	8,731	69.9	171,518.9	26.2
50-499.9	1,480	6.4	195,855.7	20.2	1,655	11.6	177,059.2	26.9	2,507	20.1	318,156.8	48.8
500+	249	1.1	521,096.5	53.8	64	0.5	270,621.2	41.1	168	1.3	160,444.9	24.5
Total	23,030		968,927.5	659	14,272		659,225.2		12,486		654,313.9	

	Las Villas				Camagüey				Oriente			
	Fincas	%	Hectares	%	Fincas	%	Hectares	%	Fincas	%	Hectares	%
0-4.9	7,240	18.0	19,454.6	0.9	3,480	18.8	8,848.6	0.4	14,922	29.0	37,917.2	1.5
5-49.9	28,863	71.8	591,759.5	29.1	10.639	57.4	261,343.4	12.1	23,610	45.9	265,999.0	10.2
50-499.9	3,617	9.0	614,277.6	30.2	3,658	19.7	698,891.2	32.3	12,286	23.9	994,732.6	38.3
500+	462	1.1	807,699.5	39.7	764	4.1	1,195,792.0	55.2	629	1.2	1,297,978.8	50.0
Total	40,182		2,033,191.1		18,541		2,164,875.2		51,447		2,596,627.6	

Hectares	Cuba			
	Fincas	%	Hectares	%
0-49.9	32,195	20.1	86,107.5	0.5
5-49.9	100,224	62.7	1,741,091.3	19.2
50-499.9	25,203	16.4	2,999,973.1	33.0
500+	2,336	1.5	4,253,632.9	46.8
Total	159,958	100.7	9,080,804.8	995

Note: The classifications by size of the second and third size groups have been modified as follows for three provinces to take account of variations in density:

Las Villas: 5-74.9 and 75-499.9
Camagüey: 5-99.9 and 100-499.9
Oriente: 5-24.9 and 25-499.9

Source: Agricultural Census, 1945, table 6.

included 3,807 non-wage temporary workers. Compare this to 229,337 non-wage (permanent and temporary) workers on what can be called "family farms", which numbered 100,224.[1] Let us assume these family farms were able to employ more or less the entire family labour force of their owners. It follows that on average they had a family labour force of 2.3 persons, and required slightly less than one extra wage worker. Such family farms employed a total of 98,910 wage workers, the vast majority of whom were temporary workers and working for less than 2.7 months a year. But as the minifundia under 5 hectares employed only 1.6 people, it follows there were some 22,263 workers "freed" from those minifundia as wage labour. This figure is small compared to the 53,693 permanent wage workers plus 423,690 temporary wage-earning opportunities on all farms.

If we assume that each holding of less than 5 hectares ("sub-family farms") disposed of 2.3 members of the labour force, then some 33.6 per cent were not employed full time by those units, but were available for work elsewhere. Decomposing this figure by province gives the following percentages:

Family labour force not employed on holdings under 5 hectares, Cuba, 1945 (percentages)

Pinar del Río	27.4
La Habana	29.0
Matanzas	32.0
Las Villas	36.3
Camagüey	40.8
Oriente	24.3
CUBA	33.6

Source: Agricultural Census, 1946, and author's estimations of size and family labour.

[1] The number of temporary non-wage workers was insignificant. I have defined family farms as holdings of between 5 and 50 hectares, except in Camagüey where they are between 5 and 75 hectares, and Oriente, where they go between 5 and 25 hectares, on account of the noticeably different densities in those two provinces.

Thus, despite a seasonal need for hired-in labour, the smallest holders were also highly dependent on hiring out their own labour for mostly seasonal wage labour for their livelihood. Furthermore, one may presume the estimate of 22,263 "surplus" workers is a minimum, since these holdings did not specialise in the same crops (especially cane) as the larger holdings; many who appear as full-time non-wage workers on them hired themselves out seasonally. Even so, there was a deficit of seasonal wage labour on large farms, filled, as many authors have pointed out, by the landless rural proletariat. However, in the light of current Brazilian and other Latin American data, what is curious is that the pressure of unemployment did not produce far more fragmentation of holdings in Cuba, and that the number of "family farms" far outstripped sub-family farms (under 5 hectares) in all provinces.

Extrapolating the data from the 1953 census backwards - by using the crude device of the inter-censal population growth rate and applying it to the various categories of the labour force - suggests there were some 260,000 non-wage workers in Cuban agriculture in 1945 (the year of reference for the 1946 Agricultural Census). This is probably a less realistic figure than the 352,372 given by the Agricultural Census, for it assumes that only one-fifth of those workers were not heads of enterprises - "self-employed", as the 1953 Census calls them. One would presume there was at least one more full-time working member of the family, especially in the light of the limited extent of extreme fragmentation of landholding. The estimate of the pure wage-earning labour force on the basis of the same extrapolation is about 429,000 which, given probable double-counting of temporary workers, is much lower than the 477,369 wage-workers given by the agricultural census. If we subtract from the figure of 429,000 the 53,700 permanent workers given by the agricultural census, and the 22,300 "excess workers" from the minifundia under 5 hectares who presumably spent much of the year on their families' holdings and were therefore employed all year, we are left with a pure rural proletariat without stable employment of some 353,000 persons, which is a large though maximum figure. Pollitt, in his "Letter to the Editor", Economía y Desarrollo (1972), states that the 1945 census probably overestimated the number of temporary wage-workers by 25 to 33 per cent; my calculation is that the overestimate was about 20 per cent.

But the apparently low level of employment on the minifundia - in comparison with what the experience of other countries might lead us to expect - still raises a problem. If unemployment was such a grave problem, why was there not a far larger population figuring as non-wage labour on these smallest holdings, or indeed on the category I have labelled "family farm"? The beginning of an answer can be found by comparing the (extrapolated) figure of 200,800 self-employed in agriculture with the 159,958 fincas in 1945. This leaves some 40,000 persons, who may have received small plots of land on medium and large farms but who appeared in the Agricultural Census as either temporary or permanent workers. They would have received plots so that employers could be sure of their labour during the peak season. If their family members are added, then perhaps a further 40,000 would also have been "peasants-cum-proletarians", classified in the Agricultural Census as permanent or temporary workers. This still leaves 273,000 seasonally unemployed workers.

The hypothesis that many workers did receive such plots is supported by the data presented by Pollitt from his 1966 survey of 1,061 household heads (Pollitt, 1979). Of those, 496 had been seasonally or permanently employed wage-workers in 1957, and 188 of those had had access to plots for their own use on the farms employing them. Interestingly, a higher proportion of the 348 seasonal workers among them (39.4 per cent) had such access than did the permanent workers (34.7 per cent). Over-all, 38 per cent had access to such plots, a figure which would yield just under 113,000 persons in 1945 (see calculation on page 385). Thus assuming those who had access to plots were not unemployed outside the peak seasons (however underemployed they may have been) the estimate of 273,000 seasonally unemployed declines to 240,000.[1] Although this is a very generous allowance, it can be made more so by adding an estimated number of family members of plot-holders who would have been employed temporarily as wage-earners even if for the remainder of the year working on plots. An allowance of one extra family member per plot would leave only 127,160 seasonally unemployed, while an allowance of 0.5 family members would leave 169,380. These figures represent respectively 17.5 per cent and 23.3 per cent of the total agricultural labour force in 1945, calculated on the basis of the 1953 census.

The puzzle remains: why did this mass of people not appear as underemployed farm-family labour, the classic resort of the poor in underdeveloped agrarian economies? My hypothesis is that many spent much of

---

[1] An equivalent 38 per cent of permanent workers who have already been subtracted from the seasonally unemployed have not been subtracted again.

An estimate of the numbers of hard-core seasonally unemployed in pre-Revolutionary Cuban agriculture

1.	Wage-earning labour force in 1945 estimated on the basis of the 1953 Demographic Census	429,000
2.	Subtract 53,700 permanent workers as stated in the 1945 Agricultural Census	375,300
3.	Subtract family members of owners of farms under 5 hectares who do not figure as family labour but were probably employed on those farms in the "dead season" (22,300)	353,000
4.	Subtract 38 per cent of the temporary wage-earning labour force who may have had plots on farms over 50 hectares - plots not registered as holdings in the 1945 Agricultural Census (112,920). (This figure is reached by taking the number of temporary workers on such farms in the 1945 Agricultural Census and subtracting 10.2 per cent to allow for double-counting.)	240,000
5.	Subtract, for the 112,090 in (4), one family member each who may have worked on the plot when not employed as a temporary wage-worker on farms over 50 hectares. (This is a very generous assumption.)	127,160
OR		
6.	Subtract from (4) half a family member for each who may have worked on the plot when also not employed as a temporary worker on farms over 50 hectares. OR	169,380
7.	On the basis of the 1953 Demographic Census the total (wage and non-wage) agricultural labour force in 1945 was 726,840. The hard-core seasonal unemployment would then have been between 17.5 per cent (see 6 above) and 23.3 per cent (see 5 above) of the labour force in 1945.	

the year in urban areas, working in what has come to be known as the "informal sector", or indeed in the formal sector. As argued below, the 1953 census gives the impression that the informal sector accounted for a substantial proportion of employment in 1943, and these people could hardly afford not to be working in the agricultural dead season. Finally, qualitative accounts of pre-Revolutionary life show that street-life was hardly inactive, even if it yielded low incomes.

The only available primary source which might clarify this question is the 1943 Population Census. It might well be asked why I have not used this before, and the reply is that it makes extremely little sense when compared either with the 1946 Agricultural Census or with the 1953 Population Census (as reported by Pollitt). The 1943 Census shows 630,356 persons in the labour force in agriculture, cattle-breeding and fishing. This would yield a 2.5 per cent annual growth rate when compared to the equivalent 1953 figure. But subdividing that 1943 figure gives the following:

1943:	Owners	Employees	Own-account	Unknown
	40,755	71,274	362,169	156,158
	6.5%	11.3%	57.5%	24.8%

1953:	Wage labour	Non-wage labour	Self-employed
	503,000	69,100	235,500
	62.3%	8.6%	29.2%

Sources: Population Census, 1943 (table 3, Grupos de industrias); Population Census, 1953 (as reported by Pollitt, 1977).

And if we refer not to the classification by branch of employment (grupos de industrias) but to the classification by occupations, it seems there were 575,798 "farmers (agricultores) and farm administrators" and 46,001 "agricultural workers".

No amount of juggling, of the kind done to conciliate the agricultural census of 1946 with the population census of 1953, can make these data comparable.

In the "tablas de industrias" of the 1943 census, we find data on the distribution of the labour force by branch of activity and by status of employment. The census is candid, for it admits that the employment status of 385,000 out of a labour force of just over one and a half million is "unknown" (se ignora). Not surprisingly, most of those were in the agricultural sector (156,000) or in the sector described as "unclassified industry and trade" (115,000). These two sectors contributed 62.1 per cent of the labour force, and 70.6 per cent of those of unknown status. And those of "unknown" status in the two sectors amounted to 17.9 per cent of the Cuban labour force.

The number in ill-defined occupations was truly enormous, especially as 20.7 per cent of the labour force was apparently employed in "unclassified industry and trade", quite apart from the 10.3 per cent of unknown status in agriculture. Now total employment opportunities given in the 1946 Agricultural Census was just under 830,000 which, subtracting my estimated 48,000 double-counted workers, leaves 782,000. This is some 152,000 more than the number of economically active persons in agriculture according to the 1943 Population Census, and that difference is close to the problematic 169,380 whose activities outside the seasonal peaks were unidentified. The hypothesis that many were in the urban labour force for this period cannot be tested, but it at least offers a possible if partial account of the divergence between the figures in the two censuses. Their presence in the urban labour force would not mean they were employed there, and one may suppose that many worked only intermittently, and/or at very low levels of productivity.

References

Aguero, N. (1977): La urbanización rural en Cuba (mimeographed).

Auroi, C. (1975): La nouvelle agriculture cubaine (Paris, Anthropos).

Booth, D. (1973): Neighbourhood committees and popular courts in the socialist transformation of Cuba Ph.D thesis (University of Surrey).

Castro, F. (1975): Report to 1st Party Congress.

Comite Estatal de Estadísticas (1977): Resumen estadístico: Sector campesino (May).

Dominguez, J. (1978): Cuba: Order and Revolution (Cambridge, Mass., Harvard University Press).

Dumont, R. (1970): Cuba: Est-il socialiste? (Paris, Seuil).

Dunn, J. (1972): Modern Revolution (London, Cambridge University Press).

Goodman, D. (1977): "The Brazilian North-east", in Journal of Peasant Studies, Oct., Vol. V, No. 1.

Gugler, J. (1980): "A minimum of urbanism and a maximum of ruralism: The Cuban experience", in International Journal of Urban and Regional Research, Vol. 4, No. 4.

Gutelman, M. (1967): L'agriculture socialisée en Cuba (Paris, Maspero).

Joshua, I. (1967): Organisation et rapports de production dans une économie de transition (Paris, Ecole pratique des hautes études, Centre d'études de planification socialiste, No.10).

Klein, E. (1980): Diferenciación social: Tendencias del empleo e ingresos agricolas, paper presented to the Santiago seminar on Employment in Peasant Economies, (Santiago, PREALC, Jan. 1980; mimeographed).

Lehmann, D. (1971): "The trajectory of the Cuban Revolution", in Journal of Development Studies, Jan., Vol. VII, No. 2.

Lehmann, D. (1979): 'Peasantisation' and proletarianisation: Recent changes in the rural sectors of Brazil and Mexico, unpublished ms.

--- (1979): "The Cuban economy in 1978", in Cambridge Journal of Economics, Vol. 3.

--- (1980a): Beyond Lenin and Chayanov: Two paths of agrarian capitalism (University of Cambridge; mimeographed).

--- (1980b): "Ni Lenin ni Chayanov", in Estudios Rurales Latinoamericanos, Jan.-Apr. Vol. III, No. 1.

--- (1980c): Peasantisation and proletarianisation: Recent changes in the rural sectors of Brazil and Mexico (University of Cambridge, ms.).

--- (1981): "Peasantisation and proletarianisation: Recent changes in the rural sectors of Brazil and Mexico", in S. Jones, P.C. Joshi and M. Murmis (eds.): Agrarian reform and rural poverty (New Delhi, Allied Publishers).

Martinez Alier, J. (1970): "The peasantry and the Cuban Revolution from the spring of 1959 to the end of 1960", in A.R.M. Carr (ed.): Latin American Affairs, St. Anthony's Papers No. 22 (Oxford University Press).

Mesa-Lago, C. (1978): Cuba in the 1970s: Pragmatism and institutionalisation (Albuquerque, New Mexico University Press).

Nelson, L. (1959): Rural Cuba (Minneapolis, Minnesota University Press).

Nove, A. (1965): The Soviet Economy (London, Allen and Unwin).

O'Connor, J. (1970): The origins of socialism in Cuba (Ithaca, Cornell University Press).

Pollitt, B. (1971): Employment plans, performance and future prospects in Cuba, Reprint Series No. 349 (Department of Applied Economics, University of Cambridge).

--- (1972): "Letter to the Editor", in Economía y Desarrollo, No. 14 (Havana).

--- (1977): "Some problems of enumerating the Cuban peasantry", in Journal of Peasant Studies, Jan., Vol. IV, No. 2.

Pollitt, B. (1979): Agrarian reform and the 'agricultural proletariat' in Cuba, 1958-1966: Some notes, Occasional Papers No. 27 (Glasgow, Institute of Latin American Studies, University of Glasgow).

Ritter, A. (1974): The economic development of revolutionary Cuba (New York, Praeger Publishers).

Silverman, B. (ed.) (1971): Man and Socialism in Cuba (New York, Atheneum).

Skocpol, T. (1979): States and social revolutions (London, Cambridge University Press).

Smelser, N. (1959): Social change in the Industrial Revolution (Chicago).

--- (1963): The sociology of economic life (Englewood Cliffs, Prentice-Hall).

United States Congress, Joint Economic Committee (1979): The Soviet economy in a period of change (Washington, DC).

Vargas, L.C. and Amador, M. (n.d.): Prevención y erradicación de la mala nutrición en Cuba (Havana).

AUTHOR INDEX

SUBJECT INDEX

Note: Abbreviations: Br. (Brazil); Col. (Colombia); Mex. (Mexico).

For Product Safety Concerns and Information please contact our EU
representative GPSR@taylorandfrancis.com
Taylor & Francis Verlag GmbH, Kaufingerstraße 24, 80331 München, Germany

www.ingramcontent.com/pod-product-compliance
Ingram Content Group UK Ltd.
Pitfield, Milton Keynes, MK11 3LW, UK
UKHW022213190926
475702UK00003B/339